THIRD EDITION

Complete Guide to Sport Education

Daryl Siedentop, PED

The Ohio State University, Professor Emeritus

Peter A. Hastie, PhD

Auburn University

Hans van der Mars, PhD

Arizona State University

HUMAN KINETICS

Library of Congress Cataloging-in-Publication Data

Names: Siedentop, Daryl, author. | Hastie, Peter A., 1959- author. | van der Mars, Hans, 1955- author.
Title: Complete guide to sport education / Daryl Siedentop, PED The Ohio State University, Professor Emeritus, Peter A. Hastie, PhD Auburn University, Hans van der Mars, PhD, Arizona State University.
Description: Third edition. | Champaign, IL : Human Kinetics, [2020] | Includes bibliographical references and index.
Identifiers: LCCN 2018045284 (print) | LCCN 2018050256 (ebook) | ISBN 9781492589327 (epub) | ISBN 9781492562528 (PDF) | ISBN 9781492562511 (print)
Subjects: LCSH: Sports for children--Study and teaching.
Classification: LCC GV709.2 (ebook) | LCC GV709.2 .S663 2020 (print) | DDC 796.083--dc23
LC record available at https://lccn.loc.gov/2018045284

ISBN: 978-1-4925-6251-1 (print)

The web addresses cited in this text were current as of December 2018, unless otherwise noted.

Acquisitions Editor: Scott Wikgren
Senior Developmental Editor: Melissa Feld
Senior Managing Editor: Anne Cole
Copyeditor: Rodelinde Albrecht
Indexer: Ferreira Indexing
Permissions Manager: Dalene Reeder
Graphic Designer: Whitney Milburn
Cover Designer: Keri Evans
Cover Design Associate: Susan Rothermel Allen
Photographs (cover): © Peter A. Hastie
Photographs (interior): © Peter A. Hastie, except as otherwise noted
Photo Production Manager: Jason Allen
Senior Art Manager: Kelly Hendren
Illustrations: © Human Kinetics, unless otherwise noted
Printer: Data Reproductions Corporation

Printed in the United States of America   10 9 8 7 6 5 4 3 2 1

The paper in this book is certified under a sustainable forestry program.

Human Kinetics
P.O. Box 5076
Champaign, IL 61825-5076
Website: www.HumanKinetics.com

In the United States, email info@hkusa.com or call 800-747-4457.
In Canada, email info@hkcanada.com.
In the United Kingdom/Europe, email hk@hkeurope.com.

For information about Human Kinetics' coverage in other areas of the world, please visit our website: **www.HumanKinetics.com**

E7250

We dedicate this book to our colleague, mentor, and close friend Daryl Siedentop as well as his wife, Bobbie.

—Peter Hastie and Hans van der Mars

Contents

Preface

The first formal introduction of the Sport Education model was in a small book published by Human Kinetics in 1994. Its title, *Sport Education: Quality PE Through Positive Sport Experiences,* is as true today as it was then. The key difference between the first edition and this latest text is that we now have a substantial amount of research and testimonials from teachers and their students to support the idea that Sport Education is indeed a valuable and motivating form of physical education. Importantly, the research and stories come from a range of grade levels, from students in the early years through those in university physical education courses. We now know what makes Sport Education so enticing to teachers and students, but we also know some key features of season design and implementation that lead to highly successful seasons.

Sport Education has always been based on the idea that small mixed-ability learning groups, what we refer to as *teams*, work together in ways that benefit all team members and help them experience success. Sport Education provides students with adequate time to develop skills and to learn to fulfill the team roles required for a successful season. Thus, Sport Education seasons are always longer than typical physical education units; for the seasonal competitions to be successful, students have more to learn than just techniques and tactics.

This latest edition has been designed to better introduce new readers to the idea of Sport Education and to give previous users of the model some contemporary ideas of ways they can expand their seasons to make them even more engaging and attractive to their students. As such, the book is presented in three parts. The first part, The What and Why of Sport Education, outlines the essential features of the Sport Education model and identifies the key aspects upon which Sport Education is based. We also show how Sport Education is different from simply copying interschool or community sport directly into physical education.

Within physical education, sport content has, in some ways, been under assault in the movement toward promoting physical activity from a public health perspective. That is, the dominance of sport content in most physical education programs has been made a scapegoat for physical education's ills. We certainly view school physical education as a primary place for helping students gain the skills and knowledge needed for leading physically active lives. However, it need not come at the expense of helping students encounter sport as a meaningful and valuable experience. From our perspective, the problem has been the way students have typically been introduced to sport. Sport Education offers a way for a more meaningful and authentic way to learn about sport and how to play it. We want to ensure that all children and youth come to view sport as something they can connect with and find meaning in.

In part II, The How of Sport Education, we introduce you to everything you need to consider when designing and implementing Sport Education seasons. These are presented in a chronological order, with the first chapters addressing the decisions you make before the season begins, followed by those aspects that arise during the first lessons of a season. The middle chapters focus on within-season issues such as teaching protocols, helping students learn their officiating roles, and developing student coaches. The final chapters address topics that are part of the whole of a Sport Education season: festivity, inclusion, and student empowerment.

Teaching Sport Education seasons is just a part of teachers' day-to-day work. Therefore, we include a new dimension in part III, Key Program Design Considerations. In this part, we introduce you to some aspects of teaching physical education that are less visible but that help to build an effective physical education program. Thus, this last set of chapters addresses various topics that go beyond the nuts and bolts of teaching Sport Education seasons.

Complete Guide to Sport Education, *Third Edition*, also includes updated web-based ancillaries. These resource materials support users of Sport Education in the planning and design of seasons. For example, some of the resources include team practice cards that both teachers and team coaches can use to plan and organize team practices. Updated assessment templates are included, allowing teachers to choose from several gameplay performance indicators (e.g., technique and tactics assessment, knowledge of rules and strategies assessment, and indicators for fair play assessment). There are also resources for teachers to use to encourage student engagement in physical activity outside of class time, using the team concept of Sport Education to encourage students to remain active after school and on weekends. All ancillary resources for this edition will be available through the Human Kinetics website. Instructors who adopt the text for their university classes will have full access to instructor materials. The students in those courses and physical education teachers who have purchased the book to implement the model in their physical education programs will have complete access to the other ancillaries. All these materials can be downloaded, edited, and printed for use in planning, implementing, and assessing Sport Education seasons. See the How to Use the Web Resource page for more information.

Daryl Siedentop, the text's lead author, is the undisputed father of Sport Education. We will be forever in his debt for envisioning a more sane sport culture for our children and youth. His articulation of the model occurred in the late 1970s and has evolved further since. We hope that you find this new edition of *Complete Guide to Sport Education* a worthy and valuable next step.

—*Peter Hastie and Hans van der Mars*

Acknowledgments

Since its start in the early 1980s, the Sport Education model has flourished worldwide, with an increasing number of physical educators, who are using the model in ever-increasingly creative ways. The numerous examples of strategies and tools identified in the text and the web resource have come from teachers who have built Sport Education into their programs. Notable teachers include Danielle Blackwell at West Albany High School in Albany, Oregon; Tracy Robertson at Hamilton High School in Chandler, Arizona; Jerry Osborne at Legacy Traditional School in Queen Creek, Arizona; Chuck Cooper at Pick Elementary School in Auburn, Alabama; and Chris Rhodes at Morris Avenue Elementary School in Opelika, Alabama. Mention must also be made of Dr. Claudio Farias in Portugal, who spent an entire school year working with seventh grade students to investigate the most critical of issues that arise when students work in teams: how to nurture student behaviors that promote a democratic, inclusive, and participatory focus. The creativity and insight of these teachers in building their own seasons and resources have made a significant contribution to the text.

As shown in this book, Sport Education offers the structure for more inclusive student experiences. Ensuring that students with special needs are truly a part of the sport experience is often a struggle for physical educators, especially if there are no paraprofessionals available. Dr. Daniel Tindall from the University of America in Ireland has published previously on the topic of inclusive practices within Sport Education for students with special needs, so we invited Dan to lend his expertise. Dan took responsibility for creating a new chapter, Meaningful Inclusion of Students With Special Needs. For that we are most thankful.

Ultimately, what counts is what our K-12 physical education colleagues create when teaching Sport Education experiences. Often working in isolation, and without much recognition, they manage to provide sport experiences that are indeed more complete and more authentic. These physical education professionals include Ryan Johnson at Legacy Traditional School in Higley, Arizona, and Peggy Robbins at Legacy Traditional School in Laveen, Arizona. We cannot thank them enough.

We also thank the teachers and students at the various schools who have contributed the wonderful images of students in action during Sport Education seasons. These photos serve to bring life to this new edition and have helped us clarify some of the key issues teachers need to consider when designing and implementing their seasons. A sincere thank-you also goes to Kristal Gonzalez, physical education teacher education major at Arizona State University, for doing the translation into Spanish for the web resource.

The staff at Human Kinetics has been instrumental in keeping us on track and assisting us in making this a high-quality text. We provide our heartfelt thanks to Scott Wikgren, the key stakeholder in the decision to move forward with this edition, and Melissa Feld, who managed the project. We also very much appreciate those at Human Kinetics involved in the production of the book for thoughtful, creative, and supportive assistance in bringing this new edition to fruition. They include Joe Buck, Kelly Hendren, Matt Harshbarger, and Jason Allen, who created the design, the illustrations, and the final layout of the text and who prepared the photos. Dalene Reeder assisted us with the process of obtaining permission to adapt certain materials previously published by other colleagues in the field. Finally, Anne Cole served as managing editor. Anne was an outstanding proofreader and ensured that the final draft to be sent to the printer was as clean and clear as it could be. The professionalism demonstrated by the entire Human Kinetics staff over the course of this revision remains unmatched!

—*Daryl Siedentop, Peter Hastie, and Hans van der Mars*

How to Use the Web Resource

The web resource for *Complete Guide to Sport Education, Third Edition,* offers numerous supporting materials for practitioners and students and is available at www.HumanKinetics.com/CompleteGuideToSportEducation. We have organized the web resource around the chapters in the text. See the next page for an abbreviated table of contents. You'll find instructions for accessing the web resource on the key code page at the very front of the book. When you go to the web resource you will find the contents listed by chapter. Select the chapter link on that page and you will be able to view and download all the resources for that chapter. We encourage you to explore all the resources.

Our primary goal in developing these resources is to support teachers and their students when planning Sport Education seasons. All resources were developed with readily available software programs within Microsoft Office. Those resources that students would use during Sport Education seasons have been translated into Spanish and can be identified by the SPA at the end of the file name.

We also recognize that teachers live in various contexts, so the materials might need to be adapted to fit their needs. We do ask users to continue to give credit to the original source.

We retained most of the supplementary materials included in the second edition of the text, with updates where appropriate. These materials include posters, score sheets, competition format templates, sample contracts, fair play materials, and assessment templates. We also included practice cards that Sport Education users can employ in organizing classwide practices and team practices. The activities on these practice cards are all games based and aid in developing students' game play in more authentic practice conditions. The web resource contains new examples of team binder content. For example, we include templates for fitness season team binders for elementary- and secondary-school levels as well as a swimming season team binder for use in high school.

For those teachers who frequently use notebook computers, tablet computers, or personal digital assistants (PDAs), several of the files that relate to such tasks as keeping score and assessing include templates (developed in Microsoft Excel) that are available in both regular print versions and electronic versions. With some practice, the management of information will get easier.

We have made every effort to ensure that the web resource is of good quality and has as few errors as possible. We are very interested in improving the existing resources, and we recognize that experienced teachers of Sport Education have developed their own excellent materials. If you find problems, have new ideas to share, or have questions about the resources included with this text, please share them with us. We wish you success in making Sport Education a regular part of your physical education program.

Peter Hastie: hastipe@auburn.edu
Hans van der Mars: hans.vandermars@asu.edu

ABBREVIATED WEB RESOURCE CONTENTS

Chapter 4 Key Features of the Sport Education Model

- Community Mapping of Physical Activity Opportunities Template
- Web-Based Teacher Content Knowledge Sources

Chapter 5 Instructional Alignment as the Road Map to Quality Season Experiences

- League Scoring System
- Planning Materials
- Season Block Plans
- Team Binder Templates

Chapter 6 Promoting Physical Activity Beyond Physical Education

- Out-of-Class Individual Physical Activity Logs
- Out-of-Class Physical Activity Team Practice Logs
- Physical Activity Step Count Logs
- Recess Resources

Chapter 7 Modifying Games and Activities

- General Game Modification Strategies
- Play Practice Content Design

Chapter 8 Designing Competition Formats

- Dual Meet Format
- Event Model Format
- Progressive Competition Format
- Round Robin Format

Chapter 9 Selecting Teams and Roles

- Selecting Teams
- Student Roles

Chapter 10 Teaching Protocols and Fair Play

- Banners and Wall Posters
- Code of Conduct
- Dispute Resolution Committee
- Sample Contracts and Pledges
- Sample Fair Play Resources

Chapter 11 Developing Competent Players

- Play Practice Action Fantasy Game Cards
- Play Practice Team Practice Cards

The What and Why of Sport Education

In the first part of this book, we outline the essential features of the Sport Education model and identify the key aspects upon which Sport Education is based. We also show how Sport Education is different from simply copying interschool or community sport directly into physical education. In chapter 1, we introduce Sport Education as a model based on the concept that small, mixed-ability learning groups, which we call *teams*, work together in ways such that all team members benefit and experience success.

Chapter 2 is designed to justify the rationale for involving students in longer units of instruction and for giving significantly more autonomy to students during lessons. Students in Sport Education have more to learn than just techniques and tactics for the seasonal competitions to be successful. In this chapter we also introduce the concept of the *teacher as the architect of the model*. In chapter 3 we present sport (taught well) as a legitimate focus for physical education and reject the artificial either/or position that says students can only be taught *either* sport skills (the skill learning perspective) *or* how to be physically active (the public health view).

Chapter 4 presents the first steps in designing a season by focusing on how best to achieve the overall goal of Sport Education, which is to develop competent, literate, and enthusiastic sport players. The outcomes we have identified contribute directly toward those broader goals. Once you have identified the goals for a season, it is important that you ensure alignment between those intended season outcomes, the content that you deliver to students to practice, and the assessment you employ to determine whether the outcomes were met. It is in chapter 5 that we present this idea of instructional alignment.

Part I closes with chapter 6, which provides an overview of how well-delivered Sport Education can contribute to the public health agenda in terms of promoting physical activity beyond the confines of school physical education.

© Human Kinetics.

Key Features of the Sport Education Model

Chapter Objective

After reading this chapter, you will be able to describe the fundamental principles of Sport Education and identify the key features of the model.

Key Concepts

- Sport Education is designed to be an engaging, developmentally appropriate form of physical education for all students.
- The term *sport* can apply to any of the physical activities included in a physical education program.
- Sport Education is not the same as out-of-school competitive sport leagues.
- The goal of Sport Education is to create competent, literate, and enthusiastic sportspersons.

Sport Education is a model for presenting authentic and developmentally appropriate sporting experiences for students in schools. *Authentic* means it involves those aspects that make sports participation fun and meaningful; *developmentally appropriate* means it engages all students in ways they can successfully participate. The key goal of Sport Education is to develop students who are competent, literate, and enthusiastic about their participation, and who therefore desire to become and stay physically active throughout their lives.

The Sport Education model was developed in the early 1990s, with a number of features that distinguish it from traditional approaches to teaching physical education.

- Sport Education units, or seasons, are longer than typical physical education units. Elementary seasons typically last from 12 to 15 class sessions whereas middle and high school seasons typically last from 18 to 20 class sessions.
- Students become members of mixed-ability teams at the start of a season and remain on those same teams throughout the season. Every effort is made to ensure that teams are as equal as possible in relation to the activity for the season.
- Students on each team learn multiple roles. While the exact roles for each season change depending on the activity, typical roles for seasons include coach, equipment manager, referee, scorekeeper, and statistician.
- Activities are typically modified so that all students can learn and be successful. Games are often small-sided versions of the parent form of the game (e.g., three-on-three soccer, two-on-two volleyball).
- The season typically consists of a series of competitions interspersed with a series of practice sessions.
- The most typical competition involves three teams. Two of the teams compete against each other while the third acts as the officiating team (i.e., referees, scorekeepers, judges).
- In Sport Education seasons, records of performances are kept and made public throughout the season. These records are used not only to determine seasonal standings and championships but also to inform students of their own skill development within the season (e.g., improved distance achieved in long jump during a track and field season, or points scored during a three-on-three basketball season).
- Season champions are typically determined by a system that can include points for items beyond just a team's win–loss record. These can include factors such as fair play, quality of officiating, or the performance of other team roles.
- The entire season is designed to be festive, and culminates in the final event that celebrates the season with awards for competition standings, student performance in various team and officiating roles, as well as fair play points.

The publication of the first Sport Education book (Siedentop, 1994) enabled physical educators around the world to learn about the model. The first large trial of Sport Education came shortly thereafter when the Hillary Commission in New Zealand funded a national trial for Sport Education in selected high schools. The trial was so successful that the New Zealand Education Department hired several trainers to serve the many schools that learned of the trial and wanted to develop Sport Education in their schools. Shortly thereafter, another trial of Sport Education was funded in Western Australia. The Western Australia trial results prompted a larger national project that was funded by the Australian Sports Commission. The evaluation results of the Western Australia project clearly showed the benefits of the model for students and the degree to which the physical education teachers reported improved effort and performances by all students.

Following the New Zealand and Australian trials, Sport Education continued to spread throughout the world, with particular interest shown in England, Japan, and South Korea, where the model is now used routinely in many schools. The research that has followed in recent years has supported these findings from a number of different schools in a number of different countries. Indeed, more than 100 published research studies show positive outcomes for both students and teachers. Table 1.1 shows some of the consistent findings across these studies. References that include most of these findings are presented in the sidebar.

Table 1.1 Summary of Sport Education Projects

Positive outcomes for teachers	Positive outcomes for students
• Many teachers find that both absenteeism and nonparticipation rates fall under Sport Education. • Teachers like the structure and routine that the model provides because it helps students to be particularly focused on learning. • Teachers appreciate the increased freedom from direct instruction, which allows them to work with individual students or teams. • Teachers find that in many cases students who were previously habitual nonparticipants become more actively involved. • It appears that Sport Education is more gender inclusive than traditional forms of physical education. • Teachers find that students improve skills in areas that were traditionally claimed as outcomes but rarely achieved in physical education. • Teachers report that participation levels are higher, skill levels improve, and students are capable of learning to effectively umpire, manage, and coach.	• Students unanimously favor the Sport Education approach over the traditional physical education approach. • Students who first experience Sport Education report that they hope their teacher would continue to use the model. • Both boys and girls report that they worked harder in Sport Education. • Students like the longer Sport Education seasons because they have more time to learn the activity, more time to play it, and more time to be with teammates. • Students enjoy being on persisting teams, express loyalty to their teams, and don't want to let their teammates down. • Students with lower ability levels report that they significantly improve their skills as a result of increased participation. • Students express and display improved attitudes toward sport as a result of their Sport Education experiences.

SPORT EDUCATION RESEARCH

The list of references that follows include the major reviews of research on Sport Education. The findings presented in table 1.1 can all be identified in one or more of these reviews.

Alexander, K., & Luckman, J. (2001). Australian teachers' perceptions and uses of the Sport Education curriculum model. *European Physical Education Review, 7*, 243-267.

Araújo, R., Mesquita, I., & Hastie, P. A. (2014). Review of the status of learning in research on Sport Education: Future research and practice. *Journal of Sports Science & Medicine, 13*, 846-858.

Hastie, P. A., Martínez, D., & Calderón, A. (2011). A review of research on Sport Education: 2004 to the present. *Physical Education and Sport Pedagogy, 16*, 103-132.

Kinchin, G. D. (2006). Sport Education: A review of the research. In: D. Kirk, D. Macdonald, & M. O'Sullivan (Eds.), *The handbook of physical education* (pp. 596-609) London: Sage.

Siedentop, D. (2002). Sport Education: A retrospective. *Journal of Teaching in Physical Education, 21*, 409-418.

Wallhead, T., & O'Sullivan, M. (2005). Sport Education: Physical education for the new millennium? *Physical Education and Sport Pedagogy, 10*, 181-210.

WHAT SPORT EDUCATION LOOKS LIKE

Table 1.2 provides an outline of an 18-lesson floor hockey season designed for a class of 36 seventh-grade students; the following scenario gives a snapshot of what a typical lesson during lessons 11 to 15 might look like.

Table 1.2   Middle School Floor Hockey Season

Lessons	Content
1	Introduction Rules of the game Beginning skills
2	Skills testing Team announcement (six teams of six) Discussion of roles (coach, fitness leader, equipment manager) Teams decide on names, mascots, and colors Teams distribute roles among team members
3-7	Whole-class skill instruction Within-team practices
8-10	Preseason scrimmages Players learn and practice duty (officiating) team roles (referee, scorekeeper, statistician)
11-15	Formal competition matches
16-17	Playoff matches
18	Championship games (competition for gold, silver, and bronze medals) Awards presentations

LESSON SCENARIO

Ms. Thomas's students enter the gym and immediately disperse to different locations, which have been designated their home areas. One student, who we learn is the fitness leader, leads his team through a series of exercises, which he had prepared prior to class. Another student from this team has collected six red hockey sticks and three pucks from the equipment area, and is giving these to the players in her team. Once the warm-up is completed, the students begin two games of two-on-one keep-off in their team area. Meanwhile, Ms. Thomas is meeting with the coaches of the six teams in the class and is reviewing some of the tactical problems she saw during matches the lesson before. Ms. Thomas asks each coach in turn to identify what they saw as the main area of need for their own team. She then provides a task sheet to each coach based upon their response. The coaches now go to lead their teams in a practice.

After 15 minutes of team practice, Ms. Thomas asks the teams to get their miniteams organized and then go to their match courts. She also tells them, "The scoreboard clock will start in two minutes, so I expect everyone to be ready; that means you too, officiating teams." On arrival at courts 1 and 2, teams of three players each from of the Blades of Wonder (with their tie-dyed T-shirts) and the Ice Foxes (with their purple headbands) take their positions for play, while players from the Flaming Sticks take their places in the roles of scorekeeper, umpire, and statistician. On courts 3 and 4, the other three teams in the class are making similar arrangements.

At the end of the lesson, all teams return to their home areas, the equipment managers return their inventory, and the referees from each match gather in front of the class. In turn, each of these officials announces the score, reports the fair play points awarded to each team, and announces the player who receives the matches' "golden puck" award for the most amazing play of the day.

From this scenario, it is possible to identify many of the six key components that characterize young people's participation in sport that are adopted in Sport Education seasons. First, the idea of a *season* is evident because the students are participating in combinations of skill practice and gameplay. There is clearly *team affiliation*, as evidenced by team names and by the teams having their own designated practice space within the gym. There is evidence of *formal competition* in that the matches are being played between specifically designated teams. Within these games, *record keeping* is taking place, with the officiating teams keeping score and compiling statistics. The element of *festivity* is found in each team's uniforms and the poster they have mounted above their team area. While the *culminating event* of the season is not witnessed in the lesson scenario, we might expect activities in the closing ceremony to be similar to the awarding of the golden puck from each game during the formal competition phase.

THE SPORT IN SPORT EDUCATION

It is important to understand that seasons of Sport Education need not to be limited to traditional team sports such as basketball, volleyball, or soccer. The model can be used for most physical activities that are included in physical education programs. Indeed, successful seasons have been conducted with gymnastics, dance, swimming, fitness, and archery as the content area. Table 1.3 shows the range of activities that have been done using the Sport Education model.

It can be seen then, that the use of the term *sport* in Sport Education follows the United Nations Educational, Scientific, and Cultural Organization's (UNESCO) concept of Sport for All. To UNESCO, the concept of sport is not restricted to competitive activities but also includes various forms of physical activity such as spontaneous games, dance, outdoor pursuits, orienteering, cycling, and physical exercise.

Table 1.3 Completed Sport Education Seasons

Activity	Sport Education seasons
Aquatics	Water polo, swimming, diving
Batting and fielding	Baseball, cricket, softball
Boules and bowling	Tenpin bowling, bocce
Dance	Dance by the decades, folk dance, aerobic dance
Skirmish	Paintball
Flying disk sports	Ultimate Frisbee
Football	Australian rules, American, rugby, soccer
Gymnastics	Artistic gymnastics, gymnastics, rope jumping
Handball	Basketball, team handball, four square, volleyball
Hockey	Field hockey, floor hockey
Mixed discipline	Biathlon
Adventure	Orienteering, bicycle safety
Weight training	Girls' weightlifting
Target sports	Archery, golf

Seasons of Sport Education need not to be limited to traditional team sports such as basketball, volleyball, or soccer. The model can be used for most physical activities that are included in physical education programs.

HOW SPORT EDUCATION DIFFERS FROM YOUTH OR INTERSCHOLASTIC SPORT

Sport Education in school physical education is not simply a mini version of how sport is typically organized and conducted in youth, community, and interscholastic sport programs. In particular, there are three fundamental differences that distinguish the two. These are best described as (1) participation requirements in that everyone plays all the time, usually in small-sided teams, (2) developmentally appropriate involvement through the use of modified games, and (3) the inclusion of diverse roles, because students do not participate only as players but take other responsibilities for the conduct of the season.

Participation Requirements

In Sport Education, all students participate equally at all points in the season. Sport Education teams have no first string and substitutes; all participants get equal playing time. Games are small-sided so that students get considerably more opportunities to learn the techniques and tactics needed to play the game well. In addition, the final competitions of a season typically involve all teams (not just the best three or four). In some cases, teachers will allocate teams to gold-, silver-, and bronze-level tournament play so that all students get to experience the excitement of postseason play. Lastly, the culminating event is arranged so that all students can take part in the final festivities, either as players or officials or as event staff, photographers, videographers, or reporters.

Developmentally Appropriate Involvement

The activities in Sport Education seasons are almost always modified to foster student success, particularly in the number of players per side and the modification of the activities themselves (e.g., lower nets or baskets, shorter fields). When activities are played in the parent form, skilled students tend to dominate and other students are much less involved (Siedentop, 1998).

Within these modified games, however, we always aim to preserve the nature of the contest. This is done by adhering to the *primary rules* of the game (what makes that game unique) while making adjustments to the *secondary rules* (those features that can be adapted without changing the essence of the game). For example, while basketball or hockey seasons in Sport Education will still involve moving a ball through dribbling and passing, and scoring by shooting into a goal, the sizes of the teams, the dimensions of the playing area, and the size of the ball and of the goals are changed to better fit the developmental capabilities of the students.

Inclusion of Diverse Roles

Finally, a major difference from other forms of child and youth sport is the diverse roles that students learn and perform in Sport Education. As mentioned, students are not only players but also coaches, managers, referees, scorekeepers, statisticians, and other roles that depend on the activity. For instance, in dance seasons, roles would include music selector, choreographer, and costume designer. We have found that the inclusion of roles during Sport Education not only helps in terms of class management but also leads to a more complete understanding of the sport studied during the season.

THE GOAL OF SPORT EDUCATION

The goal of Sport Education is to educate students to be players in the fullest sense and to help them develop as *competent*, *literate*, and *enthusiastic* sportspersons.

A *competent* sportsperson has developed sufficient skill to participate in games and activities satisfactorily, understands and can execute strategies appropriate to the complexity of the activity, and is a knowledgeable game player. Through Sport Education, students learn to be comfortable and competent performing in increasingly complex forms of sport, dance, and fitness activities. They grow in their abilities and confidence by gradually being introduced to appropriate techniques and tactics for the activity and by having ample time to improve through practices and competitions.

A *literate* sportsperson understands and values the rules, rituals, and traditions of sports and other physical activities and has learned to distinguish between good and bad practices within those activities, whether in children's sport, youth sport, school sport, or professional sport. A literate sportsperson is both a more able participant and a more discerning consumer as spectator or fan. Becoming literate about sport practices and others forms of physical activity is a prerequisite to ensuring that sport and activity programs for children and adolescents are educationally sound and contribute to a safer, saner sport and activity culture.

An *enthusiastic* sportsperson behaves in ways that preserve, protect, and enhance sport culture, whether it is a local youth sport and physical activity culture, a school sport and physical activity culture, or a community sport and physical activity culture. Enthusiastic sportspersons want to participate because they have come to value the experiences and enjoyment derived from participation. They have developed a strong sense of self-efficacy, which is a major factor in helping people to become and stay physically active throughout their lives. We would expect that students who have experienced a physical education program using the Sport Education model would be more likely to become volunteers in child and youth sport programs and to take an active role in seeing that sport and physical activity programs are widely available in their communities.

These goals are ambitious. They not only embrace the Sport Education of children and young people but can also have profound meaning for the health and vitality of the general sport and activity culture of communities, regions, and countries. As such, girls and boys who have experienced a well-done Sport Education program from fourth through twelfth grades should have the following attributes:

- be reasonably well skilled in a variety of sport, dance, and fitness activities,
- be more likely to become and stay involved in physical activities during discretionary time,
- be able to differentiate between good and bad sport practices whether in youth sport, school sport, or community sport, and
- be more likely to become engaged with local sport organizations as adults to ensure that child and youth sport programs are designed to enhance the well-being of those participating.

THE NATURE OF COMPETITION IN SPORT EDUCATION

Competition is fundamental to the sport experience, as it is related to the *pursuit of competence*. In this pursuit of competence, the contest is with oneself to surpass a previous standard of performance. It just so happens that the best way to do this is to test oneself against another individual or team. In seasons of Sport Education, we encourage students to see games not as competitions *against* someone or some team but as a process of discovering what they need to work on to become the best they can be.

Sadly however, we have all witnessed abuses of young athletes in the name of competition. Some coaches and even some parents try to convince the youngsters that a win-at-all-costs approach is most appropriate. This is in contrast to what children and adolescents have told us about what they want from their competitive experiences (Siedentop, 2002). Young people want to get better at the sport, to be with friends and make new friends, and to have fun doing it. Winning and losing do not appear to be as important to young participants as they are to some of the adult coaches and parents.

We believe in the value of developmentally appropriate competition in Sport Education. We have learned important lessons from studies of what children enjoy and value when they organize informal player-controlled games (Coakley, 2017). First, they want action, especially action that leads to scoring. Second, they want personal involvement in the action—player-controlled games have no substitutes. Third, they want a close score, which suggests that they favor evenly matched teams. Fourth, they use games to reaffirm their friendships and to make new friends. Good competition among teams always requires cooperation within teams. What is most clear is that the majority of athletes reject the notion of zero-sum competition, where one team can succeed only to the extent that the other team fails.

It is also clear that students who participate in Sport Education are more likely to develop self-efficacy for physical activity. Research shows that self-efficacy is a dominant factor for participation in and enjoyment of physical activity. Thus, in an era when the world is focusing on health issues related to overweight and obesity and focusing on increased physical activity as a primary strategy in reducing health costs, the development of self-efficacy for physical activity has become an underlying principle. Research in sport psychology has found four consistent predictors of motivated physical activity among children: (1) developing and demonstrating competence, (2) providing opportunity for autonomy and choice in activity, (3) fostering positive peer relationships, and (4) maximizing enjoyment while minimizing anxiety (Weiss, 2007).

GETTING STARTED WITH SPORT EDUCATION

The chapters that follow provide ample guidance for teachers to learn various ways of organizing their program using the Sport Education model. Our recommendation for teachers who are new to the model is to plan a basic form of the model and then gradually add to its complexity. We suggest picking an activity that you know well and that your students are likely to enjoy. As with any new approach to curriculum and instruction, it is important that the initial experiences be positive for your students and for you. The web resource includes several planning worksheets to guide you through your first effort. Start small, do it well, and then build on it. That is our advice, which comes from the many teachers we have worked with to initiate a Sport Education approach to their physical education curricula.

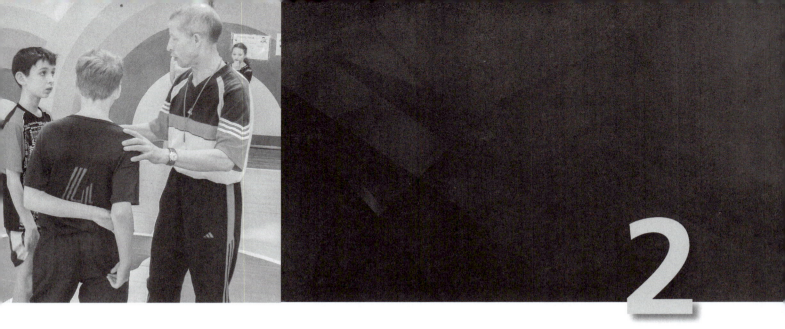

Curriculum and Instruction Foundations of Sport Education

Chapter Objective

After reading this chapter, you will be able to appreciate the rationale for involving students in longer units of instruction and for giving significantly more autonomy to students during lessons.

Key Concepts

- Sport Education is founded upon a greater depth of content coverage within fewer units across a school year.
- The instructional philosophy of Sport Education centers on developing and sustaining small, heterogeneous learning groups, which we call *teams*.
- Sport Education is an ideal format of physical education to support a twenty-first-century learner.
- While much of the in-class decision-making in Sport Education is handed over to students, the teacher is still the architect of the model.

As we saw in chapter 1, Sport Education differs from sport in that young people experience it outside of physical education in three key ways: participation requirements, the use of developmentally appropriate small-sided games, and the fact that all students have roles other than just as players. The *curricular philosophy* of Sport Education is also different from the more common unit approach, where the focus is on the development of technical skills followed by gameplay in short units with direct instruction. First, Sport Education offers a significantly deeper coverage of the content: fewer activities are taught across a given school year, allowing students to learn each activity to a greater depth than is typical in multiactivity physical education programs. The two most common reasons given for having short units of instruction in physical education are (1) that students become bored with extended lessons on one topic and (2) that it is the role of physical education to expose young people to a wide variety of activities from which they then might choose something that motivates them. In response to the first issue, it has been clearly demonstrated that students do *not* become tired of activities that they find engaging and in which they have potential ownership. The flaw in the second argument is that if physical educators provide only brief exposure to various activities, there is little time for students to develop the competency necessary for participation. Voices from students provide support for these positions. When asked to describe why they appreciate the extended length of a Sport Education season, a consistent response from students has been "because I could get really good at it, and in regular PE even if you can't do it well yet, you move on."

The second curricular feature of Sport Education is its expanded set of content goals. While the content of the traditional shorter physical education units focuses primarily, and often exclusively, on techniques and rules (and perhaps on small elements of tactics), in Sport Education the content is not only strongly focused on gameplay and tactics, but also includes learning about and practicing other roles important to how the activity is pursued outside school. This includes roles such as coaching, refereeing, scorekeeping, compiling statistics, managing teams, publicizing results, and the like. Sport Education also takes seriously the need to help students understand and appreciate the rituals and conventions of various activities and to understand the differences between good and bad sport practices. There is more to teach than just a few individual techniques. The key is that teachers communicate these expected outcomes at the outset of each season.

The *instructional philosophy* of Sport Education centers on developing and sustaining small, heterogeneous learning groups, which we call *teams*. Teams are small enough (typically comprising 6 to 10 students) so that all team members can make meaningful contributions to team goals. This applies to traditional team sports such as basketball, individual sports such as tennis and badminton, and activities such as dance, orienteering, and weight training.

Within teams, students have various roles and responsibilities, all of which contribute to the success of the team. This is perhaps best explained by Cohen and Lotan (2014, p. 6) with their comment that "when the teacher gives students a group task and allows them to struggle on their own and make mistakes, she has delegated authority. This is the first key feature of group work. Delegating authority in an instructional task is making students responsible for specific parts of their work; students are free to accomplish their task in the way they decide is best, but are still accountable to the teacher for the final product. Delegating authority does not mean that the learning process is uncontrolled; the teacher maintains control through evaluation of the final group product and of the process by which the students arrived at the final product." One of the attractive features of Sport Education is this autonomy given to students. As mentioned by an Australian tenth-grade student, "Sport Education is better than normal physical education because the teachers weren't always telling you what to do . . .

you weren't under any pressure, and this made you want to try your best. You really learned how to cooperate with other team members and it was really good sharing the responsibility with each other." Figure 2.1 provides some other examples of what the research on small learning groups states as key benefits for both teachers and students.

In Sport Education, the group product is a team's performance, not only during competitions but in their roles as officials, in their conduct regarding fair play, and in other group tasks (such as out-of-class activities) that might be provided by the teacher. Given that teams learn, practice, and compete together, it is this aspect of the *persisting team* that many students (particularly those who are lower-skilled) find particularly attractive. Because all competitions in Sport Education are team competitions, this pursuit of competence provides motivation for all students and can enhance learning. Further, it has been demonstrated that students who engage in collaborative learning and group study perform better academically, persist longer, feel better about the educational experience, and have enhanced self-esteem (Landis, 2013).

Successful group work does not simply happen when you place students into teams. Younger children and even older students who are not accustomed to the responsibilities of group work (and who may be accustomed to being the passive recipients of teacher-led management, instruction, and practice) will require a transition period to move to the small-group model. The initial tasks that teams are asked to perform should be small, and you should be prepared to assist students as they gain experience with this instructional approach. When students are moved immediately to small learning groups after experiencing only teacher-led instruction, the transition period might be chaotic. Many teachers in both the New Zealand and the Australian national high school trials chose to make this move immediately rather than gradually and reported that classes were soon unruly. However, they also reported that within several class sessions, the chaos disappeared and students were managing the seasonal chores responsibly. Several teachers thought this change was nothing short of miraculous. We believe that little can be learned from chaos; that is why we support the strategy of making a gradual transition.

The small learning group is also important for the students' personal and social development, which in turn contributes to the long-term goals of developing literate and enthusiastic sportspersons. Students first learn to become active citizens of their team. They have responsibilities, and performing their roles well is essential to team success. Thus, the citizenship they learn is not individualistic but rather related to the goals of the team. Students are required to plan and make decisions: Which team members will compete at the A-, B-, and C-levels for this competition? Who will be

Figure 2.1
BENEFITS OF SMALL-GROUP LEARNING

- Students have a stronger sense of control and ownership for their learning.
- Teachers are relieved of constant traffic-cop duties, thus opening up opportunities for content instruction and individualized feedback.
- Time on task is increased, especially during dispersed team-based practice.
- Peer support and pressure within teams serves as an accountability function.
- Students who tend to disengage are not left alone.
- It becomes more difficult for students to shy away from participation.
- Students learn to give help and to accept it.

the fitness trainer for the season? Who will be the team publicist? What should the team publicist do? How can the team do better in the next competition? Who is having problems refereeing and how can everyone else help? To address these questions, students have to carry on an organized, focused discussion; they have to make decisions about their plans and then carry out those plans. Although these skills are essential for successful adults, they are too seldom practiced in school settings.

HOW SPORT EDUCATION FITS WITH CURRENT EDUCATIONAL THOUGHT

Sport Education is wholly consistent with current trends in curriculum and instruction in schools. In particular, it fits nicely within the concept of twenty-first-century learning, which means that students master content while producing, synthesizing, and evaluating information from a wide variety of subjects and sources with an understanding of and respect for diverse cultures. Twenty-first-century learning requires that students demonstrate literacy not only the three Rs but also in the three Cs: creativity, communication, and collaboration. It is these three Cs that are an essential element of Sport Education. For example, teams need to be creative in planning, participating, and evaluating practice and performance in various team games or in activities such as fitness, gymnastics, or dance. Communication and collaboration are equally critical in team settings because decisions need to be made, from simply choosing a team name and color to more sophisticated judgments about how to practice for a specific fitness challenge or how to create routines in synchronized jump rope competition.

The Value of Authentic Learning

One of the key features of twenty-first-century learning is a focus on authenticity. With respect to Sport Education, four particular aspects stand out:

1. real life-relevance, where activities and tasks should represent those of a professional as closely as possible,
2. sustained investigation, where projects and tasks require a significant investment of time and cannot be solved in a matter of minutes or hours,
3. collaboration, in which individuals cannot achieve success alone, and
4. reflective learners, who reflect on their own learning and make choices and set targets accordingly (Pearce, 2016).

A New Role for Teachers

As a result of this new focus, traditional teacher-directed instruction, with its focus on facts and information, is being redirected toward teaching twenty-first-century skills, which focus on problem solving and on students creating and innovating with the information they have learned in the classroom. This requires teachers to move from more traditional assessments, such as quizzes and tests, to more open-ended assessment approaches, such as student portfolios.

After decades of relatively unchanged form and function, the job description of a teacher has undergone some significant transformations in a short period of time. The traditional stand-and-deliver method of instruction is being pushed out by the guide-on-the-side approach, just as the "cemetery" classroom is being replaced with creative, comfortable learning spaces.

THE CURRICULAR ROLE OF THE TEACHER IN SPORT EDUCATION

While much of the in-class decision-making in Sport Education is handed over to students, the teacher is still the architect of the model. As the career-matching platform Sokanu notes, "Architects are not just involved in the design of a building. As a licensed professional they are also responsible for public safety and overseeing of projects. Their role is important in every stage of the building's construction, from the initial concept to the opening ceremony when the building is complete." While chapter 8 provides more detail on how to organize a season of Sport Education, there are two key issues that must be resolved before planning the day-to-day features of the model. These issues relate to (a) the length of the season and (b) deciding which activities to include. For the architect, these are perhaps the equivalent of determining the budget for a project, as well as identifying the purpose of the buildings involved.

Determining the Length of a Season

At many Sport Education presentations, we have been asked, "What features of the model are most important and must be adhered to?" Our first answer is always, "The amount of time devoted to a season." At the elementary level, we have seen good Sport Education seasons done over 12 to 15 class periods lasting at least 30 to 40 minutes each. The standard amount of time at high school seems to be 20 class sessions with class periods lasting at least 45 minutes, but we have seen good examples of seasons that are longer. In high schools that use a block schedule (periods lasting anywhere from 80 to 90 minutes), a season may last 10 periods. These time allotments are adequate. As you will see in later chapters, however, if you try to do the Sport Education model in shorter seasons, you simply will not have enough time to achieve your goals.

It must be said that the Sport Education model needs no magic number of lessons to be applied. What is more important than adhering to a fixed number is to consider a number of factors when planning the curriculum. First, you must of course have sufficient time in a season for students to learn the various roles, techniques, and tactics necessary for successful participation. Second, teams must have *sufficient time to practice and compete* so that the outcomes of these competitions are what we call *good games*.

A good starting point for calculating season length is to consider the number of minutes per class and the number of classes per week to determine how long (in weeks) the season will last. If physical education is scheduled for only one day a week for 45 minutes, it makes sense to have a season last for a full semester. But if it is scheduled every day for 50 minutes and the grading period is 9 or 10 weeks, then you could plan two seasons for each grading period, using the 20-session model.

The nature of the activity and the number of goals for student achievement can also help determine the length of a season. For example, if you want to do a Sport Education fitness season, you might choose to do it for an entire semester. Teams would work toward semester-long goals in cardiorespiratory fitness, strength, body composition, and flexibility. You would organize team competitions around reaching appropriate goals in each fitness category. You could attend to flexibility in each class session, with strength and aerobic goals the focus of alternating sessions. An 18- to 20-week semester season provides sufficient time to alter body composition, strength indexes, aerobic performance, and flexibility, each of which could be a separate team competition. On the other hand, a Sport Education Frisbee golf season might be considerably shorter because the techniques and tactics are fewer and can be learned with relative ease. The competition season of dual meets followed by a championship could be done in fewer class sessions.

Dance suggests other uses of time. Sport Education dance seasons can be of regular length or last an entire semester. Dance forms can be done well in a Sport Education format. If you focused on folk dance for a season, 20 to 23 class sessions would be adequate. If, however, you wanted to do more than one form of dance (e.g., folk, square, ballroom, stomp), it could easily take an entire semester, with team champions in each of the dance forms and an overall semester champion. Richardson and Oslin (2003) described a series of three dance competitions within a nine-week season in which students met daily. The modern competition focused on solo performances within teams, the jazz competition focused on duets within teams, and the hip-hop competition focused on groups of four to six within teams. Likewise, in Spain, a class of high school students completed a 32-lesson season of three competitions focusing on contemporary dance, the traditional dances of Spain, and the dances of the world (Calderón, Hastie, Liarte, & Martínez de Ojeda, 2013).

Deciding Which Sports to Include

The second key factor that needs to be considered from the outset is the sports or games that will be included within a season or across multiple seasons. Depending upon the country, there will be courses of study for each subject area. Within physical education, these documents typically include objectives in several areas (e.g., knowledge, skill, personal development, fitness) followed by descriptions of the activities that can be taught in order to achieve those objectives. Deciding which of those activities to include in the physical education curriculum for a particular school level and school year depends on several factors, such as weather, facilities, and equipment. In larger school districts, teachers may be required to teach certain activities based on decisions made at the district level rather than at the school level.

THE INSTRUCTIONAL ROLE OF THE TEACHER IN SPORT EDUCATION

As mentioned earlier, the teacher is the architect of any Sport Education season. With respect to the tasks of architects, their work can be split into three main roles or phases: design, documentation, and construction. While the previous paragraphs focused on the design aspect, this next section will focus more on the construction (or in our case, the conduct) of lessons.

The shift toward a learner-centered approach to instruction is a learning process for both teachers and students. Teachers must actively guide this gradual shift toward more responsibility for and ownership of the Sport Education experience among students. Do not assume that teachers do no teaching in Sport Education, but realize that different types of teaching involve different responsibilities. In Sport Education, when students take on the role of team coach, referee, or manager (i.e., a nonplaying role), they need to learn what the role entails and get opportunities to practice that role. Teachers are responsible for creating an environment where students can learn to be a referee or a team manager. Officiating teams must be shown how to set up the appropriate fields or courts and equipment and must be given opportunities to practice. This all takes time and careful planning.

The difference between Sport Education and traditional physical education is that teachers also act as educational engineers. By teaching students the appropriate class

By helping students to be successful in small, mixed-ability learning groups, teachers are designing a class environment in which important outcomes are more likely to occur.

routines that ensure smooth management (see chapter 10) and by helping students to be successful in small, mixed-ability learning groups, teachers are designing a class environment in which important outcomes are more likely to occur. These outcomes include acts of personal and social responsibility that would be unlikely to occur in a class framework dominated by teacher-led instruction and practice. Most important, these outcomes are more likely to occur with students who are often unsuccessful and marginalized in physical education.

Teachers using Sport Education have frequently reported that they do more individual teaching than in a traditional model. With students responsible for more of the management and leadership of warm-ups and technique practice, teachers can move about the space and work with teams and individuals. This does not mean, however, that they never do whole-group, direct instruction.

Leading Students in Guided Practice

Whole-group direct instruction, or guided practice, is an appropriate teaching strategy in particular situations, such as during the early parts of a Sport Education season or when a new technique or tactic has to be introduced to a class. During the first lessons of the season, even when teams have been formed and team roles are assigned, as teacher, you should be in a position where the entire class can see you. You would introduce a practice task to the whole class so that teams can begin practicing the technique or tactic in their team practice space. In this format, you introduce a technique such as the drop shot in badminton. Teams then try to do the drop shot as you showed them (even if it is a shadow response without hitting the shuttlecock). Your goal in this situation is to see that all students understand the main technical features of the shot, or the critical elements. You point out common errors so students can learn to discriminate between the critical elements and common errors. As students practice, you reinforce good performance, correct major errors, and reteach the technique.

The same is true for introducing a particular tactic, such as the backdoor cut in basketball. With students gathered centrally at one of the teams' practice sites, you explain the context for and execution of the backdoor cut, giving students the opportunity to ask questions. You then organize students so they can do a walk-through of the maneuver. The goal of guided practice is to get students to the point where they can benefit from independent practice that will then be led by coaches. Though independent practice is crucial for technique development, guided practice is necessary to ensure that students will not make major technique or tactical errors once they disperse to their team practice sites.

Combinations of techniques can and should be practiced together. For example, when providing guided practice for free-throw shooting, you can also teach the techniques of boxing out and rebounding. Not only are more students actively engaged at the same time, but they are also practicing in a more authentic practice condition. The independent practice that follows can be a free-throw game in which points are scored both for making a free throw and boxing out and rebounding missed free throws. Again, this approach makes practices more gamelike.

Guided practice is also essential for teaching the duty team roles of refereeing and scorekeeping. Teachers cannot assume that students will have developed the knowledge and skills needed to be successful in these critical roles. For example, while some teams scrimmage, other teams can practice their officiating and scorekeeping skills. As teacher, you would actively monitor the players, referees, and scorekeepers. Sport Education seasons, similar to those in high school or college sport, include a preseason phase during which participants learn techniques and tactics related to the sport plus the additional managerial, refereeing, and scorekeeping duties required for the Sport Education season to be successful. Building in sufficient learning time and opportunity to learn and practice these sport-related and managerial skills during the preseason will pay dividends as the season unfolds.

Supervising Independent Practice

In the latter part of the preseason and after the teams have conducted team practices following your lead, they must be given the opportunity to practice independently as a team. During independent practice, team coaches should lead their teams in practicing techniques and tactics in their home spaces. You should carefully explain the organization for practice before dispersing students. Posters showing the critical elements and common errors of the technique or tactic are helpful. It is during team practice that students learn to work together and to help one another. The team coach provides the primary leadership for practice sessions, but you must make it clear that students are meant to help each other. Students who understand and grasp the technique or tactic quickly should be directed to provide assistance to teammates who are having trouble. Emphasize teammates helping one another and then recognize and support this when you see it occurring. During team practices, you move about the class space and offer feedback, assistance, and support to all teams. You will find that as a season gets underway, you can be of great assistance to the team coaches and help them focus their team practices on aspects of gameplay that need more attention. Thus, teachers can actually individualize their instruction where necessary.

Knowing What to Look For

Sport Education research provides convincing evidence that students like and appreciate the small-group learning model. However, at the outset, one of your primary instructional tasks is to closely supervise teams' independent practices to make sure they are practicing appropriately. As you watch the practices, ask yourself: Do the teams have a practice plan? Are they following that plan? Do they get started quickly? Are they actively engaged, or are just the higher-skilled team members involved? Are the team coaches providing the needed leadership? Do players take the lead from the team coach?

Teachers can review a team's practice plans while the fitness trainers take their teammates through their conditioning routines. We know of several teachers who have taken to using a rubber stamp that says *Approved!* after they review the practice plans that are to be kept in the team binder or portfolio. This type of monitoring shows teams that planning for quality team practices is expected. As you will see later on in more detail, this is also part of how students learn about fair play and how fair play performance is a significant factor in determining the champion team of a season.

Knowing When to Shift Focus

Since the team coaches now start leading the team practices, you can focus on teaching the activity by working with an individual team or individual players within that team. As team practices unfold, you can shift your monitoring to questions such as the following: What techniques are still lacking? What practice task might help a particular team? The more deliberate your monitoring is, the better position you are in to offer assistance to teams and individuals. As students gain more experience with Sport Education, they will be better able to work within it and profit from it. Thus, you should expect that across multiple seasons and years in Sport Education, students will become quite good at the give-and-take that characterizes small-group learning. As their capacity to work within the team concept improves, teams will become more self-directed and your supervision can shift to helping teams and individual students. You can spend more time providing teaching assistance during team practices. But do not expect such skills to develop automatically. As a teacher, you must provide ample and appropriate opportunities for students to learn to become more self-directed.

For teachers who have thus far employed a more direct style of teaching where students are almost entirely dependent on teachers' directives and commands, this gradual handing over of the reins to students may be difficult at first. However, if you have planned well, you will find that many students will surprise you with their willingness to take on leadership roles. For example, students who volunteer for the role of fitness trainer most often will have little difficulty directing their team through a series of conditioning tasks. Similarly, if the teams' equipment managers are clear on what equipment is needed and where it needs to be located, they will have little difficulty performing such tasks. As with your efforts to hold team coaches accountable for their planning, be prepared to actively monitor the fitness trainers and equipment managers. The preseason lessons will offer students multiple chances to practice performing these duties. When they do so effectively, be sure to recognize their good performances.

SUMMARY

This chapter has shown that the Sport Education model has implications for both the planning of curricula and the variety of teaching and learning experiences used in classes, as well as how this model can be used to address the national health objectives set forth for children and young people. The evidence is persuasive that students respond well both to the curricular features of Sport Education and to the kinds of learning experiences they have in their small learning groups, or teams.

Why Sport Education in Today's Context

3

Chapter Objective

After reading this chapter, you will be able to explain the central role of play in the development of children and youth and defend why and how sport belongs in physical education programs.

Key Concepts

- Humans are biologically predisposed to engage in play.
- Sport is an institutionalized form of play that is valuable and important to the development of children and youth.
- Over the past century and a half, sport has evolved globally into a dominant cultural phenomenon.
- With that prominence, sport has critical problems across all participation levels that diminish the sport experience itself.
- The reason why physical education is in a marginalized position does not lie in sport itself but rather in the manner in which it has been delivered.

This chapter will focus on why Sport Education is a legitimate curriculum and instruction model that deserves to be an integral part of today's physical education program. We first show how sport as a cultural phenomenon is rooted in play and that play is essential to the physical, social, and emotional development of children and youth. Second, we provide a brief overview of the evolution of sport from loosely played games to its highly institutionalized forms that we see today. Third, we show how sport's ever-growing dominance in society has also brought with it numerous serious problems. You will need to be able to articulate your position about these problems and recognize how in your role as physical educator you can make an important contribution to developing a healthier and saner sport culture that is accessible to all. In the final section, we argue that sport in itself is not the problem and should therefore not be dismissed as content for school physical education. As noted in chapter 1, if sport is to be a student experience to be lived, enjoyed, and meaningful, then a more authentic and more complete sport experience is needed.

SPORT AS A FORM OF PLAY

Play has been an innate part of the human experience since the beginning of time. It is seen in the earliest petroglyph drawings by Native Americans, and in the works of artists at play in world-renowned paintings. Children can been seen hard at play under even the most dismal conditions imaginable, without expensive or elaborate equipment or play areas. Scholars have made play a legitimate area of research and scholarship, which has yielded a rich body of literature about play and its critical role in the physical, social, emotional, and creative development of children and youth (Caillois, 1961; Ginsburg, 2007; Huizinga, 1955). The importance and value of play can be seen in how the school day in Finnish primary schools is structured. All children are provided 15 minutes for free unstructured play every 45 minutes. In other words, play is serious business! When you see kids by themselves in a park or on a neighborhood basketball court, do they say "Let's go practice our shooting"? No; they invariably say "Let's play." No doubt you have heard students in eighth grade physical education ask their teacher, after they have been reintroduced for the fifth time to the basic passing techniques in basketball through decontextualized and repetitive drills: "When do we play?"

Just like other species, humans are biologically predisposed to play and, as Siedentop (1980) argued, that makes their play behavior "inherently meaningful" (p. 244). It also makes play a defensible and logical focus for physical education. The same holds true for other forms of play like the arts and music. Like the man who enjoys painting on the weekend or the woman who enjoys playing the guitar in her free time, the weekend soccer player or golfer seeks out these activities because the activity is meaningful.

What characterizes play? Caillois (1961, pp. 9-10) identifies the following core characteristics of play.

1. **Play is free** in that it is voluntarily entered into.
2. **Play is separate** in that the temporal and spatial limits are defined and fixed in advance.
3. **Play is uncertain** in that its results and its course of action are not predetermined.
4. **Play is economically unproductive** in that it produces neither goods nor wealth.
5. **Play is regulated** under its own conventions, which temporarily suspend and replace ordinary laws.
6. **Play is make-believe** in that it is accompanied by a sense of being free from reality.

These characteristics need not all be present at the same time or to the same degree but can be viewed as on a continuum. If a person does not freely choose to enter into play behavior, is it still playful? Similarly, if a game is lopsided (i.e., the outcome is determined early on), is it still a playful experience? Can a professional athlete who is paid a large salary still be seen as playful when competing? We need only look at the passion and excitement among many professional athletes, who obviously are secure financially, and how important their win over the opponent is in a season-ending final.

What forms of play are there? In the earliest stages of life, infants and toddlers engage in what might be described as exploratory play. They interact with an object and see what it can do and how they can manipulate it with their body. For example, by handling blocks or sand or mud, toddlers can feel the characteristics and features of such materials; they also develop motor skills by the same token. Their attempts to repeat the same action over and over can be seen as an early form of play. Another example is when toddlers practice running and other types of locomotor skills. They look to see how fast they can go, and experiment with changing speed; they see how quickly they can change directions or come to a quick stop. They learn to navigate uneven surfaces. In tag games (a slightly more advanced form of gameplay), they practice chasing and fleeing, all the while trying to avoid crashing into others. These same actions can be seen later on in more formalized sport games. To adults, all this may seem like "only a game." We reiterate: play is serious business. It is the fundamental building block for all later engagement in other, more sophisticated games.

In the 1970s, Siedentop (1980) bucked the trend of previous physical education philosophers by arguing that physical activities (and therefore physical education) need not be justified in reaching the physical, social, moral, and mental goals that had been the focus until then. And while physical education could contribute to these other outcomes, the activities taught in physical education could be viewed as valuable and important in their own right. He laid out his argument for this in a new philosophy, which he called *Play Education*. Because Play Education was first and foremost a philosophy, it never directly impacted physical education curriculum development. It is, however, the foundation for Sport Education, which introduces students to "playful competitions" (Siedentop & van der Mars, 2012).

Sport is an institutionalized form of play (Siedentop, 1980), with all the characteristics of play still present to varying degrees. It is institutionalized in that it is highly structured (e.g., formal competitions, set times for practices, coaches) and has set boundaries in the form of rules. Measures are taken to ensure the rules are followed, by using officials. And an effort is made to ensure balanced competition, thereby creating parity between teams or competitors. When the number of participants increases and a level of governance is needed, we can say that games become institutionalized forms of play, which we call *sports* (Siedentop & van der Mars, 2012).

While sports like baseball and soccer have been around for well over a century, this institutionalization process can be seen today as well. Think in terms of the new events that have been added to the Winter Olympics in recent years (e.g., the halfpipe, big air snowboarding, freestyle skiing). Consider the rise of the summer and winter X Games. Rooted in the extreme sports of the 1980s, the popularity of the X Games was, in part, a consequence of a countermovement against the traditional sports like basketball, football, and baseball. Snowboarders, skateboarders, and BMX riders sought to break free from what they viewed as overly rigid rules and regulations within traditional sports. They sought to create their activities through experimentation, trying out what could be done on their bikes and boards. They, too, were very much at play. What is remarkable, of course, is the speed with which those forms of play have become increasingly institutionalized. Having ESPN broadcast the X Games, along with having numerous commercial sponsors, has helped these creative alternative games become institutionalized rapidly (Siedentop & van der Mars, 2012).

Physical education is an educational process that aims to improve students' knowledge of various motor play activities, as well as how to perform those activities.

If you agree that school physical education is the right program for developing physical active motor play in students, that has implications for how your programs deliver such experiences. First and foremost, physical education is an educational process that aims to change what people know and what they can do in the motor domain. It can result in one of two tendencies in students. If they come away from a unit of floor hockey or golf or swimming having experienced success, for instance; if they react favorably toward the activity and seek out additional engagement in it, we can claim that the experience has produced "subject matter approach tendencies." Conversely, if their experiences included frequent failure or ridicule and they would prefer to avoid any future contact with the activities, it would be inaccurate to call the experience *physical education*. The more appropriate label would be *physical miseducation* since it has likely produced "subject matter avoidance tendencies" (Siedentop, 1980). Put yourself in the shoes of a typical student and consider what you would want in order to develop subject matter approach tendencies toward sport.

THE EVOLUTION AND DOMINANCE OF SPORT

In the late 1800s, sport came of age in the United States. Urbanization and industrialization, along with an emerging social middle class, resulted in sport becoming increasingly institutionalized. Immigrants brought with them sports from other countries (e.g., golf and tennis). University campuses became a prime site for sport in the early twentieth century, in large part initiated by the students themselves. Attending sporting events became a major pastime. The depression following the Wall Street market crash in 1929 had caused spectatorship to decline dramatically but also gave rise to an increase in actual sport participation. World War II also influenced both amateur and professional sport, but high school and university sport continued their march to prominence. The passage of two federal laws, Title IX and Public Law 94-142, created access to sport for girls and women, and for persons with special needs, respectively.

Organized youth sport became a dominant force as participation exploded in the second half of the twentieth century. An economic perspective on this offers insight into how the youth sport landscape has changed. Drape (2018) reported that, while youth sport has been big business for a long time, the emergence of traveling teams has produced a 15 billion (U.S.) dollar annual industry, with small towns building multimillion dollar megaplex-sized youth sport facilities. These complexes can provide economic impulses to such small communities with the influx of new hotels and restaurants. King and Rothlisberger (2014) reported that families in the United States may spend as much as 10.5 percent of their annual gross income on their kids' personal trainers, equipment, and travel costs. Add to this the larger goal of getting exposure to college-level coaches and the prospect of a future athletic scholarship in college.

Few people will disagree that sport has evolved as perhaps the dominant cultural phenomenon across the globe in the last century. Consider how sport today dominates the news landscape through newspapers, television, the internet, and social media, not to mention the lucrative television contracts that are signed to broadcast major sporting events (e.g., the Olympics, major golf tournaments, the baseball World Series, the World Cup in soccer, college football in the United States, and the NFL). The rise of sport as we know and witness it today has been nothing short of remarkable.

Sport has contributed to moving the boundaries of what people are physically capable of doing. For example, consider Jesse Owens, the famous athlete who defied Nazi fervor during the 1936 Olympics by winning four gold medals. And yet his winning time in the 100 meter would not come close to qualifying him for the most recent Summer Olympics! Improvements in coaching methods, physical conditioning, and equipment have also contributed to improved performance. And while problems remain, sport participation by girls and women has risen dramatically following the passage of Title IX. Incredibly, until well into the 1970s it was commonly believed that women were not capable of running 26.2 miles. It was not until the 1984 Summer Olympics that women were allowed to compete in the marathon, with U.S. runner Joan Benoit earning the gold medal. The summer and winter Paralympics (originally only for disabled war veterans) are now commonplace, but only since 1960 and 1976, respectively.

Siedentop and van der Mars (2012) noted the many professions and other types of involvement that evolved from the rise of sport, many of which did not exist prior to the 1950s. These include athletic administration, sport broadcasting, sport journalism, sport facility management, sport medicine, athletic training, sport facility design, sport officiating, sport agents, athletic trainers, sport psychologists, sport apparel designers, sport scientists, sport photographers, and so on. The professionalization of sport is another example of its spectacular growth. The large contracts signed by athletes provide a strong stimulus for many seeking a career as an athlete, even as the odds of making it big are around one and a half to two percent. Attendance at major league baseball games continues to rise, despite labor strikes, steroid scandals, and rising ticket prices. The dominance of various forms of sports media is another barometer for how dominant (and lucrative) sport has become. In the United States, there are more than 80 national and regional sports networks, of which ESPN is the dominant source of news via multiple platforms on radio, television, the internet, and print (Smith & Hollihan, 2009; Vogan, 2015). Sports, professional leagues, and sport organizations have their own cable television networks. Canada has more than 30 sport television cable and broadcast networks, while Europe sports more than a hundred (e.g., EuroSport, SkySport).

Sport literature is also well established. Well-known athletes publish biographies (often cowritten either with ghostwrites or with sports writers). In addition, there is a plethora of sport fiction and nonfiction literature. The topics are wide-ranging, including for example, the economics of sport, social issues in sport, women and sport, and racism in sport. Sport history, sport sociology, and sport philosophy are legitimate areas of scholarly inquiry, having their own scholarly journals and conferences.

Outside the United States, governments in most other countries view sport as sufficiently important that they have a ministry of sport. Ministries of sport are charged with overseeing the development of and adherence to policies around all levels of sport (i.e., from youth and recreational sport to elite level sport). For example, they oversee investment in sport and recreation facilities, coaching education initiatives, and initiatives aimed at supporting youth, senior, and elite-level sport. The function of a ministry of sport is to ensure sport participation opportunity for all.

For many people, sport is almost a religion. Michael Novak (1992) argued that in many ways sport mirrors religion. For example, both sport and religion have distinct rituals (e.g., in tennis, opponents warm up together prior to the start of a match). Both include the use of specific clothing (i.e., uniforms and habits) that sets them apart. Both sport and religion are experienced in very personal ways, yet there is also a strong sense of community (as in the strong sense of team affiliation). Both sport and religion also have deep personal meaning for people. And finally, both carry with them a sense of power that is beyond one's control. In sport this is reflected in how a sudden burst of wind affects the flight of an arrow in archery or a ball in golf, or when a baseball takes an unexpected bad hop).

Sport has become an integral part of life for many, whether it be through participation, spectating, or other types of involvement. In many sports, participation levels continue to rise steadily. Families are willing to invest substantial amounts of money in the athletic development of their sons and daughters, sport fans are as passionate to see which players will be drafted by "their" team as they are about the team's actual performance during the season. In a word, sport has become a global behemoth. However, with that domination, numerous problems have emerged that threaten sport in multiple ways. We will highlight some of these in the next section.

PROBLEMS AND CRITICAL ISSUES IN SPORT

Based on the preceding, it might be argued that sport has us in its grip. But as a physical educator you should be cognizant of the problems that have emerged and persist in sport today and that take away from the experience itself, even though sport itself is not the cause. The actions of those in and around sport are what give rise to such questions as Who benefits from sport? Has sport become too big to fail? To what end is sport being used?

Alan Launder (2001) perhaps summarized it best when he referred to former U.S. senator, presidential candidate, and professional basketball player Bill Bradley who coined the term *third party*. This third party includes "self-serving politicians, avaricious owners, agents and promoters, cynical businesspeople, an ever more intrusive and sensationalist media, and, of course, fanatical supporters" (Launder, 2001, p. 5). Specific examples would be coaches, sport organizations (e.g., the NCAA), the leaders in these sport organizations (e.g., International Football Association Board [FIFA], the International Olympic Committee [IOC], and the United States Olympic Committee [USOC]), agents, cable television, and so forth. They are the ones who use sport for political and ideological purposes, and who look to benefit from their involvement in various ways. The gain could be money, influence, status, power, or athletic advantage. In this section, we share just some of the problems that influence the sport experience itself negatively but that may yield benefits for those around sport.

Countries continue to place financial stress on their own economies and thereby affect their social structure by investing as much as $51 billion to host the quadrennial Summer or Winter Olympics (Gelernter, 2016). In several cases, officials in the

IOC have been found to have taken bribes from representatives of countries that were looking to host the Olympics. Moreover, the recent Summer Olympics in Greece (2004) and in Brazil (2016) are good examples of two countries investing huge sums of money in the building of new athletic venues that greatly magnified the economic inequities in those countries. Both had experienced deep economic recessions and thus could hardly afford such investments, while social conditions for the economically disadvantaged got worse (Zimbalist, 2016; Zirin, 2016). And these same athletic venues generally have sat idle since then. Such decisions make sport an easy target of criticism. In their quest for Olympic medals, countries also invest millions of dollars in elite sport development. These levels of investment often limit investment in programs that support sport participation at the general population levels (Farrey, 2008; Launder, 2001).

With fair competition being the foundation of sport, it is easy to see why it is prone to cheating and corruption (Masters, 2017). Gaining an unfair athletic advantage through cheating occurs at all levels of sport. Cheating in youth sport occurs when coaches try to get a youngster on their team who is older than the maximum age allowed for that level of competition. Players may deliberately lose a game (this is called *tanking*), player-recruiting rules may be broken, coaches may be paid large sums of money by program boosters, players' grades may be changed to maintain their eligibility (see several examples documented in articles on the USA Today High School Sports website at http://usatodayhss.com/tag/cheating). Recently, a high school football coach in Arizona was found to schedule team practices as part of a so-called summer advanced physical education course, outside the period during which practices are allowed under the high school athletic association rules.

Corruption manifests itself in multiple ways as well, such as match fixing (both betting and nonbetting related), and doping (Masters, 2017). Instances of athletes being caught using banned substances have frequently grabbed the headlines in the past decades. Marion Jones, Mark McGwire, and Lance Armstrong are but a few examples of world-class athletes who were found to have cheated competitors and fans alike. Large-scale and systematic doping was an integral part of East Germany's elite sport programs (Gilbert, Grossekathöfer, Kramer, Ludwig, Pfeil, Weinreich, & Wulzinger, 2009). And Russia had most of its athletes disqualified for the same reason from the recent 2018 Winter Olympics. Officials in sports like baseball, cycling, and track and field, were slow to respond with putting measures in place to combat the use of banned substances. The World Anti-Doping Agency (WADA) is charged with testing athletes for banned substances in most international sport competitions, trying to stay ahead of the increasingly sophisticated ways in which their presence is masked. As of January 2018, there were more than 250 banned substances, including anabolic agents, beta-2 agonists, diuretics, blood manipulators, stimulants, narcotics, glucocorticoids, beta blockers, and masking agents (WADA, 2018).

Cheating and corruption continue to plague college athletics in the United States as well, notably in football and men's basketball. Examples include placing student athletes in courses that rarely (or never) meet, doctoring student athletes' transcripts, and establishing athlete-friendly academic programs to ensure athletes' eligibility (Kelderman, 2017; Stripling, 2018). While data are not readily available, oversight of universities by the National Collegiate Athletic Association (NCAA) is difficult. This is likely because the NCAA's budget for oversight of its rules is estimated to be less than 1 percent of its total budget (Branch, 2011). This likely makes cheating more common than most are willing to admit. In addition to issues of corruption and cheating, questions have been raised about the ethics around college athletes being used by the university without receiving any financial rewards. For example, the money brought in through the revenue sports (i.e., men's basketball and football) is used to fund the salaries of the tennis coach and travel cost of volleyball team at the same institution (Branch, 2011; Nocera, 2016).

Youth sport also has several critical problems. Siedentop and van der Mars (2012) as well as Coakley (2017) identified the following factors.

- *Excessive emphasis on competition.* As a result of an overemphasis on a performance ethic, both the fun factor and the focus on learning to enjoy the process of participation have diminished. Even in programs intended to be more recreational, youngsters are often pushed to seek higher levels of competition.

- *Early specialization and year-round participation.* Today, many youngsters are pushed to specialize in just one sport, and in one position (e.g. pitcher, running back) in the case of team sport. The National Association of Sport and Physical Education (NASPE) noted that specialization before the age of 15 carries more developmental risks than rewards (NASPE, 2010). For several sports, the concept of a season is almost a misnomer because youth compete on multiple teams, which results in year-round competition.

- *Increased possibility of overuse injuries.* This is especially risky in the case of younger children, whose bodies have not fully matured. For example, it is becoming increasingly common to see young baseball pitchers undergo surgery (known as Tommy John surgery) on the elbow of their pitching arm.

- *Poor quality of coaching.* Sport coaches in child and youth sport are in almost all cases volunteers. Moreover, attracting quality coaches has been found to be a problem for many youth sport leagues. While criminal background checks are now commonplace, most coaches receive little if any formal coaching education. Coaching education programs would provide the needed knowledge about and background in effective instructional strategies, developmental stages, managing parents, organization and management of games and practices, and so on. Having had personal experience in playing the sport is often regarded as the main criterion. The recent revelations on the inherent short-term and long-term risks of damage to the brain in tackle football has resulted in most U.S. State Athletic Associations now requiring high school coaches to complete concussion management modules that review the risks and assessment protocols specific to head trauma.

- *The impact of sport on family life.* Despite the ever-increasing cost of participation in sport, many families will go to great lengths to support the athletic development of their children (often with an eye toward a possible athletic scholarship to a college or a university). The prevalence of traveling teams has driven families to spend thousands of dollars on equipment, weekend travel, hotels, and meals, and the like.

- *Unequal access to sport.* The number of youth sport organizations that are funded through sponsorship from private or commercial entities has increased. Conversely, there has been a decline in the number of publicly funded child and youth sport programs (e.g., municipal parks and recreation departments). This trend contributes to the increasing inequities across socioeconomic status, race, and ethnicity because many disadvantaged families can no longer afford their child's sport participation.

- *An increase in the number of private, high-performance sport facilities that target talented young athletes.* These athletes seek to perform at the higher levels of performance in youth sport, and their parents are willing to invest substantial amounts of money to private trainers and coaches, with an eye to the future (i.e., university athletic scholarships).

- *Inappropriate involvement by parents.* Concerned about their children's success in organized youth sport, some parents act in increasingly extreme ways when advocating for them because of their views on their children's potential for future success in the sport.
- *Increased popularity of alternative sports.* Children and youth often prefer alternative action sports (e.g., BMX) to adult-controlled organized sports.

Specific to youth sport, the Aspen Institute's Sport and Society Program recently initiated Project Play 2020. This initiative brings together corporate and nonprofit organizations from areas such as sports, media, and health. This initiative is aimed at addressing several concerning trends specific to youth and their participation in sport.

- Children from homes in the lowest income bracket are far more likely to be physically inactive than those from wealthier households.
- For most sports, participation rates on a regular basis keep declining, with only gymnastics, lacrosse, and ice hockey experiencing increases between 2008 and 2016.
- The average child plays fewer than two sports; this statistic is now on a regular down cycle because of sport specialization, even though evidence shows that playing only one sport can be harmful to the body and can stunt athletic development.
- Less than one third of youth coaches are trained in competencies such as safety and sport instruction.

It is important that you, as a physical educator, are aware not only of the positive aspects that sport participation provides but also of the various problems that have arisen. Keeping current on efforts to improve the sport experience, and voicing your concerns when you see problems emerging, are important ways to combat these problems. There is a good chance that you will be put into situations where you witness very questionable sport instruction practices. How will you respond? What would you do if, in your role as sport coach, you discovered evidence of players using human growth hormones? What if you could get a player to join your team who is ineligible because of either academics or age limits? Related to this, how might you make these types of ethical dilemmas part of how you teach students about sport? Remember that one of Sport Education's objectives is for students to learn to make reasoned decisions within and about sport.

WHY SPORT SHOULD BE CENTRAL IN SCHOOL PHYSICAL EDUCATION

The ever-growing popularity of sport has resulted not only in increased opportunities for participation by many persons from childhood to senior citizens, regardless of gender, or physical ability, but also in problems that take away from the experience itself. However, you should note that this does not mean that the problems are inherent in sport itself. That is, sport engagement itself has not created the problems. It is what people (i.e., adults) have done to sport that has produced the problems. Sport is and should be an integral part of school physical education programs. As noted in chapter 1, we view sport more broadly, using the more inclusive UNESCO definition of sport, which encompasses many activities not typically viewed as sports. We cannot emphasize this enough: an education in sport should be central to school physical education. It should not only foster the development of players who can compete (regardless of level, whether recreational or more advanced) but should also enable people to contribute to creating a healthy sport culture in a host of other ways (e.g., official, administrator, coach, fitness trainer). Developing an awareness of the different ways in which fair competition is diminished through cheating (as noted earlier) reflects the ethical dimensions of sport; a perfectly legitimate area of education in sport.

In the past three decades, several trends have impacted physical education and the place of sport within it. First, there is the rollback of physical education time requirements, primarily a consequence of the ever-increasing emphasis on improving students' academic performance.

Second, there is the increased emphasis on more fitness-focused content in physical education programming. This is manifested in multiple ways. High school physical education programs now routinely schedule weight training classes for their athletic teams (van der Mars, 2017). In and of itself, this does not diminish the place of sport, and may contribute to the on-court and on-field performance of the athletes in the after-school program. But it does magnify the rather exclusionary nature of U.S. interscholastic sport programs in that it targets only a select group of students while leaving out students not deemed good enough to play on a school team.

Another way in which physical education has been affected is in the increased delivery of fitness content resulting from the emerging public health orientation in the form of "physical activity promotion." Because the number of overweight and obese children has continued to rise over the last four decades, physical educators were strongly encouraged to forgo the historically sport-dominated program focus, implying that the teaching of sport would not and could not contribute to the promotion of lifetime active living. This reflects an artificial either-or position where students can only be taught either sport skills (the skill learning perspective) or how to be physically active (the public health view). This is likely detrimental to the field, and shortchanges students' experiences. Moreover, it ignores the fact that the learning of motor play skills requires students to be physically active.

Rather than sport itself being problematic, it is the manner in which students in physical education have historically been introduced to it. Starting in mid to late elementary school grade levels, providing brief exposure to a multitude of different (sport) activities is unlikely to result in youngsters gaining any (perceived) motor competency. How many times have you seen students being asked to practice basic techniques of basketball or volleyball in fourth or fifth grade, using mostly static, drill-like practice conditions? That same scenario is then played out again in grades six, seven, and eight. There is no evidence that students must first master all the techniques of a sport in mostly drill formats before they can be successful in playing any game. The practicing of techniques is certainly important; for example, controlling the object in a game like volleyball is indeed important for successful gameplay. However, as we will show in chapter 7, such practice should occur in modified, authentic practice conditions from which transfer is more likely (e.g., through gamelike techniques challenges, modified game contexts). Moreover, there is evidence that well-designed and well-delivered Sport Education (as well as game-based instructional approaches) do produce substantial physical activity levels for students (Hastie & Trost, 2002; Pritchard, Hansen, Scarboro, & Melnic, 2015; Ward, Hastie, Wadsworth, Foote, Brock, & Hollett, 2017). Thus, the goals of teaching sport and the promotion of physical activity in school physical education are not mutually exclusive. In the next chapters, you will learn about how to design authentic sport experiences that can contribute to both.

TECHNOLOGY AND DEVELOPING PLAY BEHAVIOR

In 2017, global sales of computer games, hardware, and accessories were estimated to reach almost $110 billion. According to venturebeat.com, while total sales of computer game software and gaming hardware in the United States fell by about 2 percent, just in the month of August 2017 consumers still spent $282 million on gaming software, with EA's Madden NFL 2018 being the top-selling game. Over the last two decades, advances in technology have produced access to many forms of play behavior. The games have become more elaborate and increasingly authentic and realistic.

Why is this important for physical educators? With the ever-increasing sophistication, computer game designers capture all the essentials of sport and play: authenticity, appeal, excitement, passion, and reinforcement. Designers of computer games are masters at creating highly reinforcing games for a wide range of age groups and across a wide spectrum of different (sport) games. Designers and manufacturers target different age group markets from toddlers and preschoolers to adolescents and adults. One need only watch a toddler holding an iPad, engrossed in what is presented on the screen. Their ability to use the game's controls on the screen requires extensive and deliberate practice of their fine motor skills. As they mature, they increasingly develop approach tendencies so that they want to spend more time playing, on more advanced computer games. And this poses a serious challenge for physical education.

As a physical educator, you are competing with the gaming industry in the very domain that is your field's central target: physical, active motor play. To be sure, playing Madden NFL 2018 is very much play in its truest sense. But as exciting, authentic, and reinforcing as they are, such games are purely sedentary forms of play. This makes the task of providing physical education experiences that include the physical, cognitive, and emotional engagement of students even more important.

SUMMARY

In this chapter, we introduced you to how play behavior is critically important to the development and well-being of children and youth. That is, as humans we are meant to engage in play. In the Play Education philosophy, developed by Siedentop (1980), engaging in play (and in particular, sport) is seen as valuable and important in itself, as opposed to being used as a means to other ends such as social, physical, and emotional development. As such, it is a legitimate focus for physical education. Sport is an institutionalized form of play that has evolved into one of the most important aspects of our culture today. With its explosive growth and prominence, it has brought with it several critical problems that take away from the experience itself. We also highlighted the ever-increasing presence of technology and how it poses a serious challenge to developing students' physically active play behavior. We closed with making a case for the place of authentic sport experiences for students in school physical education.

Identifying and Selecting Season Outcomes

Chapter Objective

After reading this chapter, you will be able to identify the objectives you wish to include during a season of Sport Education.

Key Concepts

- The design of an individual season begins with asking what you would want to see during the games or competitions played at the end of the season.
- One advantage of the Sport Education format is that it allows for the pursuit of multiple outcomes that characterize the complete sports player.
- A *competent* sportsperson has both the technical capacity and the tactical understanding to satisfactorily play in a good modified game.
- A *literate* sportsperson can differentiate good and bad practices specific to the activity selected for a season.
- An *enthusiastic* sportsperson values the experiences and enjoyment derived from participation in a sport and is therefore actively engaged in all aspects of a season.

This chapter is based on the old adage, "You get what you teach." Quality physical education programs have a clear program mission, and teachers in these programs are able to communicate clearly what the program stands for and what it promises to accomplish. As we outlined in chapter 1, the mission of Sport Education is to develop competent, literate, and enthusiastic sports players. This long-term goal of the *complete sports player* can be realized through the regular and consistent achievement of short-term objectives. In this chapter, we outline all the possible outcomes that can be achieved in a season of Sport Education. Your task as a teacher is to decide which of these objectives you will prioritize during any individual season.

FIRST STEPS IN SEASON DESIGN

The design of an individual season begins with selecting specific outcomes by asking three related questions.

1. What do I want to see from my students at the end of this season?
2. How do I optimize opportunities for students to be actively engaged during my Sport Education season (both in class and beyond)?
3. How do I ensure that students will enjoy their participation during this season and feel more confident in their participation?

The best way to answer the first question is to describe what you would look for when you observe the games or competitions played at the end of the season. This is known as the end in view. In the words of Mager (1952), "the machinist does not select a tool until he knows what operation he intends to perform." In Sport Education, the end in view of an archery season would be, above all else, regular adherence to safety protocols and accurate scoring by students. In terms of shot execution, you would look for better technique, which should result in fewer arrows landing away from the targets, and perhaps tighter groupings of arrows on the target (i.e., higher total team scores). The end in view would be different for a floor hockey season (a court invasion game) compared with a badminton season (a court-divided game), a strength training season, or a dance season. In all cases, however, starting by identifying where you want to finish does provide a template upon which you can design your complete season.

The second question addresses the need to optimize the physical activity engagement of all students, not just the talented athletes, in physical education classes. How you select and design your content and class management strategies will go a long way toward giving students the best opportunities for physical activity during the season. In chapter 6, we outline numerous ways in which you can structure the elements of Sport Education to promote physical activity objectives.

The third question relates to designing tasks in which students can be successful. Consider the physical activity experiences you had growing up, whether sport-, fitness-, or dance-related. Most likely, you were drawn to those activities where you could say to yourself, "I can do this" or "This is fun." The key is that you experienced success in your initial exposure to the activities. Nothing chases students away from an activity more than being asked to practice a task that is too difficult or too strenuous. Based on the available research, it is clear that for students to adopt and value a physically active lifestyle, they must thoroughly enjoy the physical activities in which they are engaged as they develop those skills (Siedentop, 2009). Chapters 7, 8, and 11 in part II, The How of Sport Education, are written to specifically show how the use of modified games, guided practice, and graded competition are all designed to promote enjoyment and success.

SELECTING SEASON OUTCOMES

Once you have chosen a sport or activity, the most crucial step in the season design process is selecting and defining authentic, observable outcomes. An outcome is a description of what students will know and be able to do as a result of participation during the season (Siedentop & Tannehill, 2000). In Sport Education, we define outcomes as authentic (Wiggins, 1987) when they specify techniques, tactics, and knowledge that will be demonstrated in the natural context of doing the activity (i.e., during actual competition).

For example, consider the outcome of skillful passing in basketball. In a basketball season, students should learn how to recognize an open teammate who is in a position of advantage and deliver the ball to that teammate quickly with the appropriate pass (e.g., bounce pass, chest pass). This outcome requires tactical awareness (location of the open teammate who has the best advantage, as well any movement by opposing players), technique (e.g., bounce pass, chest pass), and skillfully using both in combination.

Thinking about the outcome of passing in this way will help you to design practice activities that are more likely lead to increased proficiency in passing. Having students stand some distance from each other and practice passes might be a starting point, but it is clearly just that and nothing more. At best, such tasks can serve as brief warm-ups, in which students get a feel for the ball again. To develop the techniques and tactics associated with improved passing, however, you will have to create practice situations that are dynamic and gamelike. For example, simple, modified games that have fewer players and are less complex allow for students to master beginning techniques and tactics, such as two-on-one or three-on-two basketball challenges, or games that emphasize moving to positions of advantage and executing passes.

In a weight training season, appropriate authentic outcomes would include students' technical execution of lifts with appropriate amounts of weight and their ability to track their own progress by keeping an accurate and complete training log based on their selected training goals. Being able to execute a particular lift in a technically sound and safe manner is in itself an authentic outcome. Students who try to progress too quickly and lift excessive weight likely will not be able to maintain good technique toward the end of the set and may risk injury. Similarly, maintaining a training log that is complete, accurate, and up to date is an important skill to develop as part of the broader process of self-monitoring.

As we will show in more detail in chapter 18, defining outcomes in authentic terms has implications for how you will formally assess your students. For example, having students stand 15 feet (4.6 m) from a wall and count the number of chest passes they make in 30 seconds is not an authentic assessment of passing skills. On the other hand, you could use the concept of assists in a basketball season as an authentic proxy measure for passing proficiency, because it is a common statistic kept in most basketball games. The point is that you must assess authentic outcomes in gamelike performance settings.

Outcomes should be considered not only for activity techniques and tactics but also for the knowledge and techniques that students will have to demonstrate in nonplaying roles, such as referee and scorekeeper, and their performance relative to Sport Education's fair play goals. We urge you to consider a limited set of outcomes. When educators begin to think about developing a curriculum around authentic outcomes, they often keep in mind a slogan that has become central to that approach to education: "Less is more." Too many units of instruction are best described as a mile wide and an inch deep. If you try to stuff too many outcomes into a season, you will likely be disappointed in the results.

One advantage of the Sport Education format is that it allows for the pursuit of multiple outcomes. Figure 4.1 provides a list of the outcomes that are characteristic of the complete sports player. It is up to you to decide which of these will be the priority in any one season. That decision can vary depending on the nature of the activity selected and on your students' and your own experience with Sport Education.

SPORT EDUCATION'S COMPETENCE OBJECTIVES

A *competent* sportsperson has both the technical capacity and the tactical understanding to satisfactorily play in a good modified game. Such students are also knowledgeable game players in that they can explain the rules of the game well enough to score or officiate at an in-class competition.

Develop Sport-Specific Techniques and Fitness

Good gameplay requires students to master techniques and tactics. Techniques should be taught first and then quickly put together for various tactical situations in modified gameplay. It should be obvious that students will only develop these aspects of gameplay if they are given ample opportunities to learn them gradually through the introduction of modified forms of activities such as soccer, volleyball, or folk dance. The level of play in your physical education program will not and should not be the same as what you would expect from students in interscholastic sport programs. However, that does not mean you should not have high expectations for your students. For example, there is no reason why sixth-graders cannot play basketball where they employ a good screen and roll, create space for a teammate by drawing an opponent to the outside, and make appropriate decisions on whether to shoot, dribble, or pass the ball.

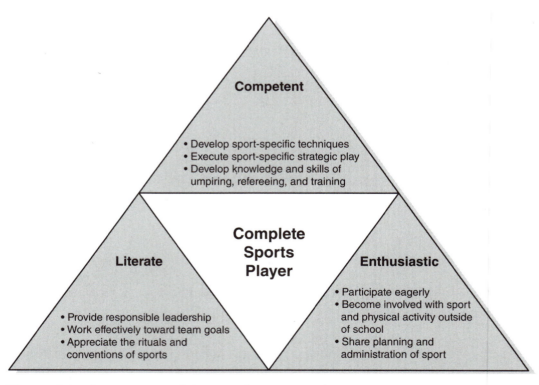

Figure 4.1 Components of the complete sports player.

You want students to be able to execute the techniques of the sport you are teaching. In volleyball, they should be able to serve, pass, set, block, and spike. In a track and field season with good instruction and ample opportunity to practice, they should be able put a shot with good form, take a smooth run-up and takeoff in the long jump, and master the hop-step-jump sequence in the triple jump. In a weight training season, you would look for technical execution in performing planks, side planks, chest presses, squats, push-ups, curl-ups, and so on. And in a dance season you would look for students to remain in time with the beat of the music, and to execute smooth transitions in moves that require a quick change of direction.

Notice that the emphasis is on the quality of the technical execution. When techniques improve, outcomes will gradually improve also. When students learn better passing technique in volleyball, they will keep the ball in play and get it to the appropriate teammate, who will have an opportunity to spike for a point. Students will come to understand that, in order to achieve the outcome goal, they must improve their techniques. Thus, even though students may initially define success in terms of baskets made in basketball, it is essential to communicate the importance of learning appropriate techniques as the quickest and best way to score points and win contests.

In principle, seasonal outcomes that focus on developing the techniques of many sports should be described relative to the execution of the technique itself and the context within which the technique is used. For example, the chest pass in basketball has discernible critical elements and phases. However, in actual gameplay, basketball players will have to contend with the actions of both teammates and defenders. This likely prevents the textbook execution in which you yourself may have been instructed. You can describe your season outcomes more holistically in terms of whether the pass actually was attempted, whether the type of pass was appropriate (e.g., chest versus bounce versus sidearm pass), and whether the target of the pass (i.e., the teammate) was appropriate given the context of the game at that moment.

In striking and fielding games, the technical execution of hitting, pitching, base running, and fielding is critical to team success. As fielders, students should learn to make good throws to bases and other fielders. Developing fluidity in approaching a ball that dropped in for a hit in the outfield, picking it up with their glove, bringing it to their throwing hand, and making the throw improves their chances of making an out or preventing a runner from advancing. Here, too, you look for students to develop consistency in the execution.

In some activities, context is less influential in terms of how techniques are executed but developing consistency in performance is essential. Such techniques are typically self-paced and are performed in relatively stable environments. Consider, for example, archery, the throwing and jumping events in track and field, the free throw in basketball, or the various shots in golf. In archery, a desired season outcome related to students' shooting technique would be to develop consistency in stance, posture, bow-arm position, anchor position, and release. When students are learning all throwing and jumping events in track and field, the sole focus can be on how to execute these events. Even with the sprint start (though it is somewhat affected by the pace of a starter's commands), the physical execution is relatively constant. In golf, students should learn the basic techniques of the swing and how those techniques are somewhat modified depending on the club used (e.g., the swing with a driver is different than the swing with a pitching wedge). Tactical issues in golf can be approximated in physical education classes but are a bit more difficult to practice without access to a golf course. Still, we have seen teachers who have been very inventive in creating hazards (i.e., bunkers, water). The outcome of a golf season would be defined in terms of consistent ball placement, address position, swing pace and rhythm, amount of backswing, and ability to strike the ball cleanly.

In court-divided games such as tennis, badminton, and pickleball, being able to control the object should remain a key focus. But you must also consider the context of the opposing player's shot (i.e., speed, angle, and placement of the shot). When describing your expectations of the level of skillful play you expect by the end of the season, therefore, you should also include how students cover the court by adjusting their position with good footwork to prepare for their shot. The same applies to executing the forearm pass or set in volleyball.

In order to help students become more proficient in executing the countless techniques in all the various sports, you yourself should have strong content knowledge of the activities. Knowing and recognizing the critical elements, common errors made by beginners, execution phases, and performance cues will put you in a better position to help students improve their technical performance. There are multiple sources you can draw from to assist you in this regard. In addition to the ample printed literature, there are countless websites where you can obtain this knowledge. For example, if your knowledge of tennis is limited, www.fuzzyyellowballs.com and www.tennis.com offer excellent free video-based lessons and graphics information that can strengthen your content knowledge. For a list of several other web-based sources of content knowledge, see the web resource. While not all YouTube postings are equal in quality, you can find ample examples of instructional videos specific to technique execution.

Appreciate and Be Able to Execute Sport-Specific Strategic Play

Successful performance in sport and other physical activities typically requires more than just performing techniques in isolation. In many activities, students will acquire competence and confidence if they are afforded the opportunity to learn to anticipate the flow of action in order to make decisions about what to do and when and where to move. That is what tactics are all about. The balance between techniques and tactics shifts from activity to activity, with tactical dimensions having a more prominent role in such games as soccer and team handball versus golf or softball. Thus, the role and relative importance of techniques and tactics are a matter of degree, not an either-or proposition. Both are necessary for skillful play to develop. An outfielder may have perfect technique when it comes to throwing a ball back to the infield, but that does little good if the throw is directed to the wrong base. Conversely, even if the throw is made to the correct base, poor technical execution may reduce the chance of an out being made or may help a runner advance to the next base anyway. Figure 4.2 provides a schematic of how different sports fit along this continuum.

Regardless of the activity, learning to make better decisions (along with the associated moves) when engaged in play is a central tactical aspect of skillful gameplay. Even though decision-making is a cognitive process, the consequences of decisions (i.e., outcomes) are reflected in the students' actions and thus are readily observable. Making better decisions in gameplay invariably leads to better games. As students grow in their capacity to make appropriate tactical decisions in games and activities, they will be more successful and their enjoyment in participating will increase.

In court-divided games (e.g., tennis, pickleball, volleyball), when you see students gaining more consistent control over the ball or the shuttle (i.e., improved technical execution), you can start focusing on the more tactical features of the game, such as coverage of the court by returning to a more central position following each shot (i.e., getting back to base position), shot placement, shot selection, and anticipation. Each of those tactical features has an underlying decision-making process. For example, how well do students recognize the actions of their opponents? Do they see that the

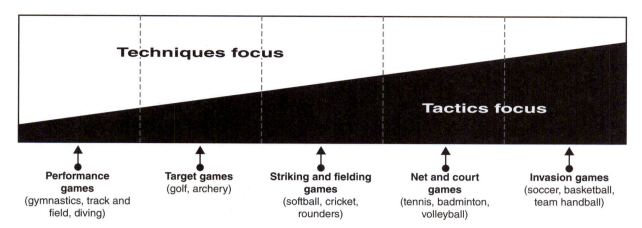

Figure 4.2   Balance between techniques and tactics across games.

opponent is slow in getting back to a central court position? Does the opponent seem to favor certain shots? Becoming better at recognizing the opponent's actions can lead to better decisions about what shot to use (e.g., passing shot versus lob versus drop shot), when to use that shot, and where to place it.

In striking and fielding games, students should learn how to throw, pitch, catch, hit, run the bases, and field ground balls. As outfielders, students should not only be able to make technically sound throws but should also learn to throw to the correct base or relay person. Outfielders should learn to back each other up on every fly ball or base hit to assist in the event the ball skips through or does not get fielded at all. In slow-pitch softball, hitters can learn to not always swing for the fences but rather look to direct a hit ball to a certain area of the field. To be a good base runner, it is not enough to be a fast runner. Students should learn what to do as a runner when a ball is hit into the outfield. Decisions on what to do then are influenced by several factors (e.g., number of outs, where the ball is hit, where the outfielders are positioned). In Sport Education, using base coaches who are learning to assist the base runners can add to the overall experience.

In invasion games (e.g., soccer, team handball, basketball), students have to anticipate the offensive or defensive movement when they are not in possession of the ball so as to get into a position of advantage for their team. Tactics can be divided into two categories. The first category includes general tactical moves. Moving to open spaces, supporting the teammate with the ball, and maintaining floor or field balance in invasion games are examples of such tactical moves. The second category of tactics includes those that are specific to offensive and defensive strategies, such as team movements in a zone defense in basketball. When a team regains possession of the ball, players have to move toward positions of advantage that will give them a good chance to score. In sports such as basketball and soccer, ball possession may switch frequently between teams because of errant passing or poor ball control, and students must be able to switch from offense to defense at a moment's notice.

Because the tactical aspects of invasion games are arguably the most complex and thus the most difficult to learn, it is critical that you provide students with practice opportunities in which they have the opportunity to put tactics in place. As an example, in one study (Romar, 1995), a teacher reported that the primary seasonal objective was for students to participate successfully in a well-played game (a wholly appropriate goal). Observations, however, showed that practice sessions were all about the techniques of dribbling, passing, shooting, and rebounding. Not a single practice task focused on tactics. The games showed the predictable results: better players dominated, no discernible offensive or defensive tactics were shown, and students were often out of place and seemingly bewildered by the pace of play and the movement of the ball. The teacher was disappointed. In Sport Education, teaching tactics is as important as teaching techniques. This lack of alignment between the season objective and the content selected by the teacher will be discussed in more detail in the next chapter.

An effective way to promote tactical development is to sequence the types of games that you present to students. For example, in soccer you can limit the number of techniques and tactics by having students start with small-sided games (e.g., one-on-one, two-on-two). Such games allow the player with the ball to practice

Successful performance in sport and other physical activities typically requires more than just performing techniques in isolation.

shielding the ball from a defender, shooting on goal, dribbling, and turning. The defender can practice going for the ball, reading the movement of the opposing player with the ball, and staying between the opponent and the goal by using good footwork. As the team size goes up (e.g., three-on-three, four-on-four, five-on-five) and field or court space increases, you can instruct students on making decisions, creating space, supporting the teammate with the ball, defending space against the opposing player, and so on.

Develop and Apply Knowledge About the Key Features of the Game or Activity

Students should be able to identify the rules in effect for a particular season, along with which penalties are appropriate when a violation or foul is called. They should also be able to accurately score a contest, and they should learn about the history of the activity and its traditions. Finally, they learn how fitness requirements vary from one activity to the next.

In Sport Education, learning the rules of the game is especially important because students will have to apply this knowledge not only as players but also as game officials once the formal competition starts. The preseason is the perfect time to learn such skills and knowledge. This is the time to form teams and to practice for the formal competition. Preseason scrimmages help students to become familiar with the game rules. Some Sport Education teachers require their students to pass the rules test in order to participate during the regular season, thus motivating teams to learn the rules. This is one approach of holding all players accountable and introduces peer accountability for players learning the rules and protocols.

In Sport Education, with its emphasis on modified games, you want to limit the number of game rules in effect for a season. Ask yourself, "How many and which rules are needed to get a good game going?" As we will show in chapter 12 on learning to officiate, keeping the game rules simple also helps students develop their officiating skills.

Many teachers include seasonal outcomes related to learning about the history of a game, critical issues in sport, or etiquette specific to the activity. In order to do this, you must bring students in direct contact with such content. For example, in a season focused on volleyball, students might learn where it was invented, for what purpose, and who the first players were. They then might learn how the sport developed and spread until it began to be played internationally.

In middle or high school programs, students could be directed to focus on controversial issues or events that transpired during international competition or on unruly spectator behavior at sporting events. For example, consider the powerful connection students can make between sport and civil rights or sport and politics when they are asked to learn about the protest by Tommie Smith and John Carlos at the medal ceremony for the 1968 Olympics or about the terrorist attacks on Israeli athletes during the 1972 Munich Olympics. In seasons where countries are the basis of team affiliation, each team can be asked to draft a written report or design a poster that reflects their knowledge of the country they represent. Such work would become part of their team portfolio. Teams could also present their posters as part of the culminating event of the season.

Students should be able to assess the specific skill and fitness requirements for successful competition in a particular sport. For example, knowing the differences in fitness conditioning required by tennis, volleyball, orienteering, and soccer is an important contribution to your students' literacy about sport. You might assign a project at an individual or team level that requires students to research the sport being studied and to identify ways in which they can improve their sport-specific fitness over a season. You might ask students to explore the contribution of various energy systems to successful performance in a sport and to design a personal training program that matches those requirements.

Develop and Apply Knowledge About Umpiring, Refereeing, and Training

Officiating and scorekeeping are central nonplaying roles in good games, and every student should have the chance to umpire, referee, or judge during a sport or activity season. As referees, students need to know how to apply the rules. However, they should also learn how, where, and when to move, how to make a call, what the possible hand signals are, and how to explain infractions to the players and scorekeepers. Referees are especially important in making sure that the game moves along quickly and that calling a foul, for example, must be done quickly with the goal of moving the game forward. Umpires and referees have to know the rules of the activity to perform their respective duties. Missing an item on a rules test has only modest consequences for a student, but a referee missing a call in a three-on-three game will spell immediate consequences for the participants. By performing as a referee or umpire, a student quickly learns the rules and violations and begins to understand how important a good referee is to the quality of the game and to the enjoyment of the competitors.

Students should also become knowledgeable about how to keep score. In Sport Education, all students are expected to serve as scorekeeper at some point during the season as part of their duty team roles. Here, too, the preseason scrimmages are the perfect time to develop such skills. Inevitably, mistakes will be made, and in most cases, their peers will alert them to the mistake. Some teachers have made accuracy in scoring a match a prerequisite to participating in the season. Others build in peer accountability strategy to ensure accuracy in scoring where a representative from each team certifies the official score sheet as accurate following each match. The score sheets provided in the web resource provide a space for this as well.

A frequent role in many seasons is that of fitness leader, whose primary responsibilities include designing warm-up activities for the team and leading the team in those warm-ups. In fitness-based seasons, this role can be expanded to helping design the fitness plans for team members. In this case, the teacher needs to support students in this role by providing appropriate resources. In most high school courses of study (at least in the United States), a key objective is for students to design personal fitness plans, and to apply principles of specificity, overload, frequency, intensity, time, and progression to physical activities.

SPORT EDUCATION'S LITERACY OBJECTIVES

A *literate* sportsperson can differentiate good and bad practices specific to the activity selected for a season. They also appreciate the value of team roles and make a commitment to ensuring they complete their tasks for the benefit of their team and of the class as a whole.

Provide Responsible Leadership

For a Sport Education season to be successful, leadership is an important objective. The student roles of coach and manager are particularly important. Each coach works with teammates to decide which team members will participate at various levels of the competition, to supervise team practices, and to resolve any conflicts that might arise within the team. Managers make sure that equipment is in the right place at the right time and that team members who are referees and scorekeepers get to the right competition venue at the right time to perform as a duty team. Not every student will be a coach or manager each season, but during the course of a school year, most students will have the opportunity to fulfill these roles. In early Sport Education experiences, teachers start with small leadership tasks and then gradually broaden the roles as students develop leadership skills.

Work Effectively With Your Team to Pursue Common Goals

Students are members of their team for the duration of a season. In most cases, team membership changes from season to season in order to ensure that teams are as even as possible in terms of the teammates' skills for the particular sport or physical activity. Teams cannot be successful unless each member of the team contributes in the role of player, in duty team roles, and in whatever role is played within the team (e.g., coach, manager, fitness leader). A major educational benefit of the Sport Education model is that students have to work together to achieve common goals, and they typically achieve that by working hard to fulfill their specific role on the team. Team camaraderie and spirit are promoted when teams create a name, color, and cheer and begin to work together to do as well as possible during the season.

Because the social dimension of Sport Education is such a significant part of the model and the success of a season, a legitimate outcome for students is to accept and act on the advice given to them by their peers. Many students have commented that this particular feature is a positive aspect of their participation. Students often report that they like their membership on a team and the support they receive from their teammates. By actively monitoring the teams' practices, you can determine how each team is getting along and be ready to intervene with teams that are not functioning as desired. Younger students experiencing Sport Education for the first time will need instruction and support from you to help them act in ways that are helpful to teammates and to avoid behavior that is harmful to teammates. This aspect of behavior development is crucial to the success of the small-group model that is at the heart of Sport Education.

Appreciate the Rituals and Conventions That Give Sports Their Unique Meanings

Part of learning a sport is coming to understand and appreciate its rituals and conventions. Why are spectators quiet in tennis and loud in basketball? What do contestants typically do at the end of a match or contest? How does a competitor show appreciation and respect for the opponents, the officials, and fans? Most important, why is fair play fundamental to a good sport experience? This objective shows that Sport Education goes beyond the techniques and tactics of an activity in order to provide students with a broader understanding of the activity in terms of the behaviors expected of good sportspersons when they compete.

Develop the Capacity to Make Reasoned Decisions About Sport Concerns

When performing their various responsibilities in Sport Education, students inevitably experience conflicts that arise within and between teams. Because fair play is an integral part of Sport Education, concerns about fair and appropriate conduct arise throughout a season. Sport Education teachers typically develop a system for resolving those conflicts, and that system includes student involvement in the resolution. Conflicts create teachable moments where students can learn how to resolve those conflicts satisfactorily.

Televised sporting events provide ample examples of athletes exhibiting inappropriate behavior toward teammates, opponents, and officials. Students in Sport Education should learn to show restraint when they believe an official has erred when deciding on a rule infraction, a goal, or a foul. This demonstration of respect goes beyond the traditional postgame handshake (although that is important to include). Daily fair play points and fair play awards for individuals and for teams throughout the season are excellent tools to reinforce these behaviors (see also the chapter 10 web resource).

Finally, you should help your students learn what it means to be *helpful and not harmful*. Teasing and bullying are often too evident in sport and physical activity settings; indeed, trash talk and taunting have evidently reached a level of acceptance in some professional sports. Events from professional sport settings can serve as excellent springboards for teaching about positive and negative sport practices. Cheating is another example of harmful behavior and comes in various forms, such as taking advantage of rules, not reporting infractions, and the like. It is useful to point out instances of cheating in the larger world of sport; for example, athletes who are charged with the use of performance-enhancing drugs serve as excellent teaching prompts for addressing good and bad sport practices. Especially in secondary school programs, you can help students become more informed by assigning them articles to read about such drugs and their related health risks, and having them debate the related issues.

Share Planning and Administration of Sport Experiences

In Sport Education, students learn a variety of roles other than performer, including coach, manager, referee, judge, statistician, trainer, and publicist. In middle and high schools, teachers often create a sport board with appointed or elected student members. The sport board plans the season and also adjudicates differences that might arise between or within teams. This typically produces two outcomes: ownership and empowerment. Students develop and show a sense of ownership for the success of their own experience and that of their classmates. Students who are empowered for the responsibilities of developing and implementing a Sport Education season take tasks more seriously and are more likely to be accountable for the success of the season. In too many physical education programs, the only responsibilities students have are to obey class rules and do what the teacher tells them to do.

SPORT EDUCATION'S ENTHUSIASM OBJECTIVES

An *enthusiastic* sportsperson values the experiences and enjoyment derived from participation in a sport, and as such is actively engaged in all aspects of a season. They also seek out opportunities for participation outside of regular physical education lessons, whether these are simply with friends in a social setting, or in programs that are available in their communities where formal competitions are scheduled. Here too, you will see a focus on fair play and why it is so critical to the total sport experience.

Actively Engage in All Aspects of Lessons

The research on Sport Education shows that student motivation to participate in the model has been overwhelmingly positive, and that for many students (particularly the lower-skilled), it is a more attractive form of physical education than their previous experiences in a teacher-directed, multiactivity curriculum. The key to achieving this enthusiasm has been students seeing that they have a greater level of curriculum ownership, particularly with regard to the roles and responsibilities that come as part of a persisting team. In other words, for students to be actively engaged in a season, they need to be given opportunities to become self-directed.

Give Their Best Effort

Giving effort is a concept that younger students need to learn. It is an integral part of developing fair play. They have to be shown what effort looks and feels like and be provided with frequent prompts about making the required effort. Also, when teams put forth good effort (even if they do not win a match) they should be rewarded with fair play points. The appropriate level of effort during practice and competition in fulfilling duty team responsibilities and team roles such as manager or coach has to be taught and emphasized, especially for young learners. Many teachers use whole-class moments or closure activities to compliment students who have shown their best effort. Some use a signal system by which students indicate their own perceived level of effort. A thumbs-up sign from students indicates that they thought they gave a great effort in class, whereas a thumbs-down sign indicates that they thought they might do better. A halfway thumb sign, which shakes up and down, indicates an undecided or partial response. Children soon become accurate monitors of their own effort levels, particularly when teachers reinforce the idea that everyone can have a bad day now and then and that the goal is for everyone to work toward good effort.

When team portfolios are developed, students can be responsible for keeping a log of their participation and learning in their roles, which includes personal reflection about their success and learning and even peer evaluations concerning their contribution to the team. They can also produce logs of their effort level for each class as a self-evaluation. Such strategies are all excellent ways of developing student awareness of what it means to put forth one's best effort.

Become Involved in Sport and Physical Activity Outside of School

The main outcome most often cited for physical education today is for students to adopt and value an active lifestyle. Physical education classes can provide some proportion of the recommended weekly accumulation of moderate to vigorous physical activity, but the more difficult task is to have the physical education experience motivate students to seek out physical activity opportunities in the community, whether by participating in community sport, working out in a fitness center, or cycling or running on their own or with friends. When your Sport Education season centers on volleyball, aerobic dance, or soccer, for example, you can not only encourage regular physical activity outside of school but also help students find out how to take part in those activities through community programs, how to access those programs, and what kinds of opportunities are available in each. This is where your knowledge of what is available in your community is essential. In this chapter's web resource, you will find a Community Mapping template to learn about what all is available in your community. Community mapping is an excellent way of exploring the many sport, fitness, and recreation options available.

One of the best predictors of students seeking out-of-school participation opportunities is their confidence in their ability to be active and the level of enjoyment they derive during activity. Think back to your own sport experiences. If you could execute the techniques of throwing, fielding, and batting and make appropriate tactical decisions in game situations, you likely felt more confident that you would be successful (i.e., a higher level of self-efficacy) and were more inclined to sign up with a softball league. Conversely, you were less likely to play in a recreational league in volleyball if you lacked confidence in your ability to serve, pass, set, spike, dig, and block. Student experiences in your program should lead them to feel confident about engaging successfully in physical activity and to enjoy that engagement. Note that physical activity at this level includes not just fitness-related activities such as running, weight training, and flexibility activities but also sport activities such as cycling, hiking, walking, orienteering, dance, and rock climbing.

Self-efficacy specific to any form of physical activity depends on the success experienced in those first opportunities for participation. The strong focus on modified learning conditions in Sport Education is more likely to help students have such positive learning opportunities (i.e., approach tendencies). The activities in which your students participate should create a strong likelihood of success, which will gradually lead to the development of self-efficacy for those activities. For this to happen, activities must have a strong fun factor. This will make the entire experience in your classes more enjoyable. Ask yourself questions such as these: Why should we expect eighth-graders to be excited about doing a static chest-pass drill when they have practiced that same drill every year since fourth grade? and How often do students say "That was fun!" as they are leaving at the end of the lesson? For students, the fun factor in physical activity cannot be underestimated. You may have strong beliefs about the quality of learning tasks that you think they need. However, if students find the tasks too challenging, too easy, lacking in meaning, dull, or boring, they will simply not be attracted to physical activity of any kind.

SUMMARY

The overall goal of Sport Education is to develop competent, literate, and enthusiastic sport players. The range of outcomes we just identified contribute directly toward those broader goals. Of course, you will not be able to address all of these Sport Education outcomes in each season. You have the flexibility to choose from this spectrum of season outcomes. The important thing is to choose appropriate outcomes in the context of the activity for each season.

Instructional Alignment as the Road Map to Quality Season Experiences

Chapter Objective

After reading this chapter, you will better understand the need to ensure alignment between your intended season outcomes, the content you deliver for students to practice, and the assessment you employ to determine whether the outcomes were met.

Key Concepts

- Developmentally appropriate outcomes should be the basis for planning and implementing Sport Education seasons.
- Content should be selected, designed, and presented so as to provide opportunities for students to engage in ways that allow them to reach the planned outcomes.
- The teacher should select and use formal formative assessments that capture student performance relative to the planned season outcomes.

Teachers' values and beliefs (along with the content knowledge they have) can be seen in their programs' overall curricular focus and the content they teach on a day-to-day basis. For example, teachers who primarily value health and fitness will mostly include activities like weight training, aerobics, yoga, and the like in their yearly plan of seasons or units. Teachers who value and know dance are more likely to include dance as the main content. Teachers who live in (rural) regions with mountains close by may be more inclined to include outdoor pursuits such as rock climbing and mountain biking.

Historically, though, most programs have reflected a sport focus. The sport culture has evolved over the past 60 years into arguably one of the most important cultural institutions. This can be seen in what Lieberman (2017) referred to as *industrialized sport*. In addition, most teachers who chose teaching physical education (and coaching) as a career did so as a consequence of their own sport experiences. Thus, they are more likely to create programs with a sport focus.

In this chapter, we focus on the central aspect of planning and implementing seasons and lessons. As shown in figure 5.1, it is critical for there to be alignment between what teachers choose as (1) the intended season learning outcomes (as introduced in the previous chapter), (2) the content (i.e., the various learning tasks) they select to teach during the season, and (3) the assessments to determine whether the intended learning outcomes are reached (e.g., Petersen & Cruz, 2004; Tannehill, van der Mars, & MacPhail, 2015). When this alignment is present, there is greater likelihood that students will practice in more meaningful ways and that teachers will be able to demonstrate that intended learning outcomes were reached based on their authentic assessments of students' performance. This is often referred to as *instructional alignment* or *constructive alignment* (e.g., Biggs, 1996; Borghouts, Slingerland, & Hearens, 2016; Tannehill et al., 2015). This chapter (along with the previous one on selecting outcomes) forms the transition between the previous chapter and the chapters in part II.

Part II focuses on the decisions teachers need to make to plan their seasons in ways that provide students the opportunity to meet the intended outcomes. Later on, in chapters 16 and 17, we highlight how Sport Education's objectives align with SHAPE

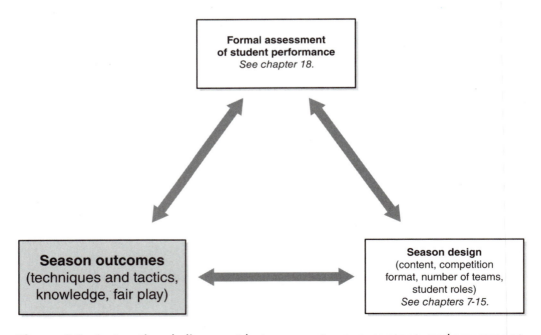

Figure 5.1 Instructional alignment between outcomes, content, and assessment.

America's current content standards (SHAPE America & AHA, 2016) and national standards, aims, and objectives developed in countries such as Australia, England, New Zealand, Portugal, and Spain.

ALIGNMENT ACROSS LEVELS

The need for alignment can be viewed across program, season, and lesson levels (see figure 5.2). At the program level, one would look for alignment between the program's overall mission or goals and the focus of the various content areas (in the form of seasons or units). This would constitute *curricular alignment*. For instance, a sample overarching goal for a program might be to develop students' skills, knowledge, and dispositions in outdoor pursuits. In that case, one would introduce students to activities like camping, hiking, rock climbing, white-water rafting, and so on. This would demonstrate clear alignment. On the other hand, if the content delivered during that school year consisted of a mix of sport, dance, fitness, and recreational activities, that would represent a clear disconnect between the stated and the enacted program goals.

Teachers choosing competency, literacy, and enthusiasm in sport as their overarching physical education program goals would design their yearly block plan by including content areas that are sport focused. That is not to say that sport (in many cases defined as traditional team sports) is the only content that teachers would include in the program offerings. As we will show, teachers have developed very creative ways of incorporating activities not generally described as sport within the Sport Education framework (e.g., weight training, fitness, dance). At the same time, we now see classroom teachers incorporating the key Sport Education features into classroom subjects such as social studies and science (see chapter 21 for more details).

A program's sport theme can also be combined with a fitness concepts theme. Curricular alignment would then manifest itself by having a mix of curricular offerings where students could choose between Sport Education seasons and Fitness for Life units (Corbin & LeMasurier, 2014). On the following pages, we first focus on the instructional alignment at the season level and then highlight the same concept at the lesson level.

SEASON-LEVEL INSTRUCTIONAL ALIGNMENT

How many times have you witnessed or participated in physical education where students ask, "Why are we doing this?" This is actually a legitimate question. When teachers teach a team handball or fitness season, we have to assume that they are goal

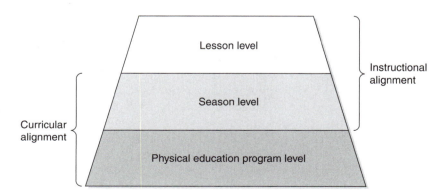

Figure 5.2   Levels of alignment.

directed and have selected appropriate learning outcomes. That is, they want students to learn meaningful skills and knowledge over the course of the season, specific to that activity. As shown in the previous chapter on season outcomes, well-delivered Sport Education has a set of legitimate and defensible season outcomes from which teachers can choose.

When we use the word *content* in the context of instructional alignment, we refer to the actual *learning experiences* that teachers present to their students. There are many managerial and organizational tasks that teachers can give their students (e.g., switching from fitness to skill-type tasks, taking attendance). But these tasks in themselves do not contribute to students' learning the subject matter (i.e., physically active motor play). Learning experiences should rather include such activities as engaging in team fitness conditioning exercises, practicing dance steps in preparation for a scheduled dance performance, or practicing maintaining ball possession in a four-on-two keep-away game.

In the first set of examples, we focused on how instructional alignment would (or would not) be present at the season level. In the next section of this chapter, we focus on instructional alignment at the lesson level. The following examples also emphasize the need to build longer seasons rather than the typical four- to eight-lesson units seen in most multiactivity (i.e., brief-exposure) physical education programming.

Instructional Alignment in Volleyball: An Example

In a seventh-grade volleyball curriculum, the teacher has three planned outcomes for students: (1) the technical outcome of consistently using a sequence of pass-set-attack (three-touch) in gameplay by the end of the season, (2) a knowledge-related outcome focused on understanding the match rules, and (3) a fair play-related outcome, focused on supporting teammates and respecting teammates and game officials.

To achieve the technical outcome, the teacher would plan for the right practice activities during the preseason by designing practice task challenges focused specifically on students handling the ball (perhaps using a trainer-ball, which is lighter), using either the forearm pass or the set, where the primary focus is on technical execution. No net would be needed for such practice tasks, but teams would need to stay within certain boundaries. Practice tasks with between-team challenges (e.g., number of consecutive touches without the ball touching the floor) would provide ample practice opportunities. Once the formal competition starts, scoring rules can be weighted toward the intended outcome as well, where a team earns bonus game points each time it uses three consecutive touches before sending the ball across the net. Scorekeepers would mark the number of bonus points earned by each team.

Developing a thorough understanding of game or match rules in effect requires repeated successful practice, not just for players but also for referees. Being able to explain the rules is necessary but not sufficient. Preseason lessons are the time for referees to learn about and practice recognizing the specific rules (and their violations) in effect during the season's competition. Referee errors (such as calling a ball that landed on the line as *out*), four touches per side, or being overly hesitant in deciding can be addressed and reviewed during brief time-outs followed by a do-over. During the season's formal competition, each team gains additional opportunities when serving as the officiating team.

To achieve the fair play outcome, the teacher would include the use of fair play points that are built directly into how the season champion is determined. This strongly encourages students to demonstrate the type of fair play behaviors the teacher wants to emphasize (e.g., respect toward teammates, opponents, and game officials). Teachers would award fair play points throughout all the season's lessons. Moreover, once referees gain experience, they can become involved in awarding fair play points upon the completion of a match.

Aligning Assessment With Season Outcomes and Content in Volleyball

In this volleyball scenario, the intended outcomes and the planned content would be properly aligned when the teacher uses both informal and formal assessment of the technical execution of the techniques used in the three consecutive touches. *Informal assessment* would consist of frequent use of specific positive and corrective verbal and nonverbal instructional feedback by teachers (and by the team coaches). Such positive feedback might include "Way to get under the ball when setting!" "You made a great platform with your forearms on that pass!" "Excellent use of your legs!" Corrective feedback examples would be "You were a little slow in squaring up to the ball." "You swung your arms a little too much on that forearm pass." "You were late in getting to that ball because you were not in a proper ready position."

Formal assessment would mean that the teacher assesses students' performance and develops actual records (also referred to as *permanent products*) of student performance. Such records play a central role in helping teachers adjust their instructional plans and designs of future volleyball seasons. Formal assessment is not used just for assigning grades at the end of a grading period. Teachers can create such permanent records using either traditional paper-and-pencil methods or electronic record-keeping tools such as smartphones or tablets. (We will address the use of such tools in more detail in chapter 18.) Teachers can develop records of students' performance in various ways. For example, they can use the match statistics the scorekeepers gather on the bonus points scored during games by employing three consecutive touches. As the season progresses, improvement in team performance would be reflected in an increase in the number of bonus points per game. Teachers can also use gameplay performance scoring guides (see figure 5.3). Scoring guides allow for assessment of student performance by scoring them on a five-

ASSESSING SETTING AND PASSING IN MODIFIED GAMEPLAY IN VOLLEYBALL

Select the term that best matches the player's performance for the observed skill or tactic.

Skill level	Level 5 EXCEEDS (competent)	Level 3 MEETS (emerging or recreational)	Level 1 DEVELOPING (struggling)
Technique: Setting and forearm passing	• Plays the ball without catching, passes with ease using an effective hip turn in the direction of the pass; does this without disrupting the flow of the game • Smooth footwork to get in position, soft touches with full body use (use of legs; on sets, appropriate full arm use with fingertip touches; forearm pass has minimal arm swings with solid platform) • Execution results in the team maintaining control of the ball	• Plays without catching most of the time, passes overhead, and uses forearm basic technique • Is reasonably accurate with less disruption to flow of game • Footwork to get in position is acceptable, touches with full body use (use of legs is adequate; fingertips are used but wrist and arms may at times be a little stiff; minimal arm swings with forearm platform) • Technical execution is reasonably good, but at times still results in loss of control of ball and side out	• Player catches the ball or may play the ball but have trouble with accuracy of passing • Footwork to get in position is lacking (late in squaring up), little use of full body, excessive slapping at ball on sets, and big arm swing on forearm passes; no appreciable use of full body • Struggles to keep the play flowing and to use the correct passing method given court position • Starts from upright position; generally late in moving to the ball • Technical execution generally results in a side out

Observed student player's name	Rating (1-5)	Observed student player's name	Rating (1-5)	Observer name:
1.		6.		
2.		7.		
3.		8.		Date:
4.		9		
5.		10.		

Figure 5.3 Gameplay scoring guide for volleyball setting and passing.

point scale from *struggling* to *exceeding standard*. Performance levels 1, 3, and 5 have observable descriptors that reflect increasing levels of technical development in using sets and forearm passes.

The knowledge outcome (referee performance in the previous example) can also be assessed informally and formally. Teachers observing gameplay throughout the preseason and the season can assess informally by again providing specific verbal and nonverbal feedback during the games and lesson closures. Examples of positive feedback would include "Great job being decisive and quick in making the call!" "Way to make the right call . . . that ball was out!" "You rock! That was a double hit by Kevin. Good call!" "Today all the referees were much better at using their hand signals!" Some examples of corrective feedback would be "You were distracted there, so you missed what happened!" "You did not use a hand signal to show the ball was out." "You were a little tentative using the whistle." Teachers can assess referee performance formally through the use of a game rules knowledge scoring guide (see figure 5.4). After a match, players can be asked to rate their referee's performance (see figure 5.5).

Alignment of the planned fair play outcome with assessment would be established when teachers provide their verbal or nonverbal feedback by targeting students' use of high-fiving their teammates, shaking hands with all officials (e.g., referee and scorekeeper) at the end of the match, and refraining from kicking the ball away after disagreeing with a referee's call. Referees can also observe inappropriate player behaviors such as taunting, verbal or physical outbursts, or refusing to acknowledge the opposing team and officials following the game.

ANALYZING KNOWLEDGE OF GAME RULES IN MODIFIED GAMEPLAY IN VOLLEYBALL

Select the term that best matches the player's performance for the observed skill or tactic.

Skill level	Level 5 EXCEEDS (competent)	Level 3 MEETS (emerging or recreational)	Level 1 DEVELOPING (struggling)
Knowledge of game rules	• Few, if any, basic rule violations (e.g., double hits, net contact, carrying ball) • Restarts game appropriately (i.e., passes ball in play) • If applicable, rotates position without needing prompts • Helps explain rule(s) in effect to teammates	• Restarts game appropriately (i.e., serves from designated position) • If applicable, rotates positions without needing prompts • When asked, knows the game score	• Appears unaware or blatantly ignores common violations (e.g., from where to serve, hits ball twice, carries ball, contacts net) • If applicable, acts uncertain or confused on where or how to rotate positions following side out • Cannot or does not recall score in game after a point is scored

Observed student player's name	Rating (1-5)	Observed student player's name	Rating (1-5)	Observer name:
1.		6.		
2.		7.		
3.		8.		Date:
4.		9		
5.		10.		

Figure 5.4 Gameplay scoring guide for volleyball knowledge of rules.

Instructional Alignment in Soccer: An Example

In a fifth-grade soccer class, the teacher selects the following season outcomes: (1) effective shooting on goal during gameplay (a technique-focused outcome), (2) providing support, showing how players not in possession of the ball should move and position themselves so that the team maintains ball possession and can move closer to the opposing team's goal upfield for a scoring chance (a tactics-focused outcome), and (3) a fair play-focused outcome aimed at teams having focused team practices and conditioning sessions.

With regard to the *shooting outcome*, teachers would need to create practice tasks that maximize opportunities for students to shoot on goals. It is important for teachers to vary shooting tasks by setting up progressively more difficult ones (e.g., variations in angles to the goal, distances, shooting out of dribbling, shooting with different parts of the foot, shooting rolling and bouncing crossing passes, shooting with or without a defender in close proximity). Shooting practice also allows for the practice not just of the technical aspects of shooting but also of the tactical dimension of decision-making that goes into shooting within gameplay (whether to shoot, when to shoot, what type of shot, etc.). Informal between-team challenges would help focus the practice and make alignment with the intended outcome of shooting evident.

The planned outcome focused on *support* would be very appropriate, especially for novices. It seeks to reduce the common problem many students have with playing their position (or *spreading out*). Despite reminders from the teacher prior to the

Player Assessment of Referee Performance					
Team:			**Final score:**		
Match: vs.					
Referee:			1 = Poor 2 = Not bad 3 = Average 4 = Good 5 = Excellent		
> > Answer questions as a team < < > > BE FAIR & HONEST < <					
	1	2	3	4	5
The referee was fair and impartial					
The referee knew the rules					
The referee was clear in his or her explanations					
Rate the overall job of this referee					

Figure 5.5 Player assessment of referee performance.

start of gameplay, most players from both teams tend to cluster right around the ball. The typical approach is for teachers to repeatedly urge players to spread out or to play their position. Alignment with the planned outcome can be established when teachers create practice conditions that mirror at least some aspects of a real game and also include a combination of some of the following developmentally appropriate game modifications. First, teachers would have students play games using a modified team size (e.g., four-on-four, five-on-five). Second, they would reduce the size of the playing field. Third, they would eliminate the use of goalies. Although playing goalie certainly keeps particular learners from clustering around the ball, the learner would not be grasping the concept of playing one's position. Fourth, teachers might intentionally create unbalanced teams (e.g., four-on-three, five-on-four). And fifth, teachers can arrange the play environment by placing multiple smaller goals set out along the end lines, as opposed to the one big goal. Any combination of these types of game modifications reflects what Launder and Piltz (2013) refer to as "shaping" gameplay practice. That is, teachers create gameplay conditions that help all players avoid clustering around the ball. It is important to note that, when having to defend two or more goals, the defense has to defend a bigger space. An extreme modification with similar intent ("spreading out") would be to use an end zone that goes the full width of the field, instead of goals. A goal (or point) would be scored when a player on the attacking team moves into the end zone and traps a pass from a teammate. Such content and learning tasks reflect a strong alignment with the intended tactical move outcome.

Students also need time to learn about and practice serving in nonplaying duty team roles such as referee and scorekeeper as well as in team roles such as coach and fitness trainer. Again, preseason is a prime time for students to practice leadership in officiating games, and to lead team practices and take their own team through conditioning exercises. Preseason is the time for teachers to observe refereeing performance and provide feedback, correct errors, and reinforce good referee decisions. During the formal competition phase of the season, students continue learning to officiate at games when serving as duty team member. Since these games or matches now count as part of the season's competition, referees need to focus even more and have good understanding of the rules as well as being able to recognize rule violations.

The preseason is also the time to form teams. As noted in chapter 2, before teams are formed for the formal competition, teachers should generally use guided practice. Toward the end of the preseason, and into the formal competition phase, teachers should direct team coaches and fitness trainers to take on more of a leadership role in planning and leading conditioning sessions and team practices, thus shifting toward using independent practice. We cannot emphasize enough that once teachers shift toward independent practice, it does not mean that the teacher is done instructing students and can sit back. On the contrary, the teacher should now work with these team leaders and provide assistance, feedback, and prompts where necessary.

Aligning Assessment With Season Outcomes and Content in Soccer

It should be clear that if shooting, support, and fair play behaviors are the intended focus in the soccer season example, teachers need to decide what assessment tool to use and build in opportunities for themselves (and, if appropriate, for the students themselves) to determine the degree to which students have progressed throughout the season. Assessing shooting on goal can be done by focusing solely on the technical execution of the shots; it could also focus on the decision-making involved in shooting on goal. When focusing on technical execution of shooting (or any other technique, for that matter), teachers would provide feedback on such aspects as how the student approaches the ball, maintains balance, uses the appropriate range of motion of the kicking leg, places the plant foot next to the ball, following through with the swing leg, and so on. If the focus were on the decision-making that led up to the shot on goal, teachers would focus on the angle from which the shot on goal was taken, the distance from the goal, and whether the shooting player had a clear line or attempted the shot while closely marked. That is, the teacher can assess whether the student opted to choose the right angle, time, and spot from where to take aim at the goal.

Similarly, students' progress in using support (the second season outcome in the previous example), can be assessed directly by using a scoring guide, as can students' fair play performance. For example, one subset of a soccer gameplay assessment scoring guide targeting the assessment of support is shown in figure 5.6 (the full scoring guide tool can be accessed in the web resource, associated with chapter 18). The scoring guides can be used throughout the season's formal competition, which makes the assessment authentic.

Needless to say, teachers can assess students' performance on all three planned outcomes informally through the frequent use of verbal or nonverbal feedback (combined with relevant technique and behavior prompts). Examples include "Way to go! You timed the shot perfectly!" "Terrific move to the outside, so you were positioned perfectly to receive the pass and move upfield!" "Great job going for the goal that was unguarded completely!" "You organized your team practice very nicely! Everyone was able to practice continuously!" "Great effort in providing good feedback to all your players! This will really help them!" "I really liked how you clearly demonstrated all the stretching and strength exercises." "Excellent plan for your conditioning today, you are using a variety of fitness components."

ASSESSING SUPPORT IN MODIFIED GAMEPLAY IN SOCCER

Select the term that best matches the player's performance for the observed skill or tactic.

Skill level	Level 5 EXCEEDS (competent)	Level 3 MEETS (emerging or recreational)	Level 1 DEVELOPING (struggling)
Tactic: Support	• Moves to support teammates on the correct angles and distance regularly • Anticipates other players' moves more consistently	• Moves to support teammates on the correct angles and distance at times • Still more reactive than anticipatory to other players' moves	• Moves little to help teammates • Moves at random • Slow (or no) response to game's action • Gets caught hiding in between players

Observed student player's name	Rating (1-5)	Observed student player's name	Rating (1-5)	Observer name:
1.		6.		
2.		7.		
3.		8.		Date:
4.		9		
5.		10.		

Figure 5.6 Gameplay scoring guide for assessing support in soccer.

In chapter 18, which focuses on the important role of assessment in teaching, we will go into more detail on why teachers cannot depend on using just the informal assessment. In order to develop the credibility of the physical education program, teachers need to make formal assessment a more habitual teaching function.

LESSON-LEVEL INSTRUCTIONAL ALIGNMENT

In this section, we shift the focus onto the instructional alignment at the lesson level. Good teachers make explicit decisions about what they wish to accomplish in individual lessons. Given the finite amount of time, here too, effective teachers generally use the less-is-more approach. It is better to have students demonstrate some progress in just a couple of areas (e.g., being able to control the ball and maintain possession, recognizing rule violations while refereeing) rather than trying to cover all the techniques in one lesson.

Teachers should strive for alignment of an individual lesson's objectives with the content they select and present. And, of course, the assessment of student performance during the lesson should link back directly to the objectives as well. The examples that follow reflect this alignment.

Lesson-Level Instructional Alignment in Basketball: An Example

In basketball, a possible season outcome could be developing the skills students need to perform as the duty team (i.e., learning how to keep score and officiate at games

Good teachers make explicit decisions about what they wish to accomplish in individual lessons.

effectively). Again, the preseason is a prime time for students to practice scorekeeping by having many opportunities to become familiar with navigating the score sheet, following the games so fouls can be recorded, and so on. Similarly, referees need to get practice in recognizing rule violations, making the calls, calling out-of-bounds, using the various hand signals, moving with the action, and the like. The key is for teachers to allocate ample time for all students to have multiple chances to serve as both scorekeepers and as referees during informal scrimmages. Having multiple scrimmages occur simultaneously increases the opportunity for students to practice these critical skills. Errors can be discussed and reviewed without their affecting the season's official competition. By allocating time for this during the preseason, teachers closely align their content with their intended season outcomes. Of course, the use of scorekeepers and referees throughout the remainder of the season reflects the instructional alignment as well.

Teachers can ensure alignment of the officiating content (keeping score and refereeing) with the season outcomes by building the duty teams' performance directly into determining the season champion by the use of duty team points. That is, the duty team points earned count toward the league standings during the formal competition. Generally, teachers award the duty team points based on their observations during the competition. Another way of strengthening alignment would be for the teams that just finished a game to assess the performance of the duty team. Following each game, the representatives of each team can be asked to certify the correctness of the score sheet with their signature. At the same time, the other players on each team can be asked to rate the referee's performance (see figure 5.5). The teacher can use this information as well to award (or deduct) duty team points.

Historically, teachers focus on just letting the students practice the role of player, leaving out any emphasis on developing scorekeeping and refereeing skills (even though these roles make the sport experience more complete and authentic). Lack of alignment would appear if teachers then opt to include the use of scorekeepers and referees but fail to formally assess students' performance in these roles.

Lesson-Level Alignment in Badminton: An Example

In badminton, placing the shuttle into open areas on the opponents' court is a critical tactical move to be learned and thus constitutes a possible season outcome. Alignment of this outcome with the lesson content would be reflected not only in how the teacher explains the why, when, and how of shot placement by providing teaching cues and brief periods of question-answer with students during gameplay, but also in setting up practice drill and game designs that give students the opportunity to recognize when to use good shuttle placement. For example, during initial drills, students could be asked to practice using angles (e.g., hitting the shuttle toward either side of the court or dropping the shuttle just over the net using drop shots). As the lesson progresses, students could be put into focused gameplay, where shots that land in the corners, or close to the side- and baselines of the opponents' court, are worth extra points.

Alignment of the assessment of shuttle placement would be present when the teacher uses *informal assessment* through verbal feedback along with related prompts during gameplay. Alignment of *formal assessment* of shuttle placement would manifest itself when teachers employ the shuttle placement-focused scoring guide shown in figure 5.7.

ASSESSING SHUTTLE PLACEMENT IN MODIFIED GAMEPLAY IN BADMINTON

Select the term that best matches the player's performance for the observed skill or tactic.

Skill level	Level 5 EXCEEDS (competent)	Level 3 MEETS (emerging or recreational)	Level 1 DEVELOPING (struggling)
Tactic: Shuttle placement	Hits shuttle to corners and either short or long, depending on opponent's court position	Can place the shuttle to spaces but only when it is hit directly to him or her	Simply aims to get shuttle back over the net without concern for specific spot on the court

Observed student player's name	Rating (1-5)	Observed student player's name	Rating (1-5)	Observer name:
1.		6.		
2.		7.		
3.		8.		Date:
4.		9		
5.		10.		

Figure 5.7 Gameplay scoring guide for assessing shuttle placement in badminton.

ADDITIONAL CONSIDERATIONS FOR ESTABLISHING INSTRUCTIONAL ALIGNMENT

If the development of players in a sport context is a goal for teachers, they should be mindful of two concepts when attempting to optimize instructional alignment in games-based content (e.g., badminton, basketball, softball, soccer). Both hail from the games-based instruction literature. They include the notion of getting a good game going (Bunker & Thorpe, 1983) and the use of working models of technique (Launder & Piltz, 2013). We will address the use of deliberate modifications in gameplay conditions in more detail in chapter 7, which highlights the important role of employing game modification for designing the game as used in formal competition as well for designing practice activities.

Getting a Good Game Going

Bunker and Thorpe (1983) remind us of the importance of presenting students with just enough and the right content to "get a good game going." For example, in volleyball the central idea behind the game is for a team to direct the ball across the net and in bounds in ways that keep the other team from keeping it in play. For that to happen, students have to learn to control the ball (i.e., by successfully directing a ball to a teammate). Attacking (i.e., spiking) and defending an attack through blocking are two techniques that have no place when students are introduced to volleyball for the first time. In soccer, there is no reason to introduce goalkeeping, throw-ins, and corner kicks in an introductory season. To foster student success in controlling and directing the ball, teachers should use developmentally appropriate practice modifications.

In golf, learning how to drive the ball from the tee is certainly a technique that should be introduced at some point in the learning process. However, here too, students can learn to control the ball through good technical execution if they focus first on putting and short iron club play. This is accomplished by practicing play from shorter distances from the hole (e.g., about a hundred yards or meters in). Practice and play with midirons could be introduced as ball control progresses.

Thus, as teachers observe the development and progress of gameplay, they can decide when and where in the process to introduce additional aspects of gameplay. The key is for teachers to give students just enough of many of the facets of gameplay in a particular sport to get a good game going.

Working Models of Technique

When teaching games, teachers should make ample use of what Launder and Piltz (2013) refer to as *working models of technique*. Working models of technique are simpler ways of executing particular techniques. For example, in tennis one might use a bounce and hit for a serve, because early on when learning to play, the real tennis serve is quite complex and more difficult to execute with consistent success. In volleyball, because of its sequential nature, many students have difficulty in successfully and consistently executing even underhand serves that clear the net and are directed into the opposing team's court. Allowing students to use a lighter ball and to execute the underhand serve from anywhere on the court (as opposed to from the baseline) would be appropriate and developmentally sound modifications while still maintaining alignment. Importantly, it would create the potential for greater success not only in serving but also in getting that good game going.

IDENTIFYING WEAK OR ABSENT INSTRUCTIONAL ALIGNMENT

The degree of instructional alignment can be determined only if (1) the teacher's intended outcomes for a particular season or lesson are known, (2) one can observe multiple lessons over the course of a season or unit, and (3) one can identify the teacher's formal and informal assessment focus. Moreover, observing a single lesson constitutes a mere snapshot of a full season. Being able to observe multiple lessons of key phases of a full season (e.g., preseason, formal competition, culminating events), creates a sort of movie, which would allow for an accurate determination of instructional alignment and allows for a better determination. Certainly, asking teachers directly about their intended outcomes and assessment plans for a full season is legitimate because it provides a better context for what is observed during any one class session.

In the earlier soccer example, lack of instructional alignment would exist if, for example, the teacher were to plan for the same three outcomes (i.e., shooting, support, and team role development) but then allocate significant class time over multiple lessons to present (and have students practice) a multitude of other skills, such as goalkeeping, throw-ins, and corner kicks. Similarly, in the volleyball example, spending large amounts of time on techniques like spiking (i.e., attacking with one hand) and blocking, given the intended outcomes, would create a lack of instructional alignment.

While these skills are an integral part of the game, it is not necessary to introduce all the various features of the game even in one full season. Trying to cover the many technical aspects of a sport (while in most cases ignoring the many tactical features) in one season is doomed to fail in getting learners to develop any level of competence, confidence, and enjoyment.

A lack of instructional alignment emerges in other ways as well, such as when teachers choose not to engage in meaningful and focused instruction throughout the course of a season. That is, teachers get their students engaged in a set of activities and then spend most of the activity time meandering around the activity area and silently observing, without offering any active instruction in the form of frequent encouragement, prompts, and feedback. The image of rolling out the ball is often used to describe this nonteaching style (Locke, 1975). There may be teachers who rationalize this approach by claiming that they have instructed their students by explaining and demonstrating the critical performance elements and getting them to practice the techniques through drills that typically lack transfer to the real activity. But once such teachers place their students in gameplay, they cease any form of active instruction because "this is their time to play."

Some objectives in Sport Education are to have students learn to self-manage and take more ownership of the season's activities by taking on selected leadership roles (e.g., fitness leader, team coach). Gradually giving team coaches more ownership of how team practices are organized places the teacher more into a role of facilitating instruction. The biggest misconception that may emerge among teachers is to think that once students take on roles such as coaches and fitness trainers, they can sit back and let the students do all the work. As noted by Siedentop and Tannehill (2000), effective teachers are those who intend students to learn (engaging in the physical activities), and who actively instruct throughout the course.

Finally, teachers may have set students up to engage in very appropriate and well-designed activities, and actively instruct throughout the lessons using frequent instructional prompts, feedback, and encouragement. They may be using lesson closures effectively by reviewing what they saw students do well and what might need more work. Thus, informal assessment is clearly present. However, the alignment would still be weak if teachers do not employ any formal assessment to document to what extent students have met the planned lesson and season outcomes.

SUMMARY

Alignment can be viewed at the curricular level as linking a physical education program's overall goals with the selected content that is mapped out in a yearly block plan. Instructional alignment can be determined at the season level and at the lesson level. The chance of students learning the needed skills and knowledge specific to physical education content is dependent at least in part on the degree to which there is instructional alignment between teachers' intended outcomes, the content-related activities they design and present to students, and the formal and informal assessment they conduct (Polikoff & Porter, 2014). A lack of alignment between these three components creates situations where students are asked to participate in a more random series of the activities without a clear link with intended outcomes.

Promoting Physical Activity Beyond Physical Education

6

Chapter Objective

After reading this chapter, you will be able to provide an overview of how well-delivered Sport Education can contribute to the public health agenda by promoting physical activity beyond the confines of school physical education.

Key Concepts

- Schools play a central role in promoting and supporting physical activity among students beyond physical education itself.
- Environmental approaches to promoting physical activity include providing expanded access, equipment, and supervision throughout the school day.
- Given the overall goals and its specific objectives, Sport Education lends itself for use in settings other than school physical education.

In this chapter, we show how the Sport Education model not only fits in with the current focus on promoting physical activity throughout the school day but also can be used in other settings, such as after-school programs, recreation leagues, or Boys and Girls clubs. Few people question the need for school-aged children and youth to acquire the skills learned in subjects like mathematics. Someone who cannot perform even the most basic math functions will have difficulty being successful in society. One the other hand, people sometimes question why subjects like physical education are or should be part of the school curriculum. In times of economic downturns or downturns in enrollment, school administrators look to reduce costs by reducing teaching positions. It is therefore important to understand why physical education should be a central school subject for every student.

Over the past three decades, evidence of increased levels of overweight and obesity has accumulated exponentially (Ogden et al., 2016). This increase is rooted in multiple causes, such as an abundance of fast food restaurants, increased food and beverage portion sizes, increased consumption of high-fat, -sugar, and -sodium foods, increased screen time, the physical layout of cities in terms of zoning, the use of cars being the primary means of transportation, and rollbacks of physical education requirements in schools (Trust for America's Health, 2013). Examples of some of the consequences of obesity include type 2 diabetes showing up in elementary school-aged children and the increased prevalence of chronic diseases such as high blood pressure, cardiovascular diseases, and high cholesterol levels. And while the levels of overweight and obesity among the nation's youth have plateaued in recent years (Ogden et al., 2016), estimates of future (severe) obesity levels raise further concerns about an even greater burden on health care systems, and the associated cost thereof (Finkelstein et al., 2012). In 2016, the national health care cost for the United States alone was estimated to reach $3.3 trillion, which is just over ten thousand dollars per person (Alonzo-Zaldivar, 2016).

Since the mid-1990s, multiple national efforts have aimed at reversing these trends. Examples include the development and publication of national physical activity recommendations and national health objectives by the U.S. Department of Health & Human Services (USDHHS, 1996, 2008, 2010, 2012, 2018) and *Educating the Student Body: Taking Physical Activity and Physical Education to School* (Kohl & Cook, 2013). Similar efforts are underway in many other industrialized countries (WHO, 2010). Taken together, these initiatives reflect the challenges of increasing physical activity levels for all. Figure 6.1 summarizes these key documents.

What is the role of school physical education programs within these broader efforts aimed at increasing the physical activity levels of children and youth? School physical education is one of only a few evidence-based interventions that positively impacts the physical activity levels of school-aged youth (Kohl & Cook, 2013; Pate et al., 2006; USDHHS, 2001). Consider that K-12 school campuses are uniquely situated to help all students learn about and how to implement the many types of physical activities. For one thing, virtually all children and youth attend schools during their formative years. Moreover, schools already have the facilities and the equipment in place and, in most cases, already have qualified and certified professionals on the premises delivering physical education programs. And so, despite the pressures placed on teachers and school administrators to improve academic performance, schools are a prime site to foster young people's instinctive drive to engage in physically active motor play (Siedentop, 1980).

Figure 6.1
KEY DOCUMENTS RELATING TO PHYSICAL ACTIVITY

National Physical Activity Recommendations

The second edition of evidence-based recommendations for physical activity was published in 2018. The document covers recommended physical activity levels for all Americans, from preschool age through older adulthood, including persons with disabilities (USDHHS, 2018). An updated review of the evidence supporting the need for physical activity is included. A key difference from previous recommendations is that individual physical activity bouts do need not be at least 10 minutes in length to provide health benefits; for adults, any amount of moderate-to-vigorous physical activity provides some health benefits.

National Physical Activity Plan

In 2016, a comprehensive plan was presented, aimed at promoting physical activity for everyone, titled the *National Physical Activity Plan*. It included strategies, tactics, and objectives drafted by experts in 10 different societal sectors, including business and industry; community, recreation, fitness, and parks; education; faith-based settings; health care; mass media; public health; sport; and transportation, land use, and community design (NPAPA, 2016).

Healthy People 2020

A set of national health objectives, first presented in 1990 and updated in 2000 and 2010, was used to track progress on a number of health indicators, including those related to physical activity (e.g., physical education, recess). Other objectives included those targeting nutrition, chronic diseases, family planning, mental health, tobacco use, and violence prevention among others. Objectives are adjusted based on results collected through national surveillance tools (USDHHS, 2008).

Educating the Student Body

This report by Kohl and Cook (2013) provides a review of the influences of physical activity and physical education on the short- and long-term physical health, cognition and brain health, and psychosocial health and development of children and adolescents. It also makes recommendations regarding approaches for strengthening and improving programs and policies for physical activity and physical education in the school environment, including before, during, and after school.

COMPREHENSIVE PHYSICAL ACTIVITY PROGRAMS IN SCHOOLS

The problems associated with student health has also given rise to global efforts to make school campuses a hub for promoting physical activity for all students throughout the school day. Finland, Ireland, Australia, Germany, Poland, Switzerland, and the United States all have initiated a whole-school approach toward this end. In the United States, SHAPE America (formerly known as AAHPERD) first proposed the framework of a Comprehensive School Physical Activity Program (CSPAP) in 2008. Together with the Centers for Disease Control and Prevention (CDC), it developed a comprehensive guide to help schools creative maximum physical activity opportunities for all students (CDC, 2013). The overarching CSPAP goal is for *all* students to be given the opportunity to reach the recommended minimum of 60 minutes of moderate to vigorous physical activity (MVPA) while at school (CDC, 2013). Full-fledged CSPAPs include five components, which are illustrated in figure 6.2.

The centerpiece CSPAP component is the physical education program. Effective physical education programs have a clear theme; for example, some programs opt to make physical fitness the curricular focus (Corbin & Le Masurier, 2014). We propose that the totality of the sport experience is an appropriate and legitimate theme for school physical education, which would make Sport Education the curricular focus.

Other student-targeted CSPAP components focus on creating physical activity opportunities before,

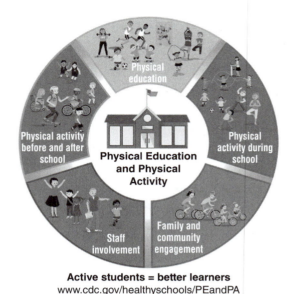

Active students = better learners
www.cdc.gov/healthyschools/PEandPA

Figure 6.2 Comprehensive physical activity program framework.

Reprinted from Centers for Disease Control and Prevention, *Increasing Physical Education and Physical Activity: A Framework for Schools* (Atlanta, GA: CDC, 2017).

during, and after school. During the before- and after-school time blocks, this could take the form of drop-in programs to accessible physical activity venues such as field space, and gymnasiums for students who arrive at school well before the start of classes. Historically, after-school programs have focused on academics, arts and crafts, and life skills. Only recently has there been a more pronounced focus on physical activity (whether through unstructured free play or more structured forms) from a programming and policy perspective (Weaver et al., 2015).

CSPAPs also include components to support engagement by school staff (i.e., teachers and support personnel), aimed at providing them with opportunities for physical activity as well as learning about topics such as wellness, fitness, and nutrition. Many workplace sites have employee wellness programs and even fitness facilities. The latter is true for most secondary schools, but schools historically have not tended to the health and wellness of their staff. In fact, there is constant and ever-increasing pressure on classroom teachers to improve students' academic performance and even to serve as surrogate parents or counselors. The increasing high-stakes accountability for teachers, where their job security is at least in part dependent on their students' academic achievement, can make for long and stressful days. Giving teachers the opportunity to engage in campus-based physical activity after school is an effective way to focus on their health and well-being.

The final component of a CSPAP focuses on family and community engagement. School campuses are a potential hub for all community members in the school's neighborhood. Parents and other adults who pay taxes that support the school system can become more invested in the school when they are provided access to the school's physical activity facilities during nonschool hours. In addition, schools are a prime venue for events such as wellness nights and health fairs, where adults from the community can learn about subjects from nutrition to food preparation, self-assessment of health and fitness, and availability of other public and commercial programs and services that focus on health, fitness, and wellness.

Public health focuses on many different dimensions of population health, including nutrition, gun violence, drug abuse, and tobacco. CSPAPs are considered school physical education's contribution to the public health of the nation as part of a larger national public health agenda aimed at improving the health of the country's citizens.

THE NATIONAL FOCUS ON PROMOTING PHYSICAL ACTIVITY

The significant rise in the number of overweight and obese children is part of the reason for the multiple efforts at all levels of government as well as in professional and scientific organizations to increase students' total daily physical activity levels (Pate et al., 2006; SHAPE America, 2013a; USDHHS, 2018). For example, the third U.S. national content standard for physical education states that students will participate regularly in physical activity with an emphasis on the need to be physically active beyond physical education classes (SHAPE America, 2013a). "Healthy People 2020," the U.S. government guide to health goals for the American population, presents national health objectives that are specific to school physical education programs (USDHHS, 2008).

In 2018, revised physical activity guidelines for the U.S. population were published that included the following physical activity recommendations for children and adolescents.

1. Children and adolescents should do 60 minutes or more of physical activity daily.

   - **Aerobic:** Most of the 60 or more minutes a day should be either moderate- or vigorous-intensity aerobic physical activity and should include vigorous-intensity physical activity at least three days a week.

   - **Muscle strengthening:** As part of their 60 or more minutes of daily physical activity, they should include muscle-strengthening physical activity on at least three days of the week.

   - **Bone strengthening:** As part of their 60 or more minutes of daily physical activity, they should include bone-strengthening physical activity on at least three days of the week.

2. It is important to encourage young people to participate in physical activities that are appropriate for their age, that are enjoyable, and that offer variety (USDHHS, 2018).

The updated National Physical Activity Plan (2016) is the most comprehensive national effort, bringing together nine sectors in American society:

1. business and industry,
2. community, recreation, and fitness and parks,
3. education,
4. faith-based settings,
5. health care,
6. mass media,
7. public health,
8. sport, and
9. transportation, land use, and community design.

The plan's overarching vision is that "[o]ne day, all Americans will be physically active, and they will live, work and play in environments that encourage and support regular physical activity." (NPAPA, 2016, p. 1) The education sector includes programs for preschool, K-12, and colleges and universities. The presence of sport as its own societal sector speaks to its prominence as a cultural institution. Figure 6.3 includes the strategies developed for the education and sport sectors.

As can be seen in figure 6.3, the goal is for schools to become places where all students can enjoy quality physical education, have access to physical activity throughout the full school day, and are taught by trained professionals. The sport sector strategies focus on ensuring that all sport programs are inclusive, are accessible to all (not just the gifted or the economically privileged), and are conducted in safe environments with minimal risk of injury and long-term illness.

Based on a careful review of this research, school physical education programs have been found to be one of the most important venues for promoting physical activity in children and adolescents (CDC, 2001). Moreover, access to school physical education lessons alone is not enough to reach the recommended daily totals of physical activity. For example, in elementary schools the amount of physical activity accumulated in elementary physical education makes up only 8 to 11 percent of the daily total (Tudor-Locke et al., 2006). CSPAPs create a school where this goal is within reach.

The promotion of CSPAPs is in some ways an effort to reclaim campus-based, out-of-class physical activity opportunities for students. For example, intramural programs were a popular physical education program component in secondary schools for many years. For various reasons (e.g., teacher contracts, financial cutbacks, increased emphasis on after-school sports) such programs have all but disappeared. This is especially troublesome since there is evidence that well-organized intramural programs are an excellent means of providing increased physical activity access for all students (Kanters et al., 2013). Physical education teachers are uniquely positioned to become the campus leaders for promoting physical activity in their regular physical education classes as well as to help create campus conditions that encourage and support physical activity for all students.

PHYSICAL ACTIVITY BEYOND PHYSICAL EDUCATION

The promotion of physical activity in physical education has become a major focus nationally and globally over the past three decades. As noted in chapter 3, the historic dominance of sport in the physical education curriculum has been pointed to as one of the main causes for many of the field's problems. This resulted in efforts to de-emphasize this focus on sport and increase the focus on fitness-related content. But there is no evidence that sport as program content in itself is the problem. Rather, we regard the manner in which sports have been taught in school physical education as the central cause. In this section, we show how Sport Education, if delivered effectively, can help students seek physical activity opportunities beyond the regular physical education lessons.

The ultimate goal for physical educators is to have their students seek out opportunities to engage in activities practiced (and learned) in physical education at times and in settings beyond the physical education lessons. For example, if students who learn to play badminton in physical education through Sport Education then go and seek out badminton before or during school (or at home), we can say that *transfer* has occurred.

Figure 6.3
NATIONAL PHYSICAL ACTIVITY PLAN STRATEGIES

Education sector strategies

- **Strategy 1**: States and school districts should adopt policies that support implementation of the Comprehensive School Physical Activity Program model.
- **Strategy 2**: Schools should provide high-quality physical education programs.
- **Strategy 3**: Providers of after-school, holiday, and vacation programs for children and youth should adopt policies and practices that ensure that participants are appropriately physically active.
- **Strategy 4**: States should adopt standards for childcare and early childhood education programs to ensure that children ages zero to five years are appropriately physically active.
- **Strategy 5**: Colleges and universities should provide students and employees with opportunities and incentives to adopt and maintain physically active lifestyles.
- **Strategy 6**: Educational institutions should provide preservice professional training and in-service professional development programs that prepare educators to deliver effective physical activity programs for students of all types.
- **Strategy 7**: Professional and scientific organizations should develop and advocate for policies that promote physical activity among all students.

Sport sector strategies

- **Strategy 1**: Sports organizations should collaborate to establish a national policy that emphasizes the importance of sports as a vehicle for promoting and sustaining a physically active population.
- **Strategy 2**: Sports organizations should establish an entity that can serve as a central resource to unify and strengthen stakeholders in the sport sector.
- **Strategy 3**: Leaders in multiple sectors should expand access to recreational spaces and quality sports programming while focusing on eliminating disparities in access based on race, ethnicity, gender, disability, socioeconomic status, geography, age, and sexual orientation.
- **Strategy 4**: Sports organizations should adopt policies and practices that promote physical activity, health, participant growth, and development of physical literacy.
- **Strategy 5**: Sports organizations should ensure that sports programs are conducted in a manner that minimizes risk of sports-related injuries and illnesses.
- **Strategy 6**: Public health agencies, in collaboration with sports organizations, should develop and implement a comprehensive surveillance system for monitoring sports participation in all segments of the population.
- **Strategy 7**: Coaches, game officials, parents, and caregivers should create safe and inclusive environments for sports participation that promote physical activity and health for youth and adult participants.
- **Strategy 8**: Sports organizations should use advances in technology to enhance the quality of the sport experience for participants.

National Physical Activity Plan Alliance (2016). U.S. National Physical Activity Plan. Retrieved from http://physicalactivityplan.org/docs/2016NPAP_Finalforwebsite.pdf

© Human Kinetics.

Sport Education, if delivered effectively, can help students seek physical activity opportunities beyond the regular physical education lessons.

Such transfer, however, does not happen automatically; it needs to be planned deliberately. That is, conditions need to be arranged so that when students are not in physical education lessons, they can still seek out needed equipment, find an appropriate location, and participate in activities taught in physical education lessons. Before school as well as during recess and lunch breaks are prime campus-based times when opportunities for physical activity can be created. In the next section, we provide various strategies that can help create the conditions for transfer from activity engagement in physical education lessons to other times on campus and beyond.

Strategies for Increasing Physical Activity Beyond Physical Education Lessons

In Sport Education, teachers can make enormous contributions to ensuring that all students make use of physical activity opportunities beyond the regular physical education lessons. They can encourage out-of-class physical activity in various ways. Out-of-class (i.e., independent) physical activity opportunities can be made available on school grounds before school, during recess and lunch, and after school. Beyond the school grounds, opportunities exist at home, in structured sport programs, in parks, at community centers, and so on. In the following sections we offer strategies for structuring the season competition, setting up the campus environment, prompting and encouragement, and self-monitoring by students.

Structuring the Season Competition

With its strong emphasis on teams learning to work together, team competition within Sport Education seasons is likely one of the strongest incentives for students to seek out physical activity beyond the regular class sessions. Out-of-class physical activity can be built directly into the season competition. In addition to the points earned as a result of games played, duty team points, and fair play points, points for out-of-class physical activity can count directly toward a team's standing in the season competition. It is important to explain this dimension of the competition clearly in the initial class sessions of the new season. Students need to learn where they can get equipment, where it needs to be stored afterward, how they can earn physical activity points, and how they should report their out-of-class activities.

As for how such points can be earned, teachers can set a point value based on the number of minutes that a team practiced during recess or lunch period, such as one physical activity point for every five minutes of time spent in team practice. Physical activity points can also be awarded to individual team members, or on the basis of how many team members participated; that is, a team that has all of its members present and participating can be awarded additional points. The teacher is the best judge of the minutes-to-points ratio.

Just as physical activity engagement is not transferred automatically from the physical education lesson to out-of-class periods, it also does not automatically transfer to times and settings away from the school campus. This means that transfer of physical activity engagement beyond the school campus also needs to be considered. Physical activity during discretionary time outside of school (e.g., time spent at home) can be integrated into the seasonal competition in physical education. Such activity can be measured using multiple tools. For example, students can be asked to keep an activity log that provides a record of the nature of the activity and the amount of physical activity time. Or they can use pedometers that can track step counts. Upper-end pedometer models like the FITStep™ Pedometer (www.gophersport.com/assessment/pedometers) can also capture the amount time spent in moderate to vigorous physical activity (MVPA). Smartphone apps also offer physical activity tracking tools. Since many if not most secondary school-aged students own smartphones, such apps would be a good way to use technology in a physical education program. Parents of elementary school-aged students could be recruited to verify their children's daily physical activity records.

This team competition approach encourages students to work on either fitness- or technique-related activities in discretionary time outside of school. In order for this strategy to succeed, it is imperative that teachers explain to students what kinds of activities count toward daily and weekly accumulation of moderate to vigorous physical activity. Needless to say, the season can be set up so that any out-of-school physical activity can count toward the total team accumulation, or it might have to be a physical activity that is specific to the current season within the physical education lessons.

Hastie et al. (2012) demonstrated how the transfer of physical activity beyond the school day is more likely to occur as part of a jump rope season with fourth-grade students. In addition to providing verbal prompts for students to practice their jump rope skill, the teacher also provided a team bonus points challenge on selected days of the season. When students practiced their jump rope skills at home and met the amount of time spent practicing set by the teacher (and certified by their parents) they earned bonus points that counted toward the team's standing in the competition. As can be seen in figure 6.4, on days when the prompting plus bonus points condition was in effect, the average step count (the indicator of students' physical activity levels) was significantly higher than for the baseline and prompting-only condition.

The use of *group contingencies* is an excellent example of how out-of-class physical activity can be encouraged and reinforced. Moreover, it represents an authentic means

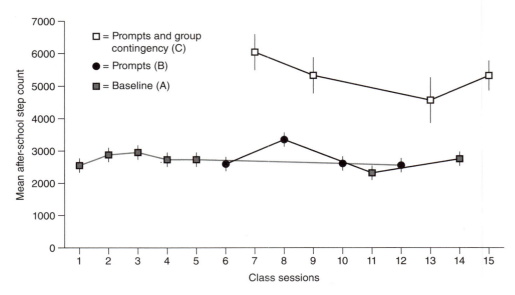

Figure 6.4 Mean after-school step counts across conditions.

Reprinted by permission from P. Hastie et al. "The Effects of Prompts and a Group-Oriented Contingency on Out-of-School Physical Activity in Elementary School-Aged Students" *Journal of Teaching in Physical Education* 31 (2012): 131-145.

of embedding it in a sport season and supports transfer from physical education classes to other times and settings.

Setting Up the Campus Environment

In all likelihood, merely prompting students to go out and be active on their own is not enough; they need to be supported in their out-of-class physical activity as well. You can help shape the school environment by providing such support in ways that address three key issues: access, equipment, and adult supervision (Lorenz et al., 2017).

First, you can create access by designating the gymnasium or parts of the outdoor activity venues as areas for independent team practices. Clearly marked signage can indicate the designated team practice area, setting it apart from other activity areas that can be used for free play by other students.

Second, you can make season-specific equipment available for use before and after school by preparing an equipment cart that is placed in the same spot every day near a designated activity area. For example, through grants or by working with Parent Teacher Organizations, all the elementary school physical education programs in Chandler, Arizona, were provided such carts, with the accompanying equipment dedicated solely to supporting campus-based physical activity beyond the physical education lessons.

Team equipment managers can be made responsible for the carts, overseeing proper use of the equipment, reporting any lost or damaged equipment, and returning the cart at the end of practice.

Some teachers may argue that equipment will get damaged, lost, or mistreated if students are given the role as equipment managers. But the proper use, treatment, and management of equipment can be built directly into the season's point system through the use of fair play points that help determine the season's champion. Repeated mistreatment or loss of equipment could result in loss of fair play points or not being allowed to practice outside of class. Once teams understand that they can earn additional fair play points, they will be more inclined to use and manage equipment appropriately.

In order for team practices held outside of physical education classes to be productive, team coaches can be asked to provide written documentation on who attended team practices and on what did or did not work well during the out-of-class team practices. Such documentation would be excellent evidence about team performance that can be shared in the team's portfolio.

Third, you can recruit other adults (e.g., playground monitors) who have lunch duty by making them aware of your goal of encouraging physical activity and seeking their assistance in this process. Typically, adult monitors see themselves as responsible only for safety and overall conduct. As long as students act safely and avoid inappropriate conduct, therefore, these monitors tend to remain passive during recess or lunch periods, and yet they are also a built-in support resource. For example, they can sign the team-based physical activity log to certify that members of a team came together to practice. For them to take on this added task of monitoring team activities they will require professional development. The willingness of physical education teachers to communicate with other staff members and teachers on campus, coupled with a little training (perhaps at staff meetings), can go a long way toward creating and supporting students' physical activity opportunities throughout the school day.

Fourth, lunch periods provide ample time for team coaches to organize one good activity that can help the team prepare for the season or for the next game. Such practices should consist of informal (but purposeful) games that are typical of the natural play patterns when children and youth gather to play a game. We strongly agree with Launder and Piltz (2013), who argued that it is within this context that learners become players through experimentation. Team coaches can be encouraged to use the team practice cards and action fantasy game cards provided in the web resource for chapter 7. Note that introducing students to a particular activity during physical education class provides a perfect opportunity for you to encourage teams to engage in that same activity during out-of-class times.

When teams play and practice by themselves, they invariably have to work through problems that may emerge between team members. A central characteristic of fair play is that all team members show up for such independent team practices. If a player misses multiple practice sessions, the team has to decide how to address this problem.

Prompting and Encouragement

Prompts serve as reminders for people to do certain things (in this case for students to be physically active on their own). For some students, that may be all that is needed. For example, once teams are formed, you can prompt, encourage, and reinforce students for practicing outside of class (e.g., during recess and lunch periods). During most lesson closures (especially early in a season), you can remind students that they can practice outside of class by joining together as a team before school, during recess, and during lunch.

Prompts also come in visual forms. The options for visual forms are endless. They can be placed in your gymnasium, hallways, locker rooms, the school newsletter, and the school or physical education program website. The key is to locate prompts strategically (i.e., in high-traffic parts of the building) so that it is almost impossible for students to miss them. For example, with the advances in digital photo technology, you (or even students) can create simple but attractive prompts in the form of photos that show your own students engaged in physical activity on the school grounds. Imagine the impact of a photo of a student in your school practicing dribbling, shooting, or curl-ups for all to see! These could be displayed on in-school reader screens or printed and posted in display cases or on bulletin boards.

Because these visual prompts tend to lose their power of attraction over time, you should change them out regularly to keep your students in tune with the overall message of your program. During recess and lunch, you can spot-check the areas where students are engaging independently in the season's activity, which you can then reinforce by personal encouragement or through the use of physical activity points that count toward the season championship.

Increasing physical activity beyond the school setting is more complex but certainly not impossible. Factors such as distance from physical activity venues or lack of transportation may be difficult barriers for students to overcome. Even if students live close to each other and close to a setting where they can all gather to practice, other factors (e.g., parental concerns about safety) may still prevent this from happening. However, more than likely, they can still be physically active on their own or with siblings, parents, or neighborhood friends. You should be knowledgeable about the possibilities and constraints for physical activity in the neighborhoods in which your students live so you can provide options for discretionary physical activity that are realistic and possible within those neighborhoods. Students in elementary schools may also stay at school and be enrolled in campus-based after-school programs. In many cases, such programs are outsourced, but have supervisory personnel that can help encourage out-of-school physical activity.

Self-Monitoring by Students

In order to award the aforementioned physical activity points in a fair manner (something that students will take seriously), you should instruct teams that earning such points is contingent on their logging out-of-class team practice time and obtaining a signature from one of the adult supervisors to verify their physical activity engagement. The web resource includes several examples of both team-based and individual out-of-class physical activity logs.

Physical activity logs can track either what the team did as a group (e.g., during on-campus times) or what individual team members did on their own time away from school. Either way, it is essential to plan this aspect of the season competition with care, because fairness in the awarding of physical activity points is central. Nothing turns students off from competition more than if they believe that it lacks fairness. Figure 6.5 shows an example of a team-based physical activity log.

Students could also be asked to keep a personal physical activity log as a form of self-monitoring (for examples, see the web resource). Self-monitoring is an effective strategy to assist a person in maintaining a physically active lifestyle. Figure 6.6 shows a sample physical activity log sheet for use by individual students. In this example, the student is asked to record when the activity took place, the type of physical activity, and how long it lasted. Note that students are not asked to record how many shots they made if practicing their basketball shooting techniques, or how many curl-ups they performed. Rather, the goal is to develop the habit of building in time every day to do something physically active, be it related specifically to the sport of the current season or something unrelated, such as riding a bike, hiking, or lifting weights. The key messages to send to students are that they can choose their own activity and that any physical activity is good activity. Having students complete a physical activity log for activities outside of class is an effective strategy for maintaining a physically active lifestyle.

Figure 6.5
SAMPLE OUT-OF-CLASS BASKETBALL TEAM PRACTICE LOG

Team name: _____

Directions: Choose at least three days this week where you come together to practice as a team. Practice can focus on physical conditioning or improving your techniques and tactics. Set realistic goals and plan your activities. Be sure to record what you did during the practice and place this completed log in your team portfolio.

Day and date	Activity planned	Objective of session (technique/tactics/conditioning)	Time spent (mins)	Team members present
Tues, Nov. 5	Three-on-three	To shoot, dribble, or pass	18	Kevin, Misty, Juan, Mark

Whether out-of-class physical activity is done individually or in teams, students should be asked to have an adult (e.g., playground supervisor, parent, guardian) sign each reported session of independent physical activity. This signature requirement provides an inexpensive way of demonstrating to significant adults (especially parents) what you are trying to accomplish in your program.

SPORT EDUCATION IN SETTINGS OTHER THAN PHYSICAL EDUCATION AND SCHOOLS

Although Sport Education was developed for school physical education programs, it is not hard to see how it might be applied in settings outside of physical education. These can include school intramural programs, campus-based after-school programs, community-based programs like Boys and Girls Club of America, parks and recreation programs, as well as basic instruction programs in colleges and universities. Here is an overview of why and how Sport Education lends itself very well to use in such settings.

First and foremost, many people between the ages of 10 and 21 have had their opportunities for effective physical education reduced in the past few decades as a result of poor state-level policy profiles, the most recent economic recession, and the extreme focus on improving academic performance (e.g., van der Mars, 2018; SHAPE-AHA,

Figure 6.6
WEEKLY SPORT AND PHYSICAL ACTIVITY SELF-REPORT LOG

Name: _____

Directions: Track the amount of time that you spend in physical activity during the week outside of school. You are encouraged to practice with your team whenever possible, but you can also count all other physical activities, such as ones listed in the left-hand column. This includes activities such as walking, in-line skating, biking, skateboarding, playing basketball, and so on.

The goal is for you to reach 60 minutes of moderate to vigorous physical activity (MVPA). The difference between moderate and vigorous levels of physical activity is determined by the intensity with which you participate in them.

Activities	Mon.	Tue.	Wed.	Thu.	Fri.	Sat.	Sun.	Total
Team practice								
Practice with a teammate								
Individual practice								
Walking								
Jogging								
Inline skating								
Bicycling								
Working out at a health club								
Swimming								
Playing golf								
Tennis								
Other								
Other								

2016). Factors in this loss of opportunity also include reductions in time allocations for physical education and recess, rollbacks in high school graduation requirements, and the increased adoption of waivers, exemptions, and substitutions for formal physical education (e.g., JROTC, marching band, interscholastic athletics). Consequently, there is a significant number of students who have had fewer, if any, regular physical education experiences.

School Intramural Programs

School intramural programs were once a common feature of school physical education programs, yet for various reasons their popularity has dwindled. This is unfortunate given that the fundamental structure of intramurals allows any student to be part of an intramural league. As noted earlier, there is evidence that intramural programs in secondary schools actually produce higher participation levels as well as higher physical activity levels among participants (Kanters et al., 2013).

It is important to note that if students are familiar with Sport Education through their experiences in their physical education classes, having a similar framework in place during intramural activities creates an opportunity for transfer. That is, they can apply the skills and knowledge gained in physical education in other settings. Moreover, it expands their opportunities for physical activity and increases their chances of solidifying their motor competency, leadership, and fair play skills. Here too, there are additional leadership opportunities for students in upper grades who might be interested in assisting with the implementation of the intramural competitions.

Campus-Based After-School Programs

While intramurals offer opportunities for sport participation during the school day, many students are on campus during the after-school hours and participate in after-school programs. Given that many school districts have outsourced the delivery of after-school programs to private companies, these programs have historically focused on providing added opportunity for students to develop academic skills (through homework), arts and crafts skills, and life skills. It is only in the last decades, when the concept of CSPAPs first emerged, that interest has increased in the promotion of physical activity during after-school time. We believe that CSPAP staff members who oversee and facilitate the after-school programs are uniquely positioned to provide delivery of physical activities during the after-school hours.

Community-Based Programs

Community-based programs such as Boys and Girls clubs and parks and recreation programs lend themselves very well as they offer a variety of sports. The Boys and Girls Club of America has a long history of serving children and youth, especially youngsters from economically disadvantaged homes. Their mission statement emphasizes a focus on developing good character and citizenship as well as on living a healthy lifestyle. In several cases, Boys and Girls clubs are located in close proximity to schools, making after-school access to them particularly easy. Boys and Girls clubs typically provide several sport-based activities. It is easy to see how creating opportunities for furthering the development of competency in performing sport activities, and the development of fair play and leadership through Sport Education-based programming, very much align with this mission.

Similarly, parks and recreation programs in the community also offer a variety of sport-based activities. These programs target a wider audience, including adults, and offer a wider array of courses. Sport programming for children and youth are also a significant component of these agencies. Here too, we can see how the fundamental features of Sport Education could be implemented successfully in such programming. For example, program staff responsible for scheduling sport leagues could be trained to employ the key features of Sport Education. Adolescents could work alongside regular staff and support the coaches for the teams to gradually infuse nonplayer roles and develop leadership skills.

Basic Instruction Programs in Higher Education

Following the elimination of required physical education courses in colleges and universities in the latter decades of the twentieth century, departments of physical education and exercise science responded by creating basic instruction programs with elective one- or two-credit physical activity courses. These programs, which have become immensely popular, include wide-ranging course options including sport, fitness, dance, and outdoor activities. Student can either continue with an activity for which they already have an affinity (e.g., softball, flag football), or they may sign up to learn a new activity (e.g., country and western dance, yoga). These programs have flourished because they are elective and, depending on the size of the university, can provide upward of 100 activity course choices.

Sport Education is ideally suited for implementation in these activity courses. First, classes usually last for an entire quarter or semester, long enough to encompass a complete program. Second, there are numerous opportunities to parallel the festive nature of intercollegiate sport that is such a big feature on many campuses. Indeed, from those sites where Sport Education has been used, students have reported that they engaged at higher rates and learned more in this format than in previous activity courses. Further, nearly all students remarked they would take another course that used this method (Bennett & Hastie, 1997; Blocker & Wahl-Alexander, 2018). The challenge then, is to train the instructors in these programs through professional development in the basic use of the Sport Education model so that all the core aspects of sport are incorporated.

SUMMARY

As with anything done well, getting out-of-class physical activity promotion going requires planning and preparation. For example, you need to prepare the activity logs (see examples in this chapter's web resource), plan how to present this process to students and their parents, decide how much weight to give to out-of-school physical activity, and build time in the lessons to spot-check the team portfolios to see whether and how well students are logging their physical activity. Making this process a regular part of how you "do" physical education will take time.

By incorporating out-of-school physical activity promotion into the physical education program, teachers not only make enormous contributions to their students' lives, they also become more visible on their school campus as leaders who create a physical activity-supportive culture and environment. Importantly, they become active partners in helping meet national health objectives. The key is to make use of the available resources that help promote your program's physical activity agenda beyond your classes.

PART II

The How of Sport Education

Attempting to implement any new form of teaching requires forethought and planning related to the key aspects of the pedagogies that need to be included. For many teachers, the Sport Education model represents a significant pedagogical shift in terms of their role in class management, organization, and task presentation. To facilitate this transition it is important that you consider several key factors in the design of Sport Education seasons. These factors should include not only curricular decisions, such as the selection of the sport or activity and the length of the season, but also pedagogical decisions related to developing festivity and facilitating management and learning when students are placed in instructional roles.

In the second part of this book we introduce you to all the aspects you need to consider when designing and implementing a season of Sport Education. These are presented in chronological order, with the first chapters addressing the decisions you make before the season begins, followed by those aspects that arise during the first lessons of a season. The middle chapters focus on within-season issues such as teaching protocols, helping students learn their officiating roles, and developing student coaches. The final chapters address topics that are part of the whole of a Sport Education season, which in this book focus on festivity, inclusion, and student empowerment.

In keeping with our metaphor of the teacher as the architect of the model, we represent the building of your program along the same lines as the construction of a house. Chapter 7 lays the foundation of the season, when you select the sport and modify it as needed to make it most suitable for your students. Chapter 8 helps you select the most appropriate combination of practices and competitions that suit the sport you have selected for the season and the amount of time you have available to complete it. In chapter 9, you will examine the various ways in which teams can be formed and the roles that students play during a season.

After laying this the foundation, you begin to build your house with in-season responsibilities, which include teaching protocols and building fair play (chapter 10) and helping students to become competent players (chapter 11) and learn to officiate and keep score (chapter 12). The upper levels of the house are where you examine strategies for making Sport Education festive, and in particular, for planning the culminating event (chapter 13).

Part II closes with two chapters that serve to empower students. In chapter 14, we present a number of approaches that can promote meaningful inclusion of students with special needs in Sport Education, while chapter 15 identifies ways in which students can be given opportunities for making decisions about the planning and administration of a season.

Modifying Games and Activities

Chapter Objective

After reading this chapter, you will be able to modify games to ensure appropriate levels of challenge for all students.

Key Concepts

- A modified game does not lessen the challenge of play.
- Five strategies are available for modifying games so that they are fun, challenging, and allow students to be successful.
- Graded competition is a way of arranging competitions so that students of similar skill levels are matched against one another. In some cases, the game forms are different across the competition levels.
- Graded competition is best used by having large teams (e.g., eight members) divide into smaller units. In these smaller competitions, the results from the various matches count equally, so the performance of the B team contributes as much to the seasonal championship as that of the A team.

This chapter focuses on the first decision you need to make when planning a season of Sport Education: identifying the sport or activity that will be the focus on the season and then deciding how to modify it for your particular student population. Figure 7.1 illustrates how the tasks involved in season design fit into the overall instructional alignment model. The chapter will discuss ways by which these sports can be modified to make them not only developmentally appropriate but also better suited to small-sided competitions that are central to the model.

The nature of a game is defined by the basic problem that needs to be solved (Almond, 1986; Siedentop, 2004). For example, the basic problem to solve in volleyball is to strike the ball over a net so that it either cannot be returned by opponents or hits the floor within bounds. The primary rules of the game define the way in which the problem is to be solved, and changing a primary rule changes the game. For example, the primary rule in volleyball is that the ball must be struck; that is, volleyball is a striking game, not a throwing and catching game. Secondary rules such as the height of the net, the size of the court, and the ball can be modified without changing the nature of the game; in fact, they *should* be changed in order to help students grow in their techniques and tactics so they will eventually be able to play the parent game. As another example, the primary rule in soccer is the handball rule, which disallows striking the ball with the hands. Secondary rules that can be manipulated, depending on the setting, include the size of the field, the size of the goal, the type of ball used, and the numbers of players on each team.

A modified game does *not* lessen the challenge of play but rather matches an appropriate level of challenge to the developmental status of the learners. Modified games also provide players with opportunities to practice techniques and tactics in situations that match their current level of learning and abilities and to do so in ways that allow them to progress toward the parent game. The web resource associated with this chapter includes multiple examples of what Launder and Piltz (2013) refer to as "shaping practice." These games-based "play practices" have students engage in gameplay in ways that emphasize both technical and tactical aspects of gameplay.

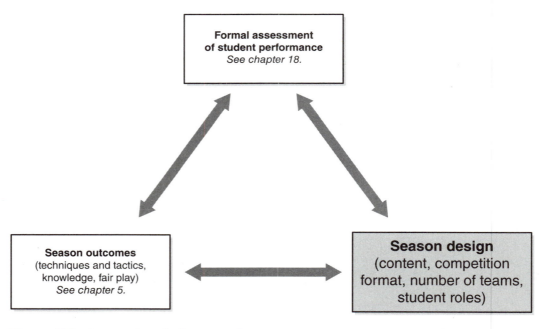

Figure 7.1 Instructional alignment between outcomes, content, and assessment.

KEY STRATEGIES FOR MODIFYING GAMES

Teachers need to keep in mind five key strategies when modifying games so that they are fun, challenging, and allow students to be successful. The modifications should be situation specific and depend on the teacher's knowledge of the students' abilities. The five strategies are to (1) make scoring easier, (2) slow the movement of the ball, (3) increase opportunities to practice techniques and tactics, (4) sequence games to enable the learning of tactics, and (5) change rules that define scoring.

Make Scoring Easier

When playing in any game or contest, students like to score. Scoring is an important way (though not the only way) to define success. It also reinforces the use of appropriate techniques and tactics. When scoring is infrequent, children tend to get frustrated. For example, when students are taught to play basketball with a 10-foot (3 m) hoop and a regulation ball in a five-a-side format, scoring is infrequent, and inappropriate techniques and tactics may be unwittingly fostered. How many volleyball games have you watched in middle school physical education with a regulation net and ball where 80 percent of the points scored are from serves that are not returned because students have no mastery over the important skill of passing? The essence of volleyball is the rally, with most scoring taking place with hits at or near the net. The most direct way to accomplish this is to eliminate the serve and start each rally with what is called a *free ball*, where either a player from the serving team or even the referee tosses an easy ball over the net.

There are many ways to increase the likelihood of scoring. For example, using lower basketball goals, larger soccer goals, and shorter rackets with larger heads (that allow for more control) all increase the appropriate use of techniques and tactics for scoring. Friendly pitchers in softball increase the pace of play and the number of hits. Balls that are softer and larger and that move through the air more slowly also tend to increase scoring through more appropriate use of offensive techniques and strategies.

Slow the Movement of the Ball

It is difficult for beginners to execute techniques if they are not in position to do so. Slowing the movement of the ball or other object gives players more time to react and move. In developing game sense (Launder, 2001), students gradually learn how to anticipate the movement of objects, teammates, and opponents, thus allowing them to move to advantageous positions that enable them to make the next play, which keeps the flow of the game moving forward. Slowing the movement of the object is particularly important in court-divided games such as volleyball, badminton, and tennis. It is of great help if the object moves more slowly while students learn to anticipate and move to appropriate positions. This same approach is also appropriate for invasion games, where the regulation ball (e.g., soccer, lacrosse, floor hockey) often moves so quickly that beginners cannot get into position to successfully continue the flow of play. There are a number of ways to accomplish this goal, but the two most important are using a friendlier, slower object and increasing the height of the net dividing the court.

Balls and other objects that move through space and along the ground more slowly than regulation balls and objects can be either purchased or made. In volleyball, you might start with a trainer ball that is 25 percent larger and 40 percent lighter than regulation before moving to a soft-touch regulation ball. Many manufacturers now produce balls and other types of equipment that are friendlier for learning techniques and tactics (see table 7.1). Moving the net higher automatically slows the pace of the game because the ball or object has to be hit on a higher trajectory to get it over the net. This allows players to move into positions that let them execute the appropriate technique and keep the flow of the game moving.

Increase Opportunities to Practice Techniques and Tactics

The most important strategy to achieve this goal is to reduce team size. In Sport Education, regulation-size teams are rarely used. Most experts who study the conditions under which techniques and tactics are learned agree that successful repetitions in a context relevant to how the technique or tactic will be used in competition are the key to improvement and eventually to students becoming skilled game players. In eleven-on-eleven soccer and six-on-six volleyball, students simply get too few opportunities to respond during the course of a game. It should be no surprise that two-on-two beach volleyball and three-on-three outdoor summer basketball competitions have become so popular: they allow for more action per player than is possible in the parent game.

In games such as basketball, volleyball, and even soccer, most of what students need to learn by way of tactics they can learn in a three-on-three format. In this format, they get more touches and more opportunities to score, which helps them to learn tactics and techniques more quickly. The reduced complexity of small-sided games also helps them to grasp the tactical nature of the games more quickly.

Striking and fielding games such as softball and cricket are notorious for their lack of involvement by many players. In a physical education class playing softball games, it would not be unusual for a number of players to touch the ball for an entire class period, and they might get just one chance to bat. Softball and cricket are sector games that can be modified to make them fun and useful for small-sided teams. Softball, for example, is played in a 90-degree sector, whereas cricket is played in a 360-degree sector. Figure 7.2 shows how a smaller sector (35 to 40 degrees) can be arranged for a modified form of softball in which students get frequent opportunities to hit and field. The use of a friendly pitcher (from either the batting team or the officiating team) makes these games move even more quickly.

Table 7.1 Enabling Learning With Modified Equipment

Equipment	Specific feature
No-string rag ball volleyballs	Balls give on impact, reduces fear, slows game
VB Trainer	40% lighter, 25% larger
VB Trainer II	25% lighter, regulation size
Softie ball	Official size and weight softball but limited flight
Rag balls	9-inch (23 cm) baseballs, 11-inch (28 cm) softballs, 16-inch (40 cm) softballs Softer, safer, slower, reduced flight
Maxi Net-N-Goal System	Can be organized for two volleyball nets at three heights, three badminton nets, three short-court tennis or racquetball nets, or three basketball goals at four heights
Mix-and-match heads and shafts	Plastic shafts at five lengths to which various heads can be attached for lacrosse or floor hockey
Hang-a-Hoop	Basketball hoop that can be hung at any height, available in regulation and large sizes

Products available from School Specialty at www.sportime.com.

In this game, called *five-a-side softball*, there are three key rules that differ from regular softball. First, the striking team pitches to its own players (there is no restriction on where this pitch is made from). Second, the ball must be hit into fair territory within two swings or the batter is out (includes air swings). Third, the ball must hit the ground before passing the imaginary (or chalked) line linking first and second base.

Once the ball is in play, all other softball rules apply (such as base running, force and tag plays, and fly ball rules). Teams play these rules for three innings (three outs per inning) and can then apply a number of options.

As variations, in the fourth inning, teams can select one player's turn in which that player is exempt from the requirement

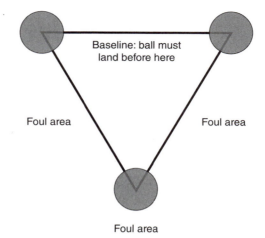

Figure 7.2 Five-a-side softball is a modified form of softball in which students get frequent opportunities to hit and field.

to hit a ground ball. In the fifth inning, teams can select one player, and each time that player bats he or she is exempt. Finally, after the fifth inning, all players are exempt from the hitting restriction.

A final suggestion to help students more easily learn techniques and tactics is to use a friendly guarding rule in both court and field invasion games. When students are beginning to learn a sport and are closely guarded by defenders, they either panic and try to get rid of the ball immediately or they try to dribble or run away from the defenders. Friendly guarding simply means that defenders must be an arm's length away from the player they are guarding. This enables the offensive player to try to execute techniques and to move more easily in a manner that is tactically appropriate. Fouls are called on students who guard more closely than an arm's length, with play resuming as quickly as possible. Friendly guarding is also a useful strategy for students to learn appropriate defensive positioning relative to the person being guarded, the flow of play, and the goal being guarded.

A strategy for ensuring friendly guarding is to incorporate a rule stating that if an offensive player is able to touch a defender, that defender must stop guarding and run to touch a sideline before resuming play. This is a particularly useful rule in games such as ultimate Frisbee or those where the player cannot move while in possession.

Sequence Games to Enable the Learning of Tactics

Invasion games present the most complex tactics for students to master. Court-divided games, such as volleyball or tennis, tend to be more predictable in their tactical demands and thus easier to master. Many students who are learning invasion games and are thrust into large teams using large spaces simply get confused and discouraged. It is no wonder that many of them quickly come to dislike invasion games. Some students are clever enough to learn to be part of the flow of the game but to stay away from the main action, often successfully hiding their lack of participation. We call these students *competent bystanders* (Tousignant & Siedentop, 1983).

The easiest way to analyze the tactics of invasion games and help students gradually become more comfortable with increasingly more complex tactics is to use a series of small-sided games. Bell and Darnell (1994) described a series of soccer competitions for elementary school children that illustrate this principle. The first competition is one-on-one and is played in a manner similar to half-court basketball. To play one-on-one successfully, students must be able to dribble, shield, and shoot while on offense and maintain defensive space and tackle on defense. In short games that are timed (3-5 minutes), students get a large number of opportunities to respond. Even inside the space of an elementary school gymnasium, it is possible to have eight such games going on simultaneously. The next competition is two-on-two played full court by simply combining two of the one-on-one spaces. In this game, the concept of tandem defending is introduced and offensive players learn passing, trapping, cutting, and floor balance. This is followed by a three-on-three competition in which goalkeeper, defender, and forward positions or two forwards and a goalkeeper are used. In the three-on-three, throw-ins, goal kicks, and corner kicks are introduced, and the tactical concepts of players maintaining floor balance, cutting to positions of advantage, and centering the ball become important. Off-the-ball play becomes more obvious both for defenders and attackers. Similar strategies could be used for court invasion games such as basketball and floor hockey. Chapter 8 provides various competition examples that use this progressive element.

The size and configuration of the game space also help determine how tactics are learned. In field invasion games especially, the space should be large relative to the number of players in order to allow more time for players to adjust to the movement of the ball, teammates, and opponents. As students progress in their game sense, the space can be made smaller so that it becomes even more important for players to value space and apply the tactics of attacking or defending. Altering spaces can also make some tactics more appropriate than others; for example, a longer, narrower space tends to produce longer passes, shots, or hits.

Change Rules That Define Scoring

Games can also be modified by changing the rules that define scoring. Since the object of the game is to outscore the opponent, this motivation can be used to emphasize the usage of certain techniques and tactics over others. We call this *differential scoring.* Teachers can modify the typical point rules to give more points for what they want students to focus on. In volleyball, awarding two points rather than one for a team that scores through a pass, set, spike pattern encourages students to use that pattern. Likewise the point system can fail to award points for aspects of play that the teacher wants to discourage. For example, in basketball, no points would be awarded for a basket scored by a player on a fast break without a teammate touching the ball. The aim here is to reduce the domination of the game by higher-skilled players.

GAME MODIFICATIONS: EVENT AND PERFORMANCE SPORTS

Performance sports are those where the performance is judged against time, distance, or height (such as racing, throwing, and jumping events in track and field and racing events in swimming) or previously established performance criteria (such as gymnastics, diving, synchronized swimming, and figure skating).

In performance activities, the primary goal is to execute the techniques themselves. In most cases, the performance is executed in a generally constant or stable environment. Therefore, the practice should focus on the technical execution itself, and modifications should relate to changes in equipment or the environment in which the performance takes place. The goal of such modifications is primarily to ease the execution, thereby increasing the chance of success, and to emphasize a particular phase of the execution.

In discus throwing, for example, such modifications could include using a weighted rod rather than an actual discus and allowing throwers to release from behind a line rather than limiting them to a restrictive discus circle. Both modifications allow for more positive and hence more motivating experiences while still reinforcing the key biomechanical features of throwing a weight (i.e., hip rotation, keeping the hands back). Following are additional examples of how many event or performance sports and activities can be modified to allow for more appropriate practice and competition.

Track and field modifications

- Long or triple jumps:
  - Use an expanded takeoff board rather than the familiar narrow board.
  - Have students run up and jump and measure from where their planted foot touched the takeoff board (or ground within an identified takeoff space).
- Discus:
  - Use a weighted rod rather than the discus.
  - Use a front line rather than a circle.
- Shot put:
  - Allow throwers to propel themselves over the starting line.
  - Allow throwers to throw backwards over the head.
- Javelin:
  - Use a blunted implement (PCV pipe inserted into a foam pool noodle works well) and count the distance by the sector it lands in (rather than measuring exact distance).
- Hurdles:
  - Use lower hurdles.
  - Modify the distance between hurdles so that students learn the appropriate step sequence (e.g., three steps or five steps) between hurdles.
  - Reduce the number of hurdles in the race.

Aquatics modifications

- Swimming:
  - Allow the use of fins for those with less skill.
  - Begin some races with swimmers already in the water (rather than diving in).
- Diving:
  - Include a category with feet-first entries.
  - Include fun categories such as biggest splash.

Cross country running

- Have varying course lengths for varying fitness levels.
- Include varying obstacles for varying fitness levels.

Gymnastics modifications

- Beam:
  - Use a lower, wider bench rather than the narrower, higher beam.
- Vault:
  - Use a lower vaulting horse.
  - Increase the number of springs under the springboard.
  - Use a mini trampoline rather than a springboard.

■ Floor exercises:
  • Allow the use of cheese-slice mats for assisting with rolls.
  • Incorporate larger mats or benches to assist in rotational movements.

GAME MODIFICATIONS: TARGET GAMES

In target sports, it is especially important for students to experience success early in the learning process. The modifications again focus on changing the environment and the equipment. Several examples are presented here that can be implemented for both practices and season competitions.

Target sport modifications

■ Archery:
  • Use bows with lower draw weights, making it easier to reach and maintain proper anchor position.
  • Use larger overall targets, or targets with larger scoring rings.
  • Reduce the distance from the shooters to the target.
■ Golf:
  • Reduce the distance from the tee to the green.
  • Increase the size of the target by making the hole a marked-off area.
  • Use modified golf balls that have a limited travel distance.
■ Ten-pin bowling:
  • Allow students to release the bowling ball closer to the pins.
  • Use the bumpers on lanes.

GAME MODIFICATIONS: WALL AND NET COURT GAMES

Significant modifications can be made to net court sports with changes in equipment, court dimensions, rule restrictions, and scoring rules. For example, slower balls in tennis and pickleball make play more continuous and hence potentially more motivating. This allows players to begin closer to targets and can lead to more success and hence enthusiasm. The following are additional examples of how net court sports can be modified to allow for more appropriate practice and competition.

Racket sport modifications

■ Tennis:
  • Use a special slow tennis ball.
  • Use a racquetball racket or a tennis racket with a shorter handle.
  • Move the serve line in from the baseline.
  • Allow only a bounce-and-hit stroke for serves.
■ Pickleball:
  • Use a slower, spongy ball rather than the regular plastic Wiffle ball.
  • Raise the net height.
  • Lengthen the baseline to allow for a lesser requirement to control power.

■ Badminton:
  • Use slower birdies.
  • Allow players to use the wider court for singles to emphasize angles.
  • Use a narrower and longer court to emphasize up-and-back play as students learn to master the clear and drop shots, which are crucial to badminton performance.

GAME MODIFICATIONS: STRIKING AND FIELDING GAMES

Softball and cricket are two examples of striking and fielding games. In these games, the key learning areas are batting, fielding, player positioning, and base running, all of which are modifiable. Examples of modifications are shown in table 7.2, which highlights changes to equipment, team size, rules, and so on.

With an eye toward increasing opportunities for appropriate practice, teachers can modify competitions and practices by employing lighter bats and balls as well as softer balls. The manner in which balls are pitched can also be modified. For example, the teacher or a player from the batting team can serve as pitcher. When machine pitching is used, the speed can be adjusted, and batters can be assured that pitches will be in the strike zone. This helps maintain the flow of the game and creates more opportunities for success. As students gain experience and base running becomes more frequent, teachers can emphasize the need for making good base running decisions by adding additional bases.

GAME MODIFICATIONS: INVASION GAMES

Invasion games are those in which a team has to gain possession of an object, move toward a specific target (progression), and score into that target. Basketball, soccer, water polo, lacrosse, flag football, and floor hockey are examples of invasion games.

To make these games more appropriate for students, you can make the following modifications: reduce the number of players on each team, reduce the size of the playing area to correspond to the number of players, reduce the number of rules, and alter secondary rules to keep the game flowing (e.g., restart rules in soccer). You can make additional alterations such as those suggested in table 7.3.

In invasion games, students can learn tactics through attacking and defending. Principles such as maintaining spacing, creating angles, and running to open spaces can help students learn attacking tactics in soccer. Invasion games such as soccer and the various forms of hockey certainly use offensive and defensive tactics that are

Table 7.2 Modifications to Striking and Fielding Games

Equipment	Batting	Fielding	Base running
• Use larger balls • Use shorter-handled bats	• Hit from a tee rather than from a pitch • Allow the batter to receive a pitch or bowl from own team • Have duty team provide a pitcher, presenting batter-friendly deliveries	• Have larger targets to hit (e.g., cricket) • Reduce the size of the sector	• Limit the stealing options

Table 7.3 Modifications for Invasion Games

Equipment	Gaining possession	Progression	Scoring
• Use larger balls • Use slower balls • Use shorter handles on striking implements (e.g., hockey sticks)	• Do not allow direct stealing of a ball • Increase the ways in which a player can gain possession	• Allow players some steps in games where none are allowed (e.g., Frisbee) • Increase the time that individual players can have possession without being penalized or in which they must make a pass • Reduce the pressure on players as they attempt to put the ball in play after an out-of-bounds play or a penalty (e.g., do not allow players to stand too close to the sideline)	• Make larger goals • Make lower goals • Consider including the opportunity to score by progressing the ball (or object) across an end line rather than into a specific goal

based on these principles but they also create more predictable movement in reaction to offensive opportunities. For example, in basketball the patterns become even more specific and player movement more predictable both on offense and defense. Teams should learn a patterned offense and either a person-to-person or a zone defense. The attacking pattern should be as simple as possible, one that can be practiced and learned.

In three-on-three basketball, a simple attacking pattern that relies on a pass and screen away tactic might be taught for use against person-to-person defenses. Students first learn the techniques of passing and catching. Offensively, they also learn the important tactic of maintaining floor balance by moving to open spaces and creating triangles. They then follow the main principle of the offense by passing to one teammate and moving away to screen for the other teammate, who cuts off that screen. The techniques needed to learn this offense are passing, catching, screening, reverse pivoting (for the screener, who then can become another target for the passer), and backdoor cutting (if the defense overplays the open player on the attacking side). Students will then learn to become aware of how defenders play against this offensive tactic. For example, do defenders switch at the screen or try to stay with their primary defensive assignment? Although the development and refinement of technique always takes a substantial amount of repetitive practice, students can learn tactics quickly once they grasp the significance and flow of the movements defined by the tactical scheme.

STUDENT-DESIGNED MODIFICATIONS

In listing the potential modifications to activities within this chapter, we may have well ignored the voices of our games consumers: our students. As Ledingham and Cox (1989) have commented,

> *At some stage in our childhood most of us will have "made games." The majority of these games have been characterized by our desire to play and create something spontaneous in response to the situation and environment. "Games Making" in this sense can encompass a wide range of games, from games we can play by ourselves, challenging our own abilities, to more recognizable forms of games involving objects, rules, opponents and team-mates. Whatever form of game*

we created the very essence of the process was the freedom from adult interference. These games were "ours" and we required no teacher to instruct or shape our innovations. (p. 14)

While teachers in some cases have involved all students in creating new games, with the class favorite being selected as the sport for a subsequent season of Sport Education (Casey & Hastie, 2011), the focus in this section is on giving students voice with regard to potential rule changes. The basis for this revolves around the concept of "thoughtful decision making" (McBride & Xiang, 2004), in which classes are characterized by ongoing discussion and debate, which lead to judgments, decisions, and compromises.

The most typical timing for involving student voice and choice is after the students have experienced the game as presented by the teacher. With experience in the original game, students have a better appreciation of what might make this a good game. As Hastie (2010) has noted, the characteristics of good games need to be explicitly presented to students, and therefore any game modification must

- contribute to *skill development*,
- be *safe*,
- *include, not eliminate*, students from participation,
- have *high participation rates*, and
- be structured so that *all children are successful and are being challenged*.

Figure 7.3 provides an example of potential student-designed modifications to the game of indoor flickerball, a noncontact sport played on a basketball court with an American football by two teams of between four and eight players on each side.

Figure 7.3
INDOOR FLICKERBALL RULES AND POTENTIAL MODIFICATIONS

Rules
- The aim of the game is to throw the football from within the three-point area so that it goes through the goal. This is worth three points.
- A shot that hits the ring (but does not travel through) is worth two points.
- A shot hitting only the backboard scores one point.
- Players can hold the ball for only five seconds and cannot travel with the ball.
- Whenever the ball hits the ground, the team that was last in possession loses that possession. That is, if a player from the Red team knocks down a pass from one Blue player to another, the Red team gains possession.

Potential Modifications: Play, Discuss, Decide
- Allow running with the ball (for so many steps? unlimited? how to stop them?).
- Shoot from anywhere, not just inside the three-point line (do the score values change?).
- Whenever the ball hits the ground, the team to touch it last loses possession.
- The team that gains control must first make a lateral or backward pass (i.e., they cannot shoot immediately).

MODIFICATIONS TO INCLUDE STUDENTS WITH DISABILITIES

A number of rule modifications can be put in place to accommodate students with disabilities. Moreover, the committee or sport board options of Sport Education provide excellent opportunities for students to investigate ways to include people with disabilities in gameplay. As a general rule, appropriate adjustments include modifying equipment, reducing or eliminating defensive pressure, eliminating time restrictions, and providing alternative scoring options. The sport board may be asked not only to develop policies of inclusion but also to outline the wording of specific rule modifications. In some cases, the sport board may require that certain restrictions be put on students without disabilities so that they may be more likely to appreciate the challenges facing those with disabilities. What is most important, however, is that the children with the disabilities themselves have the final say on any rule modifications. While they may appreciate the accommodations, many wish to play under the same rules as their classmates. In chapter 14, we share additional instructional considerations and strategies for ensuring that students with special needs are included in the season's activities in meaningful ways.

Some specific modifications to promote the success of students with disabilities are discussed next.

Modify activities to equalize competition

- Allow a student to kick or hit a stationary ball where it might otherwise be pitched.
- In volleyball, allow students to catch the ball and throw it and allow the ball to bounce.
- Allow a length of time to get to base or the goal that is commensurate with the student's abilities.
- Where indoor and outdoor venues are used concurrently, attempt to schedule the games in the gymnasium or on another smooth surface so it is easier for students to get around (i.e., avoid a grassy field).
- Involve the students with disabilities in the decisions concerning rule modifications.

Decrease distances

- Move bases closer together.
- Allow students to be closer to the target, goal, or net.
- In volleyball or badminton, allow students to serve from midcourt.

Provide more chances to score

- In basketball, allow three foul shots instead of two.
- In softball, allow four strikes instead of three.
- In target archery, allow ten arrows instead of six.

Analyze positions according to the abilities of students

- Place students with disabilities in the positions of goalie, pitcher, or other positions that require limited mobility.
- A student with a heart problem may be a goalie in soccer or a pitcher in softball.
- A single-leg amputee may be a pitcher or a first baseman.

Provide adapted equipment that makes performance easier

- Use larger bats.
- Use larger, lighter, and softer balls.
- Use larger bases that are flat, larger goals, and larger baskets.
- Use larger rackets (face and shaft).

Reprinted from Richard Hageman.

GRADED COMPETITION

In upper-elementary, middle, and high school classes, students often have vastly different experiences in many sports. Even when a season is designed around a sport that most students may never even have seen, one can expect substantial differences among students because of the carryover from sports that require similar techniques and tactics. For example, team handball is a sport many American students have never seen, let alone played. This invasion game (played indoors or outdoors) involves throwing and catching as the primary techniques, with tactical principles similar to soccer. Even if they do not know how to play team handball, students will differ in their skills of running, catching, and throwing. Students who have experience in other court or field invasion games will adjust to team handball more quickly because of the tactical similarities. Thus, heterogeneity is likely to be present even in games that are unfamiliar to nearly all students. In basketball, soccer, and volleyball (that is, sports commonly played in the United States), the heterogeneity of student backgrounds may be even more pronounced.

We suggest that you consider arranging competitions that allow all students to enjoy the game and be successful. In Sport Education, you can accomplish this by using what we call *graded competitions*, which are arranged to match students of similar skill level against one another; in some cases, even the game forms are different across the competition levels. While the essence of the team concept in Sport Education is that it contains players of different skill levels, in graded competition, each team assigns its players to A or B level competitions. For example, during a season of floor hockey, a team of eight players will create two squads of four, with each of these playing their equivalent opponent. What is important to note (and to reinforce with students), is that the results from these matches count equally, so the performance of the B team contributes as much to the seasonal championship as that of the A team.

The goal of graded competition is to create a setting where the task demands for each skill level group are better aligned to those students' needs and are set at a pace that is appropriate for the students in each group (Rink, 2006). Bygren (2016) argues that ability grouping not only benefits learning but has motivational aspects in that it helps prevent students from losing interest in a subject because the pace is too fast or too slow. Our most recent investigation of this very topic has shown that in terms of success rates, engagement rates, and playing efficiency, lower-skilled students are at a disadvantage when they play alongside higher-skilled classmates. Of particular interest is that there are also decrements in higher-skilled student success rates and efficiency in these mixed-skill conditions. In particular, while higher-skilled boys can thrive in either homogenous or mixed-level competitions, many girls as well as all students with lower skill levels benefit from playing against students of similar skill levels.

In many situations, splitting teams into smaller mini-teams is sufficient to help students learn and enjoy the game through equal competition. We suggest, however, that you consider a further refinement of this principle by having the game be somewhat different at each of the competition levels. This can be accomplished using combinations of any of the modification approaches described earlier in this chapter. Players competing in the A and B level competitions might use different balls, court sizes, or scoring rules. For example, in a game where dropping the ball (or an object like a Frisbee) results in a turn over, the B level competitions might have a one-bounce rule. Figure 7.4 shows two formats for playing invasion games like hockey, soccer, or basketball, where dribbling can be challenging for beginners. In the lower-skilled game (right image), players on the side zones can dribble without being defended. They can also pass and receive from players in the main court.

Those who argue against ability grouping believe that students classified in lower-ability groups are robbed of the opportunity to learn from their peers classified in high-ability groups. But the notion as it is applied in Sport Education is that these small-sided teams are derived from within heterogeneous groups in which there is the possibility of heterogeneous skill level practices.

In sport education, teachers can accomplish what we call *graded competition* by arranging competitions that match students of similar skill level against one another, and in some cases, even using different game forms across the competition levels.

As Hastie, Ward, and Brock (2016) note, these within-team practices can be designed so that different levels of constraints are placed on students, depending on their skill levels. In this way, and provided there is a commitment of higher-skilled students to a restructuring of power relations that foster trust and caring, there is the potential for sharing knowledge, with higher-skilled students contributing to the development of gameplay performance of lower-skilled students.

Graded competition is particularly well suited for use with individual or dual sports. For example, gymnastic competitions can have an A level and a B level for routines in order to accommodate students with varying skill levels and experiences in the sport. While all routines will require elements of balance, flight, tumbling, and changes of levels and directions, the degree of difficulty across the two levels can be varied.

Weight training seasons would see students competing in different weight categories for boys and for girls. In swimming, races could be over different distances and involve different starts to accommodate those with varying ability. Finally, in rollerblading, students could navigate obstacle courses of different lengths and difficulty levels.

With respect to net sports such as badminton, tennis, table tennis, or pickleball, A, B, and even C level competitions can be organized to allow for more appropriate competition. As mentioned earlier in this chapter, modifications can also be made to the equipment, and rule variations can be employed across the different levels.

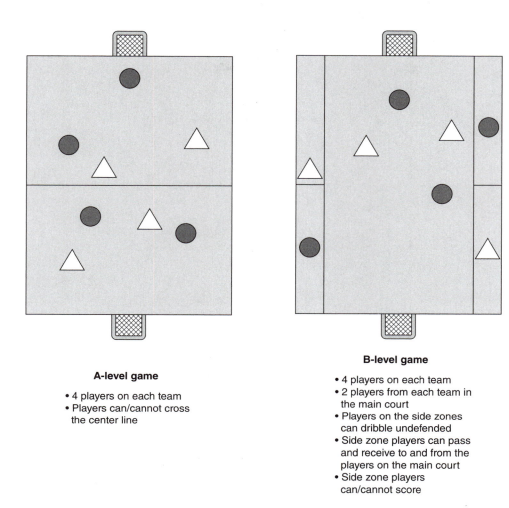

A-level game

- 4 players on each team
- Players can/cannot cross the center line

B-level game

- 4 players on each team
- 2 players from each team in the main court
- Players on the side zones can dribble undefended
- Side zone players can pass and receive to and from the players on the main court
- Side zone players can/cannot score

Figure 7.4 Different options for small-court invasion games.

SUMMARY

"Are we going to play a game today?" How many physical educators hear this from their students on a daily basis? Most students like games. They especially like friendly games in which they can participate successfully and not feel out of place or bewildered by the complexity of the game. Modified games and graded competition are a key component of Sport Education, and in this chapter we have discussed the kinds of modifications required for various categories of games and activities.

8

Designing Competition Formats

Chapter Objective

After reading this chapter, you will be able select the most appropriate combination of practices and competitions that suit the sport you have selected for the season.

Key Concepts

- The two most common competition formats are the progressive competition and the event model. Together, these can accommodate any range of sports or activities you might select for a Sport Education season.
- The progressive competition format involves teams moving through four phases, in which they first learn skills within teams, then participate in non-consequential practice games (which we call scrimmages), and then move on to formal competition and a culminating event.
- The event model consists of a series of independent competitions interspersed with team practice; this is similar to the way in which international golf and tennis tours are organized.
- To determine the season champion, you should factor in other elements besides a team's win–loss record.

In sporting competitions throughout the world, the champions in the various sports are selected in one of two ways. In the first, teams play weekly matches throughout a season to place them in a certain ranking, and this is followed by a finals series. Examples in the United States include the women's and men's National Basketball leagues and Major League Baseball. In Australia, four football codes, the Australian Netball League, the Sheffield Shield, and the Women's National Cricket League all follow this format. Throughout Europe, Asia, Africa, and South America, there are football leagues involving many divisions including the top tier Premier League (England), La Liga (Spain), the J1 League (Japan), and the Brasileirão (Brazil).

In these leagues the same game is used across the sport season, and there are no variations in rules throughout. For example, rugby in the Tri-Nations and Six-Nations competitions always consists of the 15-a-side format, while the cricket formats (1-day or T-20) retain the same playing number. We describe these seasons as following a *progressive competition format*, with the typical progression running as shown in figure 8.1.

The second common competition format is followed when the sport is conducted as a series of independent events. Examples include the various tours for golf and tennis, track and field athletics, and swimming. The various series of motor racing (NASCAR in the United States, Formula 1 internationally), also follow this format. In these cases, athletes (and sometimes teams) accumulate points based upon their performance in each of the events, and these are used to calculate either rankings or qualification for season-ending championships. In these events prize money, medals, and trophies are typically distributed after each event rather than at the end of the completed season. We describe these seasons as following an *event model*, with the typical progression running as shown in figure 8.2.

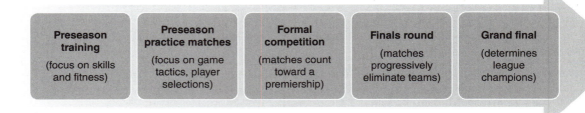

Figure 8.1 Progressive competition format sequence.

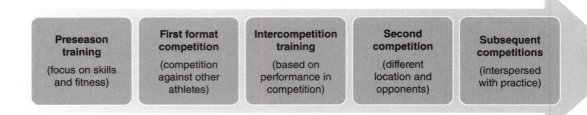

Figure 8.2 Event model competition format sequence.

PROGRESSIVE COMPETITION

The most familiar (and simple) progressive competition format is one that resembles the four phases that sports like basketball or football follow at almost any level. In the first phase (which we call *training camp*), teams are formed and then undergo a series of lessons in which they practice, learn the rules, and learn how to officiate. The second phase, the *preseason*, involves lessons in which teams play informal games whose scores do not count toward the league table and whose focus is on developing competency in officiating and in maximizing team function. The third phase is the *formal competition*, in which the game results are formally recorded in a league table along with other elements (such as fair play) that the teacher sees as relevant. The season concludes in the fourth, or *postseason*, phase, in which teams compete in playoff matches and in a culminating event that is highly festive. Table 8.1 provides a sample from a basketball three-on-three season (Hastie & Sinelnikov, 2006).

Progressive Competition for Individual or Dual Sports

The progressive competition format is not restricted to team sports such as basketball, volleyball, or hockey. Seasons of net or wall games like tennis, badminton, racquetball, and pickleball, or target games like tenpin bowling, bocce, or horseshoes can also use this format. In these situations, individuals or pairs from one team compete against equivalent individuals or pairs from their opponents. A five-member badminton team might divide into two doubles teams and a singles player, while a six-member bocce team might split into three pairs teams. A third team completes the duty responsibilities for the match. The final score in each of these contests will be either 3-0 or 2-1.

Table 8.1 Basketball Season Plan

Phase	Lesson	Content	Teacher role	Student roles
Training camp	1	Introduction Rules of the game Beginning skills	Class leader	Participant
	2	Skills testing Team announcement	Present team lists Discuss roles Discuss fair play	Determine team roles Decide on team name
	3-7	Whole-class instruction Team practices	Class leader	Participant Student coach
Preseason	8-10	Preseason practice games	Head coach	Player Student coach
Formal competition	11-15	Formal competition	Head coach Program manager	Player Student coach Duty team role
Postseason	16-17	Playoffs	Program manager	Player Student coach Duty team role
	18	Championship game Awards presentation	Program manager Master of ceremonies	Player Student coach Duty team role

Reprinted by permission from P.A. Hastie and O.A. Sinelnikov, "Russian Students' Participation in and Perceptions of a Season of Sport Education," *European Physical Education Review* 12 (2006): 131-150.

Changing the Game Across a Progressive Competition Format

The progressive competition format would be most familiar to students who follow sports competitions such as the NFL or the world football leagues, and is therefore recommended for students' (and teachers') first experiences with Sport Education. However, they do not allow the complexities of the game to be changed across the length of the season. As a result, when students have some experience with being in persisting teams with their roles and responsibilities, and have become familiar with officiating structure of Sport Education, some teachers begin to design seasons in which the matches become more and more tactically and technically advanced. This is particularly helpful for games that require students to have mastered certain ball control skills, as in floor hockey, soccer, or different racket sports. An example of a floor hockey season is provided in table 8.2.

This season begins with a two-on-two keep-away competition where the skills developed are passing and trapping and the tactical element is moving into a space. Teams play for two minutes and score one point for each successful pass. The three-on-three over-the-line competition that follows adds dribbling as a technique as well as the tactical decision whether to dribble or to pass. In this competition, teams score

Table 8.2 Hockey Season Plan

Lesson	Content	Competition format	Game rules
1	Introduction Rules of the game Beginning skills		
2	Team announcement Teams decide name and roles		
3-5	Techniques and skills of two-on-two	Within team practice	
6-8	Two-on-two competition	Two-on-two Duty team players referee Scorekeepers keep simple performance statistics	Score for each successful pass Two-minute games
9-10	Techniques and skills of three-on-three	Within-team practice	
11-13	Three-on-three competition	Three-on-three Games consist of six players with two referees and two scorekeepers	Teams score a point each time they pass to a teammate who traps the ball after it goes into an end zone
14-18	Techniques and skills of four-on-four	Within-team practice	
19-21	Six-on-six competition	Six-on-six Games consist of twelve players with two referees and two scorekeepers	Score by sending the ball into a goal Teams may have a goalkeeper
22	Championship game		

a point each time they pass to a teammate who traps the ball after it goes into an end zone (i.e., there is no goal). Finally, a six-on-six competition is played in which there is a goal and goalkeeper. Here, shooting skills are introduced, and positional play in attack and defense is also added.

The progressive competition format allows for changes in the size of the court or field, the type of implements and balls, and other features that make the particular activity progressively more advanced. For example, a beginning competition in pickleball might use slow-bounce balls, a longer and narrower court, and a service line moved closer to the net. As students become more experienced and confident, a subsequent competition can change any or all of those features. In archery, the first competition sees archers shooting from 30 feet (9 m), the second is from 50 feet (15 m), while the third competition is a clout shoot. It is up to the teacher to decide whether to have points from the early competitions count toward the season championship or to use them solely as developmental experiences.

EVENT MODEL

In the event model format, students compete in events by themselves, but all their performances count toward a collective team score. During the earliest part of the season, students work on developing the techniques and fitness levels required for successful participation in competition. For example, track athletes would practice their starts, their hurdle techniques, and their pacing skills. Swimmers would work on developing sufficient endurance to allow them to complete their events while at the same time learning and refining their strokes, turns, and starts.

The bulk of the season focuses on a series of team competitions. During the latter part of the season, teams come together in a celebratory event to contest the final championships. The number of days allocated to these final championships depends on the number of events to be completed. For example, in a cross-country season (which might include both walking and running competitions), all events may be completed in just one day with final races of varying distances. For track and field, three days may be required for the culminating event, with one day for throwing events, a second day for running events, and the final day for jumping events. During the final championships, teams would perform as competitors and also as judges, timekeepers, and in other official capacities. The teacher may ask for nominations for officials to cover all events (e.g., one for each gymnastics event) or may allocate one event (e.g., the high jump) to a specific team.

In the early stages of this event model format, competition is often limited to intrasquad events, whereby coaches help their team members determine who will represent the team in the various events. For example, in the first competition of a golf season, there might be a putting competition, a chipping competition, and a driving competition, with different players representing each team. Likewise, in the first gymnastics competition, different students might represent their teams on the beam, on the floor, and perhaps on the vault. In all cases, points are added from all team members to determine the team score.

Event Model for Fitness Activities

The event model is particularly suitable for fitness activities, where students are able to increase their strength and endurance across the course of a season. It is particularly valuable for situations in which performance is affected by size and strength, such as weightlifting. In this variation, all team members compete in the same events (e.g., bench press, clean and squat) but against those in their same weight division.

Weekly challenges are used as mini-competitions during the season, and individual team members keep personal record sheets of their workouts and lifts. Sweeney, Tannehill, and Teeters (1992) described a Sport Education strength training season for high school girls. A class of 31 girls was divided into seven teams. Four weight divisions determined the pool of students to be assigned to each team. Class A was 96 to 109 pounds (43.5-49 kg), class B was 112 to 119 pounds (51-54 kg), class C was 121 to 134 pounds (55-61 kg), and class D was 135 pounds (61 kg) and over. Weekly challenges were held, and the final competition was a team event in which the total weight lifted by a team across all events and weight divisions was used to determine the competition champion. Alternatively, the placing of each team member in each competition could be added to give a team total.

Table 8.3 shows how a fitness season for elementary school students was organized around three separate competition events (called *challenges*), where the results of each counted toward a season championship.

Relay Competitions in the Event Model

One option for the event model is to compete strictly in a relay competition. In this case, there are no individual performances but a collective team time or score. The relay format is especially appropriate for sports such as swimming, cross country, and track and field. There could be shuttle hurdle relays, shot put and long jump collective distance, and 400 and 800 relay teams.

In one season on obstacle course fitness, a class of 25 students met three times a week for six weeks. Each week followed a similar format. On day 1, all teams progressed through a series of activity stations designed by the teacher. On day 2, four teams designed their own training session while the fifth team designed the obstacle course challenge for that week. On day 3, all teams completed the obstacle course while the design team kept each team's total time as well as any penalties accrued during the course. Each week a different team designed and officiated at the course. Points were awarded each week for course completion, and the participating teams also graded the course designers on their creativity, challenge, and officiating effectiveness. This format has also been successfully used in university physical education jogging classes.

Event Model Options for Performance Activities

Throughout the text we have emphasized that Sport Education is a small-group learning model that can be used for many activities not typically considered to be sports, including outdoor activities such as snowshoeing or orienteering, exercise activities such as aerobics or jump rope, and the many forms of dance. These activities lend themselves well to the event model competition format.

Table 8.4 shows a 23-session schedule for a dance season adapted from the model described by Graves and Townsend (2000). The dance model uses *troupes* instead of *teams* to describe the student groups. The student roles include troupe leader, choreographer, fitness trainer, class dance committee representative, disc jockey, master of ceremonies, dance judge, and reviewer or critic. The season consists of five competitions, each representing a decade of popular dance forms. Teams choose the dance form they will use for each competition. The culminating event is a dance festival with each troupe picking the dance they liked best and performing it again for the class.

Table 8.3   Fitness Season Plan

Lesson 1	• Introduction to the season • Concept of challenges • Announce teams (based on earlier fitness test scores) • Complete team sheets (team names, colors, mascot)
Lesson 2	• Muscular strength and endurance lesson • Focus on MSE knowledge (reps, sets, overload) • Discuss sample exercises
Lesson 3	• MSE team practice • Examining different activities students enjoy and can do
Lesson 4	• Aerobic lesson • Focus on aerobic fitness knowledge (HR zones, intensity) • Discuss sample exercises
Lesson 5	• AER team practice • Examining different activities students enjoy and can do
Lesson 6	• Introduce challenge 1 (head to head) • Team practice and training • Begin designing first challenge
Lesson 7	• Team practice and training • Refine and finalize challenge
Lesson 8	• Challenge 1 practice run • Focus on scorekeeping
Lesson 9	• Challenge 1 formal competition • Head-to-head competition between teams (winner scores 5 points)
Lesson 10	• Introduce challenge 2 (the until challenge) • Team practice and training
Lesson 11	• Team practice and training
Lesson 12	• Team practice and training
Lesson 13	• Challenge 2 practice run • Focus on scorekeeping
Lesson 14	• Challenge 2 formal competition • Points distributed in order of team completion
Lesson 15	• Introduce challenge 3 • Team practice and training
Lesson 16	• Team practice and training
Lesson 17	• Team practice and training
Lesson 18	• Challenge 3 practice run • Full cross-fit circuit to determine cutoff times
Lesson 19	• Challenge 3 formal competition • Full cross-fit circuit with cutoff times
Lesson 20	• Present awards and final festivity

Table 8.4 Season Schedule for Popular Dance

Days	Focus
1	Form dance troupes; explain roles; review handout describing dances from various eras; show videos of selected dances
2	Troupes decide who will fulfill various roles; troupes are introduced to elementary dance techniques and rituals and traditions of dance
3-5	Dances from 1950s introduced and practiced; troupes begin to plan for 1950s dance competition (music and dance); schedule of dance competitions is posted; judging is introduced
6	1950s dance competition
7-9	Troupes practice dance they will perform in the 1960s competition
10	1960s dance competition
11-13	Troupes practice dance they will perform in 1970s competition
14	1970s dance competition
15-17	Troupes practice dance they will perform in 1980s competition
18	1980s dance competition
19-21	Troupes practice dance they will perform in 1990s competition
22	1990s dance competition
23	Dance festival and awards celebration

Adapted from a model suggested by Graves and Townsend (2000).

SETTING UP A LEAGUE SCORING SYSTEM

No matter which competition format you chose, you need to examine how you are going to determine a season champion team. One of the significant differences between Sport Education and interschool and community sport is the way in which you determine the overall season champion. In high school sport and nonschool competitions, the only thing that counts is the win–loss record. In Sport Education, the teacher has significant liberty to incorporate a number of objectives into the determination of the champion team. The sample league standings shown in table 8.5 from an eighth-grade Frisbee season show one example of how a team's win–loss record is not the sole indicator of success. The table shows how a team that wins but does not exhibit the appropriate personal and social behaviors such as playing fair (Rangers) can be outranked in total points by a team that lost more games but showed all the positive attributes of fair play and persistence (Devils). Notice how the Devils won the fewest games but finished third overall, their score boosted by excellent team organization and duty team performance. The Rangers, in contrast, finished fifth.

The example shown in table 8.5 is but one of many designs you might use. We suggest that you follow a three-step process:

1. Decide which specific features are particularly important to your season.
2. Provide a weighting for those outcomes (i.e., number of points that teams can earn per match or per lesson).
3. Design or select the instruments by which you will collect that information.

Table 8.5   Sample League Standings

Team	Win (5/win)	Tie (3/tie)	Fair play (3/match)	Organization (2/match)	Duty team (5/match)	Total points
Eagles	25	6	30	20	25	106
Tigers	25	0	30	20	22	97
Devils	15	6	28	20	25	94
Spiders	20	3	26	17	25	91
Rangers	30	0	20	16	23	89
Lions	15	3	28	18	24	88

The easiest variable to manipulate is match-play points. In head-to-head competition such as basketball or soccer, you may allocate two points for a win, one for a tie, and none for a loss. In Australian football, the ratio is win = 4, tie = 2, loss = 0, and in soccer, the common convention is win = 3, draw = 1, loss = 0. The National Hockey League now uses a system whereby teams who finish the game in regulation as a tie score one point each, but if a team wins in overtime it collects another point.

In dual sports, where teams might play a number of singles and doubles matches against another team, the points may simply be the number of matches won by each team. For example, in a five-player-per-team season involving three singles matches and one doubles match, a team could score anywhere from zero to four points depending on its total wins. If teams are tied at 2-2, you might give a bonus point to the team that won more total points (this information would be available from the score sheets and should be reported by the team statistician).

A Note on Fair Play

Fair play must be prominent in any scoring system to determine the season championship. This constitutes a built-in accountability system for you to formally assess students' fair play performance. We prefer that you start at zero points for each team and let each team accumulate fair play points.

In some leagues, teachers require teams to exhibit a certain level of fair play to become eligible for end-of-season playoffs. For example, where teams are awarded three possible points each day, a useful cutoff is 70 percent. A team thus needs to average better than two out of three (66 percent) positive outcomes for fair play throughout the course of a season to qualify. In leagues that have adopted this strategy, it is not uncommon to see captains reminding their teams (and specific

Team Name	Fitness Points	Win	Loss	Tie	Fair Play	Total Points
1. South African Zebras		7	6	3	10	18.5
2. Brazil Panthers		11	3	2	9	21
3. Denmark Disco Spiders	1	7	7	4	7	17
4. Mexican Matadors	1	4	7	5	6	13.5
5. Turkish Tie-Dye Tigers		4	10	2	10	15

Fair play must be prominent in any scoring system to determine the season championship. This constitutes a built-in accountability system for you to formally assess students' fair play performance.

players) that they need to be aware of the team's current fair play status and to be disciplined in their interactions with the officials.

Adding Team Task Points

In some elementary settings, the teacher gives teams points for accomplishing tasks in the managerial system. For instance, a team would receive one point for successful completion of each of the following tasks.

- The fitness leader brings a warm-up card to class and leads the team in their exercise routine within one minute of arriving at its designated home space.
- The equipment manager collects all the team's necessary equipment and returns it to the appropriate place in the gym at the end of a lesson.
- The mascot manager brings the team mascot to class.
- The team moves promptly and in an orderly fashion from its home space to the playing area and is ready to begin games on time.

These points are added to the scores obtained from match play. In one elementary school's flag football season, teams earned one point for each touchdown they scored, with up to four possible points added, depending on achievement of class protocols. The team points system allowed all teams to score the maximum possible for a single lesson and also served to keep the league totals close.

When using any scoring system, it is important to make the data public for all students to see. Having an up-to-date scoreboard is critical if students are to become enthusiastic about the importance of the nonplaying tasks. These points are part of determining the season champions, and not having the system public significantly reduces the authenticity of the season.

SUMMARY

Developmentally appropriate competition is a fundamentally important characteristic of Sport Education; consequently, designing the appropriate format is the link that allows students to have those beneficial competitive experiences. Different competitions take differing amounts of class time and are more suited to specific activities. In this chapter we have described the two most common formats (progressive competition and event model) that can be used to accommodate any range of sports or activities. What is central to these formats is the idea that whatever the competition format, it should involve all students equally. Table 8.6 provides a summary of a best match between the different types of activity and the different competition formats. With this table in mind, we cannot stress enough that to start with simple competition formats enables both you and your students to learn how Sport Education works. As you and your students grow more comfortable with the model, you can explore new ways to organize competitions, and students will provide feedback on how they react to the various forms of competition.

Table 8.6 Matching Sport Activities to Competition Formats

Activity type	Competition format	
	Progressive	**Event**
Invasion games: • Basketball • Team handball • Water polo	• Highly suitable • Can retain the same game form throughout or involve gradual progressions	
Racket games: • Tennis • Pickleball • Badminton	• Highly suitable • Can involve singles and doubles matches against similarly skilled opponents	
Striking and fielding games: • Softball • Rounders • Cricket	• Highly suitable • Can involve small-sided games for shorter (12-lesson) seasons • Can begin with small-sided games followed by the full format in longer seasons (>12 lessons)	
Individual target games: • Archery • Frisbee golf • Golf	• Highly suitable • Can involve singles and doubles matches against similarly skilled opponents over different difficulty courses.	Very well suited to involving three or more easily learned sports in the same season (e.g. bocce, horseshoes, shuffleboard)
Individual sports: • Track and field • Swimming • Orienteering		Highly suitable
Performance sports: • Gymnastics • Dance		Highly suitable
Fitness sports: • Aerobics • Weight training • Jump rope		Highly suitable

Courtesy of Oleg Sineinkov.

Selecting Teams and Roles

9

Chapter Objective

After reading this chapter, you will be able to identify the key processes involved in selecting teams and assigning student roles.

Key Concepts

- It is particularly helpful to have the total number of teams divisible by three.
- A key goal in determining team size is to maximize potential playing time for all students, where every effort is made to avoid having to use substitutions.
- Students can be assigned to teams by the teacher or by a collaborative process involving students as well as teachers.
- Using roles in Sport Education contributes to a more complete understanding of sport and helps produce a more literate sport player.
- Roles can relate either to the functioning of a team or to the officiating of games.
- Roles need to be clearly defined, and specific time should be allocated in the season plan to help train students in the roles they will assume.

The idea of the *persisting team* is one of the most fundamental and nonnegotiable aspects of Sport Education. Whereas in most physical education settings, teams are formed only for the duration of a game, in Sport Education students not only play together but also practice skills, develop tactics, and complete administrative tasks as a team. Researchers have noted that team affiliation is one of the most attractive features of the model (Grant, 1992; Bennett & Hastie, 1997; O'Donovan, 2003). The model was particularly effective in developing team affiliation because it allowed all students the benefits of extended team membership that might previously have been denied because of perceptions of low ability or social isolation (MacPhail et al., 2004).

The selection of team membership and the assignment of coaches to teams is an important step in building a successful Sport Education season. Once students become accustomed to the Sport Education model, this aspect of teacher planning will become much easier. Experience throughout the world has shown that students who gain experience in Sport Education become concerned about fairness in student assignment to teams.

As mentioned in chapter 7, players and performers always have more fun and more of a challenge when the outcome of a contest or event is uncertain. That is why games are better when the competitors and teams are evenly matched. With this objective achieved, the outcome of the competition will depend more on the ability of the students to work together to complete team tasks and to solve tactical and interpersonal problems than would be the case if teams were uneven. The sections that follow take you through a number of issues relating to team selection as well as the choice of roles you wish to include in a season.

DECIDING ON THE NUMBER OF TEAMS AND TEAM SIZE

Before you decide how to form student teams, you must determine how many teams are needed for the season. While team size is determined by the nature of the game and the competition format, in most cases it is most helpful to have the total number of teams *divisible by three*. This allows for two teams to play while a third assumes the responsibilities of the duty team (e.g., officiating, scorekeeping). Table 9.1 offers a scenario showing how this arrangement is particularly flexible; it comes with our recommendation.

It is not always possible to have the total number of teams divisible by three, in which case the nature of the sport and the nature of competition format will be key

Table 9.1 Three-Team Competition Organization Example

Mini-volleyball: seventh-grade coeducational class	*Six teams of four students* Sharks, Spikers, Blockbusters, Block n' Roll, Blazers, Mustangs
Early-season competition	*Two-on-two on a half court; serve from midcourt* • Court 1: Sharks vs. Spikers • Blockbusters provide two referees, two scorekeepers • Court 2: Block n' Roll vs. Blazers • Mustangs provide two referees, two scorekeepers
Late-season competition	*Four-on-four on full court; serve from the baseline* • Court 1: Blazers vs. Blockbusters • Block n' Roll provide one referee, one scorekeeper, two line judges • Court 2: Mustangs vs. Sharks • Spikers provide one referee, one scorekeeper, two line judges

factors. Two examples of possible playing and officiating combinations are shown in table 9.2. These are samples from just one match during a class. Depending upon lesson time, a second rotation might be possible.

Deciding on Team Size

A key goal in determining team size is to maximize potential playing time for all students. Every effort should be made to avoid having to use substitutions if at all possible. If you plan just a single competition with some preseason scrimmages, then a softball season might involve teams of five players, while a flag football competition might have teams of seven. Of course, class sizes are rarely perfectly divisible by a specific number so it is helpful not to be locked into an exact number for each team.

One helpful option is to embed these small-sided teams into larger teams, with team assignment determined by skill levels; this allows for a system of graded competition as described in chapter 7. For example, one softball competition might involve five players while the second has six. The use of larger teams also tends to make absences less problematic, because teams can decide which of their mini-teams will play one short.

SELECTING STUDENTS FOR TEAMS

All of our experiences in Sport Education tell us that students are extremely concerned about fairness. They want fair teams and competition that is as equal as possible. Their great interest in team selection gives you key opportunities to teach and reinforce the concept of fairness. The following suggestions for team selection have been compiled from teacher feedback based on their experiences using Sport Education.

By *even* teams, we refer not only to evenness in terms of skill but also in terms of boys and girls, students of diverse ethnicities, and potential personality conflicts. This is not to say that teachers should change team members at the first sign of discontent. Part of the process of Sport Education is that students learn to come together, experience the ups and downs of an extended season, and maximize the skills and talents of all the students on their teams.

In our experience, girls prefer being on mixed teams. This is not to say that all competitions have to be mixed gender. Although mixed-gender teams should be the norm for elementary school seasons, for some activities in middle and high schools you may choose to have boys' and girls' competitions that count equally toward the seasonal championship.

Table 9.2 Officiating Options

Sport	Teams	Competition and officials
Pickleball	Five teams of four players	• A vs. B in two doubles matches • C vs. D in two doubles matches • E: one umpire and cumulative scorekeeper on each court, one all-court timekeeper
Flag football	Four teams of seven players	• A vs. B playing seven-on-seven • C: one referee, one line judge, one field judge, one back judge, two statisticians (one per team), one down box operator • D: choice of scouting, free practice, teacher-guided practice, or film study

Who Chooses Teams?

There are no hard and fast rules concerning the selection of teams, with one exception: avoid the traditional "public auction," where two high-skilled students take turns publicly selecting players while the whole class waits, hoping they won't be the last one picked. This should never be an option in *any* physical education setting, let alone in Sport Education. Because one purpose of Sport Education is to encourage students to gradually assume more responsibility for directing and managing their own sport experiences, many teachers see opportunities for including students in the selection process.

For teachers who want to include students in the process of team selection, we provide four questions that have shown to be helpful.

1. How well do you know the students?
2. How well do the students know each other?
3. How familiar are the students with the sport chosen for the season?
4. How familiar are the students with the Sport Education model?

If you know your students well, then you will have a solid understanding of their skill level but also of their willingness to cooperate with other students, their potential for dominating team discussions, and their propensity to be good teammates. With this is mind, you would be adequately equipped to select even and balanced teams without student input.

If, on the other hand, you are working with a new class with whom you have less experience, you may want some assistance from the students. If those students have been together for an extended period, they may offer insights about collegiality, reliability, and even, in some cases, talents for sports activities of which you might not be aware.

When you ask students to assist in creating teams, it is helpful if they have experience in the sport you have chosen. In this way, they should be able to identify the skills and abilities of various students in the class as they relate to the demands of the activity. It is also helpful if they have had some experience participating in Sport Education itself, because they will have a better appreciation of the nuances of persisting teams, the demands of team roles, and the importance of team cohesion in the development of a successful season.

If you involve students in team selection, two options are available: you can work with team coaches or you can have a selection panel. When using student coaches, you must first determine how the coaches are to be chosen. Here are the three most common methods for selecting coaches.

1. You assign coaches at the beginning of the season.
2. Students apply to be coaches using written nomination forms describing their skills, talents, and leadership qualities.
3. The students in the class vote by secret ballot for the people they wish to have as coaches.

A similar process is used when a student panel assists the teacher in team selection. Students may volunteer, apply, or be voted onto this panel according to criteria determined by the teacher. Members of the panel should have some knowledge of the skills and abilities of the students in the class, and it helps if they have knowledge of the activity that will be the focus of the season.

Using Students as Selectors

Irrespective of the selection format, there are a number of factors to consider. First, all students need to be considered as selectors, not just the most skilled students, but when students are selecting teams independently of the teacher, they should have some understanding of the sport itself. Second, the teacher needs to establish clear criteria for team selection. Students should be asked to consider the skill and fitness requirements of the game, to balance the number of boys and girls on each team, and to consider the leadership abilities of the members of each team as well as possible personality conflicts. Finally, it is important that all panel discussions remain confidential. When student teams are announced in class or posted on a notice board, student names should be listed in alphabetical order rather than in the order in which they were selected.

PLACING STUDENTS INTO TEAMS

Once you have decided either to use students in team selection or do so yourself, numerous formats are available for selecting teams. Table 9.3 provides various ways to assign students to teams. Some of these involve only the teacher and can be done before the season begins. Other methods may be more appropriate once teachers and students have completed a season or two of Sport Education. In all cases, however, it is important to have students in teams as early as possible, given that a large part of the personal growth that can result from good sport experiences is intimately related to students being affiliated with a team where what they do affects the success of the team.

Preseason Allocation of Students to Teams by the Teacher

Who: Teacher independent of students
When: Before the season begins

In this option, which normally occurs when teachers know their students well, the teacher selects teams before the starts of the season. During the first lesson, the teacher announces the teams, assigns teams their home spaces, and may ask students to choose a team name and color.

Table 9.3 Methods of Team Selection

Selection method	Teacher	Selection panel	Coaches
Allocation of students to even teams	X	X	
Performance scores	X	X	X
Skills challenges	X	X	X
Tournament rankings	X	X	
3-2-1 rating system		X	X
Draft system			X
Blind draft			X

Preseason Allocation of Students to Teams by the Teacher and Students

Who: Teacher and student coaches or selection panel
When: Before the season begins

An extension of the first option is for the teacher to involve students in the selection of even teams. Students can offer valuable insight into their classmates' potential, particularly in terms of getting along with others. Using students to select teams also empowers them by giving them responsibilities. Student selectors can be appointed by the teacher or elected by their classmates using a secret ballot. As with most roles in Sport Education, if this form of selection is chosen, then all students should eventually learn the role of selector.

Performance Scores

Who: Teacher and student coaches or selection panel
When: As early as possible

In this format, scores from particular tests may be used to assign students to even teams. For example, during the early lessons of an aerobic dance season, students may perform a 1-mile (1.6 km) run or an agility course run. The times from these runs can be used to place students on teams. You can either use these data independently or involve a sport board or volunteer selectors in assigning students to teams in similar ways to those described previously.

Skill Challenges

Who: Teacher and student coaches or selection panel
When: Following initial skill instruction lessons

Similar to the method just described, teachers may conduct skills challenges or tests to gather information for placing students on teams. For example, in the early lessons of a volleyball season, students might rotate through three stations where they complete the tasks of serving, overhead passing, and continuous volleying. Likewise, in the beginning lessons of a jump rope season, students might attempt a series of jumps. The teacher or the selection committee uses the scores from these stations to place students onto even teams.

After Small Tournaments

Who: Teacher and student coaches or selection panel
When: Following a mini-tournament early in the season

In one example from a New Zealand tennis season, students participated in a short singles tournament early in the season. The results from this tournament were used to rank students and create teams for the remainder of the season. Any of the racket sports would suit this format, although one-on-one games can be created for many sports such as soccer or basketball.

Student Selection Committee Using a Rating Scale

Who: Student coaches or selection panel
When: Before the season begins

In this method, students work independently to create even teams. What is often helpful in this process is to have the students first rank all students in the class on a 3-2-1 scale, from expert to beginner. From here, the level 3 players can be allocated evenly across teams, followed by level 2 players and then level 1 players. One way of testing the evenness of teams is to check whether the total score for each team is the same as all the others. Once this is achieved, players of equal ranking can be shuffled from one team to another to balance gender and ethnicities and to avoid internal team disharmony. Teams are then announced in alphabetical order by the committee or are posted on the physical education notice board.

Draft System

Who: Student coaches
When: During the first two or three lessons

In a draft system, all players perform a series of skills before the coaches. As the students perform their skills, the coaches take notes and then conduct a conference where they select teams. In one university-level softball season, each player completed a tryout. The five coaches scouted the talent and used a draft card to tabulate the data on each student. The tryout skills included running a 60-yard (55 m) dash for time, fielding ground balls, fielding fly balls, throwing to a base, and hitting. The teacher met with the coaches at the completion of the tryouts and then set up a time to conduct the draft. The draft was conducted privately and not during class time. Each resulting team consisted of eight players. The order of drafting switched with each round so that no team got an advantage.

Coaches Conduct a Blind Draft

Who: Student coaches
When: Before the season begins

A useful method of student-only selection is to elect team coaches who then select teams in a private meeting. The coaches do not know which of those teams they will ultimately be on. It is only when they have completed team final selections that the coaches themselves are assigned to teams through a lottery. This prevents students from attempting to load up one particular team for their own benefit.

STUDENT ROLES

One of the central features of Sport Education is that students get to share in the planning and administration of their sport experiences. To accomplish these goals, Sport Education teachers create a variety of student roles for each season. When students get to learn and perform in a variety of roles besides that of player, they feel more responsible for their own participation and the success of the team. These roles also put students in positions of responsibility where successful performance contributes to the overall success of the team and the season. The purpose of this chapter is to describe those roles.

In contrast to interschool competitions or recreational leagues, during Sport Education students perform in a host of roles other than just player or performer. Students learn to be coaches, referees, and scorekeepers. In many Sport Education variations, they also learn to be managers, publicists, statisticians, and trainers. In one example from Australia, where seventh-grade students competed in a modified form of Australian Rules football, the role of sideline cameraman was added. The student cameraman followed play with a small video recorder and provided live commentary. The footage could be played back in class and students could borrow it to share with parents and friends. The roles created for students in Sport Education typically depend on the age of the students, their previous experiences in Sport Education, and the creativity of the teacher. This use of roles contributes to a more complete understanding of sport and hence a more literate sport player. The learning and practicing of roles may even contribute as a form of career education for sport-related professions.

Students report that they enjoy these nonplaying roles and take them seriously. Although some off-field chores are seen as more exciting than others (e.g., refereeing is seen by some as more attractive), studies have also shown that students show particularly high levels of commitment to these roles. Although the specific roles differ from situation to situation, here we describe two classifications of roles. The first includes those roles we believe all students should complete in each season. The second includes other roles related to the functioning of teams, or are unique to particular types of sports.

Required Roles

Table 9.4 describes the roles of *player*, *referee*, and *scorekeeper* together with the responsibilities attached to these roles. The first and most important role is that of player. Actively taking this role means making a significant contribution to one's team and to the competition. In Sport Education, all students get equal opportunity to play, and how well they play contributes to the overall success of the team. As noted in earlier chapters, the play of lower-skilled students in a graded competition counts equally to the play of the higher-skilled students.

In Sport Education, certain roles are necessary for the season to function. These mostly come into play each competition day, and so all students take some responsibility for a specific role. These required roles at a minimum include referee and scorekeeper. By *required*, we mean that all students have to learn to perform these roles well. This has significant implications for teachers planning time and strategies that allow students to learn and practice these roles. Students on the duty team also have important tasks in ensuring that contests start on time and that equipment is in place for them to do so.

Team Roles

Team roles are nonplaying roles that promote the functioning of an individual team. All teams involved in a season will have students occupying these roles, which include

Table 9.4 Roles Required of All Students Each Season

Role	Responsibilities
Player	• Make a good effort to learn techniques and tactics • Play hard and fair • Support teammates • Respect opponents and officials
Referee	• Manage the contest • Make rule decisions • Keep the contest moving without undue influence
Scorekeeper	• Record scoring performance as it occurs • Keep a running account of the status of the ongoing competition • Compile scores • Turn over final records to the appropriate person (teacher, publicist, manager, or statistician)

coach, manager, fitness leader, and trainer, among others. You choose how many of these roles to include in the Sport Education season. Typically, more roles are added as you and the students gain experience with the Sport Education model. Table 9.5 provides a number of examples for you to explore.

Many other roles may be incorporated into a Sport Education season. This category of specialist roles is virtually endless, limited only by your imagination. Any activity associated with a given sport has a legitimate place. In one Australian setting, students studied turf grass management in conjunction with their cricket season. In addition to preparing the playing field, the groundskeeper also involved students in the daily chore of collecting the dog droppings that accumulated in the popular park where classes took place. These droppings were used in the fertilizer experiments related to grass management that the students conducted in science class.

Other Officiating Roles

Apart from the fundamental referee and scorekeeper roles, different sports require other officials in order to manage contests. For example, a swimming season may incorporate starters, timekeepers, and lane judges as on-deck officials, or an event manager and scoreboard operator in administrative roles. Tables 9.6 and 9.7 list roles that relate to specific sports.

Table 9.5 Student Roles Within Teams

Role	Responsibilities
Coach	• Provide general team leadership • Direct skill and strategy practice • Help make decisions about lineups • Turn in lineups to teachers or manager
Captain	• Represent the team on the field in conversations with the officials • Provide leadership during play • Assist and encourage teammates
Manager	• Assume the administrative functions of ongoing team responsibilities • Turn in the appropriate forms • Help get team members to the right locations for their roles as performers, referees, scorekeepers, and the like
Equipment manager	• Collect and return team equipment • Collect and return playing jerseys • Inform teacher of any equipment loss or damage
Fitness leader	• Design warm-up activities for the team • Lead team warm-ups • Help design fitness plans for longer units
Trainer	• Know common injuries associated with a sport • Access first aid materials when requested • Notify the teacher of any injury during practice or competition • Aid teacher in administration of first aid and in subsequent rehabilitation
Publicist	• Compile records and statistics and publicize them • Contribute to the weekly sport sheets, the school newspaper, posters, or a specially created Sport Education newsletter
Journalist	• Write match reports • Submit reports to the publicist or other advocacy agency for the season (e.g., teacher, school administration)

Table 9.6 Specialist Roles for Team Sports

Role	Responsibilities
Invasion games (soccer, basketball, flag football)	
Timekeeper	• Know the rules concerning starting and stopping the clock • Operate the clock as instructed by the referee • Clearly indicate the end of playing periods
Statistician	• Record pertinent performance data • Compile complete data • Summarize data across competitions • Turn the summarized data over to the appropriate person (e.g., teacher, publicist, manager)
Ball retriever	• Keep up with the flow of play • Supply replacements for balls that go out of bounds • Retrieve out-of-play balls
Down markers (flag football)	• Clearly place down markers at appropriate positions • Move down makers at appropriate times • Display downs clearly to referee and players • Change down numbers on indicator boards
End-zone judges (for over-the-line games such as Frisbee or flag football)	• Signal if the ball or object legally went past the end line • Signal any defensive interference • Communicate to the statistician who made the score
Batting and fielding games (softball, cricket)	
Base umpire	• Signal safe or out for base runners • Call illegal leadoff runners
Target games (archery, bowling, golf)	
Target judge	• Determine specific point values of shots • Signal point values to scorekeeper • Signal when target is ready for resumption of shooting
Pin restacker and ball returner	• Replace struck pins to appropriate positions • Returns balls to throwing or rolling area
Safety judge	• Make sure participants are behind the shooting line • Determine when participants may resume shooting
Course marshal (golf)	• Manage flow of play between holes • Locate balls that may have gone off course • Clearly mark lost balls when located

IMPORTANT CONSIDERATIONS WHEN USING ROLES

Whichever roles are chosen for a season of sport education, five major factors need to be considered.

1. Roles needs to be clearly defined.

2. Specific time should be allocated in the season plan to help train students in the roles they will be taking.

3. Students need practice performing these roles as much as any other component of Sport Education.

Table 9.7 Specialist Roles for Individual Sports

Role	Responsibility
Performance sports (gymnastics, dance, aerobics)	
Choreographer	• Know the requirements of compulsory and optional skills • Design movement sequences for team members • Help teammates learn sequence links • Record sequences for submission to judges or scorekeepers • Help select appropriate music
Music engineer	• Check and operate the sound system • Record team members' music to be used during their sequences • Play team members' music during practice and competition
Property manager	• Store and distribute props used by the team during performances • Design and construct team props and costumes
Judge	• Score the performances of the participants • Know the criteria for the routines • Be able to justify the scores according to the set criteria
Safety monitor (gymnastics)	• Make sure the mats are stacked together • Check that the springboards do not slip
Racing sports (track events, cross country running, cross-country skiing)	
Starter	• Summon racers to start positions • Give clear preparation signals • Signal the start of races • Judge for false starts and breaks
Timekeeper	• Know the functions of stopwatches • Record scores of athletes for relevant times • Turn over racers' times to the appropriate person (e.g., teacher, coach, manager, scorekeeper, statistician)
Place judges	• Determine winners and placing participants of races • Consult timekeepers in races with close finishes • Report places to scorekeeper
Course marshals	• Help racers stay on the designated course • Report lane or area violations to referee • Give progress times to athletes • Judge legality of transitions in relays
Strength sports (weightlifting)	
Judge	• Judge legality of the lift • Assign point values where appropriate
Spotter weight loader	• Ensure safety of weightlifter by assisting where necessary • Load and unload appropriate weight onto the bar • Replace weights in designated areas

4. Some form of accountability must be present so that student performance in these crucial roles counts for something toward team success.

5. Teachers need to prepare or provide the materials needed for the roles to be fulfilled appropriately.

Clearly Defined Roles

It is important that the roles you choose are clearly defined. Students need to know exactly what the role entails, which may involve some responsibility before, during, and after a game. Many teachers prepare booklets that explain the duties of each role and describe precisely the tasks that need to be accomplished and when. At the very least, you should prepare a captain's notebook that explains all the responsibilities for that role. Teachers typically require that the booklet be returned in good shape after the season. This can be assured with a captain's contract or by having teams receive points toward the seasonal championship if they return the booklets in good condition.

Many teachers chose to develop *contracts* as methods of clearly defining a role and its responsibilities. For example, in the captain's contract, the captain first reads the contract aloud to the team and then signs the pledge. In addition, each member of that team also signs, indicating their support for the captain and acknowledging their commitment to work with the captain in positive ways during the upcoming season.

Time Allocated to Learning Roles

When designing the season plan, you need to allocate time in early season lessons for students to learn and practice their roles, especially the roles of referee and scorekeeper, roles that will eventually be taken by all the students during the season. Teachers should provide sample score sheets, statistics forms, and other forms and guides for fulfilling role responsibilities, clearly explaining the significance of the role and the expected performance.

Students must understand that they will be held accountable for their role performance.

Helping Students Practice Their Roles

Students need practice in performing these roles as much as in any other component of Sport Education. You also have to plan opportunities for students to practice these skills in the context in which they will be expected to perform these roles. Practices should come early in the season plan, so that when practice matches are scheduled early in the season, time is not spent in games that do not work. In helping students learn the roles involved in officiating a game (e.g. referee, scorekeeper, statistician, judge), it is legitimate for you to stop a practice game to check that the officials have made or recorded the appropriate response. In their very first refereeing role, students may hesitate to become assertive with their whistles, or may be indecisive in making their calls. It is your role to intervene in these games to help the official first learn the correct signals or decisions and then to support those officials as the legitimate authority of the contest. Students will improve as they come to know the activity better and gain experience and confidence in their role. When this happens, you will need to spend less time focusing on these roles.

Accountability for Role Performance

Students must understand that they will be held accountable for their role performance. We cannot expect students to apply themselves to a role unless it counts for team and individual assessment. Many teachers provide space in the season scoring system for the accomplishment of a team's administrative duties. For example, during a floor hockey season, one teacher allocated points to each team following the completion of its performance as the duty team. The points were distributed as shown in table 9.8.

Table 9.8 Point Allocation During a Floor Hockey Season

Equipment returned • Whistle and puck returned by the referee • Line judges' shirts returned • Score sheet returned • Statistics sheet returned • Pencils returned	1 point	0 points
Score sheet completed fully and accurately • Both teams' names provided • Final score indicated • Fair play points clearly indicated	1 point	0 points
Statistics sheet completed fully and accurately • Both teams' names provided • Goal tallies match the official score sheet • Goal scorers clearly indicated	1 point	0 points
Duty team evaluation (completed by the playing teams) • Did the duty team arrive at the game on time and ready? • Did the duty team get the game started on time? • Did the duty team pay attention during the game?	1 point per *yes*	
Referee evaluation (completed by the playing teams) • Did the referee know the rules? • Did the referee conduct a fair contest? • Was the referee paying attention during the game?	1 point per *yes*	

In this evaluation form, all duty team members were held responsible for actions before, during, and after the match. Many of the criteria relate to organization (e.g., getting games started on time, returning equipment and forms), while others focus more on the team's ability to perform its role in the course of a match. Both of these features of duty teams are important for the smooth running of a season.

Students can also be held individually accountable for their role performance. Many teachers include a student's performance at officiating or scoring in their course evaluation. Likewise, points may also be awarded for participation in optional activities such as membership on the sport governing board or activities as a publicist. Another important form of informal accountability is the end-of-season awards. Awards for successful completion of various roles can easily be included at the end of such ceremonies.

Preparing Materials

It is the teacher's responsibility to make sure that all the materials needed to make the season move forward smoothly are available. Many of the forms and materials needed to plan and implement a Sport Education season can be found in the web resource. These materials include not only the equipment necessary for skills practices and for gameplay but also schedules, coaches' instructions, lineup cards, results sheets, score keeping sheets, statistics sheets, cumulative statistics records, and awards. Remember that the evidence suggests that students become really involved with their season. You don't want that motivation to be reduced by not having the appropriate materials ready when they are needed.

SUMMARY

Physical educators have always asserted that their subject matter influences personal and social development, but little has been done to specifically address goals of personal and social development that are potentially embedded within the subject matter. Sport Education takes these goals seriously. The feature of multiple roles is a key part of the model that contributes to these important goals. Roles need to be defined, taught, and practiced. Students need to be held accountable for performing well in the roles, both through formal means in a seasonal point system and through informal means such as teacher feedback and recognition for improved performance. If teachers take the student roles feature of Sport Education seriously, the students will too.

Personal and social development does not happen in isolation but within an important social context. The team is the context within which personal and social development can occur in Sport Education. Heterogeneous teams require that students help and support one another if they are to be successful as a *team*. Each team member has a contribution to make. It is in the best interest of the *team* for members to help and support each other. Each team member has responsibilities. When they acquit themselves well in their various roles, their contributions are valued by teammates. We are not foolish enough to believe that all this happens automatically. It does not. It takes work. It takes good planning and support from the teacher, and when that occurs there is evidence that it can and does happen.

Teaching Protocols and Building Fair Play

Chapter Objective

After reading this chapter, you will be able to identify the importance of having specific routines for managing the transitions between the various segments in a Sport Education lesson.

Key Concepts

- Typical Sport Education lessons consist of a number of independent segments.
- The efficiency of the transitions between these segments will determine how much time can be spent practicing skills and playing games.
- Students should be taught and should master specific routines that help maximize the efficiency of the transitions between lesson segments.
- A central aspect of Sport Education is the ideal of fair play. Students need not only to be aware of fair play practices but also to demonstrate them during team practices and games.
- In teaching fair play, specific strategies need to focus on (1) developing positive and responsible membership, (2) developing positive and responsible peer leadership, and (3) reshaping the meaning of winning for legitimating different levels of participation and membership.

In chapter 2 we introduced the metaphor as the teacher as the architect of the model. Further, we pointed out that you, as the teacher, are not just involved during the planning phase; you are responsible for overseeing the implementation of a season. One critical aspect of this implementation is effective class management. Effective class management depends on the development of a series of routines that students learn and adhere to during their classes. These routines need to be taught carefully with a focus on doing the behaviors required for the routine in the least amount of time possible. When transitions run smoothly and quickly, many good things result; namely, the energy of the class is positive, available time is used productively, opportunities for disruptions are minimized, and all planned activities get to be completed. When transitions are not carefully taught and break down, lessons can seldom be completed as planned, students become frustrated, and disruptions are more likely to occur.

Once a season is underway, a typical Sport Education lesson consists of five segments. The purpose of this chapter is to outline the various managerial tasks involved in those segments and, in particular, the transitions between them. A summary of these segments is presented in figure 10.1. Routines should be created for all of the managerial tasks of these segments and transitions. Creating a predictable flow of class time is likely to require a group of routines that need to be taught and practiced until they actually *become* routine for the students. Mastery of these routines means that a maximum of class time is spent achieving desired outcomes, such as quality practice and more time for gameplay. In addition, efficient management means that extra time can be allocated to other Sport Education features, such as fair play and festivity.

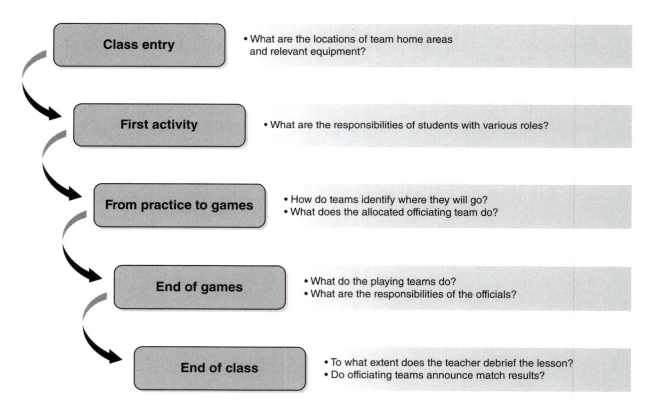

Figure 10.1 Typical class progression during a Sport Education lesson.

CLASS ENTRY AND FIRST ACTIVITY

Most physical education teachers have some sort of routine for when students first arrive for their classes. In some cases, students are instructed to read a notice board and complete an instant activity, such as jumping rope or practicing a specific skill. In others, students are expected to begin walking or running laps, or to gather in the bleachers or line up in squads. Whatever the case, the aim is to begin lessons efficiently and not waste time.

In Sport Education lessons, students will first report to their team area, which is a designated space in the gymnasium or the playing field that becomes home for the duration of the season. In gymnasiums, team areas can be designated by posting team banners along walls. On playing fields or playgrounds, they can be designated by cones or other markers, such as sections of a lined field. When teams do warm-ups, technique drills, or meet to decide player placements for competitions, they do so in their designated team area.

At the elementary level, students are likely to move from their classroom to the activity space as a group. We have found that with these students, a useful strategy is to welcome students as they enter the play area and ask random students questions, perhaps about their team name, their mascot, their team color, or their team role, or to point to their team area. Before long, the students will not ask to be told and will call this out as they walk by.

At the middle and high school levels, students are more likely to come from a locker room prior to the official start of class. In these cases, all students will still go to their team areas and begin their warm-up or skill practices. It is valuable to have the notice board close to the locker room so team captains and managers can conveniently access any required information.

The first activity immediately after arrival to class is more complex in Sport Education than in traditional lessons. This is because different students are doing different tasks depending upon their responsibilities. For example, team captains will usually report to the teacher to receive initial instructions about skill practices or to learn of the day's competitions, equipment managers will collect whatever inventory their team will need for practice, and fitness leaders will collect the fitness cards and equipment necessary to conduct the warm-up or conditioning activities.

FROM PRACTICE TO GAMES

Once students have entered the activity area, are all in their team areas, and are doing the tasks led by the teacher or by their student coach, the next transition takes them to the second lesson segment: gameplay. In the early lessons of a season the first element of this transition is the teacher's stop and start signal for attention, followed by an announcement of the upcoming games. For example, students might be notified that the Tomcats are playing the Wolves, with the Jets acting as the officials; the Eagles and the Panthers are playing against each other; and the Falcons are refereeing and keeping score.

Whether these games are nonconsequential scrimmages or formal competitions, students must know which field or court they are to report to, whether they are playing or officiating, and what materials they need to take with them to these games. Formalizing (and practicing) the routines by which students access that information results in less confusion and less wasted time.

Playing areas need to be clearly described in the very early lessons of a season. Courts and fields need to be clearly identified as 1, 2, 3, and 4, or given other labels such as north, south, east, and west. Whatever naming system used, all students need to be able to identify their locations.

When the upcoming matches are announced, the order in which teams are listed can also be relevant. For example, the first-named team might be responsible for taking the match ball to the game, or it may mean they start on one particular side of the court. Similarly, the first-named team might wear a particular color of pinnies or jerseys, or use the red hockey sticks.

While announcing all games can be time consuming, this is a recommended practice during the first lessons because the students are learning all the elements involved (i.e., teams, equipment, game locations, and officials). When the teacher sees that all teams can efficiently transfer from their own areas to the sites of gameplay, this information can be displayed in a prominent place for team captains to access. Equipment managers can also quickly identify the color of equipment their team will use during games. Some teachers use whiteboards to display this information, others write on windows with dry-erase markers, while others simply inform captains and managers as they first enter the gym.

END OF GAMES

While in most traditional physical education classes games simply end with little if any consequence, in Sport Education there are a number of important tasks that need to be completed. As in all other lesson segments, there are routines that need to be taught and learned.

These end-of-game routines differ for playing and officiating teams. The first task of the playing teams will be to shake hands with their opponents, thanking them for the opportunity to have a good game. They will then attend to equipment-related tasks. For example, in floor hockey, students will neatly line up their sticks in the goal area and hang their pinnies on the goal. In badminton, the students might give their rackets to the team equipment manager if the team has an officiating responsibility in the next game or if it is at the end of class.

At the end of a game, the officiating team will be responsible for consolidating the score sheets with the final results, tallying statistics, and then making judgments about fair play (see chapter 12 about these decisions). In some cases, where the teacher has included an evaluation of the officials in a postgame protocol, the team captains will gather to make those judgments. A further routine involves what to do with all the game-related paraphernalia. It is very useful to have a box that everything goes into and that is returned to a central place.

In lessons where more than one game is played, some teams may need to transition from their current playing area to a different one for the next contest. In this case, the routine is similar to the one where teams move from team practice to the first game. When two games are scheduled during a lesson, it is useful to have teams grouped in threes. In this way, one team plays in both games, while the other two teams alternate playing and officiating. This saves time because teams do not need to change fields or courts, and only two teams (i.e., the original officials and one team) are required to exchange equipment and roles. The other team remains in place with their original equipment.

Many teachers have had success teaching these transitions as two-minute drills, meaning that from the end of the first round of games to the beginning of the second round, both the competing teams and the duty team members will have completed all their transition duties in a two-minute span. During the early lessons, when students are still learning this transition, the time can be expanded to five minutes, but it should be gradually reduced during the preseason. The incentive for students to master this end-of-game routine is that more time can be allocated to gameplay.

CLASS CLOSURE

The final lesson segment is class closure. Sport Education teachers often like to have a formal closure to class in order to provide feedback; to recognize good performances, both in competitions and duty team responsibilities; or to preview the next lesson. As students will be dispersed across a number of play or practice areas, closure requires that students gather in one designated space. This requires a closure routine, which includes a signal for closure, instructions for storing equipment, notification of the location for meeting, and where each team should gather within this space. The closure routine should also include instructions for leaving the gymnasium or practice field and for returning to the locker facilities or the classroom. As with all routines, the closure routine needs to be taught specifically, with feedback provided in the first few weeks of the school year so that the routine becomes part of how Sport Education is done, regardless of the activity being competed and the venue in which the season is pursued.

Apart from teacher input, there may be opportunities during a closure for the officiating teams to announce the results of each game. While more common in high school and university settings, where lessons are longer, this formal process involves the officials announcing the final scores, identifying the leading players in the various statistical categories, and awarding fair play points (together with a justification for the awards).

A lesson closure can also provide an opportunity for the teacher to provide information about the next lesson. This is particularly helpful when there is an upcoming change in the phase of a season, for example when the next lesson involves a change in the competition focus from practice games to games that count toward the league table. In seasons where the event model is used, the next competition or challenge can be briefly introduced at the end of the previous lesson. Finally, in the lessons preceding the culminating event, the teacher can make announcements relative to upcoming events.

DEVELOPING POSITIVE BEHAVIOR WITHIN A CULTURE OF FAIR PLAY

Physical education has emphasized social development and character development objectives for more than 100 years, and while it has long been argued that sport builds character, we know this does not happen automatically just by engaging students in sport programs. Fortunately, the Sport Education model provides the context within which these goals can be achieved. But for Sport Education to be a site of positive responsibility, inclusion, and equitable learning environments, we need to produce season plans and individual lessons that have a democratic, inclusive, and participatory focus. Further, within these lessons there must be opportunities where fair play behaviors are addressed, together with the social (i.e., responsibility, perseverance, loyalty, and teamwork) and moral (i.e., honesty and mutual respect) properties of the sporting experience (Harvey, Kirk, & O'Donovan, 2014).

At a structural level, the basic Sport Education format of longer seasons and team membership for the duration of the season provides the motivational context within which students can learn to be good leaders, good teammates, and good competitors. They learn exactly what fair play means in the context of specific sports and other physical activities. They learn about fair play when they fulfill their roles as referees, judges, or umpires. They learn to appreciate participating in a series of *good games*, played hard and fairly by both teams. Good games are those where they can gradually learn the value of perseverance, the satisfaction of improvement, and the fulfillment that comes from contributing to a team effort and having that contribution recognized.

None of these outcomes accrues automatically; teachers and students have to work together to ensure that these outcomes prevail.

Our approach to positive responsibility is grounded in the concept of fair play. We chose this approach because fair play is recognized throughout the world as the central concept for social development in children's and youth sport. Fair play has a much broader meaning than just playing by the rules. It also means having respect for opponents, participating with the right spirit and attitude, valuing equal opportunity, and behaving responsibly as a teammate and as a player. Table 10.1 provides a list of the characteristics of fair and unfair play, while figure 10.2 gives examples of prestigious awards given by sports governing bodies. This chapter's web resource includes numerous

Table 10.1 Characteristics of Fair and Unfair Play

Fair player	Unfair player
• Follows the rules	• Tries to bend rules or cheat
• Accept officials' calls	• Argues with officials
• Compliments good play of others	• Blames mistakes on others
• Encourages teammates	• Criticizes teammates
• Plays own position	• Hogs space and dominates play
• Helps players who are less skilled	• Makes fun of players who are less skilled
• Is gracious in victory or defeat	• Gloats in victory, sulks in defeat
• Competes under control	• Loses temper frequently
• Wants everybody to succeed	• Favors only a few classmates
• Plays hard but fair	• Skirts rules to gain advantage

Reprinted by permission from P. Griffin and J. Placek. *Fair Play in the Gym: Race and Sex Equity in Physical Education* (Amherst, MA: University of Massachusetts, Women's Equity Program, 1983): 132-133.

Figure 10.2
FAIR PLAY EXAMPLES

The FIFA Fair Play Award

This award is a FIFA recognition of exemplary behavior that promotes the spirit of fair play and compassion in association football around the world. First awarded in 1987, it has been presented to individuals (including posthumously), teams, fans, spectators, football associations and federations and even entire footballing communities. One or more awards are presented annually, with there being at least one recipient each year except in 1994, when no award was presented.

The Xbox Fair Play Award in Major League Soccer

This award is given to an individual player and a team who present best overall sportsmanlike behavior in addition to receiving one of the lowest numbers of yellow and red cards, fouls, and disciplinary violations.

CIFP World Fair Play Awards

Since its foundation by UNESCO and a number of international sports governing bodies in Paris in 1963, the goal of the International Fair Play Committee has been the worldwide defense and promotion of fair play. The highly respected awards, such as trophies, diplomas, and letters of congratulations, are awarded to athletes and private individuals from all over the world selected by the CIFP for their remarkable acts of fair play or outstanding careers conducted in the spirit of fair play.

supporting resources aimed specifically at developing students' fair play skills.

STRATEGIES FOR TEACHING FAIR PLAY AND RESPONSIBILITY

Sport Education provides the context within which fair play and responsibility goals can be achieved. The affiliation of students with teams and the multiple roles students have to fulfill for a season to be successful create endless opportunities for teachers to emphasize these goals and for students to learn what it means to achieve the goals. Teams meet regularly to make decisions together, and they compete for a seasonal championship. Student referees are put in situations where they make judgments to which competitors react. These situations have the potential to create tensions, disagreements, and even confrontations, all of which become teachable moments for students not only to learn what constitutes fair play but also to come to value it.

Sport Education provides the context within which fair play and responsibility goals can be achieved.

Strategies for teaching fair play differ somewhat depending on the age and experience of the students. The overall strategy is to make fair play an important and pervasive part of all that is done throughout a Sport Education season. Farias (2017) has provided a number of useful pedagogical strategies teachers can use to promote inclusion, equity, and positive responsibility. These include (1) developing positive and responsible membership, (2) developing positive and responsible peer leadership, and (3) reshaping the meaning of winning for legitimating different levels of participation and membership.

Developing Positive and Responsible Membership

Table 10.2 lists a number of strategies teachers can use to develop positive and responsible team membership.

The Fair Play Contract

There is much to be said for creating a set of contracts for students to read carefully and sign. The fair play contract should describe the appropriate behaviors relating to respect, courtesy, positive recognition and praise, inclusiveness, fair play, effort, and hard work. While teachers often take the lead in developing such a code of conduct, there is significant benefit from having students taking an active role in its development because students are more likely to buy into rules if they have had a hand in creating them. Figure 10.3 provides an example of one such code.

Table 10.2 Pedagogical Strategies Used to Develop Positive and Responsible Team Membership

Strategy	Description	Implications and benefits
Fair play contract	A formalized agreement signed by the students and the teacher at the beginning of the Sport Education season, it sets the rules that establish the right actions and expectations for daily conduct	• At the end of the day, students will have to deal with the consequences of their actions in accordance with the rules they have established • The systematic reflection on the accomplishment of the fair play contract's goals provides the opportunity for students to constantly revisit conceptions of equity and their progression in their levels of responsibility • Students develop a collective meaning of equity and responsibility • The strategy locates the resolution of conflicts at the student level
Sport board	Consists of representatives from each of the teams participating in the season; the board members debate ideas aimed at promoting fair play	
Inclusion caretaker	Students in this role rotate in the daily monitoring of discriminatory occurrences and levels of equity; at the end of each lesson they are responsible for reporting positive or negative events to the class, or recording these data on a score chart.	

Adapted by permission from C. Farias, "Promoting Equity and Social Responsibility Within Sport Education," *Active and Healthy Journal* 24, no. 2/3 (2017): 35-42.

From this code of conduct, you can develop various fair play contracts that formalize students' commitment to the rights and responsibilities involved with the various roles they will take during a season. Following are three such contracts. The first is a general fair play agreement that is signed by each student and the teacher (figure 10.4) to formalize a commitment made by the students and their teacher. The second and third examples are contracts for coaches and referees (figures 10.5 and 10.6). These are two of the most important roles that students fulfill during the Sport Education season. Coaches are typically chosen for the length of a season, with new coaches chosen in subsequent seasons. The referee contract, however, is for all students, since they all will occupy that role at some time during the season as part of the officiating team responsibilities.

The Sport Board

In chapter 15, we outline a number of ways in which students can be given opportunities to make decisions about the planning and administration of a season. The sport board is a student group that assists the teacher with ensuring high-quality sport experiences for all students. The board's goal is to develop positive and responsible team membership, so it should be given the task of identifying mechanisms for promoting fair play and with adjudicating situations of inappropriate player behavior.

Inclusion Caretaker

One of the cornerstone goals of Sport Education—and a key difference between it and youth or interscholastic sport—is to have all students play at all times, usually in small-sided teams. In addition, Sport Education aims to be a highly inclusive pedagogical model through which students are supported by the peers and develop a sense of belonging. The research on Sport Education indicates positive outcomes, but there is

Figure 10.3
SPORT EDUCATION FAIR PLAY CODE OF CONDUCT

To ensure quality practice and contests, all players should do the following.

Participate fully and responsibly

- Be on time.
- Do your part in team and class tasks.
- Participate enthusiastically.

Give their best effort

- Try hard when practicing and playing.
- Try hard to do your duty team role well.
- Cooperate with teammates in all roles.

Show respect to teammates and opponents

- Always control your own behavior.
- Support everyone's right to participate fully.
- Try to resolve conflicts peacefully and quickly.
- Support your team and teammates in all ways.

Be a good sport

- Play by the rules and give it your best at all times.
- Respect the referees and judges.
- Show appreciation for teammates and opponents.
- Be a good sport both in winning and in losing situations.

Be helpful and not harmful

- Look for ways to be supportive of teammates.
- Avoid putting down others.
- Be willing to be a positive influence when you see put-downs or bullying.
- Always show your appreciation for good play and hard work.

still the potential for gender and status to influence students' social interactions in favor of dominant boys and higher-skilled students.

After a number of Sport Education seasons, you may wish to recruit student volunteers to be inclusion caretakers, similar to equity officers at a university or other facility. The inclusion caretaker monitors levels of equity (e.g., discrimination or inclusive behavior), identifies examples of positive or negative events, and reports these to the class during closure. This is not a permanent role; individual students rotate through this role, usually when their team is officiating.

Figure 10.4
SAMPLE FAIR PLAY AGREEMENT

Fair Play Contract for Students and Teachers

For the player:

To the best of my ability,

I, _____ , agree to

always play by the rules,

respect the decisions of the officials,

remember that I am playing because it is fun,

work at being my personal best,

encourage my teammates and recognize the good plays of my opponents,

control my temper, and

play fairly at all times.

Signature: _____ Date: _____

For the teacher:

To the best of my ability,

I, _____ , agree to

remember that students play for fun,

encourage my students to do their best,

encourage my students to be good sports,

remind students that officials are an important part of the game,

design lessons and games to maximize participation, and

remember that my actions speak louder than my words.

Signed: _____ Date: _____

Source: *Fair Play—It's Your Call!: A Resource Manual for Coaches* (p. 25) by Fair Play Canada. Copyright 1994 by Canadian Centre for Ethics in Sport.

Developing Positive and Responsible Peer Leadership

One of the key roles in Sport Education is the student coach or team captain. Early studies in Sport Education show that students who take on these roles treat them seriously, and in general try hard to develop the potential of their teams (Hastie, 2000; Kinchin, 2001). It is critical that teachers help these students develop the positive leadership skills necessary for creating a positive culture and equitable interactions in their teams. This is particularly important when those coaches are active in interscholastic or community-based sports settings. Because student coaches model their own coaches, there can tend to focus on immediate competition success rather than on mastery and equitable participation; as a result, some student voices can be silenced and participation by lower-skilled students can actually decrease (Farias, Hastie, & Mesquita, 2017).

Figure 10.5
SAMPLE COACH'S CONTRACT

Fair Play Contract for Coaches

To the best of my ability,

I, _____ , agree to

be positive with my players,

help all of my players improve their skills,

see that each player gets equal playing time,

never argue with the referee, never cheat, and never make excuses for losing,

support the team whether we are winning or losing,

model respect for the opponents and officials, and

keep winning and losing in perspective.

Signed: _____ Date: _____

Reprinted by permission from SPARC, New Zealand.

Figure 10.6
SAMPLE REFEREE CONTRACT

Fair Play Contract for Referees

To the best of my ability,

I, _____ , agree to

know the rules of the game,

be consistent and fair in my decisions,

actively keep up with the play and not get distracted,

help players understand rules by explaining decisions when appropriate, and

encourage fair play and don't tolerate foul play.

Signed: _____ Date: _____

Reprinted by permission from SPARC, New Zealand.

You need to encourage student coaches to deepen their knowledge of their team members' strengths and weaknesses in ways that allow them to build positive relationships. See chapter 11 for further suggestions for developing student coaches' instructional and positive leadership skills.

Reshaping the Meaning of Winning

In chapter 8, we explained that one of the significant differences between Sport Education and interschool and community sport is the way in which you determine the overall season champion. Whereas in school sport and community competitions, the only thing that counts is the win–loss record, in Sport Education the teacher is free to include a number of other considerations in the determining the champion team. For example, a high proportion of a team's final score can be allocated to fair play, inclusiveness, and effort.

What is critical in this reshaping of the meaning of *winning* is that students can actually see their on-going progress and achievements. You therefore need to make sure that the class league table is kept up to date, and that the various teams' relative performances are reinforced frequently.

According to Farias (2017), the reshaping of winning has two fundamental goals: to legitimate the value of different levels of participation and membership, and to create a mastery-involving climate. Similar to the way in which the league table is constructed, the award system included in the culminating event should extend beyond the team that wins the most matches or the students who top the various statistical categories. For instance, awards can be given to the most fair team, to the most improved players, to the most inclusive team, or to those students who are recognized for great hustle and effort.

SUMMARY

No matter what activity is selected for a Sport Education season, most lessons will progress through a number of independent segments. It is therefore important that, during the early lessons of a season, you put in place a number of strategies that help students efficiently and effectively transition between these segments. This chapter has outlined a number of specific routines that need to be taught and practiced until they actually become automatic for the students. The resulting predictable flow of class time allows for more time to achieve Sport Education goals.

In addition to developing class routines, you should allocate early lessons in a season to developing an ethic of fair play and social responsibility. In particular, you need to understand that many students enter Sport Education seasons with deeply rooted notions about sporting expectations and pervasive gender stereotypes (e.g., girls can't play sports), with different socioeconomic and popularity status (e.g., dominant students silencing others), as well as the "winning is everything" belief that stems from participating in extracurricular and community-based sports. With this in mind, you need to plan specific strategies in the curriculum if you want to achieve full participation by all your students.

Developing Competent Players

11

Chapter Objective

After reading this chapter, you will be able to explain how your responsibilities as a teacher gradually shift from being the primary director to that of being a facilitator.

Key Concepts

- The role of the teacher and that of the student coach change as a season progresses.
- Teachers need to model effective organizational skills for students to get the most out of their practice sessions.
- Students who take on the role of team coach need to be aware of the responsibilities of that role.
- Teachers need to design support materials such as posters or practice cards to support student coaches.
- After both the teacher and the students have experience in Sport Education, coaches' seminars are an effective way to improve the quality of student coaching.

In chapter 2, we noted that the instructional philosophy of Sport Education focuses on small, heterogeneous learning groups called *teams*. We also introduced the idea that, as a season progresses, there is a gradual shift in that students take more responsibility for and ownership of the experience. In this chapter, we emphasize the roles of the teacher and the student coach in developing competent sports players.

Figure 11.1 shows the progression of responsibilities of the teacher and the student coach during a season. The early lessons involve mostly whole class practice under the direction of the teacher, with students practicing the set tasks within their teams. Later on, teams have more autonomy as to what aspects of the game they will practice and how they can best organize their team for competitions.

An examination of the role of the teacher should make it clear that you have a definite and important teaching role during a Sport Education season; in fact, you may actually find yourself teaching more. This is because you are not only providing instruction to students but are also modeling effective instructional behaviors for student coaches. Students in the role of team coach in Sport Education may initially be excited by the prospect of coaching their team to season success, but they are unlikely to have the content knowledge or pedagogical skills necessary to be effective in their newly found instructional role (Wallhead, 2017). This chapter will take you through the individual components of figure 11.1, describing in detail the ways in which teachers and student coaches can work together to improve the sport competence of all students. It is supported by Wallhead's (2017) six strategies teachers can use to better prepare their students to

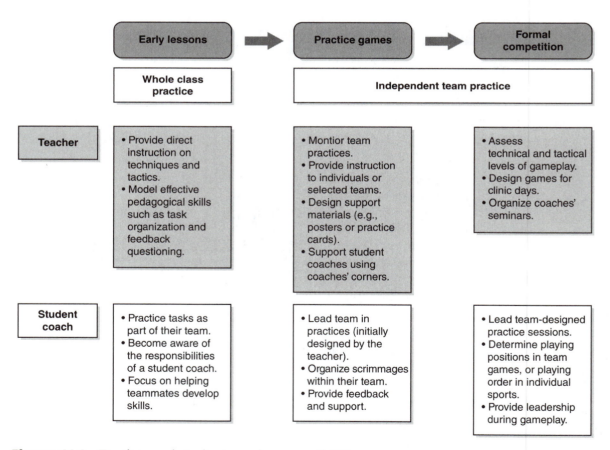

Figure 11.1 Teacher and student coach responsibilities.

fulfill the role of team coach effectively as they progress through one or more seasons of Sport Education.

Before we delve into figure 11.1, it is worth spending a few moments on the selection of student coaches. In many cases, teachers base their selection on their perception of the students' prior experiences with the sport or on their potential leadership qualities. While this strategy is particularly suitable during students' first experiences with Sport Education (because the teacher has a clearer understanding of the responsibilities of the student coach), whether these handpicked student coaches will be accepted by their peers is yet to be seen.

Wallhead (2017) suggests that an alternate approach is to give teams more voice and choice about who will ultimately be their coach. That is, rather than teams selecting their coaches on the first day of a season, the teacher includes some team-forming tasks (such as cooperative learning activities) during the early stages of a season. These tasks should be designed so that students have to work together to solve a movement problem. This gives them the opportunity to evaluate their teammates' leadership and communication skills and make a more informed choice as to the suitability of specific team members to fulfill the role of student coach. Midura and Glover (2005) provide a number of activities that challenge students to work together to achieve a common goal. As they interact verbally and physically, struggle, deal with failure, persevere, and work together to master problems, students can learn to value teamwork and individual differences, practice leadership skills, and improve listening skills.

THE TEACHER: EARLY LESSONS

During the early lessons of a season, your role will be similar to when you introduce a new technique to a class. For example, when you introduce the drop shot in badminton, your goal is to see that all students understand the main technical features or the critical elements of the shot. You point out common errors so students can learn to differentiate between the critical elements and common errors. Students then try to make the drop shot as you have shown them (even if it is a shadow response without hitting the shuttle) and as they practice you reinforce good performance, correct major errors, and reteach the technique.

The same is true for introducing a particular tactic, such as the backdoor cut in basketball. With students gathered at one of the team practice sites, you explain the context for and execution of the backdoor cut, giving students the opportunity to ask questions. You then organize the students so they can do a walk-through of the maneuver. The goal of this whole-class practice is to get students to the point where they can benefit from later independent practice that will then be led by student coaches.

Model and Provide Opportunities for Practicing Basic Pedagogical Skills

Research on student coach effectiveness in Sport Education shows that they do not possess many of the basic skills necessary for effective instruction: they take longer to get their teams organized and they spend more time demonstrating and less time instructing and providing feedback. While this should be not be unexpected, it does mean that teachers need to model specific organizational behaviors for student coaches to copy. In the earliest lessons of a season, whole-class demonstrations are particularly useful.

The second area in which you need to model is the giving of verbal and nonverbal feedback. The key here is to make explicit the learning cues for each task, so that student coaches can provide appropriate feedback where they see their teammates struggling.

Figure 11.2 provides an example of a coaching task card that includes outlines for a two-on-two flag football task. The task card includes the organizational components of the task as well as possible questions to ask players.

THE STUDENT COACH: EARLY LESSONS

During the early lessons, when instruction is led by the teacher, the student coach will participate as a regular playing team member.

Coaches' Contracts

When students take leadership positions, it is important that you provide a clear explanation of exactly what their role entails. For the student coach, this may include responsibilities prior to, during, or even after the lesson. Many teachers use contracts that specifically outline these role expectations, a sample of which is provided in figure 11.3; additional examples can be found in the web resource.

Figure 11.2
COACHING TASK CARD FOR
TWO-ON-TWO FLAG FOOTBALL

Game Format and Rules

- Groups of five (one quarterback, two receivers, and two defenders)
- No center
- Complete pass = 1 point for offense
- Incomplete pass = 1 point for defense; interception = 2 points for defense
- First team to 6 points wins the game.

Organization

- The idea is to play for the pass completion.
- As coach, you may choose if it's always 1st and 10, 1st and goal, or randomly vary the down and distance you play.
- After the completion is made, the play is finished and a new play is set up.
- Take no more than 30 seconds between each play. Teach your teammates to huddle up quickly following each play.

Questions to Ask Your Players

- What do you focus on as a defender? As a receiver? As a quarterback?
- When would you be better off throwing a shorter pass? A longer pass?
- What fake moves by opponents do you want to watch for?
- How do you keep your focus on multiple players?
- When would be the better time to go for the flag grab? Which flag?
- When would be the better time to go for the interception?

While such contracts are helpful, we have found that many students who take the role of student coach come into the Sport Education seasons with preconceived notions of coaching that were shaped by their experiences in youth sport. Moreover, some of these perceptions may not align with the teacher's educational goals for the Sport Education season. You will recall from earlier chapters that the focus of Sport Education is not solely on winning, which often leads to exclusionary practices. Both Wallhead (2017) and Farias, Hastie, and Mesquita (2016) remind us that teachers need to emphasize to student coaches that their role is to support all players on their teams but that they also need to know that you as the teacher will give them the necessary support throughout the season. They also need to be reminded that they are not expected to be perfect from the outset: like any other skill, coaching takes time, practice, and effort to become highly effective.

Helping Teammates

When teams are first formed, there will be a mix of skill, attitude toward physical education, and attitude toward the season's sport among the team members. Students are also likely to have different goals for the season. For some the focus may be on competition success while for others it may be on avoiding failure and potential embarrassment. As Farias, Hastie, and Mesquita (2017) noted, this can produce a complex interplay between students' perceptions of their place as members of their team and their level of commitment to cope with certain team dynamics. The most common outcome of these differences is that many lower-skilled students can be removed from the decision-making process, leading them to feel excluded and sometimes even causing them actually to disrupt the organization of some activities. This can result in the dominant students (including the student coach) believing that these students are not committed to the team and therefore excluding them further from team decisions.

In the earliest parts of the season, student coaches should be made aware that the central goal of Sport Education is on mastery and equitable participation, and that this is best achieved through learning to recognize the value of all players on their teams

---

Figure 11.3
SAMPLE STUDENT COACH ROLE CONTRACT

Coach Role Contract

To the best of my ability,

as team coach I, _____ , agree to

- attend all coaching briefings,
- lead the team in practice sessions,
- be enthusiastic and organized in conducting practices,
- provide help and advice to players during practices,
- listen to players' opinions and ideas for practices and games,
- know the rules of the game,
- demonstrate fair play at all times, and
- make sure *all* players are given equal opportunities to practice and participate.

Signed: _____ Date: _____

and by providing positive leadership. In particular, coaches should be encouraged to provide public recognition of the effort and ability of their lower-skilled or lower-status students.

THE TEACHER: EARLY INDEPENDENT TEAM PRACTICES

In the latter part of the preseason, after teams have conducted practices following your lead, they must be given the opportunity to practice independently as a team. During independent practice, team coaches should lead their teams in practicing techniques and tactics in their practice space. You should carefully explain the organization for practice before dispersing students. Posters showing the critical elements and common errors of the technique or tactic are helpful. It is during team practices that students learn to work together and to help one another. The student coach provides the primary leadership for practice sessions, but you must make it clear that students are meant to help each other. Students who understand and grasp the technique or tactic quickly should be directed to provide assistance to teammates who are having trouble. Emphasize teammates helping one another and then recognize and support this when you see it occurring.

In the earliest parts of the season, student coaches should be made aware that the central goal of Sport Education is on mastery and equitable participation, and that this is best achieved through learning to recognize the value of all players on their teams and by providing positive leadership.

At the outset, one of your primary instructional tasks is to closely supervise teams' independent practices to make sure they are practicing appropriately. As you watch the practices, ask yourself: Do the teams have a practice plan? Are they following that plan? Do they get started quickly? Are they actively engaged, or are just the higher-skilled team members involved? Are the team coaches providing the needed leadership? Do players take the lead from the team coach? Based on what you see happening, you can work with the various team coaches to have them help their teams work toward more effective team practices.

Providing Individual Instruction

Since the team coaches now start leading the team practices, you can focus on teaching the activity itself by working with an individual team or with individual players within that team. As team practices unfold, you can shift your monitoring to questions such as the following: What techniques are still lacking? What practice task might help a particular team? The more active and deliberate your monitoring is, the better position you are in to offer assistance to teams and individuals.

As students gain more experience with Sport Education, they will be better able to work within it and profit from it. You can therefore expect that across multiple seasons and years in Sport Education, students will become quite good at the give-and-take that characterizes small-group learning. As their capacity to work within the team concept improves, teams will become more self-directed and your supervision can shift to helping teams and individual students that may be struggling more. You can spend more time providing teaching assistance during team practices. Do not expect such self-directedness skills to develop automatically, however. As a teacher, you must provide ample and appropriate opportunities for students to learn to become more self-directed.

For teachers who have thus far employed a more direct style of teaching, where students are almost entirely dependent on their directives and commands, this gradual handing over of the reins to students may be difficult at first. However, if you plan well, you will find that many students will surprise you with their willingness to take on leadership roles.

Design Support Materials

When students are learning to play a sport, practices should mirror the conditions of the game as much as possible (e.g., either a modified form of the game or the parent game, depending on the previous experience of the students) and provide students with maximum opportunities to actively engage. You can help teams develop more focused team practices by providing them with team practice cards that they can use to organize their team practices. This chapter's web resource includes numerous examples of team practice and action fantasy cards that you can use with your students to organize and design practices. They are based on the play practice approach to developing games players (Launder & Piltz, 2013). Team coaches can then use these cards to organize their team practices. As shown in figure 11.4, team practice cards provide the necessary information for team coaches to organize a modified game, including game rules, suggested variations, scoring rules, and possible questions that they (or you) could ask team members during short breaks in the action.

Player's Side

TEAM PRACTICE CARD

Guess the Pitch: On the Line

Game format and rules:
1. Pairs of players: One hitter in batting stance and one pitcher. Hitter does not have a bat (or can have a bat, ***but is not allowed to swing at pitches***).
2. Pitcher tries to hit the strike zone (preferably the lines that outline the strike zone), while the hitter guesses whether each pitch is a strike.
3. Hitter must call the pitch "Ball!" or "Strike!" <u>BEFORE</u> it crosses home plate.
4. For the pitcher: strike = 1 pt.; strike on the line = 3 pt
5. For the hitter: Guessing a pitch correctly as either ball or strike = 1 pt
6. This can be used with underhand pitching and overhand pitching.
7. Games go to 10. Then switch roles.

Organization and modifications:
- Tape or chalk to outline strike zones on a mat that is leaning up against a wall.
- Mark off several strike zones at appropriate height and far enough apart so multiple pairs can play.
- If on open field, form groups of four, where the third person becomes catcher, and the fourth practices umpiring (i.e., calling balls and strikes).
- *Possible modification:* Use tennis balls as a substitute.
- *Possible additional challenge:* You get 20 pitches. See what percentage of those are called strike and what percentage is on the line. For example, (12 strikes/20 pitches) = 60% of pitches thrown were a strike.

Teacher or Team Coach Side

Guess the Pitch: On the Line

Teacher or team coach:
- With each practice, have specific focus (see next box).
- What do you see happening?
- Focus on what players are doing well and what is not working well.
- **Let them know!**

Focus of this practice game:
Pitcher practices:
1. Throwing strikes and preferably to the corners or edges of the strike zone
2. Hitting a ball on the sweet spot

Hitter practices:
1. Judging pitch location. (i.e., decision-making)

Catcher practices (when used in open field set-up):
1. Catching balls
2. Setting clear targets for pitcher; varying the target with every pitch
3. Adjusting glove work when catching balls

Possible questions to ask your players:
Catcher:
1. What can you do to help the pitcher hit his or her target?
2. How do you adjust to a pitch that is thrown low (e.g., on the ground)?

Hitter:
1. What pitches are harder to judge whether they are balls or strikes?
2. What can you do to keep your eye on the pitch as long as possible?

Pitcher:
1. Why is it important to vary your pitch location?
2. Why is it not a good idea to throw as hard as possible?

Figure 11.4 A team practice card, such as this one for softball, provides the necessary information for team coaches to organize a modified game.

Team practice cards are based in part on Launder and Piltz's (2013) concept of "shaping play." Teachers can shape gameplay by arranging game conditions so as to encourage students to use certain techniques and tactics. For example, in pickleball or tennis, students can play a cross-court versus down-the-line game. One player earns a bonus point when a winner is scored using a cross-court shot, while the opposing player earns the bonus point if a shot down the line is used. Thus, gameplay skills are developed by deliberately modifying any combination of game rules. With this game-oriented approach to practice, students not only practice the various strokes but also decide when the particular shot is best used. Team practice cards should be supplied to teams in their team binders at the outset of the season. You will find several examples of such practice cards in the web resource. As you gain more experience with using a game-based approach to teaching games, you will be able to develop your own practice games.

The free-throwers versus rebounders game example in basketball (see figure 11.5) shows how players are encouraged to practice multiple techniques and tactical moves. Such games provide an excellent opportunity for you to assist team coaches in getting their players to consider how and where they move to create the advantage over the opposing team as well as how and where to pass. Obviously, the defense gets ample chances to hone guarding and communication skills.

Coaches' Corner

As team coaches become more effective at organizing their teams and providing feedback, they are ready to become more independent from the teacher. As Wallhead (2017) notes, this independence should be encouraged by progressing to less-prescriptive teacher support strategies. One example of a less direct teaching strategy is the use of a coaches' corner.

Players' Side   *Teacher/Team Coach Side*

TEAM PRACTICE CARD

Free-Throwers vs. Rebounders

Free-Throwers vs. Rebounders

Teacher or team coach:
What are the tactical problems to be solved?
- *Offensive:* Maintaining possession? Transition play? Creating space? Creating scoring opportunities?
- *Defensive:* Gaining or regaining possession. Defending space or a player? Defending as a team?

Game format and rules:
1. 3 vs. 3 or 4 vs. 4
2. Free-throw team members rotate after every 4 free throws.
3. With each miss, free-throw team is allowed one follow-up shot.
4. Once each player on each team has had its free-throw turn, teams switch.
5. Watch for rough play (e.g., coming over the back).

Possible questions to ask:
Free-throw team:
- What will increase your chance of getting in a good rebound spot?
- If your team loses the rebound, what is your new responsibility?

Rebounding team:
- How do you decide where to line up along the key?
- If you do not get the rebound, what is your task?
- If your team gains possession, do not get the rebound, how can you help in transition?

Teacher or team coach:
- With each free throw, pick a gameplay dimension and one of your players.
- What do you see happening?
- Judge what your player is doing well, and what is not working well.
- **Let him or her know!**

Using time-outs:
- Ask players what might be done differently to play effectively.
- Give feedback on what is going well.

How points are scored:
Free-throwers:
- Make your free throws!
- Made free throw = 1 pt

Rebounders:
- Get your rebounds!
- Defensive rebound grabbed = 1 pt

Game variation:
- Same as above, but upon gaining possession, if the rebounding team gets ball to half-court line within 8 secs. = 2 pt.
- If the free-throw team prevents this (i.e., > 8 secs.) = 2 pt

Figure 11.5 This team practice card for basketball encourages off-the-ball movement and passing.

Usually before the lesson starts (or while peer participants are working on a previously taught task), the student coaches of each team gather with the teacher and listen to a short explanation of the expectations for the upcoming practice task. This explanation becomes less prescriptive as the season develops and should focus on knowledge, with a problem-based approach to subsequent learning tasks. During the coaches' corner, the student coaches should be provided with the organizational structure of the upcoming task but should also be presented with potential task modifications and feedback cues. The two-on-one pass and support task illustrated in figure 11.6 provides an example of task modifications that could be included in this stage of coach development. For instance, options such as a fake pass by the ball carrier or reduced limitations placed on the defender would advance the students' understanding of touch rugby game problems.

As the task progresses, the student coach should be encouraged to use questions, rather than or in addition to direct feedback statements for prompting teammates' comprehension of these game problems (e.g., Harvey, Cope, & Jones, 2016; Wallhead, 2017). Using this approach makes the student coaches more aware of different instructional strategies and also guides their teammates toward greater self-monitoring and understanding of their performance (van de Pol, Volman, & Beishuizen, 2010). The task card previously presented in figure 11.2 provides sample question prompts that could be used by the coach to teach the use of overload attacking situations. Other questions might include: When should we look to make a pass in touch rugby? and What should the support player do once they receive a pass? Such discovery-based coaching strategies serve to restructure the instructional interactions between student

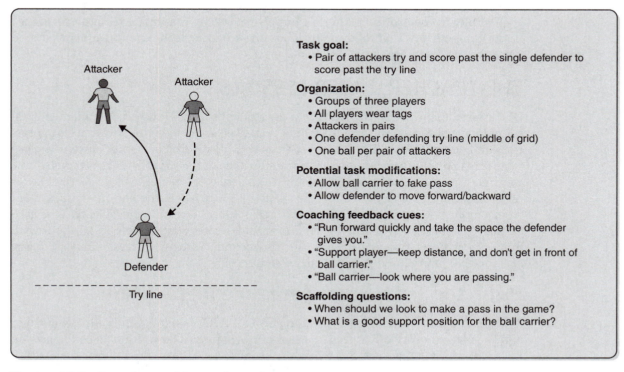

Figure 11.6   Sample coaching task card.

Reprinted by permission from T. Wallhead, "Developing Competent Games Players: Roles of the Teacher and the Student-Coach," *Active and Healthy Journal* 24, no. 2/3 (2017): 21-24.

coaches and teammates. By asking peers to formulate answers to these questions, the coaches create a dialogue between team members that helps them begin to share the responsibility for learning. As teammates develop a greater understanding of the game, they also become more able to help others in the group, which distributes some of the coaching responsibilities among the group (Farias, Hastie, & Mesquita, 2016).

THE STUDENT COACH: EARLY INDEPENDENT TEAM PRACTICES

As the season progresses from the teacher-directed focus in the early lessons to when teams are practicing independently and also participating in practice games, the role of the student coach becomes magnified. As with the early lessons, the first task of the coaches is to lead their teams in practices. While in the beginning phases of the season you will have provided the tasks to be completed, during the later, more independent practices, the teams will be given more opportunities to make decisions about how to spend their time.

It is important that student coaches are aware that they are not the only voice in the decisions about what to practice. They should be encouraged to listen to their teammates and to seek ideas from all the players, be they higher- or lower-skilled. Reminding coaches to include all students in relevant team decision-making is crucial for developing a higher sense of purpose and membership within teams.

During this second phase of the season, teams will begin taking part in intrasquad scrimmages (games within their teams) and will also participate in practice matches against other teams in the class. The student coach should have a lead role in organizing these within-team practices and making sure all players have the opportunity to participate in all the different playing positions. This not only leads to a higher level of buy-in toward the team unit but also serves to maximize team performance in the competitions that follow. The focus on providing feedback and support should continue in this phase.

THE TEACHER: LATER LESSONS

By the later lessons of Sport Education, the student coaches (and other team members) should have mastered the various managerial tasks involved with running team practices and competitions. This, in turn, frees you from being on center stage to a place where it is possible to be the guide on the side. One of the payoffs for this reduced role in directing events is the increased ability to assess the technical and tactical levels of the students' performances. While chapter 18 focuses on the notion of assessment from a more global perspective (remember that Sport Education has objectives beyond skilled gameplay), the following section will describe ways in which teachers with more Sport Education experience can incorporate informal assessments with the specific goal of enhancing skillful movement.

Using the Team Sport Assessment Procedure

The Team Sport Assessment Procedure, or TSAP (Gréhaigne, Godbout, & Bouthier, 1997), is based on two features of game performance. The first of these focuses on how a player gains possession while the second examines how a player disposes of possession. Figure 11.7 provides a simplified version of the instrument that students (or the teacher) can use to code during play. From these raw scores, the TSAP has two formulas that provide a volume of play index and an efficiency index; from these two components an overall performance score can be calculated. These data can be

Figure 11.7
MODIFIED TSAP INVASION GAME BEHAVIORS

GAINING POSSESSION OF THE BALL	
Conquered ball (CB)	• Makes an interception • Steals the ball from an opponent • Recovers the ball from an unsuccessful short on goal
Received ball (RB)	The player receives the ball from a partner and does not immediately lose control of it.
SENDING THE BALL AWAY	
Pass (P)	Pass to a teammate, then moves the ball towards the goal
Successful shot on goal (SS)	A shot that scores
Lost ball (LB)	Loses control of the ball by either (i) making a pass that is intercepted, (ii) having the ball stolen, or (iii) loses control of the ball and the other team gains possession

The computation of performance indexes and performance score:

volume of play index = CB + RB

efficiency index = CB + P + SS / 10 + LB

Performance score = (volume of play / 2) + (efficiency index × 10)

Reprinted by permission from J.-F. Gréhaigne, P.G. Godbout, and D. Bouthier, "Performance Assessment in Team Sports," *Journal of Teaching Physical Education* 16 (1997): 500-516.

used by teams to identify areas of strength or weakness and ultimately to the design of team practices that address them.

Testing of the TSAP has demonstrated that students at the grade 5 to 8 levels are capable of using the TSAP with a moderate to good level of precision and interobserver reliability, this being more so as the grade level increases (Richard, Godbout, & Gréhaigne, 2000). Given that Sport Education involves students in several roles, it makes sense to include gameplay coding as a legitimate role in any season. For example, in some Spanish schools, teachers use the players from one nonplaying team to code the performance of one student during games of modified handball.

Coaching Clinics

Alexander and Penney (2005) have introduced the idea of a coaching clinic as a way help individuals or teams with the challenges of the technical or tactical demands of the games they are playing. On clinic days (which are interspersed throughout the season), teams participate in a small-sided game that reenacts a problem the teacher has observed during previous matches. These games serve to create an overload (or unbalanced) situation (e.g., four on two or two on one) that is designed to stress specific tactical demands of the game. In this way, aspects of setting up an attack or defending critical areas become more apparent to students and help them appreciate key aspects of successful play. During these clinic games, the teacher is actively involved in asking questions such as "What should we do in this situation?" or "How did your action help or hinder your team in that last play?" A sample tactical problem for a net or wall game can be found in table 11.1.

Table 11.1 Teaching Technical and Tactical Components as Complementary

The learning intention— a tactical problem	Understand how to set up to win a rally by opening up space on the other player's court
Focus	Understand the concept of opening up (creating) space
Modified game 1	Singles rally on short length and wide (using doubles line) court
Examples of game-based questions	• What is the tactical advantage of moving your opponent? • What is the tactical advantage of hitting to space? • How do you place the shuttle to move your opponent? • How do you manipulate force as well as placement to move your opponent or hit to space? • Into what spaces can you hit the shuttle? • Where is the hardest place from which your opponent can play a return hit?
Modified game 2	Singles rally on long (using doubles court end line) and narrow half-court
Examples of game-based questions	• What is the tactical advantage of moving your opponent? • What is the tactical advantage of hitting to space? • How do you place the shuttle to move your opponent? • How do you manipulate force as well as placement to move your opponent or hit to space? • Into what spaces can you hit the shuttle? • Where is the hardest place from which your opponent can play a return hit?
Conclusion	How do you hit the shuttle to open up (create) space on the other player's court?

Reprinted by permission from S. Pill and S. Harvey, Developing Competent Players in Sport Education," *Active and Healthy Journal* 24, no. 2/3 (2017): 25-29.

After teams play these clinic games, you can follow one of two paths. One way is to have the teams spend time practicing specific techniques that would help in overall game performance. For example, if a volleyball team decides it needs to improve its serving, or a softball team decides it needs more practice in throwing cutoffs from the outfield, you can give instructions directly or via the student coach. Another way is to give the teams the opportunity to negotiate with another team to play further games, whereby they can consolidate the lessons they learned from the practice game.

Action Fantasy Cards

A variation of the team practice card that can be used on clinic days is the action fantasy game (see figure 11.8 and web resource). Launder and Piltz (2013) introduced the concept of such games to enhance play. Using the names of real athletes and teams, you create actual game scenarios for the students to enact. For example, in a court game such as tennis or pickleball, you could have Venus and Serena Williams face Maria Sharapova and Simone Halep in a doubles match. Depending on which duo is ahead in the scenario, each needs to approach the game's situation differently.

With a little creativity, you can design an endless array of game scenarios that give students the opportunity to come up with their own way of solving the problem presented. For example, in a basketball season, you might provide an NBA finals game 7 scenario in which the Los Angeles Lakers are down by four points against the Cleveland Cavaliers with 1:30 left on the clock. A team splits up into two subteams that represent the Lakers and the Cavaliers. The team coach presents the scenario (with any additional rules) to both teams. Each team gets 30 seconds to determine how to approach this game situation, and then the scenario is played out. The scenario can be repeated following a brief time-out during which each team discusses any possible

Players' Side | *Teacher or Team Coach Side*

Action Fantasy Game: Tennis

**Women's Singles
Australian Open Final**

Serena Williams (USA) vs. Maria Sharapova (Rus.)

Player Picture Here	Player Picture Here

***Rules:* Basic tennis rules in effect**
- **Best of 3 sets**
- **Modified rally scoring (i.e., 1, 2, 3, 4, 5)**
- **Sets go to 12 (no need for 2-point difference to win)**

Match status:
- **Match is tied one set all.**
- **Set 3 score: Williams, 3 and Sharapova, 4**
- **Williams has the serve.**

*If time permits, play out the scenario three times,
like a best of three.*

| **Action Fantasy Game: Singles Play
Questions to Consider** |
| --- |

Overall game plan (strategy) for each team:
- ***If ahead:*** More or less aggressive attack? Take more or fewer risks?
- ***If behind:*** More or less aggressive attack? Go for more risky shots?

What tactical moves might be critical?
- ***Offensive:*** Decision making (When to go for the winner? What shot to use? Shuttle placement. Remembering to return to base.)
- ***Defensive:*** Decision making (Where to move? Covering the entire court. Maintain position or return to base position?)
- ***Both:*** Seeing your opponent's moves. Recognizing the opponent's strengths and weaknesses. Anticipating his or her possible next actions.

Ask yourselves:
- What will the opponent's game plan most likely be?
- What should you focus on?
- What seem to be the stronger areas of play of the opponent?
- Which shots seem to cause more difficulty for the opponent?

Figure 11.8 Action fantasy cards, such as this one for tennis, are meant to give more experienced students the opportunity to solve real game problems.

adjustments. Notice again how this affords students increased involvement in how they learn to play the game: within this games-based context, both technical and tactical moves are practiced. Not only do students practice their dribbling, shooting, passing, rebounding, and catching, but they also practice defending, moving off the ball, supporting the ball handler, and making decisions on whether to shoot, drive to the basket, or focus on maintaining possession. We should note that action fantasy game scenarios are most appropriate for students who are further along in their gameplay level.

This games-based approach to practicing techniques and tactics in combination has important benefits. First, it affords students the opportunity to engage in gameplay more often, which generally motivates them more. Second, students are likely to reach higher levels of physical activity than they do in the more static, drill-based practice of isolated, out-of-context techniques so pervasive in most physical education lessons. And third, the intensity of the physical activity is likely higher during modified games. Especially given students' natural physical activity patterns, they will welcome brief time-outs, during which their team coach (or you) can address aspects of gameplay by way of a short question–answer discussion.

Coaches' Seminars

If you are interested in developing more advanced student coaching strategies, you can offer a coach education program that extends beyond the confines of the lesson or a single season of Sport Education. Coaching seminars are one strategy that has been used to great effect in developing higher-skilled student coaches in Sport Education (Araujo, Hastie, & Mesquita, 2016; Farias, Hastie, & Mesquita, 2016). These seminars occur outside of lesson time and include the student coaches watching video footage of themselves coaching and discussing their effectiveness to formulate strategies for change. These types of seminars work well when students have the opportunity to serve as coach over multiple seasons of Sport Education and thereby develop some foundational pedagogical knowledge they can refine through practice and reflection. The additional time required for the regular use of this type of coach education strategy may be beyond the constraints of your school day. However, providing an opportunity for coaches to watch themselves coach and reflect on their interactions with their teammates can be a powerful learning experience.

THE STUDENT COACH: LATER LESSONS

During the later phases of the season, teams will be given a higher level of autonomy in how they practice, based on the needs they have identified in gameplay. Student coaches could be expected at this point to bring practice plans to class. They should be primarily responsible for determining player positions within games, or in allocating individuals or pairs to represent it in different competitions (e.g., singles and doubles pairings in badminton). They should also collaborate with their teammates in making decision about who will represent the team in different events during individual sports competitions. For example, during a season of track and field, decisions need to be made as to who will enter the long jump competition and who will participate in the triple jump, or who will be throwing the javelin or representing the team in the shot put. Similarly, during a fitness season, teams will need to send students to the various exercise challenge stations.

Alexander and Penney (2005) have noted that it may not always be the teacher who decides the focus of activities during clinics. Instead, teams may request that particular tactics or techniques be placed on the practice schedule for the day. For example, players with a strong background in a sport may suggest particular tactical or technical solutions to problems they have identified. These can become a focus of the teams' activities for all or part of the clinic. It is the responsibility of student coaches to consult with their teams with respect to their preferences in these cases.

It is also critical that the student coach provide leadership during competitions by being the best models of fair play behaviors. They should also contribute very visibly to the encouragement of all team players.

SUMMARY

Within the student-centered focus of Sport Education, the development of effective student coaches is critical to the success of the model. It is therefore important that you first model effective coaching strategies, particularly in terms of task organization and providing feedback. Second, you should clearly define your expectations for coaches, particularly as they relate to including all students in team decisions and developing a sense of community. Finally, you need to develop resources that help student coaches move along a continuum from dependence to autonomy.

We want to emphasize that while you do hand over some of the instructional responsibilities to students during seasons, your role is not simply to create a season plan and then let students practice and play games. You are still responsible for the development of all students, and it is certainly legitimate to have direct involvement with students during practice and gameplay and to work with coaches during practices to help them modify tasks to make them more appropriate for their teammates.

Learning to Officiate, Keep Score, and Assess Fair Play

Chapter Objective

After reading this chapter, you will be able to identify the key teaching strategies that help students become proficient officials.

Key Concepts

- The quality of student officiating will go a long way to determining the quality of the season as a whole.
- Time needs to be allocated in the season plan for training students in officiating tasks.
- There is significant value in having all players on all teams show mastery of the rules before formal competition begins.
- In determining what statistics are kept, it is important to understand the history of the sport and to take note of the statistics that have the most meaning.
- The easiest statistics to keep are those where there is a stop in play (e.g., after goals or touchdowns).
- While officials should be asked to rate the playing teams with respect to fair play, it is also helpful to have the playing teams rate the officiating team on their performance.

As we have mentioned throughout this book, one of the defining features of Sport Education is that students take roles other than just as players. Students enjoy taking these nonplaying roles and treat them seriously. Furthermore, given appropriate opportunities to practice these roles, students show particularly high levels of commitment to them and are able to complete their allocated tasks with high degrees of success.

A second key feature of Sport Education is that students participate in formal competitions, and it is these competitions that add significant meaning to the experience. Reports from students across all grade levels (including university physical education courses) tell us that what makes Sport Education particularly attractive to students is that it is an authentic level of competition. That is, in contrast to the impromptu and unscripted ways in which games are typically organized in physical education (where teams are created ad hoc and last for perhaps only one match), games in Sport Education count toward a season championship and teams remain together to work collectively toward this goal.

Nonetheless, while students tell us that winning games is important to them in Sport Education, they also tell us that their main concern is focused on individual and team improvement and on playing hard. Quotes from vastly different contexts provide evidence for this claim. A Russian ninth-grader, Sveta, commented during an interview, "We lost today, but I think that our team played especially well today. Our team still has a spirit of a winner." And at the end of the season, her classmate Nikolai said, "Even that we took third place, I was very happy. We played tough team and others were very strong, and we gave them a battle. And more, now I could make shots when I shoot" (Sinelnikov & Hastie, 2008). A student in an American university physical education class made this entry into their team's website: "Oleg missed one of the greatest games of all time. This game was definitely one for the books. We played the Scooby Doobies and it was [one of] the closest, hardest games all semester. I'm not really upset that we lost this game; just disappointed. The score was close the entire game and we went through three full sets with every game within two points. The only thing I wish had happened different was that we had pulled it off in the end. Maybe we can still pull off the best full court game record in the class."

The relevance of these examples is that in many Sport Education seasons, the quality of student officiating will go a long way to determining the quality of the season as a whole. The officials act as the link between the fun and the quality of the competition and the learning of the nonplaying roles. This combination is designed to lead to one of the global goals of Sport Education: a more complete understanding of the nature of the sport. You should therefore give students the chance to practice the various officiating roles before scheduling games of consequence, and you must help all students understand that the primary role of the officiating team is to keep the game moving forward smoothly. It is the purpose of this chapter to outline the key teaching strategies that help students become proficient officials. Throughout the chapter, the officiating team will be called the *duty team*. This team comprises all the roles (at a minimum, those of referee and scorekeeper) whose duty it is to manage the various contests that are part of a season. However, as outlined in chapter 9, different sports and activities require a number of specialist roles (see tables 9.6 and 9.7) such as starters and timekeepers, and judges in many of the performing arts activities such as dance, gymnastics, or aerobics.

DEVELOPING QUALITY OFFICIALS

In chapter 9, a number of factors were listed with respect to helping students learn their roles. These included (1) the need for the roles to be clearly defined, (2) the allocation of time in the early lessons of a season to help train students in the roles they will be taking, (3) to provide opportunities to practice performing these roles, and (4) to have a way of holding students accountable for their role performance. The following sections outline how these factors can apply in the development of quality officials. While we limit the officials in this chapter to referees, scorekeepers, and statisticians, these strategies apply to all in-game officiating responsibilities.

Defining the Role of the Duty Team

It is important for teachers to explain the roles that referees and other officials play during contests. A helpful guide comes from Sport New Zealand, whose website explains, "Officials undertake an important role in the staging of competitions. They provide leadership and guidance to participants, ensuring that the competition is conducted in a safe and fair manner" (Sport New Zealand, 2017). Teachers should also explain that many things go into the making of a good official, but for successful seasons of Sport Education, the two key features are (1) knowing the rules of the game and (2) using the correct officiating techniques (such as giving the proper signals or accurately recording scores and statistics).

While it is not critical that students know every rule of a particular sport (the rulebook of the NFL is 85 pages, while the rules of golf expand over 230 pages), given that all students will participate in officiating roles, it is important that each one has a solid knowledge of the rules of the game. In planning a Sport Education season, the use of modified rules not only creates a more developmentally appropriate game, but is also a helpful way of assisting novice officials because there are fewer decisions for them to make. For example, to restart play in soccer, students may be allowed to kick or throw the ball to their teammates (using any form of throw) rather than being limited to the specific throwing technique seen in competitive soccer.

The rules you present to students should be a concise list of the most important aspects of the game, stated in the simplest terms possible. In some games (e.g., Ultimate), it is not necessary to have a written list of rules since they can be learned easily during play. For others, you might want to create a one-page list of key rules specific to the game, particularly in cases where most students have a good understanding of the parent game (e.g., a three-a-side modification of basketball or a chip and putt golf league).

The easiest way to make sure that all students are rules literate is to have a rules test before formal gameplay begins. We have also found that requiring each player to achieve a 100 percent score on the rules test before being allowed to play reinforces the value of knowing the rules. This allows the teacher to remind students that there should be no conflicts over the rules because everyone knows them. Figure 12.1 provides an example of how the rules of a season of floor hockey were presented to a class of sixth-grade students, and the rules test that was administered after a series of lessons covering the basic skills of dribbling, trapping and passing, and shooting.

Learning Duty Roles

In chapter 9 we stressed the importance of allocating time in the first lessons of a season for students to learn and practice their roles. Of particular importance are the lessons where students learn to officiate contests and keep score and statistics. A common and helpful beginning is to conduct a single game in which all nonplaying students are given a scoresheet and the teacher acts as the referee.

During these games, you should systematically work through the roles of the duty team as they officiate a game. First, the scorekeepers and statisticians fill in the team and player names, while the referee gathers the captains to determine which team

Figure 12.1
FLOOR HOCKEY RULES AND QUIZ

Rules

- Four-a-side (minimum one girl or boy on each four).
- Sticks may not be swung above the knee.
- A ball hit above waist height is a free push to the opposition.
- No tripping or pushing.
- If the ball is hit out by A, B gets a free push.
- You may not score directly from an out-of-bounds push.
- A goal is scored when a player pushes the ball into the goal.
- You may not kick the ball into the goal to score.
- After each goal, the teams line up on the end line and the ball is rolled to the nonscorers.
- Trapping is allowed with sticks and feet but not with hands (including the goalkeeper).
- Goalkeepers may not lie down in the crease.
- Only the goalkeeper may be in the crease.

Rules Quiz (Criterion for passing = 100 percent)

- T F You are allowed to push a player away from the ball.
- T F The goalkeeper is allowed to use his or her hands to stop the ball.
- T F Sticks must stay below the knee.
- T F After a goal, both teams come to the middle for a face-off.
- T F A player is *not* allowed to stop the ball with the feet.
- T F If the Blue team hits the ball out, the Green team gets a free push.
- T F You may trip a player if they are going to score a goal.
- T F Only the goalkeeper is allowed in the crease area.
- T F Boys may only pass to boys and girls only to girls.
- T F Teams may be all boys or all girls.

will start play. As the game begins, each time you as the referee make a decision, play stops and you demonstrate the appropriate signal to the class. You should also remind students that they need to move up and down the court or field in games such as floor hockey, Ultimate, or soccer, in order to keep in close proximity to the ball.

In these teacher-controlled games, play is stopped after a score (or a key statistical event), and all students make the appropriate record on their scoresheets. At the end of a short game, the teacher first explains what the playing teams should do with their equipment (e.g., pinnies and sticks to be lined up neatly in the goal area) and that teams will then meet to shake hands in the middle of the court or field. The teacher then directs attention towards the students who are completing the scoresheets.

In some Sport Education seasons, teachers invite officials from local associations to help students learn the finer points of positioning, while others show videos of games to illustrate how the officials move about the field and how they give their signals. The videos can also be used as sample games where all students can fill out the score or statistics sheet for what they observe. Teachers can thus assess student understanding of their responsibilities and provide feedback to correct scoring errors.

A Quick Word on Statistics

Do not make the statistics too complex and do not have too many, or students will struggle to keep up with the play. Rather, use the finite actions of the play as the statistics to be recorded. In invasion games such as basketball, flag football, or Ultimate, these may include interceptions, goals, or touchdowns, and in some cases assists. For batting and fielding games, simple statistics may include hits, runs, runs batted in for the batting team, while outs made, assists, and errors could be recorded for the fielding team. Figure 12.2 provides a sample statistics sheet from a five-a-side softball game, while there are examples of score sheets for numerous sports in the web resource.

We have also found that, where possible, it is advantageous to have two statisticians, one for each team. Particularly in games where possession can change quickly, having only one team to focus on leads to a more accurate record of match events.

In determining what statistics are kept, it is important to understand the history of the sport and to take note of the statistics that have the most meaning. Remember that we are teaching sport literacy as part of Sport Education, and we want students to understand some of the benchmark scores. In cases where the students have devised new names within their classes or schools, these may be used to develop school histories of records. As with refereeing, scorekeeping will get easier as students gain experience in Sport Education. Not only is there carryover from a seventh-grade volleyball season to an eighth-grade volleyball season, but there is also more general carryover from one sport to another as the concepts associated with scorekeeping are practiced in multiple settings.

Introducing Postmatch Protocols

In addition to learning the actions of officials during gameplay, students need to be introduced to other postmatch protocols during these first lessons. At a bare mini-

Figure 12.2
FIVE-A-SIDE SOFTBALL STATISTICS SHEET

Team	Outs	Assists	Errors	Team	Outs	Assists	Errors
Player				Player			
Player				Player			
Player				Player			
Player				Player			
Player				Player			

Out: the player making the out (e.g., receiving a throw on pass, making a tag, catching a fly ball).

Assist: a player throws the ball to a person on base who then makes an out.

Error: a mishandling error or an errant throw that prevents an out being made, or that allows a batter to advance a base.

mum, teams should line up and shake hands before returning any equipment used in the game. The officiating team should record the final scores, award fair play points, and submit their records to the teacher. As students gain more experience with Sport Education, other postmatch records can be kept. For example, the two team captains can complete an evaluation of the officials that is then submitted to the teacher along with the score and statistical sheets. Figure 12.3 shows a flowchart of how these protocols fit together to streamline the time between games. We have found it helpful to begin with a time allocation of five minutes for these postmatch tasks; with practice, this can be reduced to two minutes in time for the regular season.

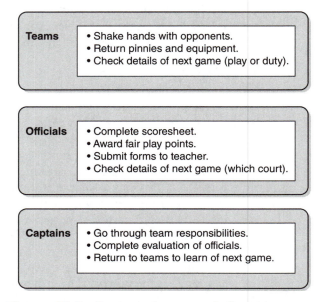

| Teams | • Shake hands with opponents.
• Return pinnies and equipment.
• Check details of next game (play or duty). |

| Officials | • Complete scoresheet.
• Award fair play points.
• Submit forms to teacher.
• Check details of next game (which court). |

| Captains | • Go through team responsibilities.
• Complete evaluation of officials.
• Return to teams to learn of next game. |

Figure 12.3 Postmatch protocols flow chart.

PRACTICING DUTY ROLES

During the third phase of learning to be good officials, students spend time carrying out their duties during complete games. These practices take place during what we call nonconsequential games, those that do not count toward the season championship. By this time, most students will have had a chance to practice keeping score or refereeing during teacher-controlled games, and should also be very familiar with the transition from team practice to gameplay (see chapter 10).

These lessons should include the completion of postmatch forms as well as live refereeing. You will still have the option of stopping a contest to reinforce a rule or an officiating signal. While some higher-skilled students might become frustrated by this stop-and-start nature of the game, you should explain that student officials are beginners; they too are learning a new skill, and hence should be treated with the same respect as others in the class who are learning new sport techniques and tactics. Intervention does not apply only to referees and line judges but also to statisticians and scorekeepers. For example, in Ultimate, a record is made both of the receiver and of the thrower of a touchdown. You can develop a protocol where the scorer and the thrower inform the statistician of their names, or you may assign this task to the referee. During the earliest lessons, you should stop play to teach or reinforce this protocol so that the more important games later in the season run smoothly. You also need to empower statisticians to stop the game and clarify a point if they are unsure of a decision. This is particularly helpful in the early stages of a season, when they are learning the scoring systems, and interruptions to games are less important. In any of these roles, when students perform well they need to be recognized and given positive feedback.

When students begin to play these practice matches, a duty team box may be prepared that includes all the equipment necessary to conduct a game. This box contains referees' jerseys, whistles, a scoreboard, score and statistics sheets, pencils, evaluation forms, and even game balls. The duty team is responsible for returning all the items to this box at the end of the competition. The manager of the team typically makes sure that this responsibility is completed successfully.

Much of your attention during these practice games should be devoted to helping the referees become more confident and competent. While some students seem naturally suited to this role, others will need closer monitoring and encouragement. Table 12.1 provides a five-stage progression for helping students to become good officials.

As with other aspects of Sport Education that are new to students, it takes time to develop competent officials. But research has found that most officiating students show high levels of compliance with the attentional requirements of their roles and also state that it is enjoyable and interesting (Layne & Hastie, 2014). Further, as students accumulate experiences in officiating roles, they not only become more accurate but begin to feel more comfortable and confident in these roles. For example, in a season involving sixth-grade students playing speedball, referees correctly called 80 percent of all possible decisions during the preseason games. Of the other 20 percent, failure to make a decision contributed 17 percent while only 3 percent were incorrect. During this learning phase, teacher intervention was needed at only 35 percent of all calls. These interventions served to clarify to all students the correct interpretation of the rule or to help the referee make the correct call. During formal competition, the referee success rating reached 94 percent, with no teacher intervention needed. It should be noted that the refereeing tasks were not complex, and referees were only required to make a decision (usually about whose throw-in it was) on the average of one every 26 seconds (Hastie, 1996).

In our work with Russian students, we have seen that they too embraced their officiating roles. Of interest in this case was that by the time they reached the formal competition stage of a season, some of them noted that they started to think beyond officiating duties and imagined themselves in the current playing situations. Dima, a good official, said, "The officiating also helps when I play. Not only now I know the rules of the game, but when officiating I can see where and to whom I would have passed the ball" (Hastie & Sinelnikov, 2006).

Table 12.1   Officiating Progression

Stage	Basketball	Volleyball or softball
Stage 1: being a player	The student is a player in the game	The student is a player in the game
Stage 2: following the teacher	The student moves with the teacher and learns about the positions on the court and following the ball	• The student stands behind the teacher and learns to make the correct judgments and signals • For base umpiring, the student takes the correct position according to the base runners and moves according to where the ball is hit
Stage 3: assistant official	The teacher is still lead official, but the student indicates fouls and other decisions	The teacher makes the call, and the student makes the appropriate signal
Stage 4: co-officials	The teacher assumes a backup role	The student tells the teacher the decision, and the teacher stops the game if the decision is correct; the student then makes the appropriate signal
Stage 5: student officials	The teacher takes no official role	The teacher takes no official role

Reprinted by permission from P.A. Hastie, "Helping Middle School Students Become Good Officials," *Journal of Teaching Elementary Physical Education,* 9, no. 4 (1988): 20-21.

Courtesy of Oleg Sinelnikov.

As with other aspects of Sport Education that are new to students, it takes time to develop competent officials. But research has found that most officiating students show high levels of compliance with the attentional requirements of their roles and also state that it is enjoyable and interesting (Layne & Hastie, 2014).

Accountability for Role Performance

As in any subject area, students will only take seriously those aspects of lessons for which they are held accountable or for which they are intrinsically motivated. We have found it helpful to have the captains of both teams complete referees' reports at the end of each match. These reports typically only involve two or three yes-or-no questions that focus on the key features that have been reinforced to students during their duty team training; knowledge, fairness, and professionalism. Figure 12.4 provides an example of a scoresheet used across a number of settings from elementary school through university. The score from this evaluation (the total of *yes* responses) becomes part of the team's total score on the league table.

Figure 12.4
OFFICIALS' EVALUATION SCORESHEET

Officiating team	Yes	No
Were the referees fair to both teams?		
Did they know the rules?		
Did the scorekeeper pay attention during the game?		

ASSESSING FAIR PLAY

We have repeatedly mentioned that fair play is critical to making games more enjoyable, and that everyone involved in the game, including players and officials, should strive to make the game fair. While the idea of acknowledging fair play is not unique to Sport Education, what *is* distinctive in the model is that fair play can become part of the formal league scoring table. Whereas FIFA and Major League Soccer present annual awards to teams and individuals with the lowest numbers of yellow or red cards, fouls, and disciplinary violations, these are independent of which team finishes as league champions.

The assessment of fair play in Sport Education is one of the extra roles taken on by the duty team in addition to their officiating responsibilities. A number of decisions need to be made concerning this assessment. These include determining the value of the fair play score, deciding how this score will be derived, and training students to assess fair play.

Determining the Value of Fair Play

The first task in designing a fair play system is to determine the extent to which fair play points will contribute to deciding the overall league champion. There are no hard and fast rules for deciding on how many points will be allocated to fair play. Many elementary school teachers foreground fair play by having it as the highest valued component of their league tables. Thus, while points may be awarded when team tasks are completed according to protocols (e.g., the fitness leader directing the warm-up, the equipment manager collecting sticks and balls), and only one point is awarded for a win, fair play might contribute as much as three points. At the other end of the spectrum, a number of university sport education seasons assess fair play daily but do not use these fair play points toward eligibility for the playoffs. In this case, if a team does not achieve 75 percent of the total fair play points available, that team does not qualify for the finals series, irrespective of that team's standing on the league table. This practice is used in a number of university intramural programs, so students in a Sport Education season should be familiar with that convention.

Awarding Fair Play Points

Following decisions concerning the weighting of fair play, the second task is to decide upon the system for awarding fair play points. Essentially we have used three different rubrics, with each one requiring a little more inference than the other. The easiest format for younger students and those with less experience with Sport Education is to simply have the officials answer a number of yes-or-no questions, with each *yes* response worth one point. Figure 12.5 provides an example of such an evaluation sheet.

Of course, the use of three questions (or these three in particular) is not set in stone. Rather, each teacher decides which attributes of fair play they want to reinforce. Other questions might include Did this team play fair and by the rules? Did this team treat the officials with respect? Did this team treat its opponent with respect? Did this team play as good sports? Did this team all play in different positions? or Did this team follow the rules? When designing these questions, it is easiest for students when all *yes* responses score a point. For instance, rather than asking Did this team argue with the officials? (where the preferred response would be *no*), we would ask Did this team accept the referees' decisions without arguing?

Figure 12.5
FAIR PLAY EVALUATION

Team name:			Team name:		
Total score:			Total score:		
	Yes	No		Yes	No
Did this team accept the referees' decisions without arguing?			Did this team accept the referees' decisions without arguing?		
Did the players on this team encourage each other?			Did the players on this team encourage each other?		
Did this team shake hands at the end of the game?			Did this team shake hands at the end of the game?		

Once students have had a number of seasons experiencing this simple yes-or-no format, they can be presented with a somewhat more elaborate format in which different points are awarded for different elements. Figure 12.6 gives an example of how various weighting can be given to the different elements of fair play, so that a score can be derived. In this case, the officiating team circles the scores that apply and then enters a total. Again, the weighting is dependent on those behaviors the teacher wants to promote more strongly.

The third version of awarding points requires students to have a more mature understanding of the implicit elements of fair play. In this case, the officiating team is asked to allocate +1, 0, or -1 points to each team. If a team does nothing wrong, does not argue with or complain about officials' decisions, and plays within the spirit at the game but at the same time does not acknowledge positive actions from its own team members or the opponents, then a score of 0 is awarded. But if negative comments are made to officials, or within or across teams, then a score of -1 is given.

In this system, to score a +1 there must be obvious examples of positive and supportive comments or actions of distinct fair play demonstrated by the playing team. Examples here would be acknowledging a rule violation (e.g., "Yes, I fouled them") or taking the opportunity to be a good sport by acknowledging a touch on a block during volleyball, or calling a ball *in* when it lands close to the line during tennis. Further, verbally recognizing achievements by teammates or opponents with comments such as "nice catch," "good shot," or "great save" would also warrant positive points.

Training Students to Recognize Fair Play

As in the other aspects of officiating, all students need to go through the same process when evaluating fair play as they do when learning how to referee, keep score, or tally statistics. They need to understand the purpose of the fair play and how it can enhance the sporting experience. And they need to see demonstrated examples of positive and negative fair play behavior so they can distinguish between these practices. For example, we have found that young elementary school students who are using the yes-or-no format might score a *no* if they saw even just a single example

Figure 12.6
OFFICIATING SCORESHEET

Team 1		Team 2	
Played fair and offered positive comments to teammates and opponents	2	Played fair and offered positive comments to teammates and opponents	2
Played within the rules	1	Played within the rules	1
Made negative comments among teammates, to officials, or opponents	-2	Made negative comments among teammates, to officials, or opponents	-2
Total		**Total**	

of the negative behavior, rather than taking the whole match in context. To address this, we have found it helpful to ask students to explain why they gave the *no* scores. You can then have a discussion about whether it was a player being overenthusiastic rather than a negative behavior that might indeed warrant a *no*. Finally, we need to teach the protocols of completing the fair play forms. As we noted earlier, one postgame task is for the officiating team to gather and consolidate the scoresheet and complete the fair play form at that time.

SUMMARY

Although several optional team roles exist in Sport Education, all students act as officials during a season. The intent of this role is for students to appreciate and learn more about the key features of a game other than simply in the role of a player, which leads to a more literate sports performer. Although considered a desired outcome of Sport Education, officiating provides a difficult challenge based on the amount of knowledge that is needed to be successful. Students are asked to make quick decisions about the play of their classmates. A good understanding of the rules and the components of gameplay are necessary for students to be able to officiate successfully. Students have to be diligent in completing their assigned tasks so their team will be successful.

As in all aspects of Sport Education that are new to students, it takes time to develop competent officials. However, research on student officiating has found that most students show high levels of compliance with the attentional requirements of their roles, and also state that it is enjoyable and interesting (Layne & Hastie, 2014). Further, as students accumulate experiences in officiating roles, they not only become more accurate but also begin to feel more comfortable and confident in the officiating roles. In our work with Russian students, we found that by the time they reached the formal competition stage of a season, some of them noted that they started to think beyond officiating duties and imagined themselves in the current playing situations. Some commented how they imagined themselves on the court in the players' roles. Students have also reported increased understanding of the rules from their roles as officials. As noted by one student during a touch football season, "If you're just playing, it doesn't really matter if you make a mistake . . . I learned more [about the rules] as a referee." As is common during Sport Education, the role of expert had shifted from the teacher to the students.

13

Making Sport Education Festive

Chapter Objective

After reading this chapter, you will be able to identify ways in which you can make your Sport Education seasons more festive.

Key Concepts

- Adding festive elements to a Sport Education season helps to make it more authentic and more significant to students.
- There are many ways to make teams special for students, thus adding to their sense of belonging and their feelings of responsibility to do their part for their team.
- Awards in Sport Education are not only for the winning teams or for the best performers. It is important for teachers to find ways to recognize effort, quality performance in various team and officiating roles, improvement, and fair play.

The word *festivity* has its origins in late fourteenth-century Old French (*festivité*) and in Latin (*festivitas*). In both cases, the common elements are *good fellowship* and *celebration of something in a joyful and exuberant way*. Festivity is included as one of the primary characteristics of Sport Education for two key reasons. First it is a central element in making the experience authentic, as sport in the real world is certainly festive. Second, this fellowship and celebration helps make the experience significant to participants.

Festivity is most obvious in grand events such as the Olympic Games, the football World Cup, or the Super Bowl of American football. But wherever we find sport, we see aspects of celebration and enthusiasm. Across the globe, be it on baseball diamonds, football fields, or basketball courts, young people are dressed in uniforms, and parents, siblings, and other relatives and friends form an audience that is enthusiastic about the play on the field. The quality of play differs dramatically depending on the age group involved, but in all cases there is an atmosphere of good cheer surrounding the competition. Likewise, road races, fun runs, triathlons, and even mud runs are now part of the sport participation culture throughout the world. A crowd gathers to applaud the racers at the starting line and local residents line the streets, encouraging all the competitors, not just the frontrunners but also the age-group runners and those in the wheelchair division. Every participant who finishes gets a T-shirt. The place winners in age groups (typically by five-year increments from 20 to 65) get trophies. All of these sporting events have a measure of festivity that adds to their importance and makes them more enjoyable for participants and spectators alike.

In many areas of the United States, high school football on Friday nights has become a sport institution with clear festival characteristics. Players run onto the field under a large school banner. Cheerleaders spark the enthusiasm of the crowd. The starting lineups are introduced as players run onto the field to the cheers of their supporters. The national anthem is often played before the game. The school band plays throughout the game and does a special performance at halftime. In many towns, a broadcast of the game is likely to be heard on the local radio. The results of the game are available in the newspaper and at various websites the next day, with particular notice paid to players who performed well and made a great effort.

A second reason why festivity is a primary defining characteristic of Sport Education is that it helps make the experience significant to participants, thus increasing the likelihood that they will pursue sport and physical activity outside the physical education program. A primary goal of many physical education programs is to increase the likelihood that students will adopt physically active lifestyles. Maintaining a healthy, physically active lifestyle requires that students value the activity and seek it out so they can continue to participate. To come to value an activity, students must have significant experiences that motivate them to pursue the activity further. Making the sport experience festive is an important way to increase its significance to those taking part.

In the United States, interscholastic sport has provided significant experiences for many girls and boys, while in other parts of the world, sports clubs take up this role. Unfortunately, many students in physical education seldom view their experiences as exciting or valuable; not only do they view physical education as insignificant but in some cases they see it as an experience to be avoided altogether. This is particularly problematic for young people in those crucial years when they are forming the value structures that will carry them into young adulthood. This is particularly true for girls and for students who are less skilled. Sport Education has been proven again and again to make a sport-based curriculum more significant to girls and to less-skilled students, and festivity is one of the characteristics of the Sport Education model that increases its potential for motivating students. The web resources associated with this chapter include numerous examples of how you can build festivity into the season.

A festive atmosphere should not be limited to the championship game at the end of a season of Sport Education but should be included on a daily basis throughout a season. All the ways we describe for making Sport Education classes more festive have been used by teachers we know or by teachers who have communicated to us their enthusiasm for the Sport Education model and what it has meant to them and to their students. We are not suggesting that you use all of these ideas, but we present enough of them so that you can choose the ones that best fit your situation. You yourself will probably find new ways to make things special for your students.

TEAMS

Putting students on teams that persist for at least the full length of the season is a significant feature of how students define fun during Sport Education It has been suggested that one of the principal reasons Sport Education is more enjoyable than typical physical education lessons is the greater opportunities for *affiliation*.

There are many ways to make teams special for students, thus adding to their sense of belonging and their feelings of responsibility to do their part for their team. First, teams should have names, and students should be allowed to choose those names, avoiding ones that project violent, sexist, derogatory, or offensive images. For instance, names such as Bullets, Killer Canines, and Redskins would not be appropriate. It is easy to be creative by using a particular feature of the sport and adding an adjective. The Flaming Pucks and the Flying Dolphins are just two examples from hockey and swimming seasons.

There are many ways to make teams special for students, thus adding to their sense of belonging and their feelings of responsibility to do their part for their team. Teams should have names, and students should be allowed to choose those names, avoiding ones that project violent, sexist, derogatory, or offensive images.

In addition to names, teams can have other elements related to their identity. From as far back as the Middle Ages, mottoes, crests, flags, and insignias were adopted as ornaments or badges on the uniforms and shields used at jousts and tournaments. These aspects are still part of the identity of schools and sports clubs today. In some countries, teams have mascots that also represent their affiliation. The numerous ways in which teams can display their identities vary from minimal expense to more costly. Table 13.1 gives examples from various Sport Education seasons.

Each team can also have a space on the bulletin board to post team results and performance statistics. Teachers can also take team pictures and post them in the team space on the bulletin board. Students should be allowed to create the team pose they would like for their team picture. Teams can also develop a motivating cheer that they perform before and after each game.

Teams typically have assigned spaces in the gymnasium or on the playing field. They go to their team space at the start of class and fulfill the designated entry routine, be it a warm-up or a skill drill. Teams can also be encouraged to practice outside of class in nonattached school time. Middle and high school teachers often have open gym times during extended lunch periods. One study from Wyoming showed an increased level of lunchtime engagement in optional practice and free play in activities during their related Sport Education season when an open gym was offered (Knowles, Wallhead, & Readdy, 2018).

Many teachers include extra practice as a way to earn points toward a seasonal championship. In some variations of Sport Education, teachers have had teams represent countries, as in Olympic sport or World Cup soccer. In these variations, teams adopt the flag, colors, and anthem of the nations they represent. All of these efforts reinforce team identity and make the experience more significant for the students.

TEAM PORTFOLIOS

Some teachers in upper-grade and university settings emphasize teams through the development of team portfolios. These portfolios allow students to demonstrate both individual and team strengths and weaknesses and summarize their growth across each season. During the course of the season, teachers can allocate time at the end of specific lessons for team members to meet and discuss progress on their portfolios.

Table 13.1 Forms of Team Affiliation

T-shirts	• Students wear pinnies in their team color • Students decide on a color and wear a headband or wristband in that color • Students create tie-dyed shirts using their selected team color • Students design logos and transfer them to T-shirts using iron-on printer paper • Teams design their own shirts and have them screen printed
Posters	• Teams design posters that identify the key attributes of their team (often used when countries are part of team names)
Flags	• Using a piece of white cotton (the size of half a pillowcase), teams create their designs using colored Sharpies (indelible marker pens) and spray these with alcohol. The alcohol causes the design to bleed into the fabric, creating attractive designs. A hem is either sewn or made with hot glue and the flag is attached to a length of half-inch PVC tube
Mascots	• Students can find and print color images of their mascots and paste these onto their team posters • Students can create graphic images of their mascots (including optional text) and print these • Students can create their own mascots using various media (papier-m,chÈ is a particularly useful medium; it is cheap and can be painted and decorated)

Portfolios usually have a cover page that includes the team's name, logo, and shirt design. Further sections include the players' names (complete with player profiles), a team philosophy, and diary entries completed by the team members. For some seasons, teams can diagram their offensive and defensive plays. All teams are welcome to include items in addition to those on the required list of artifacts. In that way, students can organize their sport experiences, take control over the layout and content of their team portfolios, and decide what kinds of learning they wish to demonstrate (Kinchin, 2001).

You can have each team designate a portfolio manager who is responsible for delegating individual responsibilities to team members to complete the portfolio, bringing the portfolio to class (or collecting it from the teacher) so that final artifacts can be included, talking to the teacher about any problems with the completion of the portfolio, and submitting the final file when it is due. Table 13.2 shows the expectations for a web-based volleyball portfolio in a university class.

AWARDS

Awards abound in Sport Education. It is important for teachers to find ways to recognize hard work, good performance, improvement, victories, and fair play. Many teachers end each class session with a meeting at which examples of good performance and fair play are pointed out. Good performance, of course, does not include only the players who performed well and the teams that showed good tactical awareness but also the duty teams that got players and equipment to the right places in a timely manner and then scored

Table 13.2 Team Portfolio Requirements

Required pages	Description
Index page	Outlines clearly, accurately, and concisely how to locate the various pages of the website and includes accurate hyperlinks to these pages; includes team logo (supplied by team manager)
Team techniques and tactics page	Includes links to players' techniques and tactics pages. Team self-analysis page includes links to players' self-analysis pages
Player biographies page	Each player provides the following items: personal information (photo, major, interests, favorite foods, quotes, etc.—anything you think might be of interest), each player's team commitment profile as judged by teammates, and each player's team role profile as judged by teammates
Team philosophy page	Discussion of how team views competition and what is important to the team
Team commitment page	Global and honest discussion and reflection on how the team worked: what happened during the season, why it happened, how problems were solved
Coach's page	Includes three formal practice plans and tips for teammates on improving basic volleyball techniques, teamwork, and communication
Manager's page	Includes a team roster page, a team schedule page that identifies opponents' team names, and dates when the team officiates
Statistician's page	Includes individual statistics page and the team record
Sports reporter's page	Includes game reports and photos of the competing and officiating teams, with creative commentary

Reprinted by permission from P.A. Hastie and O.A. Sinelnikov, "The Use of Web-Based Portfolios in College Physical Education Activity Courses," *Physical Educator* 64 (2007): 21-28.

and refereed games well, for example. It is particularly important to recognize examples of fair play. Students learn the most about the meaning of fair play when examples are pointed out to them and those who show exemplary fair play are recognized for it. Students and teams that are recognized in class do not necessarily receive trophies or certificates; rather, they are recognized in front of their classmates and publicly praised for their effort and performance. One idea is to have a fair play bulletin board and to post the names of students who have been singled out for exemplary fair play each day.

End-of-season awards are also an important part of Sport Education. Awards may be certificates and trophies of some kind. There are economical ways of developing tangible awards and trophies beyond simply printing certificates. Many teachers have taken old equipment that is somewhat worn and painted it gold, silver, and bronze to make it into a trophy. We have seen old track shoes, baseballs, and bowling pins used to create trophies that are placed in the school building after the season with team pictures alongside.

Some teachers organize a committee of representatives from each team to plan and create awards for the sport season. This approach works particularly well in a cross-disciplinary curriculum model, where students might do projects in an art class that serve the Sport Education season, for example. Coaches who fulfill their responsibilities should be recognized with a coaching award, often as a result of fulfilling a coaching contract that they sign at the start of the season. Seasonal fair play awards are powerful in reinforcing the importance of those concepts and actions. An award for most improved team gives recognition to another important concept, that of persevering in trying to improve as a group. And, of course, there is recognition of team performance. Team performance will mean something different in the different point systems teachers develop to determine the season champion. Victories will obviously be a big part of determining the champion, but there are many examples of teams with the most victories who were not the champions. This might have been because they lost fair play points, did not fulfill other obligations as duty team, or did not get as many points as they could have for practicing outside of class, and so on. The champion team and the runner-up can be recognized. These team awards go to the entire team even if the team had an A-, B-, and C-team in the seasonal competition that was graded by skill level. If the competition format is graded, then it is possible to recognize not only the overall champion and the runner-up but also the within-grade champions and runners-up. Figure 13.1 lists ideas for awards and presentations.

Figure 13.1
SAMPLE AWARDS

- Championship team
- Most improved team
- Most improved individuals (nominated by their teammates)
- Best fair play teams (teams with the highest fair play points)
- Best duty teams (teams with the highest officiating points)
- Teamwork award
- Best team cheer (voted by the class)
- Quality coaching awards
- Quality refereeing awards

CULMINATING EVENTS

All authentic sporting experiences end with a culminating event. The Super Bowl of American football and the final of the World Cup soccer competition draw millions of viewers across the world. In Australia, all AFL aficionados are aware that the grand final day occurs on the last Saturday in September. These events are not exclusive to the highest levels of professional sports; most junior leagues also have finals matches that lead to the confirmation of the premiership winners.

Consistent with its focus on inclusion, in Sport Education the end-of-season event represents the culmination of the sporting experience with one critical difference. In most sports leagues, only the two best teams get to participate in this final activity. In Sport Education, the focus is on festivity and on *full participation of all teams*. Both competitive and social outcomes are celebrated and shared among the students in the class. And so, the end-of-season event need not take place only on the final day of the competition round. Championships and other end-of-season competitions can be spread over several days. Although there may be a championship game in a tournament, there should also be games to decide the minor placings (third, fifth, seventh, etc.).

Culminating events can take many forms. Some classes treat the occasion as a purely social one while others include some activity relating to the season's competition. In all cases, however, the focus should be on the *festive* nature of the event. As Kinchin, MacPhail, and Ni Chroinin (2009) note, most teaching makes no reference to festivity and its absence contributes to the incomplete and inauthentic teaching of sport in many schools. To that end, they refer to Scheibler (1999) who claims that "in the festival, the focus is not directed to the individual but to their participation in something [an event] . . . the festival celebration is shared; participation is a sharing in an event" (pp. 151-152).

DEVELOPING CULMINATING EVENTS

The nature of the culminating event will differ depending on the sport and how the competition is organized. There are many ways to have a culminating event that involves all students, not just the two top teams. For example, if you have used a graded competition with three class teams that each have A-, B-, and C-teams competing, you would have a final competition in each of the divisions; that is, an A-level final, a B-level final, and perhaps a C-level final.

The culminating event may take several class sessions to complete if the event is held within the regular class schedule. Championship games in various divisions (e.g., singles, doubles, and mixed doubles in tennis or badminton) might take several class sessions followed by an awards and recognition session on the final day of the season. In the many cases where Sport Education is sufficiently important in the school program, special time is scheduled for a culminating event.

In developing the culminating event, it is worthwhile to consider the key features of a festival that Eichberg (2006) suggests should revolve around space, time, and atmosphere. Table 13.3 provides a summary of these elements and how they are relevant to the planning of a culminating event. A description of each element follows.

■ *Space.* While most culminating events take place on school grounds, there have been examples where larger venues are necessary, particularly when many classes (or even multiple schools) are taking part. In some cases, schools were able to conduct their festive day's competitions at an elite sporting venue, one not otherwise available for public use.

Table 13.3 Factors to Consider When Designing a Festival

Element	Particulars
Space	Location of the festival and how it is organized
Time	When the festival is planned
Energy	The practices that give the festival a particular atmosphere
Relations	The people in attendance at the festival and the relationships between them
Honors	What results come out of the festival

■ *Time.* While most individual lessons in a Sport Education season take place during scheduled class times, culminating events, by their very nature, take longer to complete. Thus, negotiations are required between the physical education and classroom staff, and in some cases, the school administration.

■ *Energy.* The festive nature of the event is limited only by the imagination of the teachers and the students involved in its planning.

■ *Relations.* A wonderful way to promote the event, and concurrently advocate for the physical education program, is to involve those from outside the regular physical education classes. At a minimum, classroom teachers, school administrators, and parents and friends can be formally invited. Further, some teachers and sport boards have invited the local press to their celebrations, and have garnered newspaper coverage of the final day's activities. Others have produced a highlights video and shown these together with a special guest speaker at a special players' breakfast.

■ *Honors.* There is almost no limit to the awards and the format of those awards that can be given at the culmination of a Sport Education season. As noted, since the goals of the model go beyond skillful play, the awards should reflect those goals. While it is certainly legitimate to honor the most outstanding team, other season components such as fair play, committee membership, skill improvement, and teamwork should also be recognized.

The Super Bowl Day at Ogletree shown in figure 13.2 is an example from an elementary school coeducational touch football season that highlights Eichberg's principles in action.

Here are some additional ideas for end-of-season culminating events from various places around the world that show the imagination teachers have demonstrated in creating end-of-season events that become significant experiences for students. We acknowledge two sources for some of these ideas. The first is Grant, Sharp, and Siedentop (1992) and the second is the teacher materials prepared for the Sport Education in Physical Education Project (SEPEP) by the Sport and Physical Activity Research Centre at Edith Cowan University in Perth, Western Australia.

1. *Schoolwide championship games.* Depending on how the competition is organized, this may involve several games between small-sided teams from each of the larger class teams who have competed in divisions that are typically varying skill levels.

2. *Awards day.* Often special guests are invited to present awards (e.g., team awards, fair play, refereeing, coaching). The guests may be school principals, community members, or sport figures. Local press representatives may be invited to garner publicity for the program and the students; the importance of regular press exposure should not be underestimated. In times of continuing time allotment and budget con-

Figure 13.2
AN ELEMENTARY SCHOOL CULMINATING EVENT IN TOUCH FOOTBALL

Super Bowl Day at Ogletree Elementary School

9:30 a.m. Tailgate party

Students, teachers, and parents have refreshments before the championship game. Students throw and catch footballs on the grass surrounding the tailgating tent.

10:00 Game-time preview

The field is marked with chalk. Student referees are in uniform and ready. A broadcasting table is set up with loudspeakers and students act as play-by-play and commentator broadcasters. Spectators are on the sidelines with teams in either end zone.

10:05 Introductions

Teams run through banners prepared by students for the occasion. The announcer introduces the players from each team. A photographer takes pictures of all introductions. Cheerleaders (boys and girls) for each team do pyramids on the sidelines. The national anthem is played.

10:10 Game begins

- The two teams that made it through the season competition to earn the right to play in the Super Bowl are each composed of one boy and three girls. Referees are chosen for their good performance throughout the season. Both team quarterbacks are girls. Play is lively, with especially good defensive play.
- At halftime, cheerleaders for each team do a prepared set of gymnastics-related cheers.
- Second-half play is equally good. Game ends in a tie. A brief overtime period is played that also ends in a tie. Teams are named co-champions. Team and individual awards are presented to players and referees.

11:00 Students return to class.

cerns, a public that is better informed of the quality of the physical education program will be more likely to support it.

3. *Great-game day.* Students enjoy drinks and snacks as they watch a great game of the sport that has been the focus of their season.

4. *Video highlights day.* Students take videos throughout the season as part of a media integration project. They edit the videos and present them to the class as part of the awards day. Internet links to these presentations can be made available to students so they can share them with their families. A variation of this is to film the championship games of the season and show them on the awards day.

5. *Visit to a local sporting venue.* A field trip to a local sporting venue for the sport of the season can show students how and where the sport is played locally. Representatives from the sport organization might describe how students can get involved in the community. Awards could be presented at the community venue rather than at school.

6. *Student–staff or student–parent game.* Students might compete against teachers or parents in the small-sided games they have played during their season. Awards can also be part of this kind of event.

7. *Between-class competitions.* As a culminating event, teams from various classes (e.g., the two sixth-grade classes in the school or the three high school classes that have done similar Sport Education seasons) can compete against each other in an intraclass format.

No matter the form of the culminating event, we encourage the involvement of all students. Here we outline one example from an elementary school hockey championship in which everyone in the class had a role in the finals and all the spectators were students and their teachers from other classes.

- Every student from the school who brought a canned food item for the Beat Bama Food Drive got a ticket to the event. (Each year before the Auburn University vs. University of Alabama football game, both cities have a competition to see which city can make the greater contribution to its local food bank.) The students could also bring posters to support their chosen team.
- Students from the participating class collected canned food and tickets.
- There was a VIP section on one side of the gym for parents, administrators, and students who brought 10 cans of food. Students from the participating class acted as security officials (wearing black T-shirts) by monitoring entry, and others acted as hosts and hostesses by serving drinks and snacks to those in VIP area.
- Press officers, some with digital cameras and others with video cameras, did live interviews with the teachers and coaches at the halftime break.
- Other attendees included officials (referees, goal judges), live team mascots, scorekeepers, and commentators.
- The game was broadcast onto the large screen in the activity area.

Culminating events can be recorded on video and used for several purposes. First, they can be uploaded to school websites, either on the entry news page or under the physical education section. Second, they can be played on televisions or large screens during open house events. Third, they can be live-streamed so that parents and friends who are unable to attend the event can follow the events online as they take place. These events can also be broadcast over the school radio and television network, with students as the commentary team and producers.

SUMMARY

Festivity is a primary characteristic of Sport Education. Let's face it: for too many students in too many places, physical education is a bore, especially for students in their transitional adolescent years. Creating a festive atmosphere for Sport Education is a reasonably low-cost endeavor. Bulletin boards, awards, and special recognition times do not have to be expensive in terms of cash outlays or teacher time. Students can and should be enlisted to help create these elements of festivity. A major potential payoff is that students get excited about their physical education experience and put more effort into the season. If they share that excitement with their parents, both the physical education program and the teacher are likely to get much more support.

© Human Kinetics

14

Meaningful Inclusion of Students With Special Needs

Chapter Objective

After reading this chapter, you will know how to employ modifications aimed at ensuring that students with special needs or disabilities have meaningful opportunities to participate successfully in Sport Education-based lessons.

Key Concepts

- Communication between the physical education teacher, the paraeducator, the student with a disability, and the student's parents and peers is critical to facilitate effective inclusion in Sport Education.
- The physical education teacher must consider teaching strategies, rule modifications, routines used during class, equipment, and environmental elements when including a student with a disability in the physical education setting.
- Adapted sport is an alternative form of play that can be valuable and important to the development of children and youth with and without disabilities.
- Engaging in adapted sport experiences allows students to develop a sense of disability awareness at some level.

The Sport Education curriculum model can serve as a useful framework within which to enhance the physical education experiences of students with disabilities. There are numerous practitioner-based papers and resources that provide useful strategies for including students with disabilities and for introducing disability sport into the physical education setting (e.g., Fittipaldi-Wert, Brock, Hastie, Arnold, & Guarino, 2009; Foley, Tindall, Lieberman, & Kim, 2007; Laughlin & Happel, 2016; Pressé, Block, Horton, & Harvey, 2011; Tindall & Foley, 2011; Tindall, Foley, & Lieberman, 2016). However, before delving into the various ways in which the Sport Education framework can be used to facilitate this inclusion or alternative sport experience, we will briefly review the legislative history and the main tenets of special education provision as they exist today in the United States. Next, we will address other issues relevant to the implementation of Sport Education for students with disabilities, including paraeducator support, knowledge of general characteristics for select areas of disability, and pedagogical considerations for adapting activities and facilitating inclusion. Then we will take a look at meaningful ways students with disabilities can participate in Sport Education as well as the role of typically developing peers who take part alongside them. Finally, we will examine disability sport as a way to further facilitate inclusion as well as to provide alternative sport experiences for *all* students through Sport Education.

ACCESS TO EDUCATION FOR STUDENTS WITH DISABILITIES

In the United States, there is a long list of federal laws advocating for the education of students with disabilities, all of which stand on the shoulders of earlier civil rights laws from the 1950s and 1960s. One early piece of legislation that many recognize as key to the protections identified in special education law today is *Brown v. Board of Education of Topeka, Kansas* (1954). In its decision, the U.S. Supreme Court declared that it was unconstitutional for educational institutions to segregate students by race.

It was during the 1970s that legislation specific to special education, and ultimately to physical education, came to fruition. Two laws that were extremely significant were the Rehabilitation Act of 1973 (Pub. L. 93-112, Section 504) and the Education for All Handicapped Children Act (EAHCA) passed in 1975 (Pub. L. 94-142). Section 504 of the Rehabilitation Act contained two crucial mandates involving any program or activity that receive financial assistance from the federal government: (1) it is illegal to the discriminate against individuals with disabilities within these programs and (2) such programs must provide equal opportunities for individuals with disabilities (Roth, Zittel, Pyfer, & Auxter, 2017; Winnick & Porretta, 2016). The EAHCA was slightly different, focusing on four areas specific to the education of persons with disabilities: (1) access to a free and appropriate education (FAPE), (2) the construction and implementation of an individualized education program or plan (IEP) for each student identified with a disability, (3) education provided in the least restrictive environment (LRE), and (4) physical education (the only subject specifically mentioned) provided as a direct educational service (Roth et al., 2017; Winnick & Porretta, 2016).

In 1990, Congress reauthorized the EAHCA, changing the title to the Individuals with Disabilities Education Act (IDEA; Pub. L. 101-476). While some minor elements of the original law were updated, the main tenets of FAPE, the IEP, LRE, and physical education as a direct educational service all remained, ensuring that education was tailored to each student's individual needs. In 1997, IDEA was again reauthorized (Pub. L. 105-17), with two sections added, highlighting the allowance of parental participation and the requirement of assessment as part of the IEP process added. Later, in 2004, IDEA was reapproved once more, but was now referred to as the Individuals with Disabilities Education Improvement Act (IDEIA, Pub. L. 108-446). It was during this time that education services would be aligned with the No Child Left Behind Act (NCLB; Pub. L. 107-110) of 2001, while also reinforcing the policy of inclusion and evidence-based education. Most recently, in December 2015, Congress amended the IDEIA through the Every Student Succeeds Act (ESSA; Pub. L. 114-95). In short, the ESSA is the reauthorization of the NCLB Act, which itself was the reauthorization of the Elementary and Secondary Education Act (ESEA; Pub. L. 89-10) of 1965.

From its original inception, the consistent goal of legislation as it pertains to special education continues to be this: to provide children with disabilities the same opportunity for an education as those students who do not have a disability. One way to ensure such educational equality is through the design and implementation of the student's Individualized Educational Plan or program (IEP). For you as the physical educator, active and sustained engagement with the IEP process is of the utmost importance.

THE USE OF IEPs AND THE ROLE THAT PHYSICAL EDUCATORS PLAY

As noted earlier, the EAHCA first mandated in 1975 that all students with disabilities receive an IEP as part of their education. Since then, this mandate has remained one of the four cornerstones of special education. Based on valid, reliable, and authentic assessment to determine the student's present level of performance in physical education content, the IEP is a working legal document prepared for a student with one or more disabilities and specifying the measurable goals and objectives in physical education that are to be achieved by that student over a set period of time. In addition to this, relevant teaching strategies, resources, supports, and the frequency and duration (minutes and days per week or stipulated time period) of physical education services necessary to achieve these goals as well as an indication of where these services are to be provided, are also identified and included as part of the plan. Some see the IEP as a useful tool in the administration and implementation of an inclusive policy. Whether viewed as a specific plan or as an overall means to facilitate schoolwide inclusion, the IEP is a contract between the school (district) and the child (and its parents or caregivers) identifying any and all services and resources deemed necessary to meet the educational goals of the student.

As part of this process, regular meetings are held with all those who have a role in the student's education. An IEP meeting therefore tends be multidisciplinary in nature and varied in terms of its membership. Two types of participants are usually present at most if not IEP meetings: those who must attend and those who attend when needed (Roth et al., 2017, pp.127-128). Periodic participants are those professionals who provide any direct or related services as part of the student's IEP. These individuals tend to be adapted physical education (APE) specialists, speech-language pathologists, occupational therapists, and mobility specialists. Other occasional participants may include the school nurse, an interpreter as required, and (if a transition from secondary school to the community is involved) any representatives from local agencies who might assist in this transition. The following individuals are required to attend each IEP meeting:

1. parents or legal guardians of the student,
2. at least one regular education teacher (if the student is participating in regular education),
3. at least one special education teacher who works directly with the student,

4. a representative of the school administration who has the authority to commit school or district resources,

5. an individual who can interpret any assessment results and provide guidance on subsequent instructional implications, and

6. anyone else the parents or school district deem necessary in assisting the student through the aforementioned direct or related services.

The student in question may also participate in the meeting whenever this is appropriate.

Because physical education is the only school subject required in the law, it is logical that you, as the physical educator, serve as the regular education teacher on a student's IEP committee. Physical education can be offered in an inclusive regular setting or as part of a specially designed or APE experience, whichever is deemed in the best interest of the student with a disability. As the expert, you can identify the appropriate content to be covered. While your role is vital to the IEP process, it is not a role that you should tackle alone, however. Support personnel, such as paraeducators, can provide additional insights.

THE ROLE OF PARAEDUCATORS

According to the National Education Association (www.nea.org), paraeducators (originally referred to as *paraprofessionals*) have provided essential support for students with disabilities for more than 40 years. The prefix *para* (derived from ancient Greek) means *alongside of* or *akin to*. Paraprofessionals in other professions, such as medicine and law, are called paramedics and paralegals; in other words, they work with and assist licensed professionals. Paraeducators serve similar functions in the educational team.

Who are paraeducators and what do they do specifically? The National Resource Center for Paraprofessionals (NRCP) coined the term paraeducator some time in the 1970s. Soon after, the NEA's Education Support Professional Quality (ESPQ) Department adopted the term to refer to a school employee who works alongside and under the supervision of a licensed or certificated educator to support and assist in providing instructional and other services to children, youth, and their families. While the licensed teacher (the educator) remains responsible for the overall conduct and management of student behavior; the design, implementation, and evaluation of the instructional program; and the general development of students, paraeducators remain an essential part of the educational process. In the past, paraeducators were primarily responsible for various administrative duties and one-on-one student assistance where necessary, with very little interaction or collaboration with the teachers, their professional counterparts. Today, most paraeducators assume broader responsibilities, spending noticeably more time working with teachers in order to provide deeper and more impactful instruction, assistance, and support to students, working in small groups as well as one-on-one. They also devote a significant amount of time to modifying materials, collecting data on students, and assisting in the planning and implementation of behavior management plans, while continuing to provide personal care assistance when necessary. Given their unique skills and training, forging positive working relationships with physical education professionals would be extremely beneficial in meeting the unique educational needs of students with disabilities (Modell, Collier, & Jackson, 2007).

According to Bryan, McCubbin, and van der Mars (2013), the role of the paraeducator in physical education is understood differently by the teacher and the paraeducator. Overall, paraeducators and physical education teachers agreed that the paraeducator role is a "constant stretching and contracting position" that moves primarily between teacher support and the care and protection of the student (Bryan et al., 2013, p.179). However, while the role appeared to be clear to paraeducators, teachers conveyed quite the opposite, noting that the paraeducator role had never been fully described to them. Additionally, Bryan and her colleagues found that teachers were unsure of their own role as it related both to the students with disabilities and to the paraeducators who accompanied them (Bryan et al., 2013, p.179). For paraeducators to feel valued, effective, and essential, the teacher plays a key role in helping them develop a sense of ownership (Lytle, Lieberman, & Aiello, 2007). Using Sport Education terminology, while the physical education teacher sometimes assumes the role of league commissioner, allowing the paraeducator to serve as a co-commissioner would go a long way in building a shared investment toward an inclusive learning experience for students with disabilities. Other ways in which you can help encourage or reinforce this investment is by introducing the paraeducator formally to your class as a co-teacher, adding the paraeducator's name on the office door, giving them appropriate clothing (e.g., collared or dry-fit shirts, shorts, warm-up pants), asking them to work with you in designing the unit or lesson plan, and perhaps inviting them to physical education in-service trainings as well as state conferences (e.g., Lytle et al., 2007; Modell et al., 2007). Anything that acknowledges the paraeducator as an equal member of the physical education team will go a long way to creating a shared and productive ownership of the learning environment.

KNOWING THE DISABILITIES

There are too many disability areas for us to go into specific detail within a single chapter. But it is important to identify and highlight some of the general yet predominant characteristics of each so as to give future and current teachers an idea of how such disabilities might present themselves in the physical education setting. Doing so will better inform teachers when using the Sport Education model with certain students with disabilities. *Predominant characteristics* refers to the common physical, cognitive, and behavioral patterns that physical educators can expect to encounter in students with one or several disabilities. What follows is a very basic overview (see table 14.1) that is by no means exhaustive, but it does provide some relevant information on the more overarching areas of disability (Roth et al., 2017; Winnick & Porretta, 2016).

FACILITATING AN INCLUSIVE SPORT EDUCATION SETTING

Physical educators often ask questions like How do I include student X with a disability in my class? or How can I adapt activities for this student? Physical education teachers have been well trained in planning and implementing logical and effective instructional strategies for students without disabilities. But teacher education programs often have only a limited focus on including of students with disabilities. Many students with disabilities can safely and successfully participate in general physical education with minimal, if any, accommodations and supports. However, some children do benefit from specially designed and logical adaptations, some of which are provided by the student or through communication with the parents. But where this is not the case, the following general approach has been shown to be effective in terms of including students with disabilities into the setting and adapting activities for them.

Sport Education provides a unique way for students to experience the content of physical education, whether it be traditional games (e.g., invasion, net-wall),

Table 14.1 Predominant Behavioral Characteristics Specific to Selected Disability Areas, and Recommended Instructional Strategies

Disability area	Predominant characteristics (psychomotor, cognitive, affective, communication)	Instructional strategies to consider
Pervasive development disorders (PDDs) (autism, Asperger's)	• Severe and pervasive impairment in several areas of growth; specifically, social interaction skills and communication skills • Significant developmental delays • Global and comprehensive language disorders • Abnormal and stereotypical behavior patterns, interests, and activities • Social isolation • Intellectual disabilities (sometimes, but not always)	• Be planned and organized. • Use management routines consistently, involving the learner and an adult engaging in a meaningful activity that requires communication. • *Applied behavior analysis (ABA):* Use a series of trials that involve instruction, a prompt, and an opportunity to respond, followed by feedback from the teacher. • *Picture exchange communication systems (PECS)* enable the student to choose or trade a picture of an item or physical activity experience for what she or he wants to do. • *Visual schedules:* Use pictures to help the student predict what will occur during the class.
Hearing impairments (HIs) and deafness	• **Hearing impairment:** Whether permanent or fluctuating, adversely affects a child's educational performance • **Deafness:** A hearing impairment so severe that the child is impaired in processing linguistic information through hearing with or without amplification, which in turn affects a child's educational performance • **Prelingual deafness:** Hearing loss before the acquisition of any linguistic or speech skills • **Postlingual deafness:** Hearing loss after having acquired speech and language skills	• Use interpreters whenever possible, remembering to make eye contact with the student rather than the interpreter. • Demonstrate first, then move the student through the pattern. • Use technology for support (e.g., PowerPoint, YouTube with subtitles activated, iPads). • Use peer-to-peer instruction, with task cards containing clear images and concise text for teaching cues, game rules, etc.
Visual impairments (VIs) and blindness	• **Congenital:** Impairment that was present at birth; the student often may have motor delays because of having been overprotected when young. • **Acquired:** Impairment that occurred after birth; the student may have had previous sight experiences that aid in motor learning; level of motor proficiency may vary. • Classifications include partially sighted, low vision, legally blind, and totally blind • Students may have issues with depth perception, field of vision, hand-eye coordination, visual memory, as well as visual-spatial development and integration	• Always address the student by first name. • Explain as well as demonstrate. • Place students at the front of the class. • Use large-print letters and numbers or Braille instructions for task cards. • Use peer tutors for active play whenever possible. • Provide kinesthetic stimulation, manually guiding students through the desired movement. • Use concrete experiences with objects and events (audible balls and bases). • Use guide wires and guide runners.

Disability area	Predominant characteristics (psychomotor, cognitive, affective, communication)	Instructional strategies to consider
Intellectual delays and disabilities (IDs)	• Significantly subaverage general intellectual functioning existing concurrently with deficits in adaptive behavior • IDs manifest during the developmental period, adversely affecting a child's educational performance • Generally categorized as mild, moderate, severe, or profound ID, based on IQ; students with mild or moderate ID would mostly likely be fully included	• Overteach content whenever possible. • Put students in a less demanding position to promote success in accomplishing tasks. • Follow the same routine daily (e.g., parts of the lesson, cues, groupings). • If possible, use peer tutors to assist and instruct students with ID, and sensitize others prior to the students arriving in class.
Learning disabilities (LDs) (dyslexia, dyscalculia, dysgraphia, dyspraxia, attention deficit hyperactivity disorder [ADHD])	• A disorder in one or more of the basic psychological processes involved in understanding or using language, spoken or written, which may manifest itself in imperfect ability to listen, think, speak, write, spell, or perform mathematical calculations • **ADHD:** Students may consistently make careless mistakes, seem not to listen or follow through on instructions, have difficulty organizing tasks or lose things necessary for tasks, and can be easily distracted. • Students may also fidget or squirm while seated, run about, climb or talk excessively, interrupt or intrude on others, or have difficulty engaging in activities quietly.	• Use station teaching. • Use a games approach to reduce the potential for failure. • Use positive behavior reinforcers (especially contingent social reinforcement). • Keep instructions to a minimum and break tasks into small learning steps. • Use a top-down, task-specific whole-part-whole teaching approach. • To increase attention, use a consistent daily routine. • Reduce extraneous stimuli; for example, keep equipment not being used out of sight. • To encourage desired behaviors, use the same visual and auditory cues for movements.
Physically disabling conditions and motor delays (cerebral palsy, amputations, walker or wheelchair users)	• Unusually slow development of fine motor or gross motor abilities. Fine motor abilities include grasping a pencil or handling a spoon. Gross motor abilities include walking, hopping, galloping, skipping, sliding, and other general movements required for sport or physical activity. • It is not uncommon for students with learning disabilities to experience motor delays (e.g., dyspraxia) as well.	• Shorten the time of games and practice sessions. • Reduce the size of the playing area. • Modify the rules of games; for example, allowing extra bounces in tennis, limited or no defense against student with movement issues, or play doubles or triples instead of singles for net or wall games (i.e., three-on-two instead of the standard two-on-two). • Use assistive devices; for example, add more wheelchairs for nondisabled peers to use during the activity.

aquatics, athletics, dance, gymnastics, or health-related fitness activities. Regardless of the framework, there are certain basic considerations for attempting to include students with disabilities. While not inclusion in and of itself, adapting activities to allow fuller participation for a student with disabilities during a Sport Education season can help facilitate an inclusive learning environment. Identifying effective teaching strategies, determining how equipment will be used, and creating and implementing consistent and effective behavior management plans and routines are all areas to be revisited. In this chapter's web resource, you will find additional information with specific resources for teachers who have students with special needs in their classes.

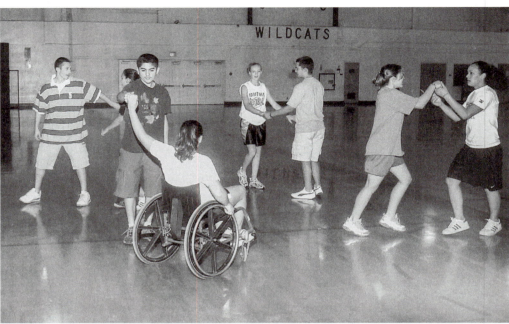

© Human Kinetics.

Sport Education provides a unique way for students to experience the content of physical education, whether it be traditional games (e.g., invasion, net-wall), aquatics, athletics, dance, gymnastics, or health-related fitness activities. Regardless of the framework, there are certain basic considerations for attempting to include students with disabilities.

Instructional Considerations for Inclusion

According to Collier (2011, p. 125), "Universal design for learning (sometimes referred to as *universal design for instruction*) suggests that instruction should be designed at the start with *all* learners in mind." In the past, most physical education teachers thought that students with disabilities or special needs require specialized curricula designed for their specific needs. But according to Friend (2008), this trend has begun to change as teachers are becoming more supportive of students with disabilities taking part in the same curriculum with their nondisabled peers, with modifications and accommodations implemented by teachers as required. Given the vast array of content covered in physical education (e.g., aquatics, track and field, dance, gymnastics, invasion and net-wall and target or striking games, outdoor adventure, and health-related activity), teachers are becoming better at using the concept of universal design to include students with disabilities in shared curricula. Specifically, they are becoming more adept at identifying, modifying, and administering as necessary the teaching strategies and management techniques employed and the equipment used to ensure learning opportunities for all students in the physical education setting.

These considerations are particularly important when you are attempting to adapt activities or facilitate the inclusion of students with disabilities into the physical education setting, whether through Sport Education or otherwise. An effective technique to help teachers include students with disabilities is through a concept and teaching resource devised by Ken Black (2004) as part of an initiative with the Disability Sport Unit of the Australian Sports Commission. Black developed the *Disability Education Program (DEP) Activity Cards* resource. The content on the cards is based on the

TREE principle, which serves as a starting point for teachers when planning for and teaching students with disabilities. Similar to the activity modifications highlighted by Lieberman and Houston-Wilson (2018), the TREE principle prompts educators to consider

- which **teaching styles and strategies** might work best for a student with a particular disability,
- what **rule** modifications would most effectively permit the student to engage in the activity or sport,
- what **equipment** should be used and how it could be modified, and
- what **environmental** factors should be considered.

It is important to note that although a link to the DEP cards is provided in the references section, finding the resource itself can be difficult. Fortunately, the TREE principles have been included as part of the *Best Start: Inclusive Schools Project* from the Irish Wheelchair Association – Sport (Niland, Barry, Dempsey, & Daly, 2010). This is a free resource and much easier to locate.

Teaching Styles and Strategies

When planning and delivering lessons, teachers must do so in a way that will maximize everyone's learning while at the same time cater for the ability level of all. A difficult task indeed. For example, teacher-directed instruction (also referred to as direct teaching) is more effective for certain students with disabilities than other instructional strategies such as peer-reciprocal, small group, or cooperative learning. While Sport Education is designed to move the learning environment from more teacher-led to student-led instruction and learning, the way teaching strategies are used can be helpful, depending on how students with a disability can best engage as well as by what means they can adapt. For example, students with intellectual disabilities tend to need more straightforward direction from the teacher, usually with a command-style or practice-style approach (Mosston, 1992). In command style, the teacher clearly says or demonstrates what is to be learned or accomplished and the students copy it. In practice style, the teacher explains or demonstrates the task and the students perform practice trials either on their own or with peers. The difference between the two styles is that the practice style does permit some decision-making by the students. The same approach can be used for students with other disabilities, such as visual impairments or blindness, hearing impairments or deafness, learning disabilities, or physical disabilities and motor delays. For students with mild levels of autism, instruction should be provided together with visual displays. Oral instruction alone may pose problems for students who have difficulty processing language, require extra time to complete tasks, or struggle to block out background stimulation. Using visual aids in conjunction with direct instruction helps the student to focus better on the task, so this approach may be more appropriate than peer teaching, small group, or cooperative learning approaches. Students with autism may eventually respond to such teaching strategies, but you should generally begin with more direct-teaching and visual approaches for such students.

Rules and Routines

During practice, game or match rules can be changed in order to assist both students with disabilities and those who are lower skilled. Initially, what is important is the execution of the skill. Examples of rule modifications that can help increase the success of students with disabilities include allowing extra bounces in tennis or allowing double dribbles and extra steps (traveling) or increased distances between opposing players when defending or attempting to score in basketball. Other examples include closer tee-off areas or increased par (number of throws) for each hole in disc golf, no offsides in soccer, requiring students without disabilities to use their nondominant hand when dribbling a basketball, holding onto a peer when performing balance skills in a gymnastics routine, and minimizing the distance of the orienteering route for those with visual impairments or movement issues. As the student progresses, the teacher can make the activities more complex by further adjusting or even adding rules when they are ready. If effective, such rule changes during practice can also be added to actual competition. (For more examples of such modifications, see chapter 7.)

Routines are another important aspect of the TREE principle. For many students with pervasive development disorders (autism) or intellectual delays, clear and consistent routines are essential in helping them understand or engage during class. Routines can be managerial routines designed for the whole class to follow or other routines that may be specific for students with disabilities. Managerial routines include how a teacher starts and ends a class, takes attendance, moves students into and out of groups, signals for attention (freeze), and places equipment in the gymnasium, as well as the process for students to get and return equipment and determine a home position for the equipment. Specific routines for students with disabilities are those that allow them to engage in a more comfortable, consistent, and productive way. Examples of these routines for students with autism or intellectual delay include having when things occur consistently in a particular order during the lesson or making sure each task or activity has a clear beginning and end before moving on to something else. Though considered a teaching strategy as well, the use of a token boards reward system can also serve as a useful routine: the student receives a token when a positive behavior is displayed or a task is completed correctly. There is a reward for a certain number of tokens earned, for example, free time in the gym, using the computer, activity of the student's choice, and so on.

Regardless of the type used, routines must be well planned and clear for all to understand, they must become regular in their use, and they must happen predictably in the same order each time. The absence of clear and consistent routines is more likely to result in students with autism or intellectual delays being confused or getting frustrated, which contributes to a lack of engagement. To help avoid this, you are strongly advised to consult with the parents of the student, as well as with the paraeducators and other classroom teachers working with them, to identify any routines used at home or elsewhere throughout the school day. Doing so will allow you to incorporate similar (or the same) routines into your physical education lessons.

Equipment

Not all equipment can be used as originally intended by students with disabilities. Some equipment may be too heavy, too long, or too fast for students to practice with or use in general. For this reason, you should consider equipment options that will allow students (depending on their disability) to practice or participate in a way that suits them. One helpful approach is to have students experiment with different types of equipment to determine an appropriate starting point. Doing so allows students with disabilities to experience the differences this creates when practicing techniques or playing in games, modified or otherwise. If it makes technique practice or gameplay challenging but still achievable, you (and ultimately the student) have a place to begin in terms of progression up to what is required for effective participation in the future.

When determining how equipment can be used for students with disabilities, you should consider what Healy (2013) referred to as the *Five Ss of Equipment Adaptation* (size, sound, support, surface, and speed). In terms of *size*, all equipment can be adapted in order to allow the user to be more successful. For example, ball size can be adapted so the students can throw, kick, or strike more efficiently. A smaller ball may be used during gameplay for students who cannot effectively grip, pass, or throw a normal-sized ball. Conversely, a larger ball may be needed in soccer for students who have coordination difficulties. Other size considerations for equipment could also include different-sized targets such as hoops, goals, and nets. With larger targets, students with visual impairments or general coordination issues may be more successful in their practice attempts. Likewise, the size (and weight) of striking implements should be considered, taking into account the level of grip strength and overall strength that students with motor control issues may possess. For example, students with strength issues may experience more success by using a shorter and lighter bat, racquet, or hurley (*camán*), a striking implement used in hurling or camogie, a sport played in Ireland. The size of the surface area of a striking implement could also contribute to a student's success in making contact with an object (e.g., a cricket bat, or fat bat, instead of a regulation softball bat).

For the aspect of *sound*, equipment that makes noise can be of great benefit for students with visual impairments. According to Healy (2013), sound can be added to targets, cones, and other equipment by using simple things like security beepers or bells that can be fastened to equipment using Velcro or tape. Special throwing equipment, such as flying discs or balls that make sound, can be purchased from equipment vendors. If budget is tight, a bell or beads can easily be inserted into the ball with little alteration or damage to it. A *support* form of adaptation can be particularly useful when you are teaching activities that involve striking a ball with a bat or target games like bowling or bocce. For example, in the case of practicing striking, you can place the ball on a tee or suspend it with a string. For bowling or bocce, you may use a ramp, allowing students with motor development issues the ability to line up or target their attempt. In these examples, the batting tee and the ramp are forms of support. The next aspect you should consider is the *surface* of certain pieces of equipment. Adapting the surface can greatly improve its use for many students, especially for those with visual impairments and fine motor issues. For those with visual impairments, equipment that includes bright colors as part of the surface area will help them to see it more clearly. For students with fine motor skill issues, wrapping the handles of bats and racquets with tape or a coarse thin rope, for example, will allow them to grip it more efficiently. Likewise, equipment that uses Velcro can greatly assist students when practicing both throwing (Velcro grip) and catching (Velcro target) skills. Lastly, reducing the *speed* of some equipment can greatly assist students with a variety of different disabilities. Ball type, in particular, often needs to be adapted so that it moves more slowly for easier catching, kicking, or striking. In volleyball, for example, if the regulation size ball still moves too fast for students with visual or coordination impairments, you might introduce a beach ball that may vary in size as well, allowing greater chances for the student to track, defend, and make contact during practice or gameplay. In badminton or table tennis, a balloon can used instead of a shuttlecock or a table tennis ball. Most physical education equipment companies now offer a wide variety of modified balls that differ in trajectory, speed, and amount of bounce.

Environment

The last aspect of the TREE principle is the *environment* in which instruction occurs, both in the gymnasium and on the field. This is a unique aspect; it may include considerations similar to the teaching strategies and rules and routines aspects of the TREE principle. When planning and organizing class activities, you should consider some simple changes in the setup that may make the whole learning environment more acceptable for all students. One example is the level of sound (specifically the use of music) for students who have pervasive development disorders (autism) or visual impairments. Students with autism may either overreact or pay no attention whatsoever to many ordinary sensations, smells, sights, and, in the physical education environment, sounds. This is because such individuals process sensory information much differently than those who do not have the disorder. Therefore, you will want to be mindful of how you use music. For example, students with autism might not be able to screen out extraneous noises; conversely, they might find certain sounds very uncomfortable and distracting, which causes them to exhibit a noticeable level of anxiety or to become irritable, placing their hands over their ears in reaction.

Another example of environment is the surface area on which students practice or the shape of the playing area in general. Students who use a wheelchair or a walker for mobility may have great difficulty on the soccer pitch, so it might be more appropriate to practice and play on a harder surface, like a tennis court or the gym floor. Likewise, if the playing area is too big, say for softball or cricket, you should consider shortening the distance between bases or the amount of the field to cover while on defense. For students with visual impairments or blindness, you could alter the floor's texture by using a Poly Spot or a rug taped to the floor with special gymnasium tape to mark the area where exercises are to be completed. Likewise, to identify boundaries, you can place a rubber carpet or doormat runner along the wall in the gym or on the playing field so students with a visual impairment will know when they have stepped out of bounds. This approach is particularly useful in the gym setting because it alerts students that a wall or object is nearby and they need to slow down and stop. Designing an effective environment for all students can be challenging, but you can have students without disabilities (i.e., team members) assist you. Moreover, by talking with students with a disability, their parents, and the other students in the class, you can identify many considerations and modifications to suit all.

BEHAVIOR MANAGEMENT CONSIDERATIONS

Effective and consistent behavior management strategies are essential to facilitating an inclusive environment. Students tend to go off task for a number of reasons. They may be experiencing problems at home; they could be tired, bored, lonely, frustrated, depressed, or angry at someone; or they may just want to annoy the teacher. Whatever the reason, you must have a plan in place to teach and reinforce appropriate behavior in the physical education setting and beyond. It is essential that you know the potential triggers that cause students to misbehave, and have strategies in place to remove such triggers or to de-escalate behaviors once the misbehavior has been triggered. Specific triggers for many students typically include having a change in their normal routine, feeling that they cannot complete a task adequately (fear of failure and embarrassment) or that the task is too easy (becoming bored), being ignored or having their feelings hurt by others, being bullied at school, or possibly experiencing physical or verbal abuse at home. Regardless of the reason, these triggers often originate in the home but become exacerbated at school in the form of behavior issues. This is particularly important for all students and you can address it through the TREE principle; specifically, through your teaching strategies and rules, routines, and expectations (RREs) as a way to structure the learning environment. It is most important to practice behavior management and RREs early and often at the beginning of each term.

Introducing such concepts as a five-finger contract or player-team contracts as part of Sport Education has proven to be effective in providing a shared responsibility not only for how students will behave toward each other but also how the teacher and the students will interact. A five-finger contract is a form of a full value contract, an agreement whereby individuals seek to create the most effective learning environment for all participants. The students and the teacher are asked to agree on a set of behavioral guidelines as a way to ensure that everyone understands what is expected and what is accepted. In the five-finger contract, each finger represents a different guideline, which can change depending on the class. An example of a contract might include the following: the *thumb* could represent creating value for yourself and others for each activity, the *index finger* could represent taking care of yourself (looking out for number one), the *middle finger* is pretty universal and could instead represent no putdowns or having respect others, the *ring finger* could stand for commitment to each other or to faithfully trying new things, and the *pinky finger* could stand for helping others or looking out for the little guy (those who are out of their comfort zone and need support). Prior to introducing the behavior contract, it would be helpful for you to meet with the parents of students with particular disabilities to identify any potential modifications to the contract or approach. We also recommend that you include the paraeducators and utilize their expertise when designing and implementing any behavior management plan.

MEANINGFUL PARTICIPATION IN SPORT EDUCATION FOR STUDENTS WITH DISABILITIES

When implementing the Sport Education model, you must consider how students with disabilities will participate to the fullest extent possible in both player and nonplayer roles. Equitable competition as players or performers for students with disabilities will vary depending on their level of disability. Originating in the Paralympic movement, equitable competition is the assessment, classification, and grouping of athletes with mild, moderate, or severe physical, intellectual, and visual disabilities into sports classes according to how much their impairment affects their ability to carry out the fundamental activities in a specific sport. Doing so provides a structure for fair and equitable competition within adapted (disability) sport. While such a system is not necessary in the physical education setting, the concept is still important for students with disabilities participating as players or performers (and even as nonplayers) alongside their nondisabled peers.

So that you can provide a meaningful player or performer role for students with disabilities, we strongly recommend that you learn as much as possible about the student's abilities and preferences of engagement with peers before they enter the physical education setting. This can be done in many ways, but the most effective is by talking with the parents first and with the student soon afterward. Many parents of children with disabilities would agree that, while they may not be experts in the particular area of disability, they *are* experts in how the disability impacts their child. If at all possible, it would be beneficial for you to meet with the parents prior to the student attending class, especially if the student is new to the school. In most cases, parents are happy to speak to the teacher separately at first and, if desired, to the entire class afterwards. This allows the student's peers to ask questions and prepare to welcome their new classmate. Even if the student is not new to the school, possibly having grown up with their peers through elementary school, having a parent address the class can still be very helpful. After talking with the parents, you should talk to the student and ask them how they want, or think they want, to participate. After this, the parents and the student should have a conversation with the class, especially with the student's Sport Education team. Together, the teacher, the other students, and even the student with the disability can decide on ways in which to the latter can effectively participate in both player and nonplayer roles. For example, the students may decide to alter the rules of the game by having no defense assigned to the student with a disability or by having another teammate push a student in a wheelchair or catch a pass for a student with motor delays such as cerebral palsy during invasion-style games. Or the students could decide to play different versions of a game; for example, during a soccer season, teams playing against another team that includes a student with a visual impairment may choose to all play blindfolded five-a-side soccer with a ball that makes noise. Whatever the modifications, students can work together to find practical ways to include teammates with disabilities in both practice and gameplay. The key is to determine how you can create a more equitable environment.

There are also many ways students with disabilities can contribute to their team in a nonplaying role. Either on their own or with some help from teammates, students with a disability are more than able to serve as captains, trainers, nutritionists, statisticians, publicists, scouts, referees, scorekeepers, and so on. It is extremely important, however, that you not fall into the trap of having the Sport Education experience for students with a disability revolve solely around nonplayer roles. All too often, they are locked into the scorekeeper or statistician role for the entire season and never see any actual playing time. While this seems like a logical way for them to contribute to their team, it should not be the first or only way. Here too, the teacher, the other students, and the student with a disability can work together to find ways to assist their teammate in completing nonplayer roles. For instance, students with intellectual delays or learning disabilities may have a teammate sit or stand beside them while undertaking the scorekeeping and refereeing roles. Likewise, students may help their teammate who is acting as the team publicist conduct interviews when creating player biographies or team updates. The same approach can be adopted for setting the eating plan as the team nutritionist, the warm-up and cool-down routines as the team trainer, or when entering data into a computer as the team statistician. With this increased level of cooperation among teammates, students with disabilities can generally undertake any of the nonplayer roles with ease. It is important to ensure that the typically developing peers only assist their teammates whenever possible but do not complete the task for their teammate instead of the teammate doing it themselves.

THE ROLE OF TYPICALLY DEVELOPING PEERS WITHIN SPORT EDUCATION

The role that typically developing peers (i.e., students without disabilities) play during an inclusive Sport Education season is critical to its success. As alluded to earlier in the chapter, depending on their level of ability, students with disabilities can engage in Sport Education in both player and nonplayer roles through the TREE principles: appropriate teaching strategies, rule modifications, specialized equipment, and various environmental considerations. Regardless of the approach, students without disabilities can greatly assist their classmate with this engagement in many practical ways.

In the context of player or performer roles, peers without disabilities should understand and faithfully adhere to any rule changes during practice and gameplay. For example, during practice sessions, teams can prepare using scenarios in which players are allowed to take extra steps when dribbling a basketball or extra bounces during a pickleball game. Likewise, players without disabilities should be encouraged to participate in practice sessions and gameplay at a speed that allows success for their classmate with a disability. With your assistance, teams can devise more appropriate defensive strategies when competing against a team or player with a disability, such as purposely playing a very lackadaisical defense, playing defense with one less player, or possibly not having a defender at all. Whatever the case, faithfully following newly adapted rules or participating at an appropriate level throughout the season are two ways students can demonstrate caring, understanding, and patience, ultimately earning valuable fair play points for this behavior.

Typically developing peers can also earn team points in many different ways in the context of nonplayer roles. Again with your guidance, nondisabled peers can help teammates with disabilities to complete duties such as captain or co-captain, trainer, nutritionist, publicist, statistician, referee, and so on. For example, a student with a disability might need help in completing the duties of statistician. This assistance can come from a teammate who sits with the student and helps input the data. Nondisabled peers can even ask their teammates with disabilities to assist them in completing their own roles and duties. Likewise, students with similar roles, but from different teams, can also help each other to complete various duties and tasks. In the aforementioned example, statisticians from two separate teams (one student with a disability and one without) can work together to enter game results and play stats into the Excel spreadsheet on the computer. The same approaches can be used for other roles as well. A team nutritionist, for example, may receive help from a teammate (either with or without disabilities) to construct a healthy eating plan for the team, or nutritionists (one with a disability and one without) from two different teams can work in tandem to complete the same task. Regardless of the situation, duties within the various roles must be completed and students should be encouraged to help each other fulfill these duties. In this way, students begin to understand that not helping teammates (with or without disabilities) who might be struggling to complete their tasks is an undesirable characteristic of any truly successful team, and diminishes the fair play culture you are attempting to create.

ADAPTED SPORT

Adapted sport, sometimes referred to as disability sport, consists of sports created or altered to meet the needs of individuals with disabilities. The term *adapted sport* includes disability sport (e.g., deaf sports), which typically focuses on segregated participation in regular or adapted sport (Winnick & Porretta, 2016). Because many disabled sports are based on existing able-bodied sports modified to meet the needs of persons with a disability, they are sometimes referred to as adapted sports. An example would be rugby as a regular sport and wheelchair rugby as an adapted sport. Not all disabled sports are adaptable, however. A number of sports specifically created for persons with disabilities have no equivalent nondisabled sport (e.g., goalball).

Using adapted sport and Sport Education as a framework to introduce typically developing peers to issues surrounding disability can be a unique and beneficial aspect of an effective and worthwhile physical education program. It can help shape and reinforce students' positive attitudes and perceptions toward their peers with disabilities. Research conducted by Loovis and Loovis (1997), Ellery, Rauschenbach, and Stewart (2000), Panagiotou, et al. (2008), and Tindall (2013) all demonstrated that providing students with empathy experiences through adapted sport can be an excellent way to develop in them what Wilson and Lieberman (2000) identify as *disability awareness*. There are three developmental levels through which by participation in adapted sport students (and teachers) gain *exposure* to various disability-related issues as they pertain to sport (Level I), *experience* what others with certain disabilities might go through when trying to engage in sport (Level II), and demonstrate *advocacy and ownership* (Level III) for persons with disabilities that extends beyond sport and the school setting in general.

Through Sport Education, physical education teachers can introduce adapted sport to students (both those with and without disabilities) in two distinct ways (Davis, 2011). The first is to provide the experience to students without disabilities as a standalone adapted sport unit or season; possibly through the lens and theme of the Paralympic Games. Different from the Special Olympics, where competitions are held primarily for individuals with intellectual delays, the Paralympics is a series of international contests for athletes with physical disabilities, associated with and held immediately following the Summer and Winter Olympic Games. Persons with physical disabilities and impairments (e.g., cerebral palsy, ataxia, amputees, wheelchair users) and visual impairments (including blindness) primarily compete in the Paralympics (Paralympics.org, 2013). Examples of adapted sports that are both interesting and easy to facilitate using Sport Education include sit-volleyball, goalball, wheelchair basketball, five-a-side (blind) soccer, and beep baseball (this last is not a Paralympic sport). Laughlin and Happel (2016) offer a nice example of how goalball can be offered specifically through Sport Education.

The second way to introduce adapted sport centers on students with disabilities who participate with their nondisabled peers as part of the Sport Education season. A student who uses a wheelchair, one with cerebral palsy, or one with a mild level of intellectual delay as a characteristic of Down Syndrome could all be included in a regular physical education class. In these instances, as part of combined unit, adapted sports could be added to the original version of the sport. For example, sit-volleyball could be added as an aspect of a volleyball season, wheelchair basketball or wheelchair rugby could be incorporated as part of a basketball or rugby unit, or beep baseball as part of a softball unit. Regardless of the approach, adding an adapted sport as a standalone or modified season can provide a new range of opportunities for teachers to engage all students in Sport Education in more meaningful ways. This can lead to more positive attitudes toward disability and inclusion as well as to a more in-depth appreciation of sport.

SUMMARY

In this chapter, we provided a brief overview of key education legislation for students with disabilities relevant to physical education, with particular attention paid to the IEP process, the physical educator's role in the process, and the benefits of working together with paraeducators. The majority of the chapter, however, highlighted ways in which students with disabilities and special needs can be included in a Sport Education season. Overall, there are many factors that affect teaching in the area of physical education, through Sport Education or otherwise. Teachers who can considerately, creatively, and effectively use many different and logical approaches to meet the specific needs of students with disabilities are more likely to experience success. With this in mind, the notion of universal design and the aforementioned TREE principles are critical to this success. The use of logical and appropriate teaching strategies, rule and equipment modifications and adaptions, classwide and specific routines for students with disabilities, and environmental considerations must all be taken into account in relation to both player and nonplayer roles. These considerations are critical not only for students with disabilities but also for their nondisabled peers, who must also understand their role in the inclusive Sport Education setting. Finally, we closed with making a case for the place of adapted sport experiences for students with and without disabilities as a means to further deepen the Sport Education experience in a more contextualized way.

Promoting Student Voice and Choice

Chapter Objective

After reading this chapter, you will be able to identify ways in which students can be given opportunities for making decisions about the planning and administration of a season.

Key Concepts

- Teachers who use autonomy-supportive motivating styles (rather than controlling styles) tend to produce classes in which there are higher levels of engagement, in which students show greater persistence during tasks, and where students report they are more intrinsically motivated.
- Sport Education is a particularly suitable way for teachers to incorporate students' ideas and recommendations.
- Giving students autonomy is a key factor in enhancing the motivation of students toward physical education.
- A number of built-in aspects of Sport Education allow students to make decisions independently of the teacher.
- Incorporating a sport board or student committees allows the teacher to give the students responsibility for the conduct of specific seasons.
- After significant experience with the model, students are capable of creating their own Sport Education seasons with minimal input from the teacher.

Across all subject areas, be it math, social studies, or physical education, teachers motivate students by adopting interpersonal styles that range from highly controlling to highly autonomy-supportive. Controlling teachers generally set a specific agenda for students to follow and then use directives and extrinsic motivators to encourage students toward that agenda. Typical language includes "you should follow the guidelines," "you have to," and "you are expected to." Autonomy-supportive teachers on the other hand, generally invite, welcome, and incorporate students' thoughts, feelings, and behaviors into the flow of lessons. In their case, typical language includes "you can choose," "you might want to," and "what ideas do you have about?"

Motivating style is important because students of autonomy-supportive teachers display markedly more positive classroom functioning and educational outcomes than do students of controlling teachers. In other words, students whose teachers are autonomy-supportive show higher levels of engagement in classes, greater persistence during tasks, higher levels of learning, and greater satisfaction from their experiences (Su & Reeve, 2011).

And yet, many teachers persist with controlling behaviors despite the overwhelming evidence that it undermines positive outcomes. Reasons can include pressure from school administrators and parents, or perceived student lack of motivation. Still other influences arise from within the teachers themselves because they believe that controlling motivating strategies are more effective than are autonomy-supportive ones. This is especially the case when teachers enter the classroom with a controlling motivation of their own.

As we have noted with respect to student roles, one of the main goals of Sport Education is for students to share in the planning and administration of their sport experiences. This sharing is one way in which the teacher can create a more autonomy-supportive class environment. Indeed, research has suggested that students' increased enthusiasm for Sport Education could be attributed to the fact that much of the decision-making and control of the experience was determined by the students themselves (Grant, 1992; Hastie, 1998).

Figure 15.1 outlines a so-called stairway of autonomy showing how teachers can provide opportunities for students to take responsibility for various aspects in a season of Sport Education. At the base level are those built-in elements that appear across all seasons, including the decisions students make about their team identity (e.g., name, colors, mascot, chant), and about which students will take upon the different team and officiating roles. Teams are also given a degree of autonomy in terms of how they will practice, and what aspects of the game they wish to focus on. In cases of graded competitions, students are given the authority to decide who will represent them in different contests. The remainder of this chapter explores the three higher levels of autonomy that can be given to students once they have experience with Sport Education: (1) incorporating a sport board, (2) involving students as committee members who make decisions about selected elements of a season, and (3) giving student full autonomy in creating a season on their own.

SPORT BOARD

Many teachers choose to include a sport board as a feature of their Sport Education seasons. The sport board is a student group that assists the teacher with ensuring high quality sport experiences for all students. This can be a unique and very powerful feature of a Sport Education season, especially in middle and secondary school programs.

The sport board operates in a way similar to the teen advisory boards frequently used by libraries, museums, hospitals, and local councils. For example, library teen advisory boards typically provide input on book selection and collection development, contribute to blogs or other library publications, volunteer at events, organize community service projects, or organize and promote an author visit. Duties of the sport board can include planning the competitions with the teacher, dealing with disputes or student requests,

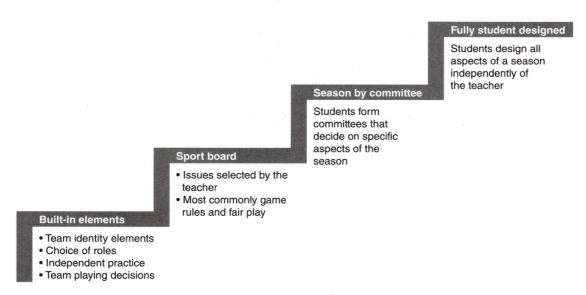

Figure 15.1 The stairway of autonomy.

meeting with the teacher to share ideas and feedback from students, providing positive role models for teams, planning the culminating event, and ensuring the smooth day-to-day functioning of the program. Table 15.1 provides some examples of these functions.

The main benefit of incorporating a sport board into Sport Education is that students see the running of a season through a different set of lenses and can therefore offer a fresh set of eyes. The goal of library advisory boards is to help young people feel more connected to the library and become more involved lifelong library users. Likewise, in Sport Education, the goal is to give young people a voice in creating and sustaining their sport experience, which in turn will tend to encourage them to continue their participation outside of school.

Once you have decided to include a sport board, you must give careful attention to how you introduce the students to the function and expectations of the board and to the process of selecting the board members. Here are some suggestions for establishing a sport board.

- Wait to include a sport board until you and your students have completed several full Sport Education seasons. They will be better prepared to take on more ownership when they have mastered some initial levels of responsibility.

- The sport board selection should occur during the earliest lessons of a new season.

- The number of sport board members should generally equal the number of teams involved in the competition.

- The process for selecting sport board members should be clearly explained.

- Regardless of which selection process is used, teachers should provide a clear overview of the types of skills, dispositions, and expectations come with being an effective board member.

- Given the critical role of the sport board, you should offer this overview of expectations prior to the actual selection process.

- Across multiple seasons, be sure that board membership changes regularly so as to avoid having the same students repeatedly serve in this capacity.

Table 15.1 Possible Duties of a Sport Board

Duty	Examples
Advise the teacher on policies governing the Sport Education season	• Create policies for team names • Make suggestions about rule changes following the preseason competition • Create an equity policy with respect to team leadership positions
Make decisions regarding fair play	• Discuss options for awarding fair play points • Adjudicate situations of inappropriate player behavior
Plan and decide on the competition schedule	• Decide the length of games • Determine the number of divisions in larger classes • Advise on the format of the playoffs
Plan and prepare the culminating event	• Determine which awards will be given • Invite guest speakers • Communicate with local media concerning the event
Promote the season throughout the school	• Create and update a Sport Education website • Write press releases for the school news channel

How to Select the Sport Board

Having students participate in the process of selecting sport board members offers them a great opportunity to be involved in shaping a governing body for the sport season, and thus have greater ownership of the total sport experience. Depending on your knowledge of the student group, you can use one of the following processes to select the board: (1) students can *volunteer* for board membership, (2) students can *apply* for board membership, or (3) students can *vote* for board member nominees. Figure 15.2 provides a step-by-step explanation for each process. Note that option 1 (asking for volunteers) is the quickest way to select members.

Be sure to provide a clear explanation of the roles and responsibilities of a board member. Remind the students that board membership involves a willingness to spend time in meetings and discussions outside of regular class time. Figure 15.3 provides some ideas that might be useful in helping to set up meeting times.

A Fair Play Commission

Even if you prefer not to adopt the complete sport board concept, you may wish to use a group of students for dispute resolution. This group can meet to make decisions concerning violations of fair play rules or to respond to complaints from officials. An extract from interviews with a ninth-grade student shows how effective such a committee can be.

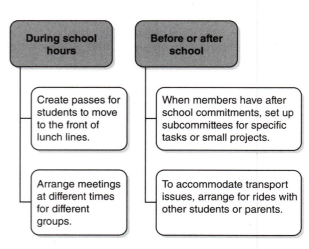

Figure 15.3 Promoting attendance at meetings.

Figure 15.2
STEPS FOR SELECTING THE SPORT BOARD

1. Students Volunteer for Board Membership

- Announce the number of volunteers you need.
- Ask for that number of volunteers to come to the front of the class.
- If more students come forward than needed, have all the volunteers turn away from the rest of the group.
- Ask the rest of the group to voice their opinion on the best candidates by raising their hands.

2. Students Apply for Board Membership

- Give students enough time to learn about the role, functions, and duties of sport board members.
- Publish role description and expectations (e.g., by posting them on the Sport Education bulletin board).
- Give students time to fill out an application for board membership.
- Select the best candidates, according to the expectations, your knowledge of the applicants, and any previous experience they have.

3. Students Vote for Board Member Nominees

- Have students nominate possible sport board members (they should be allowed to nominate themselves).
- Post the nominations.
- Choosing from the posted nominations, students then list on a piece of paper, in descending order of preference, the names of those students they believe would serve effectively on the board.
- Select the best candidates, according to the expectations, your knowledge of the candidates, and any previous experience they have.
- Count all the votes. If you need, say, five members, announce the names of the five students who received the most votes.

So far we've only had like one complaint that we had to deal with and that was only swearing, so we just made that person have a suspension for two games. I don't think she wants to swear again because otherwise she will let her team down, but she didn't mind being taken off because she knew she swore. The little shock we've given her will make sure that she won't do that in the future because she knows the consequences now (Carlson & Hastie, 1997, p. 185).

A SPORT EDUCATION SEASON DEVELOPED BY COMMITTEES

An extension of the sport board is to include all students in the decision-making process through the use of committees. Most of the time allocated to committee work is during the earliest lessons of the season, but there may be moments throughout the season when students are required to meet. The scenario outlined in the following paragraphs describes how a class of seventh-grade boys designed a season of floor hockey (Carlson & Hastie, 2003).

All students became members of one of four committees that served to oversee the development of the season: (1) rules, (2) competition, (3) administration, and (4) judiciary. Full details of these committees' responsibilities are shown in table 15.2. During the first lesson of the season, the students were given the descriptions of these committees and were able to select membership in one of them. While there was no limit to the number of students on any one committee, membership was quite well balanced across the four.

During the first five minutes of these lessons, each committee was given one specific problem to discuss and resolve. Table 15.3 provides some sample issues discussed by these committees. The most typical progression during committee meetings involved one student reading the day's task, followed by a gathering of opinions from the members. In the larger committees, the reader would normally act as de facto chair, synthesizing the varied responses into some agreement. In the smaller committees, most of the students presented an idea, and then they would come to some agreement, particularly if one of the ideas sounded particularly attractive. This was indeed the case when one student suggested that team names be limited to those of the National Hockey League teams, thereby avoiding any problems.

Following the separate meetings, the students would all gather to listen to the resolutions of the various committees. Here, the teacher provided more leadership, and developed a specific protocol, acting essentially as the house speaker. One student representative would present his committee's findings, and the teacher would first clarify the outcome and its implications, then ask for comments from the floor, and finally, ask for general agreement. Rarely (on fewer than three occasions) was a vote required.

An analysis of the students' opinions about the structure of the season showed that the individual items that produced the most favorable responses related to the students being involved in determining the structure of the game. While the students thought

Table 15.2   Committee Responsibilities

Committee	Responsibility
Rules	• All issues and decisions relating to the playing rules of the game • Determination of playing boundaries
Competition	• All issues and decisions relating to the conduct of play • Number of games per lesson • Time length of games • Finals competition format
Administration	• Ethical issues, including appropriateness of team names • Season awards: type and criteria
Judiciary	All issues and decisions relating to sportsmanship, player behavior, and appropriate class conduct

Table 15.3 Committee Issues and Responses

Committee	Sample issues and responses
Rules	**Q. What are the restrictions on what the goalkeeper can do to defend the goal?** *A. The goalie can wear a softball glove to help in defense. This is so he or she can sprawl on the floor to cover up the ball without getting injured. A face-off follows.* **Q. Do you want to have any rules about offside?** *A. No player may progress past the offside line until the ball first clearly passes this line.*
Competition	**Q. What end-of-season awards might we give for this season?** *A. Most valuable player, most fair player, highest goal scorer, best goalie, best referee.* **Q. How are you going to work out who gets these awards? What methods are needed to score them?** *A. At the end of each game, teams will select the MVP and the MFP from the other team. Other awards can be from the score sheets.*
Administration	**Q. What standards are we going to put in place for team names? What sorts of names are not suitable?** *A. Teams may pick one of the names from the National Hockey League.*
Judiciary	**Q. Yesterday, Team A did not return their puck or their ball. What should be the consequence of this for today's practice?** *A. The other team starts with one goal.*

Students who participated in season planning through committees noted a significant lack of conflict during the course of the season. Of particular interest was the notion that "since we made up the rules and how the game was to be played, everyone understood them—they were clear, and so no one had any business getting into arguments and fights."

it was a good idea to have some involvement in many of the planning features of the hockey season, they also believed they learned something by being on a committee, particularly as their opinion was at least recognized.

On a more general level, three major themes came to light from the season. First, students felt they had particular ownership over the season. They frequently referred to the season as "ours," noting that "what happened during the unit was because we wanted it that way—not some teacher just coming in there and telling us what to do." As a result of this ownership, many students said they felt a sense of commitment to the season since it was, in effect, theirs. Because they had made the rules as well as the decisions as to how the season would work, they also felt protective role of the season's well-being. As one student commented, "You know we weren't going to allow anyone to spoil the season by goofing off or not taking it seriously. We had a responsibility to make it work, since we made it up in the first place."

Many students also noted a significant lack of conflict during the course of the season. Of particular interest was the notion that "since we made up the rules and how the game was to be played, everyone understood them—they were clear, and so no one had any business getting into arguments and fights."

A SPORT EDUCATION SEASON CREATED EXCLUSIVELY BY STUDENTS

Once students and teachers have had considerable experience with Sport Education and can appreciate the nuances of the model, there is little reason why students should not be given the authority to design all aspects of an entire season. In keeping with the spirit of the model, however, the students should be committed to having persisting teams, taking on roles other than player, keeping records, and participating in formal competitions that lead to a culminating event. The scenario outlined in the following paragraphs describes how a class of eighth-grade students designed a season of flag football (Wahl-Alexander, Curtner-Smith, & Sinelnikov, 2016).

Similar to their previous seasons, the students were committed to having an extensive period allocated to the same sport, and hence the season consisted of 24 45-minute lessons over eight weeks. This was divided into a preseason and a regular season, and involved postseason gameplay with an all-star game, all culminating in a Super Bowl. A celebratory party and awards ceremony followed. Roles included captain, coach, equipment manager, statistician, and equity officer, all of which the students had experiences in previous seasons. A blind ballot was used to select the coaches for each team, and these coaches then selected their teams through a draft. A fair play point system, which consisted of cheering for one's own team and not trash-talking, was also incorporated. Table 15.4 shows the overall plan for the season.

An inspection of table 15.4 shows some differences in the sequence of events from a teacher-developed season, First, the 18 students took three lessons in which they engaged in whole-group discussions in order to come up with several alternative solutions to a particular issue. Lessons 9 and 17 were also allocated to class discussions in which they first reviewed the season to that point and consolidated the rules for the upcoming competition. Lesson 17 focused on the activities involved in the culminating event.

In the main, class discussions followed a consistent pattern. First, an issue was raised and the students considered alternatives, which were then put to a vote. When the outcomes were not unanimous, further discussion followed, so that class members could explain their positions on particular issues. A second vote followed, with the majority decision being the final outcome. The teacher's role was to help the students

Table 15.4 The Sport Education Season Plan

Class period	Description
1-3	Select sport, create teams, select team colors, allocate roles, decide on rules and field dimensions, create posters and fair play statistics sheets
4-5	Practice
6-8	Preseason games
9	Student meeting to discuss season to date, possible trades, and rule changes
10-16	Regular season games
17	Discussion of playoff format, Super Bowl, and party and awards ceremony
18	Skills challenge
19-22	Play-offs
23	All-star game
24	Super Bowl and party and awards ceremony

Reprinted by permission from Z. Wahl-Alexander, M. Curtner-Smith, and O. Sinelnikov, "Influence of a Purposefully Negotiated Season of Sport Education on One Teacher and His Pupils," *European Physical Education Review* 22, no. 4 (2116): 450-464.

appreciate some of the implications of their decisions. While not intervening on issues such as gameplay or the sport selected for the season, he did ask questions when he saw issues of inequity, safety, or situations that might compromise student learning.

In addition to the formal class meetings, the students also made sure there was an opportunity for anyone in the class to note concerns about how things were going and to make suggestions for further changes once the season had started. These informal meetings typically took place in the locker room after class; one student would explain his or her idea and, after discussion, a vote followed. The four main topics raised during these sessions were concerned with unfair and uneven teams, rule changes or modifications, field dimensions, and the gameplay schedule. Of particular interest in this season was that the solutions to most of the issue were generated by the equity officer, who happened to be one of the lower-skilled students in the class.

THE TEACHER'S ROLE IN CREATING AUTONOMY-SUPPORTIVE ENVIRONMENTS

In making the initial decision about giving students voice and choice, you must first decide on the level of autonomy you will give your students. A good first question to ask yourself is whether you really care what they come up with. You may hope the season progresses in one particular direction, but this may be compromised when students come up with an alternative path. As Carlson and Hastie (2003) note, your answer to this will give you an idea of what, for you, are the fundamental, nonnegotiable features of the season. It is then important that you communicate these to students in the initial discussions. For example, hockey was the sport selected by the teacher during the committee-based season, and in this season as well as in the fully student-designed flag football season the students were required to include the fundamental features of Sport Education.

When giving students the authority to design their own seasons, you must also be prepared to allocate extra lessons to give students enough time to research the sport of their choice or to deliberate and vote on each aspect over which they are given authority. As noted, these can include issues such as team selection and affiliation, the modification of rules, and playing dimensions. As noted, in the flag football season described in this chapter, the first three lessons were allocated to these features.

Your second decision is to determine the extent to which you will direct student decision-making. That is, you need to first determine whether to have a direct involvement in leading the process or to leave this to a debriefing following the outcomes. In the particular hockey season described, the teacher was more directly involved in that he presented a limited situation for the students to discuss. In the flag football season, the teacher used a more informal questioning technique, mostly with the goal of keeping the students focused on design tasks.

SUMMARY

Owen (1996) notes that citizenship involves a range of roles that individuals can play in forming, maintaining, and changing their communities. Giving students the opportunity to take charge and make decisions about their Sport Education experiences allows them to participate in all three roles. What is critical, however, is to act upon student input and make their contributions a legitimate part of the season. To be given a voice but having that voice make no difference may be more profoundly alienating than having no voice at all.

The few studies of purposefully negotiated curricula in physical education in general, and in Sport Education specifically, have yielded mainly positive results. The studies have shown that student learning is not compromised by giving them autonomy; rather, more students become motivated and engaged.

PART III

Key Program Design Considerations

The reality of the school as a workplace is that teachers have many additional, much less visible, roles and responsibilities. The casual observer does not easily recognize these, which leads to the common misconception that a teacher's work consists of no more than teaching lessons and grading students' work. As a physical educator, your additional roles and responsibilities are specific to the physical education program to which you must attend. If you teach in an elementary school you will in most cases be the sole person in charge of the program. In secondary programs, on the other hand, you will have to work together with colleagues. Getting all the teachers in a secondary program to be on the same page with a common focus and goal is not always easy.

In part III, we introduce you to some of the less obvious aspects of teaching physical education, which together help to build a quality and effective program. This last set of chapters addresses various aspects that in some ways go beyond the nuts and bolts of teaching a Sport Education-based season. In keeping with our architectural metaphor, this third part represents the less visible parts of a house—the plumbing, electrical, and mechanical systems; pipes, wires, sewer lines, and vents are critical to a well-functioning house. The topics addressed in part III ensure that a Sport Education model fits comfortably into a complete physical education program.

In chapter 16, we address how Sport Education's competency, literacy, and enthusiasm objectives link with U.S. content standards. Understanding this link is especially important if, when you advocate and promote your program, you are asked to articulate why your program is central to the development to the whole student. And because Sport Education has made inroads in numerous other countries, we introduce in chapter 17 the same link with aims and learning outcomes developed in several other countries.

Chapter 18 focuses on the need for physical education programs to integrate ongoing formative-formal assessment of student performance on your selected season outcomes. This is especially critical because physical education in general has fallen short of demonstrating that it is a legitimate subject in schools. In chapter 19, we focus on the need for you to decide on a clear mission, theme, and focus for your physical education program. This has implications for what content you select to deliver and how you plan your total program for the year and, in particular, where your Sport

Education seasons fit into your curriculum. Chapter 20 introduces you to the need for developing program-level policies and procedures as well as the management and organization of equipment and supplies (including managing your equipment budget). It also suggests ways to implement safety measures in cases of program- or school-level emergencies. The chapter closes with important information specific to your legal responsibilities. Understanding them and knowing how you can avoid actions that might result in being held legally liable is of paramount importance.

Part III closes with chapter 21, which gives examples of how you can connect with your classroom colleagues and integrate classroom content (e.g., art, math, science) with your Sport Education program. Collaborating with classroom teachers is a powerful way of showing how your program does indeed play a vital role in the school.

Sport Education's Link With U.S. Content Standards

16

Chapter Objective

After reading this chapter, you will be able to articulate how the Sport Education objectives link with, and how Sport Education can contribute to, meeting U.S. national content standards.

Key Concepts

- SHAPE America's national content standards (along the related grade-level outcomes) reflect what primary and postprimary (K-12) students should learn through their school physical education experiences.
- Sport Education's competency-, literacy-, and enthusiasm-related objectives are linked to varying degrees with SHAPE America's content standards.
- Recognizing and being able to explain these links is important for you to be able to promote and defend the quality of your physical education program

In this chapter, we highlight how Sport Education's short-term competency, literacy, and enthusiasm objectives align with the SHAPE America content standards (SHAPE America, 2013a). By clarifying these links, we will make it clear how Sport Education incorporates outcomes that are legitimate and defensible to the public (i.e., parents and policymakers).

In the 1990s, the National Association for Sport and Physical Education (NASPE) developed the first set of national content standards (NASPE, 1995). Content standards (also referred to as *outcomes*) indicate what students should demonstrate in terms of their skills, knowledge, and dispositions as a consequence of their K-12 physical education experience (Tannehill et al., 2015). The most recent revised content standards are presented in table 16.1 (SHAPE America, 2013a). Grade level outcomes were also developed for each of the five standards, providing more detailed specifications on how well and under what conditions students should be able to show what they know, can do, and value, across grade levels (SHAPE America, 2013b). That is, the grade level outcomes (also referred to as *performance standards*) focus on the qual-

Table 16.1 SHAPE America's 2013 National Content Standards Link With Sport Education's Objectives

SHAPE America content standards: A physically literate individual...	Sport Education competency (C), literacy (L) and enthusiasm (E) objectives
Standard 1: demonstrates competency in a variety of motor skills and movement patterns	SE-C 1. Develop sport-specific techniques and fitness SE-C 2. Appreciate and be able to execute sport-specific strategic play SE-C 3. Develop and apply knowledge about the key features of the game or activity
Standard 2: applies knowledge of concepts, principles, strategies, and tactics related to movement and performance	SE-C 1. Develop sport-specific techniques and fitness SE-C 2. Appreciate and be able to execute sport-specific strategic play SE-C 4. Develop and apply knowledge about umpiring, refereeing, and training
Standard 3: demonstrates the knowledge and skills to achieve and maintain a health-enhancing level of physical activity and fitness	SE-C 1. Develop sport-specific techniques and fitness SE-C 4. Develop and apply knowledge about umpiring, refereeing, and training
Standard 4: exhibits responsible personal and social behavior that respects self and others	SE-L 5. Provide responsible leadership SE-L 6. Work effectively with your team to pursue common goals SE-L 7. Appreciate the rituals and conventions that give sports their unique meanings SE-L 8. Develop the capacity to make reasoned decisions about sport concerns SE-L 9. Share in the planning and administration of sport experiences SE-E 10. Actively engage in all aspects of lessons SE-E 11. Give their best effort
Standard 5: recognizes the value of physical activity for health, enjoyment, challenge, self-expression, and social interaction	SE-L 6. Work effectively in a group toward common goals SE-L 7. Appreciate the rituals and conventions that give sports their unique meanings SE-L 9. Share in the planning and administration of sport experiences SE-E 10. Actively engage in all aspects of lessons SE-E 11. Give their best effort SE-E 12. Become involved in sport and physical activity outside of school

ity of the performance. It is important not to confuse the *content* standards with the *performance* standards.

The development of content standards is a direct consequence of what is called s*tandards-based education.* As noted by MacPhail (2015), standards-based education seeks to "clarify what schools and teachers are trying to accomplish . . ." (p. 22). In standards-based education, the desired student learning outcomes become the starting point from which teachers organize and plan their curriculum, content, instruction, and assessments. In the U.S., individual states have also developed their own state-level content standards. Typically, though, these are patterned after the national content standards. In the next chapter, we will also show how Sport Education fits within the national learning aims and outcomes developed in other countries.

Compared to mathematics standards, for example, the content standards for physical education are stated in more general terms, so that teachers can articulate how a single season's objectives, along with the selected content and assessments, align with them. But it would be a misunderstanding for teachers to think they would need to revamp their program completely just because they are asked to employ standards-based education. The purpose of content standards is to allow teachers to focus their program and unit planning, instruction, and assessments on developmentally appropriate outcomes.

In the following section, we show how Sport Education's objectives align with SHAPE America's content standards. This will clarify how teachers who use Sport Education are in fact teaching toward the national content standards.

HOW SPORT EDUCATION'S OBJECTIVES LINK WITH U.S. CONTENT STANDARDS

The breadth of focus in the U.S. content standards has a long history. Since the early twentieth century, physical education in the U.S. has sought to develop students' motor skills, physical fitness, and the knowledge that underpins these. As well, the field has long claimed that school physical education is a prime factor in their social development and has long touted a focus on the affective learning domain.

How do Sport Education's objectives align with SHAPE America's content standards? Sport Education seeks to make students' sport experiences more complete and authentic. As shown in chapter 1, Sport Education has three overarching goals: the development of sport *competency, literacy,* and *enthusiasm.* These are broad, long-term targets. At the more short-term, program level, Sport Education has 12 objectives that fall under these three goals (see chapter 5). Their alignment with SHAPE America's five content standards is presented in table 16.1. On the next few pages, we describe these alignments links in more detail.

CONTENT STANDARD 1: DEMONSTRATES COMPETENCY IN A VARIETY OF MOTOR SKILLS AND MOVEMENT PATTERNS

SHAPE America's first content standard focuses on students learning to execute fundamental motor skills in the early grades (i.e., K-2 or 3), and execute more activity-specific movements in various environments (e.g., sport, aquatics, dance, fitness, outdoor pursuits) as they mature into adolescence. This content standard focuses on the *psychomotor domain* of learning (i.e., the degree to which people learn to command physical movement). If students are to remain active in sports like soccer, badminton, or softball beyond their formative years (a desirable and defensible objective), they will need to develop a level of competence in using the specific techniques. For example, someone who can control the shuttle in badminton using the various strokes and get it to fly in the desired direction (and at the appropriate angles and speed) is more likely to say Yes when invited to join a city league. Similarly, effectively handling a soccer ball through trapping, passing, and shooting is part of becoming a more competent player. Thus, Sport Education's competency objective to *develop sport-specific techniques and fitness* aligns directly with SHAPE America's first content standard.

Sport Education's competency objective of *appreciating and being able to execute strategic play specific to a sport or game* also aligns directly with SHAPE America's first content standard. *Strategic play* reflects team performance based on a plan of action decided on prior to the start of a game and on any necessary adjustment to the plan based on how the game develops. Strategies are different from tactical moves. The former reflect a general plan of action whereas the latter reflect specific players' actions based on what is happening in a game at any given moment. Strategic play does not occur only in team games like soccer and basketball; it is also an integral part of individual sports such as golf or tennis.

A strategic plan of action is based on what is known about the opponent's tendencies and weaknesses and the environmental conditions. For example, a known weakness in a tennis player (e.g., net play, poor backhand) could prompt opposing players to take advantage of it. In basketball, a team known for being poor in shooting from long range allows the opposing team to adjust their defensive play. Relative to environmental conditions, an example would be a situation in disc golf where the player would need to make adjustments given a strong wind.

As games progress and circumstances change, teams and players need to alter their strategic approaches. The reasons for such adjustments might include getting an unexpected lead late in a game, an injury to one of the players, or a player being sent off because of extreme foul play. For example, a team leading in a soccer, football, or team handball game, with little time left in the game, likely would concentrate on more defensive play with the goal of maintaining possession, perhaps shifting one or more players to a primarily defensive role. In response, the team that is behind would then likely take more risks and play more aggressively by moving more players into the offensive half of the court or field.

It is important to note that strategy is critical in both traditionally team-based sports and in sports typically described as individual sports. For example, strategic play in golf would be reflected when players with a three-stroke lead and only a few holes left start to play a little less aggressively. For example, they are more likely to lay up their second shot on a par five with sand traps or water in front of the hole, instead of going for the green in two shots. In softball, outfielders of a team with a one-run lead late in the game would likely play deeper in the outfield to avoid doubles or triples. Conversely, with a large lead in later innings, outfielders should focus on getting outs. That is, on a base hit with a runner on second base, the player should go to second base (instead of throwing the ball home to keep the run from scoring) so the hitter does not advance to second base and get into scoring position.

Sport Education's third competency objective (*develop and apply knowledge about the key features of the game or activity*) also links directly with the first content standard. As we have shown throughout this book, students experience all practice as well as formal competitions under modified learning conditions (see especially chapter 7). Students benefit little from learning contexts typically seen in more advanced levels of experience because these are far too complex. Teachers have many options for combining technical and tactical practice in modified and gameplay conditions that are at appropriate levels of difficulty and complexity. Modifications range from reduced court or field size to modified equipment, adjusted scoring rules, team sizes, and so on. Sport Education's golden rule is that competitions are not designed using the parent game (e.g., full-court five-on-five basketball or six-on-six volleyball on regulation courts with regular net height). In mid- to upper-elementary grade levels, netcourt games can be played on very small courts (e.g., 20 x 12 ft or 6.1 x 3.66 m) with nets as low as 1 or 2 feet (30-60 cm).

An example of developmentally appropriate practice in a netcourt game context is to build the competition around cooperative technique-rally challenges. At mid-elementary or primary grade levels, a cooperative competition would focus on improving control of the ball. Partners in each team are challenged to sustain the longest possible rallies using (a) specified technique(s) within a certain time limit (e.g., 3 minutes) keeping the ball inbounds. Duty team members would be responsible for counting the touches per rally. The longest rally scores from each set of partners in each team would be added together to come up with a total team score.

In the case of a net-court game, using different balls (or raising the net) can help slow the game down. Slowing the game down is especially important in the early stages of learning. A slower-moving ball in volleyball would buy a learner more time to get into a better position to direct the ball. Raising the net a little higher in volleyball would also help slow the game down, reduce attempts at spiking the ball (a more advanced technique), and encourage more upward trajectories when passing across the net to unguarded areas on the opposing team's half-open areas.

In softball (a striking-and-fielding game), depending on the level of experience, game conditions could be modified by using timed innings (instead of the standard three outs), having teams pitch to themselves, adding extra bases, or creating scoring opportunities for the team in the field by getting as many outs as possible (e.g., catching a fly ball or making an out at a base). The tactical complexity in softball can be simplified by eliminating the making outs at individual bases. Instead, the fielding team is to move the ball to the catcher who downs the ball on home plate. Any base runner who is not on a base would be called out.

CONTENT STANDARD 2: APPLIES KNOWLEDGE OF CONCEPTS, PRINCIPLES, STRATEGIES, AND TACTICS RELATED TO MOVEMENT AND PERFORMANCE

SHAPE America's second content standard focuses on how students execute movement that reflects "knowledge in action" (also referred to as "understanding") about underlying concepts, principles, strategies, and tactics. This standard focuses on the *cognitive domain* of learning. Being able to use the activity-specific techniques alone (see Standard 1 in the preceding section) is not enough to become a player (i.e., one who has game sense). The knowledge-in-action focus is critical here. For example, in basketball, understanding the basic rules entails more than being able to explain what is meant by violations like travel, double dribble, or 3-second on a written test or through a verbal check. True understanding is reflected when students avoid violating these rules as players or call them correctly when serving as referee; that is when they demonstrate knowledge in action.

Other examples of knowledge in action include putting enough force on a passed ball in soccer and directing it perfectly ahead of the person moving into open space. A tennis or badminton player who, when at the net, chooses the drop shot only when the opponent is still deep in the backcourt truly understands the concept of shot selection and placement. In a track event, middle-distance runners who preserve enough energy to use a strong sprint toward the end of a race demonstrate an understanding of pacing. In a Sport Education fitness season, a team that discusses and decides to have each team player be responsible for different numbers of push-ups based on their physical capabilities (rather than every team member being expected to do the same amount) demonstrates understanding of the concept of strategizing for success.

A key underlying concept is the need for students to learn to make good decisions. That is, all actions in active motor play (physical education's primary domain) have underlying decisions. Learning to make better decisions in action requires numerous opportunities to practice making those decisions.

In striking-and-fielding games like softball, technical execution is still dominant, but the game situation changes with every pitch or hitter. Decision-making is critical because players need to consider factors like the number of outs, the hitter, the score in the game, the outfielders' position, and where a ball is hit. For example, fielders need to adjust their position, base runners need to decide whether to take the extra base, outfielders need to decide to which base to throw the ball.

As we showed in in more detail in chapter 11, Sport Education focuses on developing competent sports players. This requires more than just the development of the critical techniques and learning about the tactical aspects of play. Clearly, all of Sport Education's competency objectives (i.e., *Develop sport-specific techniques and fitness*, *Appreciate and be able to execute sport-specific strategic play*, *Develop and apply knowledge about the key features of the game or activity*, and *Develop and apply knowledge about umpiring, refereeing, and training*) align with SHAPE America's second content standard.

CONTENT STANDARD 3: DEMONSTRATES THE KNOWLEDGE AND SKILLS TO ACHIEVE AND MAINTAIN A HEALTH-ENHANCING LEVEL OF PHYSICAL ACTIVITY AND FITNESS

SHAPE America's third content standard aligns primarily with Sport Education's competency objectives *Develop sport-specific techniques and fitness*, and *Develop and apply knowledge about umpiring, refereeing, and training*. Through Sport Education, students should learn how fitness demands differ from one sport to the next (e.g., soccer, tennis, archery, golf) in a matter of degree. For example, being able to adjust one's position continuously on a field in soccer, team handball, or basketball and intersperse that with short- to medium-length bouts of sprints is different from the primary fitness demands in archery, where muscular strength in the core and upper body is emphasized more than cardiorespiratory (i.e., aerobic) endurance.

In badminton, players need to be able to return quickly to base position and switch direction again quickly to reach an opponent's shot placed in a short or deep corner. Conditioning needs for learning to play golf are different again. Flexibility in the core and shoulders is key in golf since it contributes to better swing execution. It is also important for students to learn that engaging in appropriate (i.e., activity-specific) conditioning will help prevent injury.

Actually improving students' physical fitness level is beyond the reach of Sport Education, given the time and frequency allocated to school physical education. Rather, the goal is for students to learn what would be the types of exercises appropriate for being successful in specific activities. That is, they should learn what the appropriate muscular strength and agility exercises are for participating successfully in softball versus badminton.

Sport Education should focus on promoting physical activity within and beyond the lessons. This would occur in the form of team-based fitness conditioning sessions

Sport Education has a distinct focus on promoting physical activity within and beyond the physical education lessons.

within the lessons, led first by the teacher during the preseasons and by the teams' fitness or conditioning trainer. Teachers should also encourage teams to practice beyond the physical education lessons. Students could practice individually, or team members might get together for a team practice during the school day while on campus (e.g., during recess or lunch periods). Depending on how far apart students live from each other and from access to transportation, they could be encouraged to get together during discretionary times away from campus (i.e., at home in the afternoons on school days or on weekends). In chapter 6 we showed how this focus on promoting physical activity beyond the lessons can be built directly into a season.

CONTENT STANDARD 4: EXHIBITS RESPONSIBLE PERSONAL AND SOCIAL BEHAVIOR THAT RESPECTS SELF AND OTHERS

The following Sport Education's Literacy objectives are linked to varying degrees with SHAPE America's fourth content standard:

- *Work effectively with your team to pursue common goals*
- *Appreciate the rituals and conventions that give sports their unique meanings*
- *Develop the capacity to make reasoned decisions about sport concerns*
- *Share in the planning and administration of sport experiences*

The link with working together toward common goals is perhaps the most obvious one. In Sport Education, we emphasize the need to form balanced teams. And teams compete to determine which team wins the season's championship, the ultimate goal.

That goal requires contributions from all team members in both player and nonplayer roles. Performance in both roles affects the team's performance in the season competition through fair play points. But you should be mindful of how teams can also set other goals. For example, in basketball, in early season games teams may have been prone to committing fouls or turnovers, or taking too many shots from outside the three-point arc. Making improvements in such areas can contribute to overall gameplay. In flag football, teams with lots of interceptions (i.e., a turnover), can focus on reducing those. In pickleball or tennis, if players commit a lot of unforced errors, this can be an area for improvement. More focused practice on the technical execution of the various strokes, or choosing better shots, can help reduce the number of unforced errors.

Sport Education includes a strong focus on developing fair play behavior among students. Historically referred to as *sportsmanship*, fair play is more comprehensive in nature in that is focuses not just on how players conduct themselves during gameplay, but also on the many other facets of students' social behavior. Physical education has a long history of espousing students' social development as a primary area of learning outcomes. And, despite all the evidence to the contrary, many continue to assume that prosocial behavior develops automatically by virtue of participating in sport. We take the position that acting in socially supportive ways is learned behavior. We noted the following five fair play goals.

1. ***Participate fully and responsibly.*** Be on time. Be responsible in fulfilling your team and class tasks and responsibilities. Participate with enthusiasm.

2. ***Give your best effort.*** Sport is always at its best when all competitors give a full effort. Teams work well when all teammates make a good effort in their roles. All students benefit when referees, scorekeepers, duty teams, coaches, and managers make a good effort to cooperate with each other.

3. ***Respect the rights and feelings of teammates and opponents.*** Students should maintain self-control, show respect for teammates and opponents, and participate fully and fairly in practices and competitions. When conflicts do arise, students should respect and value ways to resolve those conflicts peacefully.

4. ***Be a good sport.*** Play hard and play by the rules. Respect those who enforce the rules. Appreciate the efforts of teammates and opponents. Be graceful in victory and dignified in defeat.

5. ***Be helpful and not harmful.*** Look for ways to help teammates. Avoid putting down others or bullying. Express appreciation for good play and tasks well done.

The following examples highlight what fair play looks like when observed in students in action in Sport Education, and how it links directly with the fourth SHAPE America content standard. The degree to which students perform their nonplaying roles of referee, scorekeeper, team coach, publicist, or equipment manager fall under fair play performance. Fair play also includes the way students support each other and demonstrate respect to the teams and officials, as well as the degree to which they put forth effort not just during gameplay but also during team practices.

Opportunities to shape fair play behavior occur elsewhere as well. Teams are groups of heterogeneous members, each with unique histories and experiences. The goal of teams is for all members to work in the same direction toward a common goal. Tension can easily arise within a team when team members have disagreements or disputes. Such instances form good teaching moments in terms of how differences between team members can and need to be resolved.

Sport is such an important cultural phenomenon in most countries that critical and controversial issues will surface during class. With sport news ever present via the Internet, students will invariably learn about such issues as ableism, racism, sexism, homophobia, use of performance-enhancing drugs (PEDs), different types of cheating, and the way in which sport and politics are intertwined. And they will discuss these topics with each other and with you. They will form and share opinions about specific events.

Another good example of fair play in sport is the issue of cheating (see also chapter 3). Perhaps nothing exemplifies fair play more than the idea of playing by the rules. While the goal of sport is to win a game or match (and ultimately a season's championship), the *essence* of sport is fairness. The rules in games and sport set the boundaries of acceptable conduct for all involved. Nothing upsets students more than seeing fair play violated, where one performer or one team gains an unfair advantage. Already in primary (i.e., elementary) grade levels, teachers can emphasize the problems surrounding cheating. The types of cheating that arise may be less sophisticated, but they will provide a springboard for brief discussions. In a badminton season, the scorekeeper might not be paying close attention, or might favor one of the players who is his or her friend, and thus not keep score accurately. When the match is over, if the opposing player(s) were paying attention, there might be disagreements on the final score. In soccer, a referee might be more lenient toward one team on purpose. Players may not give full effort during team practices or during gameplay. These are all different ways in which fair play is reduced, diminishing the experience for everyone else on the team.

As students move into secondary school physical education, you can also address some of the critical issues noted above in various ways. For example, in a secondary weight training season, students can be asked to do an out-of-class writing assignment focused on the pros and cons of using PEDs. Based on research with self-reporting tools, use of legal and illegal PEDs is not as prevalent as one might assume. Estimates of PED-use hovers around 5 percent, is more prevalent among boys, and is used not just for enhancing performance in athletics but also for improving one's body image (e.g., Darkes, Collins, Cohen, & Gwartney, 2013; Dodge & Jaccard, 2006; Mayo Clinic, 2015; Pope, Wood, Rogol, Nyberg, Bowers, & Bhasin, 2013). Dodge and Jaccard (2006) noted that there is widespread misperception about the use of PEDs being safe and that their adverse effects can be managed. In their in-depth review, Pope, Khalsa, and Bhasin (2017) reported adverse effects on cardiovascular function, increased occurrence of psychiatric and various behavioral symptoms, and increased risk of addiction. Given the changing landscape in high school physical education programming, with strength conditioning having become the primary content that caters mostly to the schools' athletes (van der Mars, 2017), it is even more important that physical educators become well informed about PEDs.

Other examples of learning to make reasoned decisions about sport include issues surrounding fan behavior at sport events, player conduct toward fans during games, the consequences of repeated subconcussive head trauma in sports like football, or whether athletes should or should not speak out about social issues (e.g., unequal pay for female professional athletes or racial injustice). As a physical educator, you are uniquely situated to help students become more informed, so it is important that you develop (and articulate) your own position on such issues and events, and understand the basis for the perspectives that students share.

Finally, there is the objective of students learning to *Share in the planning and administration of sport experiences.* As students gain experience in well-delivered Sport Education, you should give them the opportunity to take increased ownership and responsibility for various aspects of seasons by giving them a voice in how seasons or lessons or tasks within lessons are structured (e.g., Farias et al., 2017; Ward et al., 2017). One way to do this is to expand the features of nonplaying roles, for example by letting team coaches start designing and organizing their own team practices as opposed to using practice plans you have provided. Similarly, fitness leaders could design their team's fitness conditioning exercises, or dance or fitness teams could design their own dance routines or fitness challenges, or team publicists who have the technology skills might design a class-level team website or Facebook page that highlights aspects of the various teams' identity and performance.

Examples of more advanced levels of ownership of planning and administering seasons would be to build in a rules committee. Students on this committee would get to decide on the rules of general class conduct for the upcoming season and set the consequences for breaking such rules. When students get to set their own rules of conduct, they are less likely to argue with each other. You could also form a student-led competition committee, which would be asked to decide on season competition aspects such as how many games would be scheduled per lesson, how many game points would be earned after a win, a draw, or a loss. For example, typically in sport competition, the winning team would earn two points, the losing team would not earn a game point, and a draw (i.e., a tie) would result in both teams earning one point. But when students get to oversee how the competition is structured, they might decide that in a game with a final score of 4 to 3, the winning team would earn four game points and the losing team would earn three points. A draw of 3 to 3 would thus result in each team getting three points.

Yet another example of advanced levels of ownership might be the inclusion of a sports panel (e.g., Farias, 2017; Harvey et al., 2014). Students on the sports panel could be tasked with making decisions about certain issues (e.g., game protests, what awards would be made part of the season, what the consequence would be for players who were sent off for extreme inappropriate conduct during a season's game). For example, a student who engaged in overly aggressive physical play might be suspended for the next three games. The player sent off would then appear before the judiciary. The judiciary (made up of students representing all teams) would hear the plea from the student to have the suspension reduced or waived.

CONTENT STANDARD 5: RECOGNIZES THE VALUE OF PHYSICAL ACTIVITY FOR HEALTH, ENJOYMENT, CHALLENGE, SELF-EXPRESSION, AND SOCIAL INTERACTION

SHAPE America's fifth content standard focuses primarily on the affective learning domain, that is, the degree to which engaging in physical activities becomes an important, meaningful, and important way to spend one's time. A student who, rather than staying home and playing FIFA 2017, goes out and actually plays a game of soccer (either recreationally or as part of a formal competition) can confidently be said to value physical activity, exhibiting approach tendencies toward soccer. That is, it is important to this student to get to play soccer.

Sport Education's broader goal of developing enthusiasm for sport (broadly defined) is partially reflected in its more specific literacy objectives of *Work effectively with your team to pursue common goals, Appreciate the rituals and conventions that give sports their unique meanings,* as well as the enthusiasm objective of *Become involved with sport and physical activity outside of school.* The camaraderie that develops between team members in sport during the formative years is an important factor that may contribute to people seeking out similar experiences beyond their school years.

SPORT EDUCATION'S OBJECTIVES AND GRADE-LEVEL OUTCOMES

As noted at the beginning of this chapter, for each of the five content standards, SHAPE America has also developed grade-level outcomes (SHAPE America, 2013b). A review of these grade-level outcomes reveals how the intended outcomes become more advanced across grade levels. That is, students are expected to demonstrate their skills and knowledge under increasingly complex conditions. As we have emphasized throughout parts I and II of this text, you, as a physical educator, should be very mindful about the season outcomes you select, what type of competition format you use, what equipment you select, what rules you want students to learn, and so on, depending on the developmental level of your students.

HOW IMPORTANT IS THE LINK BETWEEN CONTENT STANDARDS AND SPORT EDUCATION'S OBJECTIVES?

Just like the American Medical Association (AMA) for physicians and the American Bar Association (ABA) for attorneys, SHAPE America is the premier professional association that sets the bar for what students should know and be able to do. Being knowledgeable about Sport Education's objectives and how they link with the national content standards is an integral part of being a professional physical educator.

Teachers in language arts or mathematics do not have to spend time or energy defending their subject's presence in the school's curriculum. Nobody questions the importance of their subjects. By contrast, as a physical educator you will frequently find yourself in a position where you need to defend your program in the school. This makes your use of appropriate teaching practices even more important.

Going back to our architect of the model image, with you as the architect of seasons, you will see that designing seasons that are instructionally aligned will help you in such efforts. As a season architect, your selection of developmentally appropriate season outcomes and appropriately designed season content and structure helps create conditions for your students to develop sport competence, literacy, and enthusiasm. And, as we will show in chapter 18, building in a formal assessment of your students' performance and knowledge will enable you to demonstrate that you deliver a high-quality program in which students are meeting the national content standards.

SUMMARY

The SHAPE America physical education content standards are a guide for the teacher as to what you should expect your students to know and be able to do upon completion of the formal primary and postprimary (K-12) education. These content standards are stated in more broad terms, allowing for different curriculum and instruction models to be used to help students meet the standards. To show how Sport Education is linked with the national Content standards, we showed how its competency, literacy, and enthusiasm objectives are linked to the national content standards.

Keren Su/Lonely Planet Images/Getty Images

17

Sport Education's Link With International Outcomes

Chapter Objective

After reading this chapter, you will be able to articulate how the Sport Education objectives link with, and how Sport Education can contribute to, meeting international goals and outcomes.

Key Concepts

- Sport Education is an internationally known and widely used curriculum and instructional model.
- The development of national goals, aims, and outcomes in other countries is overseen by the education departments in their respective national government, which is fundamentally different from how the U.S. content standards are developed and approved.
- There are similarities across different countries, with a strong focus on both sport-related and health-related national goals, aims, and outcomes.

Since its conception in the early 1980s, Sport Education has made significant inroads in countries beyond the United States. The model has been implemented widely in countries such as Australia, England, Ireland, and New Zealand. In recent years, Sport Education has been introduced in Portugal, Spain, Korea, and Japan as well. This development warrants a closer look at how Sport Education objectives align with the national aims or outcomes that other countries set for students in physical education.

Like the United States, other countries have developed physical education aims (depending on the country, these are also referred to as *outcomes* or *objectives*), but there are differences in how these are developed and approved. For example, in the United States, physical education's national association (SHAPE America) has developed the content standards (SHAPE America, 2013). The association recruits a panel of experts from the field who draft the content standards. The draft is then presented to the field, from which input is sought through public meetings at national conventions and through web-based feedback from members of the national association. Most U.S. states develop state-level content standards and the accompanying grade-level outcomes, which frequently mirror the national content standards.

In most other countries, it is the national government (through its ministry of education) that recruits experts in physical education. The key difference is that the national government (as opposed to the country's national professional association) oversees the development, revision process, and final approval. The formulation of national objectives is based on how the physical education profession has evolved over time in each country. Moreover, these national objectives also reflect their respective political, social, cultural, and educational contexts, without necessarily considering Sport Education-specific objectives. Yet, as we will show, in most cases the national outcomes focus on students' physical, social, and emotional development.

However, while not identical in history, structure, and focus, it is hard not to see how Sport Education's objectives align quite well. The comparisons we present in this chapter's tables reflect a matter of degree and emphasis. In just a few cases, the national outcomes of other countries may not align with Sport Education's objectives. Just like in the U.S., national outcomes, aims, and objectives of the countries included here are revised and updated periodically. Those listed here were current

Sport Education is an internationally known and widely used curriculum and instructional model.

Figure 17.1
SPORT EDUCATION'S COMPETENCY, LITERACY, AND ENTHUSIASM OBJECTIVES

Competency Objectives

SE-C 1. Develop sport-specific techniques and fitness.

SE-C 2. Appreciate and be able to execute sport-specific strategic play.

SE-C 3. Develop and apply knowledge about the key features of the game or activity.

SE-C 4. Develop and apply knowledge about umpiring, refereeing, and training.

Literacy Objectives

SE-L 5. Provide responsible leadership.

SE-L 6. Work effectively with your team to pursue common goals.

SE-L 7. Appreciate the rituals and conventions that give sports their unique meanings.

SE-L 8. Develop the capacity to make reasoned decisions about sport concerns.

SE-L 9. Share in the planning and administration of sport experiences.

Enthusiasm Objectives

SE-E 10. Actively engage in all aspects of lessons.

SE-E 11. Give your best effort.

SE-E 12. Become involved in sport and physical activity outside of school.

---

as of August 2018. Sport Education's competency (C), Literacy (L), and Enthusiasm (E) objectives introduced in chapter 5 are revisited in figure 17.1 to help guide you in reviewing their link with the national outcomes in the countries covered.

AUSTRALIA

In 2015 and 2017, the Australian Curriculum, Assessment, and Reporting Authority (ACARA) published its *Sequence of Content* and *Achievement*, respectively (ACARA, 2015, 2017) for Australian students from foundation (equivalent to kindergarten in the U.S.) to year 10. The *Sequence of Content* includes outcomes for the foundation, as well as those for subsequent pairs of years (equivalent to U.S. grade levels).

The *Sequence of Achievement* was described as follows:

> *By the end of Year 10, students critically analyze contextual factors that influence identities, relationships, decisions and behaviors. They analyze the impact attitudes and beliefs about diversity have on community connection and wellbeing. They evaluate the outcomes of emotional responses to different situations. Students access, synthesize and apply health information from credible sources to propose and justify responses to health situations. Students propose and evaluate interventions to improve fitness and physical activity levels in their communities. They examine the role physical activity has played historically in defining cultures and cultural identities.*

Students demonstrate leadership, fair play and cooperation across a range of movement and health contexts. They apply decision-making and problem-solving skills when taking action to enhance their own and others' health, safety and wellbeing. They apply and transfer movement concepts and strategies to new and challenging movement situations. They apply criteria to make judgements about and refine their own and others' specialized movement skills and movement performances. They work collaboratively to design and apply solutions to movement challenges." (ACARA, 2017, p. 2)

Table 17.1 reflects the link between Sport Education's objectives and Australia's learning outcomes (called *sequence of content*) for years 9 and 10 across two areas, (1) personal, social, and community health and (2) movement and physical activity.

Table 17.1 Alignment Between Sport Education's Objectives and Australia's National Physical Education Learning Outcomes

Sequence of content	Sport Education objectives
Personal, social, and community health	
Evaluate factors that shape identities and critically analyze how individuals impact the identities of others	SE-C 4 SE-L 6 SE-L 8
Examine the impact of changes and transitions on relationships	
Plan, rehearse, and evaluate options (including CPR and first aid) for managing situations where their own or others' health, safety, and wellbeing may be at short or long-term risk	
Propose, practice and evaluate responses in situations where external influences may impact on their ability to make healthy and safe choices	
Investigate how empathy and ethical decision making contribute to respectful relationships	
Evaluate situations and propose appropriate emotional responses and then reflect on possible outcomes of different responses	
Critically analyze and apply health information from a range of sources to health decisions and situations	
Movement and physical activity	
Provide and apply feedback to develop and refine specialized movement skills in a range of challenging movement situations	SE-C 1, 2, 3
Develop, implement, and evaluate movement concepts and strategies for successful outcomes with and without equipment	SE-C 1, 2, 3
Design, implement, and evaluate personalized plans for improving or maintaining their own and others' physical activity and fitness levels	SE-C 1, 4
Analyze the impact of effort, space, time, objects, and people when composing and performing movement sequences	SE-C 1, 2, 3
Examine the role physical activity, outdoor recreation, and sport play in the lives of Australians and investigate how this has changed over time	SE-L 7
Devise, implement, and refine strategies demonstrating leadership and collaboration skills when working in groups or teams	SE-L 5, 6
Transfer understanding from previous movement experiences to create solutions to movement challenges	SE-C 1, 2, 3
Reflect on how fair play and ethical behavior can influence the outcomes of movement activities	SE-L 7, 8 SE-E 10, 11

Adapted from Australian Curriculum, Assessment, and Reporting Authority (ACARA), *The Australian Curriculum-Health and Physical Education-Year 10* (Sydney, Australia, 2015).

ENGLAND

The Qualifications and Curriculum Authority (QCA, 2007) in England identified three overall aims for all education subjects taught in English schools. They include (1) successful learners who enjoy learning, make progress, and achieve, (2) confident individuals who are able to live safe, healthy, and fulfilling lives, and (3) responsible citizens who make a positive contribution to society.

In addition, the report noted the central role of physical education in schools, stating that "PE develops pupils' competence and confidence to take part in a range of physical activities that become a central part of their lives, both in and out of school" (QCA, 2007, p. 189). In table 17. 2, we show the link between Sport Education's objectives

Table 17.2 Alignment Between Sport Education's Objectives and England's National Physical Education Learning Outcomes

Skills and processes	Sport Education objectives
Developing skills in physical activity	
Refine and adapt skills into techniques	SE-C 1, 2, 3
Develop the range of skills they use	SE-C 1, 2, 3
Develop the precision, control, and fluency of their skills	SE-C 1, 2, 3
Making and applying decisions	
Select and use tactics, strategies, and compositional ideas effectively in different creative, competitive, and challenge-type contexts	SE-C 2, 3
Refine and adapt ideas and plans in response to changing circumstances	SE-C 2, 3
Plan and implement what needs practicing to be more effective in performance	SE-C 1, 2, 3
Recognize hazards and make decisions about how to control any risks to themselves and others	SE-C 1, 2, 3
Developing physical and mental capacity	
Develop their physical strength, stamina, speed, and flexibility to cope with the demands of different activities	SE-C 1, 4
Develop their mental determination to succeed	N/A
Evaluating and improving	
Analyze performances, identifying strengths and weaknesses	SE-C 1, 2, 4
Make decisions about what to do to improve their performance and the performance of others	SE-C 1, 2, 4
Act on these decisions in future performances	SE-C 1, 2 SE-E 12
Be clear about what they want to achieve in their own work and what they have actually achieved	SE-L 6
Making informed choices about healthy, active lifestyles	
Identify the types of activity they are best suited to	SE-C 4
Identify the types of role they would like to take on	SE-C 4 SE-L 6
Make choices about their involvement in healthy physical activity	SE-E 10, 11

Adapted from Qualifications and Curriculum Authority (QCA), *Physical Education-Programme of Study for Key Stage 3 and Attainment Target* (London: Crown, 2007).

and England's 16 skills and processes (i.e., student learning outcomes) grouped in the following five areas: (1) developing skills in physical activity, (2) making and applying decisions, (3) developing physical and mental capacity, (4) evaluating and improving, and (5) making informed choices about healthy, active lifestyles.

IRELAND

In 2011, the Irish Department of Education and Skills put forth its senior cycle (i.e., students between the ages of 15 and 18) education curriculum. The National Council for Curriculum and Assessment (NCCA) described the overall aim for physical education in the senior cycle as follows: "to support learners' confident, enjoyable and informed participation in physical activity now and in the future" (NCCA, 2011, p. 9). Sport Education is one of several curriculum and instructional models around which the senior cycle curriculum was built; other models included adventure education, teaching personal and social responsibility, and teaching games for understanding. The senior cycle physical education syllabus also includes a focus on health-related physical fitness and on contemporary issues in physical activity.

Teachers can opt to design their program using stand-alone models or combine models (e.g., Sport Education and health-related physical fitness), and design units of work accordingly. In table 17.3 we show Ireland's senior cycle physical education objectives specific to Sport Education and the link to Sport Education's objectives specific to other models is beyond the scope of this text.

NEW ZEALAND

New Zealand's Ministry of Education (2007) published its national curriculum, which includes student-focused achievement objectives for physical education. They are grouped in four general areas: (1) personal health and development, (2) movement concepts and motor skills, (3) relationships with other people, and (4) healthy communities and environments. Like the grade-level outcomes developed by SHAPE America, achievement objectives were developed across eight levels. Table 17.4 shows New Zealand's level eight (16-18 age group) achievement objectives and how they align with alignment with Sport Education's objectives.

PORTUGAL

In recent years, the Sport Education model has become a focus of study in Portuguese schools. Portugal's educational system is organized into three levels: preschool (3-6 years old); elementary school, which includes first cycle (grades 1-4, ages 5-11), second cycle (grades 5-6, ages 10-13), and third cycle (grades 7-9, ages 12-16); and secondary school (grades 10-12).

Physical education is compulsory only from the second cycle through secondary school; it is almost nonexistent at the preschool level. Local counties are responsible for paying for physical education to be offered to students in the first cycle. Not unlike

Table 17.3 Alignment Between Sport Education's Objectives and Ireland's Senior Cycle Physical Education Aims and Learning Objectives

Students learn about	Students should be able to	Sport Education objectives
Roles and responsibilities	• undertake different playing and nonplaying roles in the selected physical activity	SE-C 1, 2, 3 SE-L 5, 9
Being an effective team member	• participate as an effective member of a team toward a common goal, e.g., culminating event, display, performance	SE-C 1, 2, 3 SE-L 6, 9 SE-E 10,
	• respect the group fair play contract	SE-C 1, 2, 3
Effective personal performance	• demonstrate the skills, techniques, and strategies of the activity to the best of their ability	SE-C 1, 2, 3
	• observe the rituals and conventions of the activity	SE-L 7
	• adhere to the safety requirements of the activity	SE-C 6, 8
	• develop the fitness requirements for the selected physical activity	SE-C 1, 2, 3
	• incorporate a variety of techniques, choreographic principles, and approaches to group work in their dance or gymnastic performance	SE-C 1, 2, 3
	• demonstrate an understanding of aesthetic and artistic considerations in the design of the performance	SE-C 1, 2, 3
	• work creatively with props in dance and small and large apparatus in gymnastics	SE-C 1, 2, 3
Culminating physical activity event	• organize a culminating event for the selected physical activity	SE-L 9 SE-E 10
	• reflect on their own experience of organizing and participating in a culminating event from an individual or a group perspective	
Physical activity opportunities beyond the physical activity class	• document related physical activity opportunities beyond the physical education class with a view to active participation in at least one	SE-E 12
Common sport injuries and their rehabilitation, first aid procedures	• prepare a group presentation detailing common injuries in the chosen activity, including first aid procedures and rehabilitation.	N/A

Adapted from National Council for Curriculum and Assessment (NCCA), *Physical Education Framework*, 2018.

in the United States, the richer the county, the more time children will have for physical and motor activities in secondary school. The grade that students earn in physical education does not count toward their secondary school average grade, which affects students' access to the university courses of their choice. Table 17.5 includes the second and third cycle general physical education objectives common to all activities (i.e., sports, fitness, dance).

Table 17.4 Alignment Between Sport Education's Objectives and New Zealand's National Physical Education Learning Outcomes

Achievement objectives	Sport Education objectives
Personal health and development	
Personal growth and development: critically evaluate a range of qualitative and quantitative data to devise strategies to meet their current and future needs for well-being	SE-C 1, 4 SE-E 12
Regular physical activity: critically examine commercial products and programs that promote physical activity and relate this to personal participation in programs intended to meet their current well-being needs	SE-C 4 SE-L 8
Safety management: critically analyze dilemmas and contemporary ethical issues that influence their own health and safety and that of other people	SE-L 8
Personal identity: critically analyze the impacts that conceptions of personal, cultural, and national identity have on people's well-being	SE-L 8
Movement concepts and motor skills	
Movement skills: devise, apply, and evaluate strategies to improve physical activity performance for themselves and others	SE-L 8
Positive attitudes: devise, apply, and appraise strategies through which they and other people can participate responsibly in challenging physical situations	SE-C 1, 2, 3
Science and technology: critically analyze and experience the application of scientific and technological knowledge and resources to physical activity in a range of environments	SE-L 6 SE-E 10, 11
Challenges and social and cultural factors: devise and apply strategies to ensure that social and cultural needs are met in personal and group physical activities	SE-C 3 SE-L 5, 6, 9
Relationships with other people	
Relationships: critically analyze the dynamics of effective relationships in a range of social contexts	SE-C 2, 3, 4 SE-L 8
Identity, sensitivity, and respect: critically analyze attitudes, values, and behaviors that contribute to conflict and identify and describe ways of creating more harmonious relationships	SE-L 5, 6, 7, 8
Interpersonal skills: analyze and evaluate attitudes and interpersonal skills that enable people to participate fully and effectively as community members in various situations	SE-L 5, 6
Healthy communities and environments	
Societal attitudes and values: critically analyze societal attitudes and practices and legislation influencing contemporary health and sporting issues, in relation to the need to promote mentally healthy and physically safe communities	SE-L 5, 6, 8
Community resources: establish and justify priorities for equitable distribution of available health and recreational resources and advocate change where necessary	SE-L 5, 6 SE-E 10, 11
Rights, responsibilities, and laws: demonstrate the use of health promotion strategies by implementing a plan of action to enhance the well-being of the school, community, or environment	SE-E 10, 11
People and the environment: critically analyze the interrelationships between people, industry, technology, and legislation on aspects of environmental health	SE-E 12

Based on information from Ministry of Education, *The New Zealand Curriculum for English-Medium Teaching and Learning in Years 1-13* (Wellington: Ministry of Education, 2007).

Table 17.5 Alignment Between Sport Education's Objectives and Portugal's National Physical Education Objectives

Learning objectives	Sport Education objectives
To participate successfully in all situations toward achieving individual and group success, students will • respect their peers, either teammates or opponents • accept peer teaching help toward self-improvement, and show tolerance toward others' difficulties and options • cooperate in learning and organizational situations, selecting actions favorable to success, safety, and good relational climate during class activities	SE-L 5, 6, 9
Analyze and interpret the performance of the selected physical activities, applying the knowledge about technique, organization and participation, sports ethics, etc.	SE-C 1, 2, 3, 4 SE-L 8
To know and apply hygiene care, along with knowledge of personal and others' safety and of ways to preserve the material resources	N/A
To elevate the functional level of the general and basic coordination and conditional capacities, particularly long-term endurance, fast power, complex and simplified reaction speed, execution and frequency of motor movements, flexibility, endurance power, and general skills	SE-C 1, 4
Raise the functional level of the general health- and skill-related fitness capacities, in particular muscular endurance, muscular strength, power, and reaction time of general and specific skills	SE-C 1, 4
Know and apply various processes for improvement and maintenance of physical fitness in an independent way in their daily lives	SE-E 12
Know and interpret health and risk factors associated with the practice of physical activities, and apply hygiene and safety rules	N/A

Adapted and translated from Ministry of Education, *Programa EducaÁ, o Fisica-Plano de OrganizÁ, o do Ensino Aprendizagem* (Organizational plan for teaching-and-learning: Physical Education Program), 1998.

We thank Dr. Cláudio Farias (University of Porto Portugal) for his assistance with translating the national documents from Portugal.

SCOTLAND

In 2016, the Scottish Government published its national Experiences and Outcomes. The introduction noted that

> *Physical education provides learners with a platform from which they can build physical competences, improve aspects of fitness, and develop personal and interpersonal skills and attributes. It enables learners to develop the concepts and skills necessary for participation in a wide range of physical activity, sport, dance, and outdoor learning, and enhances their physical wellbeing in preparation for leading a fulfilling, active and healthy lifestyle... Learning in, through and about physical education is enhanced by participating on a regular basis in a wide range of purposeful, challenging, progressive, and enjoyable physical activities with choice built in for all learners. The Scottish Government expects schools to continue to work towards the*

provision of at least two hours of good quality physical education for every child, every week. (Smarter Scotland-Scottish Government, 2016, p. 5)

The last statement is particularly noteworthy in that schools across all grade levels are expected to provide 120 minutes of physical education per week.

Education Scotland also recognizes the importance of creating physical activity opportunities beyond the physical education lessons:

In addition to planned physical education sessions, physical activity and sport take place in the classroom, in the school, during travel such as walking and cycling, in the outdoor environment and in the community. Learning in, through and about physical activity and sport is enhanced by participating in a wide range of purposeful and enjoyable physical pursuits at break times, lunchtimes, within and beyond the place of learning. The experiences and outcomes are intended to establish a pattern

Table 17.6 Alignment Between Sport Education's Objectives and Scotland's National Physical Education Student Learning Outcomes

Student learning outcomes	Sport Education objectives
Movement skills, competencies, and concepts	
As I encounter a variety of challenges and contexts for learning, I am encouraged and supported to demonstrate my ability to select and apply a wide range of complex movement skills and strategies, creatively, accurately and with consistency and control.	SE-C 1, 2, 3
I can organize my time to practice, consolidate, and refine my skills to achieve my highest quality performance in a range of contexts. I am developing and sustaining my level of performance across all aspects of fitness.	SE-C 1, 2, 3, 4
Cooperation and competition	
While learning together, and in leadership situations, I can • experience different roles and take responsibility in organizing a physical event and • contribute to a supportive and inclusive environment and demonstrate behavior that contributes to fair play.	SE-L 5, 6, 9
Evaluating and appreciating	
I can • observe closely, reflect, describe, and analyze key aspects of my own and others' performances, • make informed judgments specific to an activity, and • monitor and take responsibility for improving my own performance based on recognition of personal strengths and development needs.	SE-C 1, 2, 3, 4
I continue to enjoy daily participation in moderate to vigorous physical activity and sport and can demonstrate my understanding that it can • contribute to and promote my learning, • develop my fitness and physical and mental well-being, • develop my social skills, positive attitudes, and values, and • make an important contribution to living a healthy lifestyle.	SE-E 12

Adapted from Smarter Scotland-Scottish Government, *Curriculum for Excellence: Health and Well-Being* (Edinburgh, Scotland, 2016).

of daily physical activity which, research has shown, is most likely to lead to sustained physical activity in adult life. Experiences and outcomes should also open up opportunities for learners to participate and perform at their highest level in sport and, if interested, pursue careers in the health and leisure industries. (Smarter Scotland-Scottish Government, 2016 , p. 7)

Furthermore, Scottish physical education programs are directed to have a strong focus on future health: "Learners develop an understanding of their physical health and the contribution made by participation in physical education, physical activity and sport to keeping them healthy and preparing them for life beyond school." (Smarter Scotland-Scottish Government, 2016, p. 9)

In table 17.6, we share Scotland's outcomes specific to physical education and their link with Sport Education's objectives.

SPAIN

Teachers in Spanish schools teach core subjects (e.g., natural sciences, mathematics, social sciences, language, second language), specific subjects (which include physical education), and free choice subjects that can be chosen by the 19 individual states. Weekly minutes for the core subjects are set by the national government, while the individual states have the flexibility to set the weekly minutes for the specific subjects.

In Spain, physical education is taught at both the primary (ages 6-12) and the postprimary (ages 12-16) school level. Postsecondary physical education is taught to 17-year-old students. In primary grade levels, instruction in physical education is provided by classroom teachers while in postprimary schools it is provided by certified physical education specialists. The postprimary school physical education curriculum targets development in five main areas: (1) body image and perception, (2) fundamental motor skills, (3) dance and physical arts activities, (4) health-related physical activity, and (5) games and sports.

Spain's general aims for physical education at the postprimary school level include the following.

- Reinforce and further develop the physical education knowledge, understanding, skills, and competencies acquired at primary level.
- Provide the resources that enable students to reach an adequate level of motor competence, to be autonomous and practice regular physical activity that lead to healthy lifestyle habits.
- The student is skillful and competent, which means acquiring a repertoire of relevant motor responses to situations showing coordination, balance, control, harmony, and fluidity of movements or rhythm in performances.

Spain's national physical education student learning outcomes under these general aims are presented in table 17.7, where we show their alignment with Sport Education's objectives. Each outcome includes specific success criteria that teachers are to use to determine the degree of student learning on that outcome.

Table 17.7 Alignment Between Sport Education's Objectives and Spain's National Physical Education Aims

National student learning outcomes	Sport Education objectives
Primary school outcomes	
Practice learning experiences with a variety of stimuli and spatiotemporal conditions by selecting and combining the basic motor skills and adapting them to the conditions laid down in an effective manner	SE-C 1, 2
Use the expressive resources of body and movement, aesthetically and creatively, communicating feelings, emotions, and ideas	SE-C 1, 3
Resolve elementary tactical challenges of play and physical activities, with or without opposition, applying principles and rules to solve driving situations, acting as individual, coordinated, and cooperative, and playing the different functions in games and activities	SE-C 1, 2, 3 SE-L 5, 6
Connect the specific concepts of physical education and the input in other areas with the practice of physical sports and artistic expressive activities	SE-C 2
Recognize the effects of physical exercise, hygiene, food, and postural habits on health and welfare, demonstrating a responsible attitude toward the self	SE-C 1, 4
Enhance the level of physical abilities by adjusting the intensity and duration of effort and considering its possibilities and its relationship to health	SE-C 1
Rate, accept, and respect the individual's bodily reality and that of others, showing a critical and reflective attitude	N/A
Know and value the diversity of physical, recreational, sporting, and artistic activities	SE-C 2, 3
Stay consistently critical, from the perspective of both participant and spectator, of potential conflict situations arising, participating in discussions, and accepting the opinions of others	SE-L 8
Express respect toward the natural environment in games and activities in the open air, identifying and carrying out concrete actions aimed at their preservation	SE-L 5, 12
Identify and internalize the importance of prevention, recovery, and safety measures in carrying out the practice of physical activity	SE-C 4, 8
Extract and produce information related to topics of interest in the stage (i.e., grade level) and share it, using certain sources of information, and making use of the technologies of information and communication as a source of support to the area	SE-C 4
Demonstrate responsible personal and social behavior, respecting self and others in physical activities and games, accepting the established rules and acting with interest and individual initiative and teamwork	SE-L 5

National student learning outcomes	Sport Education objectives
Postprimary school outcomes	
Resolve individual physical activities situations by applying the technical foundations and specific skills of the proposed sport activities, in real or adapted conditions	SE-C 1, 2
Interpret and produce artistic movement actions using techniques of body expression and other resources	SE-C 2
Resolve collective situations of opposition, collaboration, or collaboration-opposition, using the most appropriate strategies based on relevant stimuli	SE-C 2
Recognize the factors involved in movements and mechanisms of control of the intensity of physical activity, by applying them to the practice and relating them to health	SE-C 1, 2, 4
Develop physical abilities according to the personal possibilities and within the margins of health, showing an attitude of self-control and effort	SE-C 1, 4
Develop activities of each of the phases of the lesson, related to its characteristics	SE-C 3, 4
Recognize the possibilities of sport and dance activities as forms of social inclusion, facilitating the removal of barriers to the participation of others regardless characteristics, collaborating with others and accepting their contributions	SE-C 3 SE-L 6
Recognize the possibilities that offer sport activities as forms of active leisure and responsible use of the environment	SE-C 3 SE-E 12
Be aware of the difficulties and risks during participation in sport and dance activities	SE-C 3
Use information technologies and communication in the learning process, to search, analyze, and select relevant information, preparing documents, and making presentations	SE-C 3

Adapted and translated from Ley Org·nica 8/2013 de 9 de diciembre para la Mejora de la Calidad Educativa (LOMCE) [Organic Law 8/2013, 9 December, to improve quality of education (LOMCE)]; Real Decreto 126/2014, de 28 de febrero, por el que se establece el currìculo b·sico de la EducaciÛn Primaria [Royal Decree126/2014, 28 February, of the establishment of the basic curriculum of Primary Education]; Real Decreto 1105/2014, de 26 de Diciembre, por el que se establece el currìculo b·sico de la EducaciÛn Secundaria Obligatoria y del Bachillerato [Royal Decree1105/2014, 26 December, of the establishment of the basic curriculum of Compulsory Secondary Education and Baccalaureate]

We thank Dr. Antonio Calderon (University of Limerick, Limerick, Ireland), and Dr. Norma Teresa Martín Sanz (IES Miguel Romero Esteo, M·laga, Spain) for their assistance with translating the national documents from Spain.

SUMMARY

In this chapter, we showed how Sport Education has become widely known as a curriculum and instruction model in numerous countries around the globe. There are differences across the countries from the cultural, social, and political perspective. Moreover, there are fundamental differences in the governance and oversight of education. Like the United States, however, most countries have developed national aims or outcomes for physical education and there are significant similarities between them. Most countries target national outcomes toward development in the physical, social, and affective domains, with an emphasis on content in sport, health, fitness, and artistic and expressive movement (e.g., in dance). Using Sport Education's competency, literacy, and enthusiasm objectives, we showed how these, to varying degrees, align with the published national physical education outcomes in Australia, England, Ireland, New Zealand, Portugal, Scotland, and Spain.

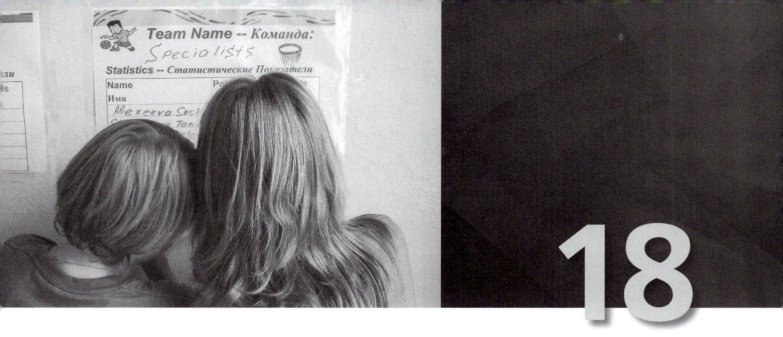

Building Program Credibility and Legitimacy Through Assessment

Chapter Objective

After reading this chapter and practicing the use of the recommended assessment tools strategies, you will be able to articulate the role and importance of assessment and engage in both informal and formal assessment for informing instructional practice and demonstrating student learning.

Key Concepts

- Assessment of students is a teaching function aimed at determining student performance and progress in learning tasks, including subject matter and managerial and social tasks.
- Well-delivered Sport Education provides increased time and opportunity for teachers to conduct both formal and informal assessment.
- Formal-formative assessment is critical in developing credible evidence regarding the quality of physical education programs.
- Formal-formative assessment of student performance should be conducted in authentic contexts (i.e., during actual games, contests, or performance situations).

As noted in chapter 5, instructional alignment is present when the lesson (and season) content that you select is aligned with your intended season outcomes, and when your informal and formal assessments link directly with these same outcomes (see figure 18.1). This chapter focuses on the third component of the instructional alignment—the process of assessment. The end goal is that, through assessment, you put yourself in a position to develop credible information about student performance in your program.

ASSESSMENT DEFINED

Assessment is defined as the "variety of tasks and settings where students are given opportunities to demonstrate their knowledge, skill, understanding, and application of content in a context that allows continued learning and growth" (Siedentop & Tannehill, 2000, pp. 178-179). Assessment requires some form of measurement, whether it is through your observations of students while performing as players or in duty team roles or on written tests, or through student work products such as records of physical activity during discretionary time. Students can also be part of assessment efforts. Assessment is a core teaching function; it yields important information about where your students are in the learning process and about the effectiveness of your instructional efforts.

You can assess students both informally and formally. Assessment is informal when you observe students and provide positive feedback, corrective feedback, prompts, and encouragement. Frequent use of this type of assessment is critical in supporting students' learning. Well-timed and properly targeted feedback can help students move toward competence. It can also help you in deciding when to move on to a new practice task, what content to select for future lessons, how to modify a certain activity to make it either more challenging or easier, when to transition to help students progress as they engage in learning activities, and so on.

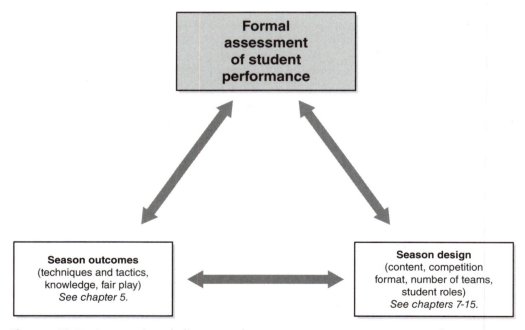

Figure 18.1 Instructional alignment between outcomes, content, and assessment.

Your assessment becomes formal when you develop a permanent product or record of your students' performance. Whether your school district employs traditional letter grades or a standards-based approach, you are expected to do formal assessment. When a parent or an administrator asks about the grade of a specific student, you should be able to provide credible evidence that led to that grade. In other words, your assessments must result in a permanent record of performance. Traditionally, physical education teachers have used either written tests or skill tests at the end of a unit. In Sport Education, however, we recommend ongoing assessments aimed at helping your students progress as they participate in the various learning tasks of a season.

ASSESSMENT IN SPORT EDUCATION

Given that Sport Education seasons are typically longer than traditional units, and because Sport Education classes tend to be highly structured, with student coaches and managers occupying key roles, you will be able to spend more of your time observing students as they perform techniques, tactics, and their roles as referees, scorekeepers, managers, fitness leaders, and the like.

The structure of Sport Education seasons, which emphasizes authentic competition, also allows for ample *authentic assessment*, that is, assessment tasks that resemble how that task is done in the larger world (Siedentop, 1994). Assessing students in tasks that are not gamelike therefore makes little sense. Instead, rather than having to commit a full class session at the end of a unit to give a skills test that bears little resemblance to actual performance, you can use both preseason and regular season matches to formally assess students' performance in their multiple roles under these authentic, gamelike learning conditions.

The culminating events in performance sports like dance or gymnastics present perfect opportunities for authentic assessment. As Wiggins (1987) notes, "We speak of such a final challenge as an 'exhibition.' It is a 'test' in the sense that the big game on

© Human Kinetics.

Sport Education offers increased opportunities for regular assessment that can be used for giving feedback, marking progress, and contributing to a final assessment.

opening night is a 'test.' Unlike the conventional 'final,' the exhibition—like a piano recital or a play—lets the performer show off or 'exhibit' what he or she knows" (p. 15). In Sport Education, these exhibitions could include, for instance, the balance beam routines during a competition day. During a dance season, after several days of the troupes practicing the dance routine (designed either by you or by the troupes themselves), the exhibition is the performance of a line dance or hip-hop routine in front of judges on the day of the formal competition. Such assessments are important because they mark the achievement of season-specific outcomes. Still, judging a team or an athlete solely on a single performance at the end of a season does not provide data that are as valid as performance across the length of a season.

As we have noted, Sport Education offers increased opportunities for regular assessment that can be used for giving feedback, marking progress, and contributing to a final assessment. Because Sport Education seasons involve frequent participation in games and performance situations, and all those situations involve small teams or groups, students will get many more opportunities to use and practice the techniques and tactical moves, giving you more time to observe and assess their performance. As you can see, this is far different from the typical physical education setting, in which large teams and low accountability for performance allow many students to participate at a marginal level.

INFUSING AUTHENTIC AND WORKABLE ASSESSMENTS INTO SEASONS

Effective assessment within one season involves a four-step process. The first step is for you to select specific and authentic season outcomes (see chapter 4). The second step is to select assessment tools that provide the needed quality information about students' performance specific to the selected outcomes. The third step is to use the assessment tools throughout the season to collect student performance data. The fourth step is to document student outcomes. This last step is important in that it becomes the basis for making any needed changes in the program, content selection, or instructional strategies; for assigning student grades; and for program promotion.

Step 1: Select Authentic Season Outcomes

The broad menu of season outcomes outlined in chapter 4 provides you with ample choices, but we recommend that you select just a few for any one season. For a single season, you should select no more than three season outcomes, which would be the focus of your formal assessment. For example, you could select one technique or tactical performance outcome, one outcome related to fair play, and one outcome related to performance in a nonplaying role (e.g., officiating). Given the increased focus around the globe on increasing students' physical activity levels, we recommend that you also include assessments of the amount of physical activity students engage in and the degree to which they enjoy and feel confident about their skills.

Step 2: Select Appropriate Assessment Tools

With season outcomes selected, you need to select or design tools to assess achievement of those outcomes. Table 18.1 gives an overview of the assessment tools from which you can choose. This chapter's web resource suggests tools for assessing the various areas of student performance such as scoring guides, checklists and rating scales, written tests, and team portfolios.

Scoring guides are records of students' performance in the actual game activities. Checklists usually offer a yes-or-no format in relation to student demonstration of specific criteria while rating scales indicate the degree or frequency of the behaviors, skills, or strategies displayed by the student. These tools can be used by students to rate their peers' performance, as we saw in the postgame assessment of fair play and refereeing performance in chapter 12. In some cases, written tests can be useful. As also noted in chapter 12, you can require each team to pass a written test on the game rules that will be in effect during the season. Until they pass that test, they are limited to using class time for team practices. (It obviously makes no sense to use a written rules test at the end of a season.) Team portfolios are excellent tools for students to gather and organize their performance evidence.

Although we encourage student participation in assessment of peers, you as the teacher still have the primary responsibility to develop credible evidence of student performance. If you and your students have extensive experience in Sport Education, you may involve them in developing the tools for specific situations. For example, you may ask students to develop a checklist that measures fair play or the contribution in duty roles to one's team. In addition, self-assessment of fair play and enjoyment is a legitimate tool for measuring Sport Education outcomes.

Step 3: Use Assessment Tools Throughout the Season

Once you have selected specific student outcomes and the associated assessment tools for the season, you need to build in class time to conduct these assessments. As we have noted, Sport Education has a strong emphasis on students learning to manage their own seasons. If students are not engaged as players or performers, they officiate or keep score or scout opposing teams and players. Both preseason and regular season matches offer excellent opportunities to formally assess students' performance in their multiple roles under authentic learning conditions. The key is to make use of the full season. With the longer season, students have more than one opportunity to demonstrate where they are in developing as competent, literate, and enthusiastic sportspersons. To that end, we offer the following strategies regarding the *what*, *when*, *how often*, and *who* of formal-formative assessment, as well as for *remembering to assess*.

Table 18.1 Assessment Tool Options Across Sport Education Season Outcomes

Types of season outcomes	Assessment tool type			
	Scoring guides	Checklists and rating scales	Written tests	Team portfolios
Gameplay performance (techniques, tactics, player and team statistics)	X			X
Fair play performance	X	X		
Duty team performance (e.g., officiating or scorekeeping)		X		X
Knowledge of sport or activity, knowledge of rules, knowledge of scoring procedures	X		X	X
In-class physical activity		X		
Out-of-class physical activity				X

What to Assess

Limit the number of learning outcomes by selecting no more than three outcomes during any one season. The assessment tool shown in figure 18.2 reflects a broad range of legitimate season outcomes. For formal assessment, you could select one or two outcomes that would cover technique and tactical execution (e.g., shot execution, court coverage) and knowledge of game rules or fair play behavior. It is also acceptable to assess different students in the same class on different aspects of gameplay. For example, you might assess some students on court coverage and shot execution while assessing others on shot execution and shot placement.

In a soccer season, you could select guarding and support (both off-the-ball moves) as the gameplay performance outcomes. In addition, you could select scorekeeping or a knowledge-related project about the country represented (a cognitive outcome) plus out-of-class physical activity. Needless to say, you can still informally assess other aspects of student performance. The key is that, at season's end, you have evidence that your students not only were present, on time, and dressed appropriately, but also to what extent they progressed toward the intended outcomes of the season.

When and How Often to Assess

There is evidence that teachers can effectively and reliably build in formal assessment throughout their lessons (van der Mars, Timken, & McNamee 2018; van der Mars, McNamee, & Timken 2018). Ongoing formal-formative assessment has multiple benefits. First, gathering formal assessment data throughout the season avoids the need for scheduling testing days. The formal assessment is embedded within the regular class activities (e.g., warm-up, team practice, competition); that is, when you observe a student and determine his or her level of performance in supporting teammates in a soccer game, you would record your observation as such.

Writing this information down also sets the scene for you to offer a correction, prompt, or reinforcement, or initiate a short bout of Q-and-A. For example, in a basketball season, some students persist in shooting from behind the three-point arc with little success while teammates are wide open and closer to the basket. If developing tactical skills (e.g., decision-making) were a primary outcome for that season, you would score those students lower on that aspect of gameplay because they are not yet recognizing or accepting that there are teammates who may be in a better shooting position. At the same time, you would provide them with feedback or prompt them to look for teammates who were in a better position to shoot. You can also employ what Harvey et al. (2016) referred to as a "debate of ideas." Debates of ideas reflect the use of questioning techniques to aid students in developing deeper understanding of their actions. Recording students' levels of performance is also a trigger for informal assessment.

It is important to note that, when assessing throughout the entire season, you can adjust your ratings of student performance made earlier in the season if you see that students are clearly progressing in one or more gameplay areas.

Whom to Assess

When formally assessing students throughout the season, there is no pressure to assess all students in one day. During any given lesson, you could formally assess just one team or a small group of target students from various teams. Using periodic spot-checks, you can observe selected students in their games (or duty team roles) and judge their performance based on the levels described in the scoring guides.

Knowing that you need not assess all students in one class period should make the assessment function more manageable. Again from the perspective of starting small, we suggest you start with formally assessing only one team during one lesson. Across multiple seasons, you should be able to observe and record performance information for each student and use that information as the basis for determining grades or scoring students relative to state or national content standards.

As you gain experience with ongoing formal-formative assessment, you will start making better judgments in less time. Imagine a regular day in a tennis season where students are engaged in match play or serving in a duty team capacity. How many students do you think you can observe for short periods of time? You will find that as you become more competent in assessing students' learning you will be able to observe and record more quickly, thus having more complete coverage of more students.

All students (not just the higher-skilled ones) deserve your attention through encouragement, feedback, and questioning. For the purpose of formal assessment, however, your knowledge of your students will help determine which students may require more attention. For example, you likely will need less time to judge the level of play of a student who is already a varsity team tennis player, so you will be able to focus your assessment (and instruction) on those who are less experienced.

Remembering to Assess

It is essential that the assessment teaching function becomes habitual rather than an afterthought. Still, teachers have to attend to so many things during class that formal assessment is easily forgotten. The MotivAider (www.habitchange.com) is an excellent prompting tool to remind you to observe and judge target students' performance and mark down a record thereof. Worn on waistband or belt, this is a countdown timer that vibrates for 3 to 5 seconds at the end of each interval (e.g., 120 seconds). When you have had some practice assessing your students with the aid of this prompter, and it has become a habit, you may no longer need this prompting device.

Step 4: Document Student Outcomes

Once student performance data have been collected, you need to design a report form in which student achievement can be summarized. You will need to decide the weight (or percentage) to give to each area of performance for which you have documented evidence. An example of how students' performance can be weighted for the purpose of assigning a grade, which includes a focus on actual performance, is shown in figure 18.2. Note that fair play performance also encompasses the typical managerial performance indicators (attendance, dress, being on time). If you find that students' overall

Figure 18.2
SAMPLE GRADE WEIGHTING (100 POINTS MAXIMUM)

Category	Points
League play (4 at 10 points each)	40
Fair play performance (including attendance, dress, punctuality)	20
Knowledge and understanding	20
Duty team performance (4 at 5 points each)	20

class conduct needs further improvement, you can give greater weight to their fair play performance than to their performance in actual league play.

TYPES OF ASSESSMENT TOOLS

As a physical educator, you can choose from various assessment tools. With each type, some practice will be required to get comfortable with its use. Four types of assessment tools are discussed here: scoring guides; checklists and rating scales; team portfolios; and written tests. Some of these can be used by students, as well.

Scoring Guides

Scoring guides are completed while observing students' actions during gameplay or performances that are part of the season. They provide descriptions of students' performance across a number of levels. Figure 18.3 includes two examples of portions of scoring guides, one for assessing ball placement in pickleball, and one for assessing support by players not in possession of the puck in floor hockey. In these examples, performance levels range from struggling (level 1) to exceeding (level 5). Scoring guides (see this chapter's web resource) take a holistic approach, and give teachers the choice of which aspects of gameplay to assess formally. That is, they include technical and tactical aspects of gameplay, knowledge of game rules, and a fair play component.

Scoring guides are flexible. You can choose the specific gameplay dimensions of most interest during a season. For example, you might assess student's performance on technical and tactical aspects of gameplay, on their knowledge of the game rules in their role as player, or on their fair play behavior. For a formal assessment, you should select only those dimensions that are aligned with your planned season outcomes. A number of examples of gameplay performance scales for sports and activities can be found in the web resource. They come in Word and Excel formats. The Excel version also includes space for you to record students' performance on the managerial performance indicators of attendance, punctuality, and dress, with performance across selected season outcomes linked in a single file.

In figure 18.4 we present a scoring guide template for use in a strength conditioning season, where the assessment is focused primarily on students executing technically correct strength exercises, general etiquette and conduct in the weight room, the documenting of lifts performed, and a possible out-of-class assignment. When students track their progress, it reflects a form of formative-formal assessment. As you monitor the class, you can spot-check five or six students (or a particular team) to determine whether they know how to track their progress. Such individual progress charts can be made part of the team portfolio, which is made available for review by you.

Checklists and Rating Scales

Checklists and rating scales are particularly useful in assessing student performance as they complete their officiating and other team roles. Figure 18.5 shows a simple checklist completed by team captains at the end of games, while the referee performance rating scale in figure 18.6 is completed by the players on the participating teams. This rating scale gives you (and the referees) important feedback about their performance. Because all students will at some point be in the role of referee, they are likely to take the evaluation more seriously, knowing that they too will be evaluated.

Developing strong fair play behaviors warrants ongoing evaluation, with checklists and rating scales that are legitimate tools for assessment. The instruments presented in figures 12.4 and 12.5 in chapter 12 show two good examples.

Figure 18.3
SCORING GUIDES FOR ASSESSING PICKLEBALL BALL PLACEMENT AND FLOOR HOCKEY SUPPORT

Pickleball Ball Placement

Select the term that best matches the player's performance for the observed skill or tactic.

Technique or skill level	Level 5 Exceeds (competent)	Level 3 Meets (emerging or recreational)	Level 1 Developing (struggling)
Tactic: Ball placement	Ball is hit to the corners and is either short or long dependent upon opponent's court position	Is able to place the ball to spaces when it's hit directly to the player	• Aim of ball placement is to simply get the ball back over the net, without concern for a specific spot on the court • Returns the ball in most cases, but with little account for placement

Floor Hockey Support

Select the term that best matches the player's performance for the observed skill or tactic.

Technique or skill level	Level 5 Exceeds (competent)	Level 3 Meets (emerging or recreational)	Level 1 Developing (struggling)
Tactic: Off-the-ball or puck play (support)	• Moves to help teammates at effective angles and distances within offensive plan • Moves to open passing lanes or space • Draws opponent's defense out of position, using V-cuts and L-cuts	• At times, moves to help teammates in moving ball or puck up-court, but sometimes misses the right angle or distance • Still more reactive than anticipatory to other players' moves • At times, still lingers between or behind opponents, but does try to correct • Only sporadic moves are aimed at drawing opponent's defense out of position, using V-cuts and L-cuts	• Moves with uncertainty; appears at random and confused • Does not respond or slowly responds to the game's action • Looks lost or avoids ball or puck • Gets caught "hiding" in between or behind other players

Figure 18.4
SCORING GUIDE FOR ASSESSING STRENGTH CONDITIONING PERFORMANCE

Select the number that best matches the student's performance for the observed strength tasks.

Teacher: _____ Class: _____

Strength conditioning area assessed	PERFORMANCE LEVEL	
	Exceeds performance standard 4	**Meets performance standard** 3
Lift technique execution: ___ Core ___ Upper body ___ Lower body	• Uses proper weight according to skill level and season goals • *Throughout a set:* • Uses three Ss (i.e., slow, smooth, steady) appropriately • Proper hand-foot-trunk position is maintained • With dynamic lifts, ROM is utilized fully • Exhales on exertion and inhales on recovery • With both dynamic and static exercises (e.g., planks), body position is properly maintained	• Uses proper weight • *Throughout a set:* • On most reps, uses three Ss (i.e., slow, smooth, steady) appropriately • Proper hand-foot-trunk position is maintained • Only minor body alignment changes as fatigue sets in (continues to own the movement) • With dynamic lifts, ROM is utilized fully on most reps • Exhales on exertion and inhales on recovery • With both dynamic and static exercises (e.g., planks), body position is maintained in most reps and time
Weight training etiquette and general class conduct	• Handles all equipment with care. • Cleans up stations after use • Helps peers with attentive spotting and coaching • Lets others work in • Time lag between sets is appropriate • Socializing is at appropriate level (i.e., does not detract) • Focused on completing with appropriate intensity and good quality sets and reps or serving as spotter • Employs safety equipment at all times	• Uses equipment appropriately • Cleans up stations after use • Helps others with spotting at times. • Lets others work in • Socializing is appropriate and nondisruptive • Time lag between sets is acceptable • Is focused on completing own sets and reps, but spotting is spotty • Employs safety equipment at all times
Training log	• Lift record is complete and correct • Info is thorough and detailed • Includes all required lifts and choice lifts (sets, reps, and weight) • Consistent use of muscle balance using appropriate relative balance between movements (push–pull) or muscle groups (e.g., chest–back, quads–glutes–hamstrings)	• Includes all required lifts (sets, reps, and weight) • Lift record is complete and correct • Uses muscle balance with inconsistent use of ratios (working to the weaker muscle)
Summary report	• Submits draft report for initial feedback • Seeks advice and input • Substance is extensive and focused • Detailed self-reflection • Well organized • Extensive supporting sources • Could serve as model for future students	• Submits draft report for initial feedback • Seeks advice and input • Reasonable substance • Some reflection is included • Well organized • Some supporting sources

	PERFORMANCE LEVEL	
Strength conditioning area assessed	**Progressing toward performance standard** 2	**Well below performance standard** 1
Lift technique execution: ___ Core ___ Upper body ___ Lower body	• Weight too heavy or light • *Throughout a set:* • Lift pace or cadence is either too fast or uneven, with some loss of control through much of the set (e.g., weights are still slammed down on release) • Hand–foot–trunk position is established and maintained • Noticeable change as fatigue sets in • With dynamic lifts, partial ROM is utilized • Breathing pattern still inconsistent • With both dynamic and static exercises (e.g., planks), body position is maintained in most reps • Body is jerked out of position during later reps	• Weight too heavy or too light • *Throughout a set:* • Lift pace or cadence is too fast early on, uncontrolled or uneven throughout much of the set (i.e., weights slammed on release) • Hand–foot position is inappropriate or inconsistent • With dynamic lifts, ROM used is limited • With static exercises, body is not positioned properly • Holds breath on exertion; breathes between reps • Body is jerked out of position during later reps
Weight training etiquette and general class conduct	• Uses equipment appropriately • Station clean-up is inconsistent • Disrupts or interrupts others • Spots sparingly • Time spent socializing is less dominant • Inconsistent safety equipment use	• Mishandles equipment • Leaves stations without cleaning up • Disrupts or interrupts others • Neglects spotting duties • Excessive noise • Excessive time lag between sets • Socializing is a primary activity
Training log	• Records info on some required lifts (sets and reps), but no choice lifts • Has correct information, but some data still missing • Uses muscle balance on some lifts but not on others	• Does not record info on completed sets and reps (i.e., not kept up-to-date) • Leaves card behind at station or loses card • No use of muscle balance, no ratio addressed
Summary report	• Submits no draft version for screening • Little or incomplete substance • Few, if any, supporting sources • Organization reflects some planning • Effort is there	• Does not submit report, or submits report that reflects complete lack of substance, organization, and effort

Figure 18.5
EVALUATION OF OFFICIALS

Officiating team	Yes	No
Were the referees fair to both teams?		
Did they know the rules?		
Did the scorekeeper pay attention during the game?		

Figure 18.6
TEAM ASSESSMENT OF REFEREE PERFORMANCE

Team: _____ Final score: _____

Match: _____ vs. _____

Referee: _____

- Answer questions as a team.
- Be fair and honest.

	1 Poor	2 Not bad	3 Average	4 Good	5 Excellent
The referee was fair and impartial.					
The referee knew the rules.					
The referee was clear in explanations.					

Team Portfolios

Some teachers have students develop team portfolios to document their participation and performance in Sport Education, and these portfolios can be used to assess student performance and learning as well. Portfolios can represent evidence of their motor, cognitive, and emotional engagement. For example, they can be organized to include sections for individual player statistics, team statistics, written team practice plans, written fitness trainer conditioning plans, action photos, team photo, player bios and photos, and any out-of-class written reports (e.g., game summary reports or reports on the sporting history of a country if the competition is held between countries). As the season progresses, teams would be expected to add evidence to their portfolio. Kinchin (2001) provided one example of a portfolio that was designed to show students' achievement in relation to the Sport Education goals of competence, literacy, and enthusiasm (see table 18.2).

Table 18.2 Assessing Achievement of Sport Education Season Outcomes

Artifact	Competence	Literacy	Enthusiasm
Self-assessment of performance	X		
Rules test		X	
Fair play awards			X
Peer skills test	X		
Role evaluation		X	
Activity log or diary			X

Reprinted with permission from: G.D. Kinchin, "Using Team Portfolios During a Sport Education Season," *Journal of Physical Education, Recreation & Dance* 72, no. 2 (2001): 41-44. DOI: 10.1080/07303084.2001.10605834

A portfolio consists of a number of artifacts, which are any product that provides evidence of progress, experience, and achievements. In Sport Education, examples of artifacts include written tests, score sheets, written or electronic reports, worksheets, team and player photos, action photos, team statistics forms, flags, player profiles, and so on.

It should be noted that a team portfolio is a *student-created product,* and all team members have certain responsibilities to contribute to building the portfolio and prepare it for subsequent review by you, the teacher. You should make it clear that each team documents what each team member contributed to the total portfolio. This can help ensure that individual team members actually work as a team on such assignments. For example, the team statistician could be asked to enter the game statistics from individual games and update the individual player and team statistics. The score sheets completed during competition also provide direct performance indicators. The team publicist would oversee compiling of the photos taken and add captions to give context to each photo. He or she could also provide the player bios. The coach and fitness leaders would place their respective practice and conditioning plans in a designated section. If teams or individual players practice outside of class, they could include their practice activity logs as well. One example is provided in figure 6.5, and the web resource includes several examples of activity logs that teams (or individual players) can complete and use as evidence.

Teachers using Sport Education have also collaborated with their classroom colleagues by integrating classroom content (see chapter 21 for more an in-depth overview and examples). For example, in a season where students compete as different nations they might be asked to write reports on their nation (by way of a link with social studies). Reporting on famous athletes in the history of a sport (history) or on the life and habitat of the animal after which the team is named (biology or life science) would also be ways to assess student knowledge. Another idea is to have each team represent a disease (e.g., malaria, diphtheria, typhoid). For their health education class, your students could write a report on the disease their team represents. This chapter's web resource includes a template for assessing such work. The focus of the assessment is the quality of the work in terms of content, depth, accuracy, layout, organization, and writing (i.e., spelling, grammar).

Written Tests

Students' knowledge can be assessed in multiple ways, including observation of knowledge in action (as noted earlier), as well as artifacts such as written tests and quizzes, worksheets, and out-of-class assignments. Traditionally, teachers have relied on written tests to assess students' knowledge of the rules of a sport. Written tests take up precious class time that could instead be devoted to authentic learning activities where students can demonstrate their knowledge and understanding of the rules either as players or as officials. For example, in basketball, you can directly observe how well both players and referees understand the traveling rule (a primary rule) based on the number of times that violation is committed and called. For documenting your students' knowledge of game rules, we strongly recommend that you assess their knowledge in action. The scoring guides included in the web resource include an option for assessing knowledge in action.

ASSESSING IN-CLASS PHYSICAL ACTIVITY

You can choose from several tools to assess your students' in-class physical activity, such as direct observation, pedometers, heart rate monitors, and smartphones. The choice of tool depends in part on cost and ease of use.

Direct Observation

If the purchase of electronic devices is not an option, you can still collect evidence of student physical activity levels using direct observation. Direct observation is a valid means of collecting data on physical activity (McKenzie & van der Mars, 2015). You can select three students and, at set time intervals (e.g., between 90 and 120 seconds), quickly scan the selected students and determine whether they are engaged in moderate to vigorous physical activity (MVPA). This observation tactic is called *momentary time sampling*. At the end of each interval you take a snapshot of what the three students are doing and make a yes-or-no decision. A student lying down, sitting, or standing would be sedentary. A student engaged in activity that requires energy expenditure of at least brisk walking would be scored as engaged in MVPA.

You would select a new trio of students each time you assessed this season outcome. In a 50-minute lesson with an observation interval of 90 seconds, you would obtain just over 30 samples, which provides an accurate estimate of students' MVPA levels. It takes some practice, but is an excellent low-cost approach to assessment. The paper-and-pencil recording card is shown in figure 18.7.

Pedometers

Pedometers are a well-accepted and reliable tool for tracking physical activity levels. They are worn on the waistband or belt just above the right hip or in the back. They are relatively inexpensive and can be used for tracking physical activity during physical education classes and beyond. The technology behind pedometers has progressed to the point that you can select from those that count only steps, those that count steps and time accumulated in physical activity, and those that track time accumulated in MVPA. The latter feature is based on the number of steps taken per minute. You can set the minimum number of steps needed for the activity to be considered at least moderate in intensity. Tracking time accumulated in MVPA during physical education classes is a legitimate but minimal indicator of program quality. Having

Student MVPA Assessment (120 sec interval)

Date: 3/23   Grade: 8   Teacher: J.V.

Students: Jose   , Ciara   , David

Activity: Team warm-ups and conditioning; season games

MVPA = Moderate to vigorous physical activity

(Definition: Brisk walking or any activity that would require more energy than a brisk walk, including strength exercises such as curl-ups and push-ups.)

Y = MVPA; N = No MVPA

Name:	Jose	Ciara	David
1.	Ⓨ/ N	Ⓨ/ N	Ⓨ/ N
2.	Ⓨ/ N	Ⓨ/ N	Ⓨ/ N
3.	Y /Ⓝ	Ⓨ/ N	Ⓨ/ N
4.	Ⓨ/ N	Y /Ⓝ	Ⓨ/ N
5.	Y /Ⓝ	Y /Ⓝ	Y /Ⓝ
6.	Y /Ⓝ	Y /Ⓝ	Y /Ⓝ
7.	Y /Ⓝ	Ⓨ/ N	Y /Ⓝ
8.	Ⓨ/ N	Y /Ⓝ	Y /Ⓝ
9.	Ⓨ/ N	Ⓨ/ N	Y /Ⓝ
10.	Y /Ⓝ	Ⓨ/ N	Ⓨ/ N
11.	Ⓨ/ N	Ⓨ/ N	Ⓨ/ N
12.	Ⓨ/ N	Y /Ⓝ	Ⓨ/ N
13.	Y /Ⓝ	Y /Ⓝ	Ⓨ/ N
14.	Ⓨ/ N	Ⓨ/ N	Y /Ⓝ
15.	Ⓨ/ N	Y /Ⓝ	Ⓨ/ N
Total # Ys:	9/15 = 60%	8/15 = 53%	9/15 = 60%

Figure 18.7 A moderate to vigorous physical activity (MVPA) worksheet uses an observation tactic called momentary time sampling. Every 120 seconds, teachers quickly assess whether or not their students are engaged in MVPA.

such evidence allows you to gauge how your students' activity levels compares with the national recommended levels (Kohl & Cook, 2013).

A full set of pedometers can give you a good measure of class activity levels. With some practice and guidance, students can learn to attach a pedometer, and return it without much delay when the measurement episode ends. Separate recording forms that students can use to track their in-class physical activity can be found in this chapter's web resource.

Smartphone Apps

Smartphones are commonplace in today's world. Schools and school districts have established policies regarding students' use of smartphones while on campus. Clearly they can be a distraction but their use can also be justified, for example when students are properly introduced to one of the many physical activity tracking apps.

There are many fitness and wellness apps, each offering different features. Accuracy will vary across apps, so it helps if all the students use the same one. Apps can play an important role students' overall fitness and activity plan when they monitor their activity levels (either in step counts or in time spent in physical activity) over extended periods of time.

ASSESSING OUT-OF-CLASS PHYSICAL ACTIVITY

It is important to promote and support students' physical activity during your lessons. However, it is equally (if not more) important to encourage students to engage in activity beyond the class (e.g., during recess, lunch period, before and after school). The web resource includes several assessment tools that teams (and individual players on a team) can use to track their out-of-class physical activity. Students can be asked to document when they were active, what they did for activity, with whom, and for how long they were active. These would be excellent examples of team or player artifacts that can be placed in the team's portfolio as evidence of performance.

Smart phone apps are also an excellent physical activity tracking tool for use during students' discretionary times. The web resource includes spreadsheet templates for various grade levels from primary through post-secondary that allow students to set step count goals and track their physical activity levels by tracking their cumulative step counts across days. Step count results are graphed automatically. Table 18.3 and figure 18.8 reflect the data entry and graphic output for a high school student.

MAKING A CASE FOR YOUR PROGRAM

Your students, their parents, and your school's administration are all key people who should know about your program. Through report cards, all will get some indication of student progress and performance in physical education. But beyond that, physical education programs must find ways to garner attention and recognition from the public. Teachers who have gathered good data on what their students know and can do are in a stronger position to promote and advocate for their role in the school cur-

Table 18.3 Output From a Spreadsheet Physical Activity Log for Use by Students

Cumulative daily goal (steps): 9,800				
Day	Date	Cumulative daily step goal	Actual steps	Cumulative actual steps
Monday	4/24/18	9,800	9,834	9,834
Tuesday	4/25/18	19,600	12,651	22,485
Wednesday	4/26/18	29,400	13,943	36,428
Thursday	4/27/18	39,200	8,934	45,362
Friday	4/28/18	49,000	3,461	48,823
Saturday	4/29/18	58,800	12,569	61,392
Sunday	4/30/18	68,600	11,128	72,520
Monday	5/1/18	78,400	9,367	81,887
Tuesday	5/2/18	88,200	12,498	94,385
Wednesday	5/3/18	98,000	14,497	108,882
Thursday	5/4/18	107,800	13,402	122,284
Friday	5/5/18	117,600	11,602	133,886
Saturday	5/6/18	127,400	10,383	144,269
Sunday	5/7/18	137,200	12,451	156,720
		Daily average (actual steps):	11,194	

riculum. The following five key strategies will help you make the case for your physical education program to significant constituents (i.e., school and district administrators, parents, and classroom teachers).

1. Have credible information to share about the accomplishments of your program.

First and foremost, you have to be able to show that your program is accomplishing its goals and objectives. Ongoing formal assessment should go a long way toward providing you with the needed information. Without it, you will be limited to making general claims for which you have no specific support.

2. Prepare to share with anyone, anytime, anyplace.

Whenever and wherever possible, take every opportunity to be proactive and share the accomplishments of your program. Encounters with administrators and parents can be formal. They include staff meetings, school board meetings, parent–teacher organization (PTO) meetings, parent–teacher conferences, school open houses, curriculum nights, and physical education demonstration nights. When at these meetings, have a plan of what information you can share about your program. Sharing your efforts and accomplishments with your colleagues during faculty meetings (or in passing) also increases their awareness of the mission and accomplishments of your program.

Informal opportunities to advocate for your program are equally important. Chance encounters with parents around campus or in the community are great opportunities to let them know what is going on in your program and to report on their child. We know of teachers who make it a point to make four or five phone calls each week to parents or guardians of a small group of students and share the students' accomplishments. Imagine the parents' surprise to receive such news! Playing matches that are part of your culminating events during a school assembly is another excellent way of demonstrating what your students have accomplished. If possible, invite the local newspaper to your opening day or the culminating event of a season. There is no off-season for being proactive in promoting and advocating for your program!

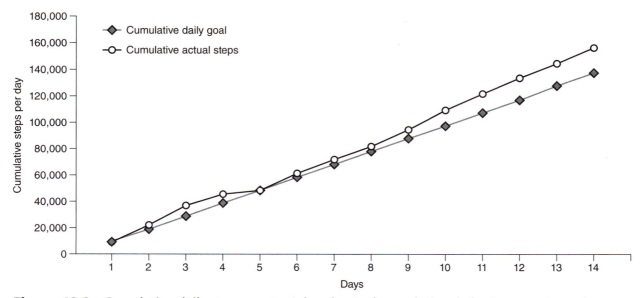

Figure 18.8 Cumulative daily step count goal and actual cumulative daily step count graph.

3. Use all possible venues.

There are so many ways to share information about students' performance and accomplishments. In programs where students have more experience with Sport Education, their effort in publicizing the season can reach well beyond the gym. The school newsletter, the school's website (or your own physical education program's website), and display boards in the school building are excellent places to show your season results. With students becoming more and more tech savvy, their publicity roles can include using those places to display artifacts of the season (e.g., action photos, league standings, player profiles).

4. Invite significant people to your season events.

Throughout the season, consider inviting any of the significant parties. In elementary schools, classroom teachers typically use the physical education class period for their own planning. They may be willing to come and witness how their students do in physical education during such special events.

More so in elementary school programs, parents often visit school and observe their children in class events. Once they witness the energy, passion, and enthusiasm of students as they participate in a Sport Education season, they will become more aware of your programming efforts. They may even be willing to serve as volunteer assistants.

School and district administrators have busy work schedules, but standing invitations (with e-mail reminders) may increase the likelihood that they will attend a regular season day or a culminating event. Imagine their reaction when they see motivated, self-directed students who demonstrate well-played matches or performances. Good administrators will remember and recognize such efforts. Those who witness a physical education program that has focus, energy, and a positive impact on students are more likely to support such programs.

5. Regularly attend meetings of your school's PTO, site council, and school wellness council.

Each of these groups is involved in the well-being of students in the schools. Any time you can get the ear of these committee members, you have an opportunity to advocate for your program. Too often, the only time school board members see physical educators at their monthly meetings is when physical education programs are targeted for cutbacks. Your active engagement in such meetings will be noticed (as will a lack of involvement).

SUMMARY

Historically, physical education programs have not had what Lund and Veal (2008) refer to as a *culture of assessment* in the sense that teachers have not regarded assessment as a central teaching function. In this chapter, we have shown the link between assessment and the selected season outcomes, and have offered strategies to make assessment a more manageable process. We have also provided ways in which such information can be used for promoting and advocating for your physical education program to parents and school- or district-level policy makers (i.e., principals, district superintendents, and district school boards).

Organizing a Sport Education-Themed Physical Education Program

Chapter Objective

After reading this chapter, you will be able to identify the value of program mission statements, program themes, and yearly block plans.

Key Concepts

- A program theme reflects the central focus of the program, and includes content (i.e., seasons or units) that reflect coherence in what students experience as they complete the program.
- Examples of program themes include sport, fitness, outdoor pursuits, or personal and social responsibility. These themes reflect teachers' values and beliefs as well as their expertise specific to what they can and prefer to teach.
- Program mission statements inform people as to what the program aims to accomplish with all the students in the school.
- Establishing a physical education program mission and theme allows teachers to defend a physical education program to their school's administrative team.
- A yearly block plan provides a calendar of when seasons are scheduled, who is assigned to teach them, how long each one will last, and which activity area will be used.

In chapter 2 we introduced the metaphor of *physical educators as architects*. In this chapter, we want to draw your attention to the need to have a strong foundation. In three sections, we present strategies for organizing your physical education program with a theme around Sport Education. First, we introduce the need for developing a clear program mission statement. Second, we address the need to select and organize your program's content around a distinct theme that runs through the program, while keeping in mind Sport Education's curricular philosophy. Third, we address the need to develop and maintain a yearly block plan.

DEVELOPING A PROGRAM MISSION STATEMENT

Through their experiences in the physical education program, all students will develop physically, socially, and emotionally to ensure they are equipped with the needed skills and knowledge to grow into informed, healthy, and active young adults.

We pledge that our students at Mission Junior High School will become skillful in a variety of physical activities that will help them be active for a lifetime.

These are just two examples of possible program mission statements. In the lobby of most schools, some type of mission statement is posted somewhere that informs people of what the school stands for and what it aims to accomplish. A physical education program should have its own program mission statement, posted and advertised prominently. The statement becomes a compass for you as you plan, deliver, and assess the program. A well-crafted program mission statement should set your program apart from other programs.

What are the core characteristics of a sound program mission statement? First, it is usually a short (one- or two-sentence) statement that conveys what the program aims to accomplish with its students. Long mission statements tend to be cumbersome and soon forgotten. Second, it should inspire its readers be motivated and want to learn more about the program and what happens within it. Third, it is a more general statement that could easily be connected to the current national or state content standards (see chapters 16 and 17). Fourth, it should be inclusive of all students, regardless of their (dis-)abilities, incoming skill levels, aptitudes, and gender, ethnic, and racial heritage. Fifth, it should link with the more specific program goals, meaningful student experiences in the program (i.e., the units or seasons), the instructional strategies employed, and how teachers assess students and the program itself. Sixth, it allows teachers to explain how the program's mission is reflected in the more specific program goals, and what meaningful experiences they provide in the program (i.e., the units or seasons), the instructional strategies they employ, and how they assess students and the program itself. Finally, the statement should not make claims that it cannot reasonably meet. Rather, it should reflect what the staff in the program views as its main strengths.

Mission statements are dynamic, not static, concepts. It is important that the physical education staff take inventory at regular intervals (i.e., every couple of years) in order to determine whether the program is delivered in a way that matches what is claimed in the mission statement. This will keep it from becoming a stale and empty statement. Look back at the two program mission examples. Do they meet most of the criteria listed here?

Ideally, a school district would have a mission statement for all its physical education programs at each of the three school levels (i.e., elementary, middle or junior high, and high school). In reality, few districts dictate a specific curriculum and instruction model, leaving it up to individual schools to decide on how to organize and build their respective programs. A program mission statement should therefore be developed by the entire school's physical education staff. All teachers in the program should have input into what the program stands for and how they each contribute to the mission. This is especially important for new teachers hired to join the staff.

ESTABLISHING A DISTINCT PROGRAM THEME

Reflect on your own physical education experiences when you were in school. Can you recall your physical education having a distinct theme? Can you honestly state that you learned something valuable and meaningful because of your participation in it? Do you believe that all students would view these experiences in similar ways? Having a distinct program theme and organizing the content accordingly will help your program remain focused. It will also help you avoid having a program that is a repeat of the same short units that are nothing more than a smorgasbord of content and that have little if any focus on providing students with meaningful learning experiences.

A quality physical education program is one whose content reflects a distinct program theme (Tannehill et al., 2015). That is, there is coherence in what students experience as they complete the program. Examples of program themes include sport, fitness, outdoor pursuits, or personal and social responsibility. An agreed-upon program theme reflects and is determined by multiple factors. Key factors include the local topography and climate, teachers' values and beliefs, and their expertise specific to what they can teach. For example, teachers with a strong content background in outdoor pursuits and who live in more mountainous regions would most likely build a program aimed at developing students' skills and knowledge through activities such as hiking, climbing, mountain biking, canoeing, and fly-fishing. Similarly, teachers who value and believe in the importance of physical fitness and who have strong content knowledge in this area are more likely to develop a fitness-themed program. These teachers might consider incorporating the Fitness for Life model (Corbin & Le Masurier, 2014), which includes content offerings aimed at helping students become informed fitness consumers. Teachers with both broad and in-depth content background in sport would likely make sport the central theme, and so Sport Education would be the logical curricular approach to build students' competency, literacy, and enthusiasm for sport. Choosing a fitness- or outdoor-themed program does not mean that the principles embedded in Sport Education cannot be used. Throughout this text, we have made reference to several examples of how Sport Education can be used with content not typically described as sport.

Can Programs Have More Than One Theme?

In most cases, because they are the only teacher in the program, physical educators in elementary schools can put their own stamp on how a program is organized. Later in this chapter we will provide more detail on how an elementary program can be structured around a theme.

Depending on the school size, secondary school programs may have anywhere from three to six physical education teachers on staff. It is not uncommon for teachers in one program to have differing values and beliefs about what the program theme and focus should be and what content should be included. This does not mean that the physical education program cannot have a distinct theme. Moreover, programs can have a dual theme. For example, over the last three decades there has been a shift in physical education programming, given the growing interest in the promotion of physical activity from a health perspective. As a result, we have seen an increased emphasis on building in more physical fitness content in K-12 programs. We view a dual-themed focus on Sport Education and Fitness for Life (Corbin & Le Masurier, 2014; Corbin, Le Masurier, & Lambdin, 2018) as a natural and defensible blend. Two examples of a junior high program with a dual-themed focus are presented in Tables 19.1 and 19.2. Table 19.1 shows a program for a school where physical education is offered every day and in both grade levels, but only for one semester (i.e., 18 weeks, in either fall or spring). Table 19.2 includes a junior high school program with physical education offered every day in both grade levels over the full year. Later on in this chapter (see tables 19.5 and 19.6), when we address the use of yearly block plans, we will present another example of a dual-themed sport and fitness program in a junior high school.

In high schools, graduation requirements for physical education vary from district to district. In many districts, high school students have physical education for only two semesters or less. Moreover, the length of high schools classes varies, depending on their school's schedule. While some schools employ a standard 50-minute lesson schedule; others, where the block system is in place, have lessons lasting from 75 to 90 minutes. Still other schools use a combination of these two schedules. Also common are schools that follow an A-B format (often named after the school colors, e.g., Blue and White or Green and Gold), which results in students having physical education every other day.

Table 19.1 Dual Focus Fitness for Life and Sport Education Semester Plan

Week	Student text content	Mon	Tues	Wed	Thurs	Fri
1	FFL ch. 1	1.1	1.2	1.3	1.4	1.5
2	FFL ch. 2	2.1	2.2	2.3	2.4	2.5
3	FFL ch. 3	3.1	3.2	3.3	3.4	3.5
4	SE season 1	SE season 1	SE season 1	SE season 1	SE season 1	SE season 1
5	SE season 1	SE season 1	SE season 1	SE season 1	SE season 1	SE season 1
6	SE season 1	SE season 1	SE season 1	SE season 1	SE season 1	SE season 1
7	FFL ch. 4	4.1	4.2	4.3	4.4	4.5
8	FFL ch. 5	5.1	5.2	5.3	5.4	5.5
9	FFL ch. 6	6.1	6.2	6.3	6.4	6.5
10	SE season 2	SE season 2	SE season 2	SE season 2	SE season 2	SE season 2
11	SE season 2	SE season 2	SE season 2	SE season 2	SE season 2	SE season 2
12	SE season 2	SE season 2	SE season 2	SE season 2	SE season 2	SE season 2
13	FFL ch. 7	7.1	7.2	7.3	7.4	7.5
14	FFL ch. 8	8.1	8.2	8.3	8.4	8.5
15	FFL ch. 9	9.1	9.2	9.3	9.4	9.5
16	SE season 3	SE season 3	SE season 3	SE season 3	SE season 3	SE season 3
17	SE season 3	SE season 3	SE season 3	SE season 3	SE season 3	SE season 3
18	SE season 3	SE season 3	SE season 3	SE season 3	SE season 3	SE season 3

Table 19.2   Dual Focus Fitness for Life and Sport Education Yearly Plan

Week	Student text content	Mon	Tues	Wed	Thurs	Fri
1	N/A	Program orientation	Program orientation	Team building challenges	Team building challenges	Team building challenges
2	FFL ch. 1	Organizational lesson 1	Organizational lesson 2	Organizational lesson 3	FFL 1.1	FFL 1.2
3	FFL ch. 1	FFL 1.3	FFL 1.4	FFL 1.5	SE season 1	SE season 1
4	FFL ch. 1	SE season 1	SE season 1	SE season 1	SE season 1	SE season 1
5	FFL ch. 2	SE season 1	SE season 1	SE season 1	SE season 1	SE season 1
6	FFL ch. 3	SE season 1	SE season 1	SE season 1	SE season 1	SE season 1
7	SE season 1	SE season 1	SE season 1	SE season 1	SE season 1	SE season 1
8	FFL ch. 2	FFL 2.1	FFL 2.2	FFL 2.3	FFL 2.4	FFL 2.5
9	FFL ch. 3	FFL 3.1	FFL 3.2	FFL 3.3	FFL 3.4	FFL 3.5
10	SE season 2	SE season 2	SE season 2	SE season 2	SE season 2	SE season 2
11	SE season 2	SE season 2	SE season 2	SE season 2	SE season 2	SE season 2
12	SE season 2	SE season 2	SE season 2	SE season 2	SE season 2	SE season 2
13	SE season 3	SE season 3	SE season 2	SE season 3	SE season 3	SE season 3
14	SE season 3	SE season 3	SE season 2	SE season 3	SE season 3	SE season 3
15	SE season 3	SE season 3	SE season 2	SE season 3	SE season 3	SE season 3
16	FFL ch. 4	FFL 4.1	FFL 4.2	FFL 4.3	FFL 4.4	FFL 4.5
17	FFL ch. 5	FFL 5.1	FFL 5.2	FFL 5.3	FFL 5.4	FFL 5.5
18	SE season 4	SE season 4	SE season 4	SE season 4	SE season 4	SE season 4
19	SE season 4	SE season 4	SE season 4	SE season 4	SE season 4	SE season 4
19	SE season 4	SE season 4	SE season 4	SE season 4	SE season 4	SE season 4
21	SE season 5	SE season 5	SE season 5	SE season 5	SE season 5	SE season 5
22	SE season 5	SE season 5	SE season 5	SE season 5	SE season 5	SE season 5
23	SE season 5	SE season 5	SE season 5	SE season 5	SE season 5	SE season 5
24	FFL ch. 6	FFL 6.1	FFL 6.2	FFL 6.3	FFL 6.4	FFL 6.5
25	FFL ch. 7	FFL 7.1	FFL 7.2	FFL 7.3	FFL 7.4	FFL 7.5
26	SE season 6	SE season 6	SE season 6	SE season 6	SE season 6	SE season 6
27	SE season 6	SE season 6	SE season 6	SE season 6	SE season 6	SE season 6
28	SE season 6	SE season 6	SE season 6	SE season 6	SE season 6	SE season 6
29	SE season 7	SE season 7	SE season 7	SE season 7	SE season 7	SE season 7
30	SE season 7	SE season 7	SE season 7	SE season 7	SE season 7	SE season 7
31	FFL ch. 8	FFL 8.1	FFL 8.2	FFL 8.3	FFL 8.4	FFL 8.5
32	FFL ch. 8	FFL 9.1	FFL 9.2	FFL 9.3	FFL 9.4	FFL 9.5
33	SE season 8	SE season 8	SE season 8	SE season 8	SE season 8	SE season 8
34	SE season 8	SE season 8	SE season 8	SE season 8	SE season 8	SE season 8
35	SE season 8	SE season 8	SE season 8	SE season 8	SE season 8	SE season 8
36	Finals week	Finals week	Finals week	Finals week	Finals week	Finals week

© Human Kinetics.

These high school students are completing fitness-related self-assessments as part of a Fitness for Life unit within a course that includes various Sport Education seasons.

In high schools with a one-year (i.e., two-semester) physical education requirement, a logical approach to creating a sport and fitness concepts dual-themed program is for all students to complete the Fitness for Life course in one semester, and use the second semester to choose a course that includes various Sport Education seasons. In this chapter's web resource, we provide examples of how these two content areas could be integrated over the course of two consecutive semesters. You may not be able to cover the entire set of chapters included in the Fitness for Life program. However, if your program provides positive experiences in the first two courses, that may attract students to an additional elective credit course titled Advanced Physical Education, during which the dual-theme focus is continued, or a single sport or fitness theme is extended.

SELECTING AND ORGANIZING THE PROGRAM CONTENT

The feature of Sport Education that most affects how a program is organized is that seasons are longer than typical physical education units. As we frequently point out, Sport Education emphasizes both depth of coverage and sufficient time for students to improve during the season. The other important factor, of course, is the amount of curricular time assigned to physical education. Curricular time is determined both by the frequency of physical education classes—daily, once, twice, three or four times per week—and by the length of the class session, which might range from 30 minutes in a third grade class to two hours in a high school that uses block scheduling. These factors also reflect the variety of school scheduling formats and demonstrate how both traditional sports and other activities such as weight training and dance can be incorporated.

We have always advised Sport Education teachers to err in the direction of planning for more rather than less time. As teachers, we all tend to underestimate the time it takes students to master techniques and tactics and to learn to use them in well-played games. Here are two Sport Education curriculum design examples, one from the elementary school level and one from the high school level.

An Elementary School Example

Darnell (1994) described an elementary curriculum in which the year started with a short fitness unit that was followed by five Sport Education seasons. The program operated on a four-day rotating schedule (i.e., students participated in physical education every fourth day), and classes lasted 50 minutes. The length of each season was typically 12 class sessions. This meant that each season had a maximum of 600 class minutes, and occupied a little more than 9 weeks of the school schedule. The fitness unit served two purposes. First, it allowed the teacher to get to know the students and to see them in various fitness activities, providing evidence pertinent to placing students on teams that would be as evenly matched as possible. Second, it allowed the teacher to introduce principles of fitness and determine the various fitness levels of the students.

The Sport Education curriculum included soccer, basketball, volleyball, gymnastics, and track and field. These are important international sports, but they each have different characteristics that, taken together, make for a coherent, balanced Sport Education curriculum. The program had five Sport Education seasons per school year, each of which allowed sufficient time for students to accomplish significant outcomes. In addition, the activities were repeated at subsequent grade levels, although not always in exactly the same form. The total amount of curricular time devoted to helping students become competent and confident in these activities was adequate to achieve the intended outcomes.

A High School Example

Dugas (1994) described a high school physical education program where Sport Education was used as one element in the curriculum. Although physical education was required, in this model students could choose their physical education classes. The school year was divided into four nine-week grading periods. The seasons were fall, early winter, late winter, and spring. Students could choose their activity from three categories: Sport Education, recreation, or fitness (see table 19.3). The activities in the recreation and fitness offerings could also be done using the Sport Education model, although in this school they were not.

Within the Sport Education category, students could choose between team and individual sports (see table 19.4). An effort was made to have activities in the Sport Education category that corresponded with the availability of similar activities in the larger local sport culture. For team sport, flag football and cross country were offered in the fall; volleyball and soccer in the early winter; basketball and swimming in the late winter; and softball, baseball, and track and field in the spring. Individual sport offerings included tennis, archery, fencing, badminton, golf, bowling, racquetball, riflery, and table tennis. The length of these seasons was sufficient for students to accomplish significant improvement in techniques and tactics and for teams to learn to work together to achieve team goals.

Table 19.3 Yearly Physical Education Activities in Three Areas

Sport Education	Fitness activities	Recreational activities
Racquet sports • Badminton • Racquetball • Table tennis • Tennis Target sports • Archery • Bowling • Golf • Fencing • Riflery Team sports • Volleyball • Track and field • Baseball • Softball • Cross country • Soccer	Weight training Aerobic dance Aerobic activities	Swimming • Beginning swimming • Intermediate swimming • Lifesaving Recreational activities • Square and folk dancing • Backpacking and hiking • Recreational boating

Adapted from Dugas, 1994.

Table 19.4 Seasonal Sport Education Schedule

Season	Team sports	Individual sports
Fall	Flag football Cross country	Tennis Archery Table tennis
Early winter	Volleyball Soccer	Fencing Bowling Badminton Racquetball
Late winter	Basketball Swimming	Fencing Bowling Racquetball Riflery
Spring	Baseball Softball Track and field	Badminton Golf Archery

Determining Season Length

What is the appropriate length for a Sport Education season? In the national curriculum trial of Sport Education in Australian high schools, the recommended format was 20 class periods, with two sessions per week for 10 weeks, resulting in four seasons each school year. This format grew out of the New Zealand national curriculum project in 10th-grade physical education, where schools had to commit to seasons lasting at least 20 class sessions to be involved in the trial (Grant, 1992). Consequently, 20 class sessions have become the recommended norm at the high school level (Mohr, Townsend, & Bulger, 2001).

A Sport Education-themed program needs no magic number of lessons to be applied, but you do need to consider several factors when planning the curriculum. First, students must have *sufficient time to learn the various roles* in a season, techniques, and tactics necessary for successful participation. Teams must have *sufficient time to practice and compete.* Calculate season length based on the number of minutes per class and the number of classes per week to determine how long (in weeks) the season will last. If physical education is only scheduled one day a week for 45 minutes, it makes sense to have a season last for a full semester. If physical education is scheduled every day for 50 minutes, and the grading period is 9 to 10 weeks, then you could plan two seasons for each grading period, using the 20-session model or one season lasting 40 sessions.

Second, the *nature of the activity* and the number of *planned season outcomes* can also help determine the length of a season. For example, in a Sport Education fitness season, you might choose to do it for an entire semester. Teams would work toward semester-long goals in cardiorespiratory fitness, strength, body composition, and flexibility. You would organize team competitions around reaching appropriate goals in each fitness category. You could attend to flexibility in each class session, with strength and aerobic goals the focus of alternating sessions. An 18- to 20-week semester season provides sufficient time to alter body composition, strength indexes, aerobic performance, and flexibility, each of which could be a separate team competition. Conversely, a Sport Education-based Frisbee golf season might be considerably shorter, because the techniques and tactics are fewer and can be learned with relative ease. A round robin competition followed by a championship could be done in fewer class sessions.

Dance suggests other uses of time. Sport Education-based dance seasons could be of regular length or last an entire semester. Dance forms lend themselves well to a Sport Education format. If you focused on folk dance for a season, 20 class sessions could be adequate. If, however, you wanted to include more than one form of dance (e.g., folk, square, ballroom), it could easily take an entire semester, with team champions in each of the dance forms and an overall semester champion. Richardson and Oslin (2003) described a series of three dance competitions within a nine-week season in which students met daily. The modern competition focused on solo performances within teams, the jazz competition focused on duets within teams, and the hip-hop competition focused on groups of four to six within teams.

These examples reflect a fundamentally different organization of content from what has been and is the norm in most physical education programs, where teachers opt to deliver units that may only be 5 to 10 lessons, based on the notion that students should only be provided with brief exposures to as many as 15 different activities. When first learning about Sport Education, some physical education teachers believe that their students will become bored by the longer seasons, but the many evaluations of well-taught Sport Education completed worldwide provide no evidence of this. To the contrary, their interest tends to grow as the season progresses, largely because the matches, games, and performances are more exciting and meaningful. Moreover, students who might otherwise have felt marginalized reported feeling more valued and were more actively engaged throughout the seasons.

Deciding Which Activities to Include

Most U.S. school districts have a district course of study for each subject matter. This graded course of study typically includes objectives in several areas (e.g., knowledge, skill, personal development, and fitness) followed by descriptions of the activities that can be taught to achieve those objectives. Deciding which of those activities to include in the physical education curriculum for a particular school level and school year depends on several factors, such as weather, facilities, and equipment. In larger school districts, teachers may be required to teach certain activities based on decisions made at the district level rather than at the school level. What follows are three examples of how programs have been built around Sport Education at various school levels.

Sample Elementary School Sport Education Program

One can argue that at the elementary school level, children should experience a range of activities, each of which has a particular emphasis in terms of technical and tactical demands. Darnell (1994) described such a rationale for her elementary curriculum. As described earlier, the school year for third through fifth grades started with a fitness unit that was used to assess student skills and fitness and to establish expectations for fitness that lasted throughout the school year, much like a theme. The bulk of the school year was composed of five Sport Education seasons: soccer, basketball, volleyball, track and field, and gymnastics.

Soccer was chosen because it emphasizes manipulating an object with the feet. It is a field invasion game (like field hockey, lacrosse, and speedball) that requires offensive and defensive tactics, with frequent unpredictable changes from offense to defense and vice versa. It is also a highly active game with a strong cardiorespiratory component, and it can be played indoors or out with little equipment. It is an important international sport that is increasingly popular in the U.S. across children, adolescents, and adults.

Basketball was chosen because it emphasizes manipulating an object with the hands. It is a court invasion game (similar to team handball) with techniques and tactics that are more patterned than in soccer. It too has frequent offensive and defensive changes. It is played widely in youth and adult recreational settings and can be played indoors or out with little equipment.

Volleyball was chosen because it is a game of striking skills using the hands and arms. It is a court-divided game (similar to tennis and badminton) with techniques and tactics that are more predictable than in invasion games. It is played widely in recreational settings and is increasingly available to young people and adults in the community. It can be played indoors or out with little equipment. Variations such as beach volleyball have become increasingly popular.

Track and field was chosen because it caters to a wide variety of skills and interests. Some track and field events require speed, others require endurance, and still others require strength. The primary techniques are running, jumping, and throwing, all of which can be used in a variety of sport activities. Track and field allows for competitions against standards and previous best performances, as well as individual and team competitions. It can contribute to both cardiorespiratory and strength improvements. Furthermore, it is an important international sport.

Gymnastics was chosen because it emphasizes total-body assembly and inversion. Upper-body strength is required for several of the events. Gymnastics has a high aesthetic content, and requires judging to determine performance outcomes. Events require strength, balance, flexibility, and sometimes creativity. In many events the performance is a routine created by the competitor. The creation of routines allows students the opportunity to plan and create their own variations.

In the third- through fifth-grade model, the sport was repeated for three grade levels, allowing students to make substantial progress toward competence in that sport. The yearly progression, however, does not always have to be conceptualized as a repeat of the same form of the sport in the same situation. For example, in gymnastics, students could learn rhythmic gymnastics in one year, acrosport (a form of gymnastics where teams create group-based poses that require balance, coordination, strength, and teamwork) in the second year, and Olympic gymnastics in the third year. In soccer, one year could be done indoors in small spaces and another could be done outdoors in larger spaces, along with gradually increasing team sizes (i.e., from three-on-three to four-on-four to five-on-five).

The description and rationale for these activities shows a coherent logic for the selection of activities composing a third- through fifth-grade elementary Sport Education program. At other levels and in other situations, you would use a different logic to select sports and other activities. For example, your Sport Education curriculum might include folk dance, aerobic dance, weightlifting, and orienteering. The point is that in Sport Education, you can develop a customized curriculum with a logical choice of activities for a year and for an entire school program.

Sample Middle School Sport Education Program

In the middle school, cross-curricular integration is often a significant element of how a curriculum is organized and taught. Sport Education offers tremendous opportunities for such curricular integration, which will be addressed in more detail in chapter 21. It can also help teachers increase the visibility of their program to others in the school. One example of curricular integration would be an Olympics-themed Sport Education season (Siedentop, 1994). In this variation of Sport Education, students are members of teams that represent nations. This focus on global sport is enhanced if teams for a particular season represent nations from all the continents. Students remain on their teams for at least one semester, so several seasons can be completed in various Olympic sports. The range of Olympic sports allows you to choose activities for which your space and equipment are adequate. It should be easy to see how such a season would be especially meaningful during Olympic years. For example, as shown in figure 19.1, you might include a modified form of curling as an event during the winter season.

Such an approach allows physical educators to work closely with teachers in other classroom subjects as well. Teams adopt their nation's colors, flag, and national anthem. Team members can study their nation's music, art, poetry, history, economic structure,

Figure 19.1 Modified curling.

political system, and literature as homework, all coordinated with their work in social studies classes. They can enter their reports and other artifacts in their team portfolio. An Olympic Committee can be chosen to govern the seasonal competitions during the semester. Representatives from each nation can form a committee to design and make Olympic awards as an art project. Students can study the sports of the nation they represent and learn about the nation's history of success in sport and its major sport heroes and heroines. They can also learn about the country's geography, food, music, and art. These examples in social studies, literature, art, and music reflect the countless ways in which physical education can be part of authentic cross-curricular integration of subjects.

To enhance the Olympic theme, each team can be required to understand and make their nation's flag and learn their national anthem. One student can be chosen to take the athletes' pledge and another to take the officials' pledge. Students can create replicas of gold, silver, and bronze medals, which can be awarded for individual and team performances depending on the sports competed. The entire experience can end with a festive closing ceremony.

Sample High School Sport Education Program

In an ideal situation, a school district would have articulation between the elementary, middle, and high school physical education programs. Thus, selection of activities at the high school level would be influenced by what students experienced at the earlier levels. High school physical education works best when students have options for choosing their activities. We do not suggest that physical education should not be required, but rather that students be able to select activities from among those offered to fulfill the graduation requirement.

As students grow older, differences in their sport skills and backgrounds tend to widen. If students do not have the opportunity to choose a particular activity, consider offering activities that are less familiar and thus reduce these variances. With coeducational classes, gender is also a factor. There is substantial evidence that girls are often marginalized in coeducational classes. One way to remedy this problem is to form coeducational teams but have multiple competitions; that is, a girls' competition, a boys' competition, and a coeducational competition. In tennis, for example, you could have girls' singles and doubles, boys' singles and doubles, and mixed doubles. In flag football, you could have separate boys' and girls' round robin league competitions followed by a coeducational league competition.

The high school model by Dugas (1994) described earlier in this chapter is one attractive way to organize an elective curriculum. Adventure activities also lend themselves well to the small, heterogeneous learning groups of Sport Education. Differences in requirements between states and between districts within states tend to dictate the flexibility that physical education teachers have in planning a Sport Education-themed program at the high school level. We reiterate, however, our profound belief that elective programs are likely to be much more successful than programs where students are simply assigned to a physical education class based on time available in their class schedule and with no knowledge about what activities will be available in that class.

Recent developments in U.S. high school physical education programs have changed the daily program offerings. Increasingly, the typical high school physical education program consists of weight training courses that target schools' athletic teams (van der Mars, 2017). Therefore, it is important that the courses still viewed as regular physical education are delivered in such a way that they have a clear theme and provide authentic and more complete sport experiences.

DEVELOPING A YEARLY BLOCK PLAN

Once a physical education staff has decided on what content to include, and how long the seasons will be, they should develop a yearly block plan. This is a calendar showing when units or seasons are scheduled, who will teach each one, how long they will last, and which activity area will be used. A yearly block plan is important for several reasons. First, all teachers should know what they are expected to teach throughout the school year. This is especially important for newly hired staff. Second, it is important for demonstrating to the rest of the school (notably the administrators) that the program is well planned and organized. Third, it allows for making the needed adjustments if schedule changes are needed. For example, events like assemblies, science fairs, school photo shoots, assemblies, blood drives, or other special events generally get scheduled in the school gymnasiums, thus displacing the class scheduled in there. If your block plan is well laid out, you can share it with your school's administration and staff so that if the gymnasium is needed for a special event, the administration can notify the physical education staff in time to make any needed adjustments.

Yearly block plans generally include information about

- the lessons needed for the typical opening of the school year (e.g., program orientation, locker distribution, setting program expectations, establishing management routines, etc.),
- the final lesson needed at the end of the school year (e.g., collection of locker locks, cleaning out of lockers, etc.),
- scheduled vacation periods and national holidays,
- the start and end dates of the seasons,
- the teachers assigned to teach each season or unit, and
- the activity area where each season or unit will be taught (e.g., whether basketball will be taught in the indoor gymnasium or on the outdoor courts).

Tables 19.5 and 19.6 include examples of a Sport Education-themed junior high school program. Beyond the required health education courses often taught by physical educators, the program had a distinct dual sport and fitness education theme in that students in seventh grade experienced net-court game seasons (e.g., badminton, tennis, volleyball) and a fitness season. In eighth grade, in addition to the health education courses, students experienced invasion games (e.g., basketball, floor hockey, soccer) as well as fitness-focused seasons. Importantly, this schedule of offerings is defensible to all your constituents (i.e., students, administrators, and parents) and its underlying rationale can be easily explained.

SUMMARY

In this chapter, we have presented key strategies for organizing a physical education program with Sport Education as a central theme. We introduced the need for the school's physical education staff to develop consensus on the program's mission. This allows for selecting and organizing the content in seasons or units that allow enough time for students to learn (supporting Sport Education's underlying less-is-more curricular philosophy), while keeping in mind the need for developing a distinct theme. A final step in organizing the program is to build a yearly block plan that serves as a flight plan for all physical education staff and that can also ensure that adjustments can be made in the event of the school's administration needing to use physical activity areas for special events.

Table 19.5 Lincoln Junior High School Physical Education Program, School Year 2017-2018, Grade 7

Classes meet daily (M-F)		Wickman		Camacho		Bachman		Levinson	
Week	Date	Activity	Location	Activity	Location	Activity	Location	Activity	Location
0	8/1-8/5	Meetings and planning		Meetings and planning		Meetings and planning		Meetings and planning	
1-3*	8/8-8/26	FFL ch. 1-2	Classroom	Fitness	Second gym	FFL ch. 1-2	Classroom	Badminton	Main gym
4-6	8/29-9/16	FFL ch. 3	Classroom	Fitness	Second gym	FFL ch. 3	Classroom	Pickleball	Main gym
7-9	9/19-10/7	FFL ch. 4-5	Classroom	Fitness	Second gym	FFL ch. 4-5	Classroom	Volleyball	Main gym
Fall break	10/10-10/14	No classes							
10-12	10/17-11/4	Bowling	Second gym	Badminton	Main gym	Fitness	Second gym	FFL ch. 1-2	Classroom
13-15	11/7-11/23	Team run	Track	Pickleball	Main gym	Fitness	Second gym	FFL ch. 3	Classroom
16-18	11/26-12/16	Orienteering	Campus	Volleyball	Main gym	Fitness	Second gym	FFL ch. 4-5	Classroom
Winter break	12/19-1/1	No classes							
19-21	1/2-1/20	Badminton	Main gym	Bowling	Second gym	Bowling	Second gym	Fitness	Second gym
22-24	1/23-2/10	Pickleball	Main gym	Team run	Track	Team run	Track	Fitness	Second gym
25-27	2/13-3/3	Volleyball	Main gym	Orienteering	Campus	Orienteering	Campus	Fitness	Second gym
Spring break	3/6-3/10	No classes							
28-30	3/13-3/31	Fitness	Second gym	FFL ch. 1-2	Classroom	Badminton	Main gym	Bowling	Second gym
31-33	4/3-4/21	Fitness	Second gym	FFL ch. 3	Classroom	Pickleball	Main gym	Team run	Track
34-36	4/24-5/12	Fitness	Second gym	FFL ch. 4-5	Classroom	Volleyball	Main gym	Orienteering	Campus
37**	5/15-5/19	Makeup exams		Makeup exams		Makeup exams		Makeup exams	

*Includes one day for program orientation.

**Includes time for equipment and locker return.

Table 19.6 Lincoln Junior High School Physical Education Program, School Year 2017-2018, Grade 8

Classes meet daily (M-F)		Wickman		Camacho		Bachman		Levinson	
Week	Date	Activity	Location	Activity	Location	Activity	Location	Activity	Location
0	8/1-8/5	Meetings and planning		Meetings and planning		Meetings and planning		Meetings and planning	
1-3*	8/8-8/26	Basketball	Main gym	Fitness	Second gym	FFL ch. 6	Classroom	Weight training	Weight room
4-6	8/29-9/16	Floor hockey	Hardtop	Fitness	Second gym	FFL ch. 7-8	Classroom	Dance	Main gym
7-9	9/19-10/7	Soccer	FB field	Fitness	Second gym	FFL ch. 9	Classroom	Student designed games	Main gym
Fall break	10/10-10/14	*No classes*							
10-12	10/17-11/4	FFL ch. 6	Classroom	Weight training	Weight room	Basketball	Main gym	Fitness	Second gym
13-15	11/7-11/23	FFL ch. 7-8	Classroom	Dance	Main gym	Floor hockey	Hardtop	Fitness	Second gym
16-18	11/26-12/16	FFL ch. 9	Classroom	Student-designated games	Main gym	Soccer	FB field	Fitness	Second gym
Winter break	12/19-1/1	*No classes*							
19-21	1/2-1/20	Fitness	Second gym	Basketball	Main gym	Weight training	Weight room	FFL ch. 6	Classroom
22-24	1/23-2/10	Fitness	Second gym	Floor hockey	Hardtop	Dance	Main gym	FFL ch. 7-8	Classroom
25-27	2/13-3/3	Fitness	Second gym	Soccer	FB field	Student-designated games	Main gym	FFL ch. 9	Classroom
Spring break	3/6-3/10	*No classes*							
28-30	3/13-3/31	Weight training	Weight room	FFL ch. 6	Classroom	Fitness	Second gym	Basketball	Main gym
31-33	4/3-4/21	Dance	Main gym	FFL ch. 7-8	Classroom	Fitness	Second gym	Floor hockey	Hardtop
34-36	4/24-5/12	Student-designated games	Main gym	FFL ch. 9	Classroom	Fitness	Second gym	Soccer	FB field
37**	5/15-5/19	Makeup exams		Makeup exams		Makeup exams		Makeup exams	

*Includes one day for program orientation.

**Includes time for equipment and locker return.

Managing a Sport Education Program

Chapter Objective

After reading this chapter and its related resources, you will develop a better understanding of the need for developing program-level policies, how to manage and budget for your equipment and supplies, as well as your professional and legal responsibilities.

Key Concepts

- Establishing program-level policies and procedures ensure consistency in its day-to-day delivery.
- Management of equipment, facilities, and supplies is critical to the effective delivery of high-quality instruction, and ensures student safety.
- Teachers are members of a profession that brings with it important legal and professional responsibilities. Failure to meet these may have important legal consequences.

In this chapter, we introduce key areas for which physical educators need to plan to ensure smooth and safe operation of the overall physical education program. Generally, these job aspects are much less visible to first-year physical educators, and may not have been a central focus of their teacher preparation program. However, all require ongoing attention. The selected areas include (1) the development of program-level policies, (2) a plan for managing the program's equipment, facilities, and supplies, and (3) a plan to ensure proper supervision and safety to limit risks of liability. The importance of these cannot be underestimated.

DEVELOPING PROGRAM POLICIES AND PROCEDURES

Physical education programs must have a set of program-level policies that can guide teachers when they have to address certain events. Policies are rules that an organization and the people within it are supposed to live by. In our case, this refers both to the teachers and to their students. The policies specific to the physical education program generally are decided on by the physical education staff (with input from the school's administration). In addition, and for obvious reasons, they cannot go against school-level or district-level policies. And in secondary schools, with multiple physical education teachers, program-level policies are important to help ensure that all teachers apply and enforce them consistently. In the next paragraphs, we present the main areas for which teachers must develop policies to govern the program.

Student Information Relevant to Physical Education

Physical education teachers should be aware of any possible health conditions and disablities of their students. In a perfect world, the school administration would have a system in place to alert all teachers in the school about any health condition (e.g., epilepsy, Type I diabetes) or disability (e.g., autism, cerebral palsy) from which students suffer. In the real world, teachers may not find out about such conditions until they are faced with a student having, for example, an epileptic seizure. The level of severity of a documented disability such as autism spectrum disorder (ASD) varies. This is reflected in the wide variation in the symptoms, dysfunctions, and impairments in communication as well as behavioral and social skills. In milder forms of ASD, the symptoms may be less obvious, and teachers may not detect these patterns of behavior. But if teachers are keenly aware of which students have specific conditions or disablities, and they have the needed skill and knowledge on how to work with such students effectively, possible problems can be prevented. Chapter 14 included more specific information on how teachers can make accommodations for students with special needs.

Clearly, it is important for the physical education program to set up a process by which all teachers in the program are fully informed as to which of their students might have a health condition or disabilty. In fact, the physical education staff may be in a better position to know of such conditions because they are likely to be on the team of school staff members that works on developing or adjusting the students' individualized education program (IEP).

Use of Mobile Phones

It is difficult to recall a time before school-aged students were equipped with their own mobile phones. At any moment of dicretionary time during the school day, students can be found on their phones, busily browsing the Internet or texting with peers. Schools generally have set policies in place regarding students' use of mobile phones during the school day. For physical education, mobile phones can be a potentially powerful instructional tool. For example, there are several useful skill analysis apps that allow for recording skill execution or gameplay that can be can used as a mean showing what student are doing well or what they still need to work on when learning to perform techniques, tactics, and so on.

Unfortunately, mobile phones can also be used to compromise students' psychological safety. Bullying of students is certainly nothing new, but ready access to mobile phones has given rise to cyberbullying, which is much more difficult to detect by school staff and may have deadly consequences. You need to decide whether and how you introduce the use of mobile phones. One possible alternative for the use of skill analysis apps would be to purchase tablets that are the property of the program.

Temporary Excuses from Physical Activity

At times, students will need to be kept out of participation in class on account of illness or injury. You need to develop rules and procedures for managing not only students who are temporarily unable to participate in the physical activities of physical education class, but also those who will be out of action for an extended period of time. In developing these policies, you need to consider whether and how you will manage makeup work (e.g., a quiz or an out-of-class written assignment) that the student will have missed.

Students who are out for an extended period of time (e.g., a broken leg, severely injured knee) should be expected to complete some type of relevant and meaningful alternative assignment. In such cases, it is important that you inform the parents of these alternative arrangments. Just as you would provide a substitute teacher with a lesson plan if you have to be absent, you should develop a menu of alternative assignments ready to present to the student, rather than having to make something up at the last minute. Parents should also be informed about your policy regarding requests (along with acceptable reasons) for a student's temporary absence from physical activities, and what if any documentation is needed to explain the reason for this absence.

Attendance and Tardiness

What procedure will you use to take attendance, so that it does not mean the excessive loss of valuable learning time? And what is your policy regarding students' attendance? How many excused absences? Unexcused absences? What about tardies? What are the consequences of being absent or tardy? Do you allow makeup opportunities? If so, how? How much? How will you keep track of all this?

Exemptions, Substitutions, and Waivers Policy

Unless there is state-level policy, the decision on whether students can be exempted from or use a substitution for fulfilling the physical education requirements in high schools rests with the district. High school students may be exempt from physical education by participating in alternative activities such as athletics, marching band, or Junior Reserve Officers' Training Corps (JROTC). Or they might be exempt on religious grounds. While physical educators have no decision-making role here, it is important that you develop a strong stance on this issue. If this issue is brought forth for consideration by your school board in your district, what would be your arguments against allowing exemptions or substitutions? Is there any credible evidence that marching band, JROTC, or after-school athletics can address the physical education content standards (SHAPE America, 2013)? Actually, there is evidence that students are substantially more active in physical education than during JROTC classes (Lounsbery, Holt, Monnat, Funk, & McKenzie, 2014).

Emergency Planning

Teachers, students, and staff members are apt to experience emergency situations on a regular basis. Some of these impact the entire school while others are program-specific. Examples of school-level emergencies include fires, hostage taking, student abductions, gunfire that occurs in the neighborhood, or, as has been happening with increasing frequency since the mid-1990s, on-campus shootings. This last example shakes everyone at the core, so it is not surprising that schools are now often perceived as very dangerous places. Difficult as it may be to believe, however, schools are in fact very safe places for students, teachers, support staff, and administrators. Still, you do need to be prepared for both types of emergencies.

School-Level Emergencies

Even shootings that occur in the immediate vicinity of a school campus will, in most cases, result in schools going into lockdown mode. Districts and schools have set protocols in place for managing such emergencies through evacuations (e.g., in the case of fires) or lockdowns (e.g., if an armed person is near or on the school campus). Physical educators should be aware of all these protocols and how to assist with executing them. The following sidebar includes an example of a red emergency flip chart posted throughout schools. It includes the steps that teachers are expected to take across a variety of school-level emergencies. Physical education facilities are larger, so it is more difficult to monitor the movement (and whereabouts) of students in the case of school-wide emergencies. You will therefore need to be doubly vigilant in monitoring students during these very stressful situations. School districts have extensive school safety plans. See the sidebars for a list of safety guidelines from the Chandler, Arizona, Unified School District and a list of safety resource from the same district.

Greenberg and LoBianco (2020) recommend that all physical educators (or at least one physical educator in every secondary school) should be members their school safety plan committee. This will ensure that they are aware of emergency plans and of any updates to it. In addition, they should be provided with a communication device to allow swift action and information sharing when there is an emergency. The protocols outlined in the following sidebar are good examples of what actions teachers need to take during such emergencies. By definition, emergencies are unpredictable, so it is almost impossible to anticipate every possible scenario. Because of this, you will find that emergency plans are revised and updated frequently (often immediately following an emergency). Although fire drills and evacuation drills disrupt teachers' opportunity to teach and students' opportunity to learn, they are an integral part of school safety measures.

Program-Level Emergencies

Program-level emergencies include student injuries and fights. Though not common, they require the shift teacher's response.

Student Injuries All physical activity has the inherent risks of injury. There are three key areas to which you as a teacher need to attend. First, you will need to do everything to minimize the risk of injury through appropriate use of equipment (i.e., using equipment appropriate to the age and development of the students) and facilities, appropriate instructional task designs and progressions, and appropriate management of students.

SAFETY GUIDELINES FOR TEACHERS

Chandler, Arizona, Unified School District's Red Emergency Flip Chart

Fire Drill and Evacuation Procedures

In Classroom With Students

1. Teachers or staff escort students to designated evacuation area (see map in room).
2. Take emergency materials including roll book and keys.
3. Turn out lights.
4. Move 500 feet away from building, face away from building, and remain there until directed.
5. Display color-coded sign after taking attendance. Green: all students accounted for. Red: students missing or emergency situation.
6. Maintain students in a line that is orderly and composed.
7. **Do not** release any student to a parent without administrator authorization.
8. Return to classroom when all clear is announced.

Out of Classroom

1. If at lunch, students should leave food and immediately exit the room, proceed to designated evacuation area.
2. If in the restroom, students should exit and proceed immediately to the designated evacuation area and report to their teacher.
3. During a passing period (if applicable) students will immediately exit the building and report to their previous period teacher in the designated evacuation area.

Lockdown Procedures

1. Front office will issue lockdown order. (Note: anyone can call for a lockdown.)
2. Direct all students, staff, and visitors into classrooms or secure rooms.
3. Lock door, turn off lights and TV, close blinds, or cover interior windows.
4. Direct students to sit down on floor out of line of sight from doors and windows.
5. If directed, take attendance and email names of students unaccounted for to the respective administrator.
6. **No Talking.**
7. **Do not open the door** under any circumstances.
8. The primary form of communication from classrooms will be via email; telephones will be utilized only in emergency situations.
9. Remain in lockdown status until the incident commander makes an announcement giving the all clear signal.

(continued)

Safety Guidelines for Teachers   *(continued)*

Unauthorized Person(s)

1. Notify principal.

2. Have another staff member accompany you, direct the person to the office to sign in and obtain a volunteer or visitor's badge.

3. If they do not have a legitimate reason to be on campus, ask them to leave and escort them to an exit.

4. If noncompliant, proceed to a safe area and call police.

5. Call the principal with details of the situation: physical description including clothing, the type of behavior the individual is exhibiting, and where he/she was last seen. Office will send security to approach the person and direct them to the office.

6. Lockdown procedures will be followed if deemed necessary by site administration.

An Unauthorized Person Enters Your Classroom

1. Contact security and have them escort the person to the front office to sign in and obtain a volunteer or visitor badge.

2. As soon as the individual leaves, call the principal to alert them and provide a physical description.

3. If the individual refuses to leave, contact the principal and ask for security.

A Child Is Abducted
*** Call 911.

1. Call the principal with as many details as possible, including description of the person(s), vehicle used, direction it was headed, and license plate number.

2. Document all details you can remember.

3. Assist the office staff and attending officer with next action steps.

A Hostage Situation Occurs
*** Call 911.

1. Call the principal with all known details.

2. Principal or police department will dictate ensuing procedures for lockdown.

3. **Remain calm** and keep students calm.

Suicide Threat

1. Notify the principal about the situation including any known details.

2. Do not leave the student alone until administration and counselor have arrived.

3. Administration and counselor will notify involved teachers of ensuing action.

(continued)

You Suspect Someone Has a Weapon on Campus

*** Call 911.

1. Notify the principal immediately.

2. Have the principal and school resource officer (SRO) question the suspected student, staff member, or visitor.

3. Accompany suspect to a private office and wait for police.

4. Inform suspect of their rights and why you are conducting a search.

5. Conduct search with police or SRO.

6. If suspect threatens you with a weapon, do not try to disarm them.

   a. Back away with arms up, talk to the suspect in a calm voice.

   b. Call 911.

   c. Send for the principal immediately.

A Gun Has Been Discharged

***Call 911.

1. Notify the principal for immediate assistance. The principal will determine need for immediate lockdown and make notification.

2. If someone is injured, use common sense to stop bleeding or keep the person breathing.

3. Help those who arrive to assist or remove other students from the situation.

4. If there are no injuries, remove as many students as possible. Don't touch the gun. Protect the scene for police investigation.

Emergency Procedures and Responsibilities

- Administration will review their emergency plan with all staff prior to the commencement of each school year.

- All staff members will be familiar with the location and accessibility of the nearest fire exits, extinguisher, and automated external defibrillators (AEDs).

Teachers are responsible for:

- Informing each of their classes of the expected procedures within the first week of school and the first week of each grading period.

- Making sure students are aware of evacuation procedures, evacuation routes, and alternate evacuation routes.

- Orienting new students who have entered the class throughout the year of the plan and procedures within one week of the student entering the class.

- Making sure that an emergency exit map is posted at each exit of their classroom. If one is not present, they are to inform their principal so that one may be provided.

(continued)

Safety Guidelines for Teachers *(continued)*

- Communicating any relevant changes in emergency procedures to students within one week following notification of the change.
- Having an explanation of evacuation and lockdown procedures and expectations available for a substitute teacher.
- Maintain a current class list with contact information for all classes taught.

You Become Aware of a Bomb or the Threat of a Bomb

1. Notify principal at once, giving as many details as you can. The principal or designee will determine what procedures should be followed.

2. If it is a written message, handle it no more than absolutely necessary to preserve fingerprints.

3. If a suspicious object is found, **do not touch it**! Notify principal. A law enforcement officer will determine course of action.

4. Do not use cell phones or electronic devices if aware of a bomb threat to campus.

5. Follow all emergency evacuation procedures prescribed by administration or law enforcement officials

If you receive a phone call informing you of a bomb:

1. Do not hang up.

2. Document the threat noting the time and exact words of caller, background noises, description of the voice, sex, age if apparent, tone, and dialect.

3. Ask specific questions. Try to keep the caller talking.

4. Notify principal immediately and wait for further instructions.

Courtesy of Chandler Unified School District.

Second, you need to be vigilant in ensuring that your students are supervised at all times. This does not apply only to your lessons. In elementary schools, physical educators are responsible for the care of students from the moment they are dropped off at the gym until the classroom teacher comes and picks the students up at the end lesson's end. If a classroom teacher is late in picking up the students, you may not leave that group alone while you start your next class. In secondary school programs, physical educators are responsible for supervising the students from the moment they enter the hallways or locker rooms until the start of passing time, when students move to the next class. Often locker rooms filled with upwards of 60 or 70 students are difficult to monitor because of their layout. Imagine the problems that would be caused if, between classes, all the teachers were sitting in the staff office checking email or watching sport highlights on the Internet and a fight were to break out somewhere in the locker room.

Third, you need a plan for what to do if an injury does occur. In the absence of a protocol (or if you do not follow the protocol that is in place), you open yourself to

SAFETY RESOURCES FOR SCHOOL STAFF IN CHANDLER, ARIZONA, UNIFIED SCHOOL DISTRICT

- Board Policy JIH—Student Interrogations, Searches, and Arrests
- Board Policy JIH-EB—Form for Signature When Arresting or Placing Student into Custody
- Board Policy JIH-EC—Form for Signature of Interviewing Officer
- Board Policy JIH-ED—Form for Parental Consent to Interview Student by Law Enforcement Officers
- Bomb Threat Checklist
- CUSD Red Emergency Flip Chart
- Community Education Safety Binder
- Elementary School Bus Riders Identification
- Emergency Action Flowchart Contact Numbers
- Emergency Notification Flowchart
- Evacuation Preparation and Consideration
- Evacuation Questions and Answers
- Fire Safety Self-Inspection Custodian Checklist
- Fire Safety Self-Inspection Sprinkler Checklist
- Go Bags for Nurses and Health Assistants
- Go Bags for Principals
- Go Bags for Teachers
- Graffiti Reporting Procedures
- License Plate Awareness
- Lockdown Contact Information
- Lockdown Procedures
- Lockdown Procedures for Every Room
- Lockdown Protocol School Sites
- Lost Student Guidelines
- Modified Lockdown Procedures
- Parent and Student Transportation Agreement
- Rules of the Road Around Ryan Elementary
- Safety Quick Documents Template
- School Security Officer (SSO) Core Job Functions
- School Security Officer (SSO) Overview of Program
- Self-Injury Protocol
- Sex Offender Notification Flowchart
- Substitute Teacher Binder
- Suicide Prevention Overview

Courtesy of the Chandler Unified School District.

possible lawsuits in such a situation. Ask yourself: What do you need to do if, during a regular class activity, two students collide and hit their heads? What do you do when a student goes down during a volleyball game and injures an ankle? Is it a sprain? Is it broken? What would be your plan of action? If a student suffers a sizable cut above the eye and bleeds profusely, how do you stop the bleeding and manage the cleanup? If a student breaks a leg, how do you manage the other students in the class? How will you notify the school nurse and the office personnel? How and when do the parents or guardians need to be notified? Where is your first aid kit located? How often is the kit checked to ensure that it is still fully stocked? Nowadays, many teachers wear a hip pouch with basic first aid supplies. Moreover, with outdoor physical activity facilities in secondary schools being increasingly widespread, physical educators should insist on having a walkie-talkie. Your school may also be equipped with an automated external defibrillator (AED) device. If one is available, you will be expected to become certified in its use.

Many school districts have begun using a protocol whereby teachers are not allowed to treat or even move an injured student, especially when the injury appears more severe. (There is a risk of teachers or school officials being sued for possible mishandling the situation.) If your school is located in an urban or a suburban area, emergency medical teams will generally arrive within minutes. In more rural areas, though, it may take longer. It then becomes essential that you can recognize symptoms related to the injury, safely make the injured student more comfortable, and brief the emergency medical team on the type of injury. It is therefore imperative that you complete and maintain currency in certifications for first aid, cardiopulmonary resuscitation (CPR), and water safety instructor (WSI). You will then be better equipped to detect the type and severity of injuries, and make better decisions on how to manage and monitor it, while still managing the rest of the class.

In the case of an injury, you will be required to complete an incident or accident report (based on school and district policy). Generally, such reports will require you to note the type of event (i.e., who, what, when, where), the type and severity of the injury, who was supervising the area at the time, where the student was transported to, how and when the parents were informed of their child's injury, and so on. You will need to find out what those present at the incident witnessed. This highlights the need for every physical educator to be intimately familiar with the school and district policies and protocols. An example of an accident report form can be found in the web resource for this chapter.

Finally, with the technology available, most schools now have all documented conditions (including diagnosed special needs) available online. You should be keenly aware of which students suffer from diabetes, epilepsy, asthma, and other conditions such as an allergy to peanuts or beestings. Moreover, you need to know whether there is consent from parents to have school personnel administer medication or provide other treatments if needed. Most every class that you teach is likely to have one or more students with special needs. If your school does not automatically provide information about the disability for every student in your classes, you will want to seek this out. There is no longer any excuse for you not to be aware of which students have documented special needs, including type, severity, actions to avoid, and so on.

Student Fights   In general, fights among students are uncommon, but they also constitute an emergency. Typically, fights will occur outside of regular classes. In secondary schools, they are more likely to occur in the locker room or during passing times. This again serves as a reminder for you and your colleagues to actively supervise these areas and times. Here too, teachers need to have a plan of action. Should you get between the two fighting students? What is the risk that you yourself will get injured if you attempt to stop the fight? If the fight is between two students who vary widely in weight and height, which one would you attempt to restrain and pull away from the other? Do other staff members need to be called in to assist?

MANAGEMENT OF EQUIPMENT, FACILITIES, AND SUPPLIES

With the possible exception of classrooms used to teach high school chemistry, no other academic program in schools requires as much vigilance to ensure the safety of equipment and facilities as does physical education. Here too you want to have a protocol for periodic safety checks on all equipment and facilities. In secondary schools, the athletic director has a similar responsibility to ensure safe use of these for athletic events. Close collaboration is needed between the two programs.

Normal wear and tear is inherent to equipment, especially when it is used frequently. For example, the popularity of weight training in secondary schools has increased the use of that equipment, so it requires more frequent safety checks. In the case of outdoor facilities, fields may develop uneven play surfaces that can result in higher rates of ankle, knee, or hip injuries. And despite their increasing popularity, even artifical turf fields are not immune to wear and tear. Equipment safety is compromised when, for example floor hockey sticks develop cracks. Equipment carts will develop defective wheels, and cables in a school weight room will fray. In older

Courtesy of Jonathan Thompson.

With the possible exception of classrooms used to teach high school chemistry, no other academic program in schools requires as much vigilance to ensure the safety of equipment and facilities as does physical education.

school facilities, gymnasium floors may wear to the point where a nail might stick up just far enough to cause serious cuts if a student dives for a ball during a volleyball match. These examples are just some that, if left undetected or unattended, can cause serious injuries. Again, this might result in parents bringing a lawsuit to cover any medical cost. As with planning and preparing for emergencies, it is imperative to have a plan in place to ensure the safe working condition of your equipment and facilites. What will you do to ensure that your equipment and facilities are safe?

Additional logistical issues surrounding equipment include keeping an updated inventory of what equipment is available, keeping equipment organized and stored properly, minimizing the disappearance or loss of equipment, and handling of its possible use by students outside of regular classes, as part of maximizing students' opportunities for recreational physical activity. Physical education equipment budgets are typically very limited. This raises the issue of the quality of the equipment you should consider when requesting a purchase. Better quality (and appropriately treated and maintained) equipment should last about 10 years. You need to decide whether to buy better quality equipment in smaller quantities, or the opposite, recognizing that you will soon have added replacement costs on account of equipment breakage. Maintaining an equipment inventory may appear mundane, but it is important to the smooth running of a physical education program.

Keeping an accurate inventory of all available and functional equipment is essential. Few things will frustrate you more than walking into your equipment room, expecting to take the equipment you need for your classses, only to find that much of it is either missing or not in working order. Especially in secondary school programs with multiple teachers having acess to and using the equipment, it is important that all the teachers support each other and the program's department head in accounting for all equipment. What would you do if after teaching a tennis season you determined that your inventory of tennis balls has been reduced by six balls? Why did this happen? You must be vigilant in ensuring that if you start with 12 basketballs at the beginning of class, by class end your teams' equipment managers work together to make sure that all are returned.

Maintaining an organized equipment storage room ensures easy access and return. It is easy to pull different pieces of equipment off the shelves and place it in a cart prior to the start of classes. Returning all the equipment to its proper place after use is just as important. Leaving it stored in the cart may cause problems later on for you and your colleagues, when equipment is not found where it is expected to be.

Doing regular equipment inventory checks (e.g., once a semester) includes monitoring both its quantity and its possible disrepair status. Finally, you should mark all your equipment clearly as belonging to your program. This is especially critical if others use your facility outside of school hours. In this chapter's web resource, we provide a sample equipment inventory checklist template.

As a physical educator, you are also responsible for ensuring the safety and functionality of facilities (i.e., permanent structures and spaces), such as playing fields, fencing, lighting, and motorized baskets. Any problems you may discover will likely require action on the part of the school's or district's facility management personnel. Just like regular checks on equipment, frequent sweeps of facilities are necessary to ensure safety and functionality. You should therefore be aware of the contact persons and procedures necessary to start any repairs to facilities.

Use of Equipment and Facilities by Students Beyond Physical Education

The increased focus on creating expanded physical activity opportunities for students on campus beyond the regular physical education lessons highlights the need to give students access to equipment before, during, and after school. For this reason, you should set up a process for distribution and return of equipment. To maximize opportunity for physical activity during such times, set aside a certain amount of varied equipment, offering activity choices, and place it in a dedicated area. Ideally, this is equipment dedicated solely to recreational play outside of the physical education lessons and placed in a sturdy cart that can be rolled to any of the areas made accessible for play. Students could use this equipment for holding team practices or for purely informal recreational play. Consider the following questions when planning for students' use of this equipment: Who may borrow the equipment? How will you manage the checking out and checking in of equipment? On which days of the week will equipment be made available?

A related issue is that of how facilities may or may not be used for certain activities (either during the school day or outside of school hours). The scheduling of activities is in the hands of the administration, so you need to work closely with your school's administration on this issue. The school likely has priorities for determining who can use specific activity spaces, and school groups (e.g., athletic teams, school clubs) most always get priority over outside groups (e.g., other clubs, religious organizations). You want to be involved in the decision-making process on what policies are in effect for outside groups who wish to rent the school's activity spaces. For example, what activities and equipment may or may not be used?

PROGRAM BUDGETING

Since budgets for physical education programs are generally very small, it is important to maintain the quantity and functionality of what you already have. Here are some steps you can take to make the best use of what budget your school's administation makes available.

First, based on your equipment inventory, you need to set priorities on what new equipment should be purchased, including that which would replace old or damaged items. Your priority list might look something like this: (1) high (we really need this, it is critical), (2) medium (this would be nice to have), and (3) low (if money were no object).

The following questions will help you prioritize your equipment purchase. First, do you have enough equipment items (e.g., volleyballs, hockey sticks) to provide maximum practice opportunities? The rule historically has been one that every student student should have his or her own piece of equipment. This is a good rule of thumb for use in elementary school programs for practicing fundamental motor skills in the early grade levels. However, by grade 4, you likely do not need a basketball or volleyball for every student. Teams of six or eight students in a volleyball or basketball season can practice their techniques and tactical moves quite effectively with just two balls per team, as long as they are provided with the right activity designs (e.g., for practicing passing and providing support in four-on-one, or for three-on-two possession games, with or without shooting on a goal or a basket).

Second, how often will the equipment be used? Will you be using the desired equipment on a regular basis? And (specifically in secondary school programs) will this new equipment be of use just to one or to all the teachers in the program? Teachers might wish to get a particular piece of equipment, but end up not using it much after a while (once the novelty wears off). Remember that quipment companies regularly roll out and aggressively market new equipment.

Third, how much of your equipment is no longer safe to use, and thus in need of replacement? Regular wear and tear (or inappropriate use) may make equipment no longer usable. If it is frequently used, it should rise to the highest priority level. In addition, maintaining well-stocked first aid kits should also be a high priority.

Fourth, what can the program afford? Equipment with high price tags likely will need to be of lower priority. On the other hand, a PA system that provides better communication in an old gymnasium with terrible acoustics might be a worthwhile investment.

Fifth, will this purchase help the delivery of the program content equitably? Certain activities require more equipment than others. For example, do you really need 10 more basketballs or soccer balls? Perhaps the purchase of some more tennis racquets or pickleball paddles is more warranted. Key considerations for planning equipment purchases should be (1) how this will help the program meet its mission, (2) how it will ensure sound teaching and learning practices, and (3) whether it will ensure student safety. This chapter's web resources include an equipment priority request template.

Finally, despite the typically minimal funds available from your school's administration and district, you do have options for expanding your inventory. First, it pays to build connections with leaders from local organizations and businesses (e.g., sporting goods, the health and fitness industry). Once you establish these connections, they may consider donating equipment and supplies. Second, in secondary schools, your interscholastic sport program generally has ample quality equipment. Coaches may be willing to donate equipment that is a few years old but still in good working order. Third, you can generate additional funding. In an elementary school, you can tap into the school's parent–teacher organzation (PTO), a built-in source of funding to which you can turn annually. It has funds to distribute dedicated specifically to support teachers. We have found that many physical educators have not tapped into this source of funding. Typically, all you need to do is draft a formal written request, in which you outline what you would like to purchase, how much you need, how you would use it, and how your students will benefit from its use. The latter is really your rationale for why you need this equipment. For example, puchasing a set of quality pedometers for the class might well wipe out your entire year's equipment budget, but a proposal to the school's PTO could put that purchase within your reach. For example, to enrich student experiences in a Sport Education season, the physical education staff at Santan Junior High school in the Chandler district recently secured US$750 by writing a district-level grant to purchase T-shirts and medals for their flag football season's culminating event.

Another example of a potential added funding stream is to find local or regional grant programs that have funding opportunities on an annual or rolling basis. A US$500 grant program may not seem worth it, but it would help you gradually move your program forward. There are many organizations (e.g., the National Football League [NFL], United States Tennis Association [USTA]) that make monetary and material resources available to schools.

In part because of frequent district budget shortfalls, schools have had to rely on countless annual fundraisers. The annual "Jump Rope for Heart" and "Hoops for Heart" fundraisers have been popular for years. They support a most worthy cause: reducing the threat of heart disease. However, they require a lot of time and energy. Instead, you could organize a fundraiser that is much smaller in scope but where all the funds raised come back to the program. Fundraiser events like a jog-a-thon and free throw challenges can be a good source of supplementary funding.

SUPERVISION, SAFETY, AND LIABILITY

The topics of supervision, safety, and liability are closely connected to the professional and legal responsibilities of physical educators. Here we first provide a brief overview of basic legal terms and then offer guidelines and strategies for minimizing the risks of getting into situations where they may be found to have fallen short of these responsibilities.

Basic Legal Terms

In most cases, legal liability results from teachers' breach of duty through acts of malfeasance or negligence. As a licensed professional physical educator, you are expected to anticipate the negative consequences of inappropriate or dangerous actions. Whether you can be held legally liable is determined by considering duty of care, breach of duty, proximate cause, and damages. If legal action is taken by parents on behalf of an injured student (the plaintiff), their attorney must show proof that the conduct and actions of the teacher (defendant) were the cause of the injury. You should be informed about basic concepts and terms around legal liability.

■ **Malfeasance.** Malfeasance occurs when a teacher knowingly does something wrong (legally or morally). The key word here is *knowingly*. This is different from doing something wrong by mistake (which is called misfeasance) or through negligence. An example of malfeasance would be if a teacher used physical activity for punishment, while knowing that the state has a law forbidding this practice. Another example would be if a teacher continued to use a piece of equipment that they know is not safe to use (e.g., frayed cables on weight machines, damaged floor hockey sticks).

■ **Negligence.** Negligence occurs when a teacher's actions fall below the level of care that is expected. The following are examples of negligence. A teacher starts texting a message or takes a phone call during a class while students are engaged in activities and is distracted from his or her expected role of instructing and monitoring the students' activities. A teacher who asks a class of 9-year-old students to engage in excessively intense fitness activities. A teacher who fails to introduce proper safety instructions or measures. If a student is injured during a situation like this, the teacher could be held liable.

■ **Duty of care.** This refers to the expectation that teachers (and other school staff) are expected to act according to accepted standards of conduct. As in other professions, such as nursing, law, or medicine, teachers are expected to conduct themselves in a professional manner. A teacher's negligence would be determined by comparing his or her actions against those of teachers deemed to be in good standing.

■ **Breach of duty.** Breach of duty occurs when teachers fail to follow required duties (e.g., supervision of students, using appropriate instructional task progressions).

■ **Proximate cause.** Failure of a teacher to demonstrate the expected standard of care must be proven to have caused the student's injury.

■ **Damages.** For there to be liability, there must be physical or financial damages or both. If these are not present, then there can be no liability.

■ **Foreseeability.** As a licensed physical education teacher, you are expected to anticipate the possible harmful consequences of actions and to do everything you can to avoid such actions. For example, knowingly putting too many students in close proximity to tennis racquets or golf clubs increases the likelihood of student injuries. For example, specific to a Sport Education-based tennis context, the risk of injury can be reduced significantly because of Sport Education's built-in use of nonplaying roles (e.g., officials, scorekeepers, line judges). This means that fewer students will have racquets in their hands, yet are still cognitively engaged. The latter is also an integral part of learning about sport.

Safety Considerations Specific to Physical Education

The following sidebar presents three scenarios. For each of these, put yourself in the shoes of the teachers and the parents of the students. How would you navigate the situations that arose because of the teachers' actions?

These scenarios all include issues surrounding safety, supervision, and potential liability. The physical education setting is more difficult compared to regular classroom settings in terms of preventing physical injuries. Physical educators must be especially mindful of the importance of creating safe learning conditions, and vigilant in their supervision of students. Compared to regular classrooms, the physical activity areas (e.g., gymnasiums, tennis courts, fields) are larger, and the goal is for students to engage in physical movement, which carries inherent risks of physical injuries. Moreover, some venues are more difficult to supervise, not because of their size but by the nature of the setting. For example, weight rooms in high schools have become increasingly expansive, with lots of equipment that can obstruct a teacher's view of what is going on. The locker room in secondary schools is another area that can be difficult to supervise at times because of its layout. Physical educators should do everything in their power to minimize the risk of being sued for negligence.

Most school districts have an office of risk management. The central purpose of this office is to keep the district and its employees from being held liable. For example, if the district sees an increase in student injuries in a specific activity (e.g., floor hockey, or mountain biking), the district, on the advice of the office of risk management, may choose no longer to allow this activity to be taught in any of its physical education programs (see, for example, the Resources sidebar). If you wanted to incorporate a unit of golf or mountain biking or indoor climbing, your principal would likely direct you to meet with personnel in the office of risk management to review the anticipated risks of injuries associated with such activities. Student safety can also be compromised when your school's indoor and outdoor physical activity areas fall into disrepair. This, too, can be a consequence either of regular wear and tear of or deliberate destruction. At times, you might choose to do your own repairs, but best practice would be for you to contact your district-level office of facilities management and get the district personnel to resolve the safety hazard.

Finding yourself accused of negligence is a very stressful situation and it is a very expensive process. You have options, however, to protect yourself financially. First, you can become a member of your state's or one of the national teacher unions or your national professional organization (SHAPE America). The national unions include the American Federation of Teachers (AFT) and the National Education Association (NEA). Membership in the unions and SHAPE America includes the benefit of reduced fees for professional liability insurance. Coverage can go as high as $2,000,000. Like car insurance, you may not ever need it, but if a lawsuit is filed, you are covered financially.

SAFETY CONSIDERATION SCENARIOS

Scenario 1: Class Size and Activity Design

During a volleyball unit, with a coeducational class of 34 students, the teacher organizes a single game between two teams of 17 students with a net at regular height and one ball. The teacher observes the game and calls out the score following each completed play. The teacher provides little, if any, guidance (e.g., through instructional feedback, encouragement, technical or tactical prompts) to students to help them develop or improve gameplay. While few, if any, actual rallies ensue, at one point in the game, the ball is placed in a cluster of players on one side of the net. Multiple students converge by moving to the ball. In the attempt to play the ball, two students' heads collide, and one student falls to the ground and lies motionless. The teacher calls 911. The student regains consciousness after a little while, but is transported to the hospital for further tests. Although the head injury turns out to be less severe than originally believed, the student ends up being hospitalized for well over a week. The student's parents retain an attorney to get the teacher and the school district to cover the cost of the hospitalization.

Should the teacher and the district be held responsible for the cost incurred by the family?

Scenario 2: Physical Activity and Adult Supervision

During a 40-minute lunch period at a middle school, a group of students, after eating lunch, heads to one of the fields to play soccer. The soccer ball is provided by one of the physical education teachers as part of a lunchtime expanded physical activity program. The teacher and the assistant principal supervise the students attending the lunchtime program, checking for safety, general student conduct, and treatment of equipment. The student group divides up into two teams of six, sets up small goals, and commences a game. At one point during the game, one player trips over the leg of another player from the other team, and stumbles to the ground. The left tibia of the player who tripped and fell turns out to be broken.

If the parents of the injured student were to retain an attorney, could the teacher and possibly the principal and the district be held liable?

Scenario 3: Content Selection

Melissa is a certified physical educator who works at Sloane Valley Middle School. She teaches in a district that has an established, school board-approved physical education curriculum. While attending her state association's annual convention, she learns about an exciting new activity that involves the use of Ripstiks. Ripstiks are skateboards with only a single wheel in the front and one in the back. In addition, the board on which the user stands splits in half, with a strong spring connecting the two halves, which allows for torque. With a persuasive presentation, Melissa makes a request to her school's PTO to fund the purchase of 30 Ripstiks. The PTO agrees to make the funds available.

Melissa plans a short unit of the use of this new equipment, including extensive time spent on safety matters related its use, as suggested by the manufacturer. Her first day goes smoothly, and the students are excited about the new activity. But on day two of the unit, a student has a bad fall, in which he suffers a serious shoulder injury.

The injury results in significant medical costs, including surgery, hospital stay, and rehabilitation. The family of the student has no health insurance. An attorney is hired to determine whether the teacher, the principal, and the district could be found liable. The attorney representing the parents determines that the new unit on Ripstiks is not a sanctioned activity in the district-approved curriculum.

Should the teacher and possibly the principal and the district be held liable?

RESOURCES FOR TEACHERS SPECIFIC TO ETHICAL CONDUCT AND TO LEGAL RIGHTS AND RESPONSIBILITIES

- https://www.aaeteachers.org/index.php/about-us/aae-code-of-ethics
- http://education.findlaw.com
- http://www.educationrights.com/teacherrights.php
- https://www.lawyers.com/legal-info/research/education-law/teachers-have-many-responsibilities-to-their-students.html
- https://prezi.com/byvuxrdyrhcl/legal-and-ethical-responsibilities-of-educators/

Related Resources Specific to Ethical Conduct and to Legal Rights and Responsibilities

Teachers are members of a profession. With that membership come legal rights and responsibilities, and teachers are expected to behave ethically. Teachers should become aware of their legal rights and responsibilities because they affect most aspects of their work from the moment of signing their contract. The web resources in the sidebar provide more specific information about teachers' rights and responsibilities.

SUMMARY

In this chapter, we introduced you to several professional and legal responsibilities that go well beyond the act of teaching your classes. Delivering a quality physical education program includes more than having a well-designed, thematic curriculum. For the program to be delivered smoothly and consistently, you should have specific program-level policies that help you handle issues like managing attendance and equipment, budgeting for equipment and supplies, and emergencies such as student injuries and fights. When you enter the teaching profession, you also enter a legal commitment to provide a legal level of care for your students that ensures their safety. This requires you to be informed about the many instructional, managerial, and logistical strategies involved in minimizing the risks of injury.

Integrating Classroom Content With Sport Education

21

Chapter Objective

After reading this chapter, you will be able to identify ways in which you can reinforce lessons from the classroom in a season of Sport Education.

Key Concepts

- One of the major dangers in attempting to integrate classroom content with physical education is that the subject matter from both areas can become trivialized.
- Physical education teachers need to consult with classroom teachers to discover their current topics of study.
- Integration with Sport Education should take account of the grade level expectations for classroom work.
- The parallel form of integration is particularly suited to Sport Education. In a parallel design, teachers sequence their lessons to correspond to lessons in the other discipline.
- Sport Education is particularly suited to incorporating an Olympic Values curriculum.

Many educators have suggested that schools need to consider implementing more integrated or interdisciplinary curricula as a way of helping students apply their learning outside of school. This chapter will show how grade-level academic goals in subjects such as mathematics, science, literature, art, and music, among others, can be integrated with a Sport Education season, how Sport Education material can be used in classroom subjects, and how the concept of *parallel design* of curriculum integration can easily be achieved through the Sport Education model.

Integrating content from the classroom can be organized on a number of different levels. These levels are determined by the extent to which the classroom and physical education content is connected around a particular topic or theme. These connections have been described as "connected, shared, or partnered" (Purcell-Cone, Werner, & Cone 2009). An example of a *connected* example would involve showing students the location of the Philippines when introducing the subject of tinikling. In a *shared* case, you would continue to discuss the origin of tinikling and its representation of the buff-banded rail, or tinikling bird, as it dances in the rice fields in the Philippines. In social studies, students might learn more about agricultural societies and rice farming. Finally, in a *partnered* case, the focus might be on sustainable agriculture, with students exploring how various forms of farming and pest eradication affect the environment. To revisit our example, the tinikling dances mimic the movement of the tinikling heron dodging the bamboo traps set by farmers.

Irrespective of the level of connections, one of the major dangers of trying to integrate with physical education lies in trivialising the classroom content. While a sixth-grade physical education teacher might (in good faith) ask teams to create a drawing or painting of their team mascot in Sport Education, the appropriate art content for this grade might be nontraditional media and techniques such as collage, weaving, wire sculpture, or clay reliefs. Your first step should therefore be to seek the advice of the classroom teacher who is familiar with the curriculum guides.

THE CONCEPT OF PARALLEL DESIGN

In deciding whether to make connections across subjects, Ackerman (1989) urges us to consider two specific questions: (1) Does it make intellectual sense to integrate certain parts of the curriculum? and (2) Does it make practical sense, all things considered? Expanding these questions, Ackerman suggests we must first decide whether each subject *should* devote a portion of instructional time to the project, and whether students would learn the content better if it were taught separately.

One form of curriculum integration that has been found to answer these questions in the positive is referred to as a *parallel design*. In a parallel design, teachers sequence their lessons to correspond to lessons in the other discipline. The content itself does not change, but it is coordinated so that both subject areas are taught concurrently. This maintains the validity of each area while simultaneously relating studies in one subject with the other. Placek (1992) describes this organization as "separate but contributing." The following three scenarios give examples of parallel seasons. The first uses the progressive competition format (see chapter 8), while the second uses the progressive format where the dance content becomes more sophisticated. The third example is from a season that follows the event model format.

Parallel Soccer–Social Studies Season

A class of students is participating in a season of soccer while at the same time studying Europe in social studies. Each of the teams in this Sport Education soccer season identifies with one European country. The soccer team name is taken from a premier league team in their adopted country. Students are required not only to take the name of this team but also to adopt the team colors, mascot, and the city they represent in that country. As a special project, the team writes to the chambers of commerce of these cities (or searches the Internet) to get details about the history, geography, and economics of the city and country.

Parallel Dance–Music and Social Studies Season

This season, titled "Stomp: Exploring Music, Dance, and Culture" sees contributions by teachers in physical education, music, and social studies to bring to life the struggles of oppressed minority groups and their efforts to express themselves through unique music and movement. The central theme involves replicating the percussive dance form called *stomp* that is popular in major cities where there are significant Caribbean immigrant populations.

During music lessons, the students improvise instruments from ordinary household utensils. They then develop and refine percussive skills using these instruments. The lessons include segments that examine differences in cadence, accent, and beat. In social studies, the students examine the role of expressive movement and dance in minority cultures, particularly those who have a history of being oppressed. They learn of the countries that immigrants come from and the countries to which they immigrate and what their living conditions are.

The Sport Education season sees students in teams of four in which they learn step forms and design and practice short dance sequences and longer routines. At first, the accompaniment is just the sounds students make with their feet, but each week a team is allowed to add one new instrument of accompaniment. Teams may use whatever they wish as long as it is a basic household item (e.g., trash-can lid, broom, saucepan).

Friday is performance day, when teams present versions of their continually growing routine, while the other days of the week are used for skill development and routine design. On competition Fridays, one representative from each team acts on a judging panel, which awards points based on choreography, technique, and coordination among group members.

Weekly points are accumulated for progressively more points, and the final production counts for the largest number of points toward the seasonal championship. The season culminates with a final performance that includes costumes and that other classes are invited to watch.

Parallel Cross Country Running–Geography Season

Students in social studies are focusing on reading and drawing maps, with a particular emphasis on the concept of scale. In this case the concurrent Sport Education season is a cross-country running season. Using a topographic map of the school grounds, the students plan various courses for use during each Friday's cross-country team competition. Each week a different team acts as the host and plans the route. Using the school map, the students not only design the course but also determine its distance by means of the scale on the map. The students check the accuracy of their scale drawing by physically checking the length of the course with a measuring wheel. The organizing team hands out maps of the course two days before competition so that all teams can walk or run the course in order to become familiar with the geography and determine their strategy.

A SCHOOL-WIDE PARALLEL SPORT EDUCATION SEASON

The following season was conducted at an elementary school in Alabama in which students from grades 2 through 5 participated in a season called the *Biome Project*. This season provided an integrated curriculum within life sciences, art, technology, and physical education. It was designed around the central theme of biodiversity and habitat. Gymnastics was the physical education content used for the season, and in each grade, students practiced the skills and designed floor, vault, and balance beam routines.

Each of the seven classes that attended physical education represented one of the earth's large stable terrestrial ecosystems known as *biomes*: tundra, desert, tropical rainforest, deciduous forest, grassland, freshwater, and ocean. The students in each class became members of one of six teams: birds, mammals, reptiles, fish, amphibians, and arthropods.

Once students were allocated to a species group, they had to identify an animal of that species that lived within their biome to represent their team. For instance, students in the second-grade class representing deserts had to find a bird, mammal, or other species that lived in the desert. The fifth-grade grassland class had team names such as the Coyotes, Eagles, Fly Catchers, and Dung Beetles. The students went to great lengths to find animals that were accurate representatives but also were creative and unique. Once the classroom teacher verified the animal, each team had to construct a mascot of that animal and bring it to physical education class each day.

The competition during the season was both within classes (within biome) and across grades (across species). The teacher constructed a league table that could be read both horizontally and vertically. While the Birds team from one third-grade class was in fourth place, it was still part of a larger Birds team that was placed second across the entire league. To help facilitate this affiliation, the principal scheduled, for example, special Reptile lunches: instead of attending lunch with their classmates, students from all the Reptile teams (grades 2-5) had lunch together. Similar lunches were planned for all species groups. Further, on some days, instead of two third-grade classes attending physical education together, one fifth-grade and one third-grade class attended together. In this lesson, all the students from the Bird teams would practice together, with the older students providing feedback and designing routines with their younger teammates. On other days, fourth-grade students would attend with second-grade students, again with the older students acting as tutors within species teams.

To promote the life sciences curriculum content, all teachers in the school agreed to complete their section of the grade-level course of study at this time during the season. Additionally, six large posters (one for each species) were posted on the walls of the motor skills room, where teams could earn bonus points for making contributions about their specific animal. These contributions included photos or drawings of the animal as well as other pertinent information. For example, each day the physical education teacher posed a question about the animal that was in accord with the course of study for that grade. While the second-grade students were asked to identify what their animals ate and where they lived, the third-grade students described the survival tactics of their animal. The fourth-grade students explored the full biological name of their animal and some details of its taxonomic hierarchy, while the fifth-grade students described some of their animal's basic physiology. Because these posters were highly visible in the room that also doubled as the school cafeteria, there was considerable competition across biomes and species to contribute good work.

For the culminating event of the biomes project, all of the students from the school (including first grade) were bused to the town recreation center, where the final competition of the gymnastics league was staged. Each teacher in the school became a member of a team and sat and cheered with that team during the competition. All teams were allocated a specific color (e.g., all Birds wore yellow, all Fish wore blue), and each team was encouraged to make posters. Selected fifth-grade students who were not competing in one of the event finals dressed in complete mascot costume.

To involve as many students as possible during the culminating event, students took the roles of competitor, judge, scorekeeper, equipment supervisor, runner (to take scores from event locations to the central score desk), and VIP host (where parents and central-office officials could watch the event, complete with refreshments). Between rotations, second- and third-grade students known as information officers gave brief summaries of their animal, using a microphone. At the end of the competition, awards were given for the best overall biome as well as for the champion species. These were presented by members of the gymnastics team from the local university.

The following sections provide a step-by-step regression of how to create a Sport Education season that can reinforce classroom content while promoting team affiliation and connectedness between subjects.

Determine the Subject Area and Identify Key Elements of Classroom Work

In this beginning phase, the physical education teacher connects with the classroom teacher to determine which area of their curriculum is in particular need of reinforcement. At the same time, they negotiate the amount of time each will allocate for specific research and reporting of results: how often the teacher will provide the physical educator with content challenges, how often the classroom teacher will allocate specific time for research, and how often the physical educator will allot time for students to update their poster boards. Of course, where the classroom teacher also acts as the physical education teacher, there is considerably more flexibility in this process.

Determine the Organizing Framework for Team Affiliation

In the biome project, the consistent teams were the various animal species (birds, reptiles, etc.), with each team then being responsible for selecting its subspecies depending upon its habitat. In another season completed by the same teacher, the focus was on math. Here the central team names represented the key content domains of that curriculum, such as fractions, money, and time. In this case, team names had to reflect the implications of the topic, for example Bad Credit and Bouncing Checks. Table 21.1 provides some examples of these frameworks.

Determine the Academic Tasks and the Level of Contribution by Teams

In the biome project, all teams received the same question, and the task was to apply it to their particular animal. For example, the third grade teams were asked to determine who eats whom and who gets eaten by whom. In the math season, however, the tasks were specific to each content area, with the fractions teams receiving different questions from those on the operation team. A further difference was that the life

Table 21.1 Sample Organizing Frameworks for Parallel Sport Education Seasons

Content area	Sample team groups	Possible questions
Biomes (life sciences)	• The seven major groups include tundra, desert, tropical rainforest, deciduous forest, grassland, freshwater, and ocean • Teams in each biome include birds, reptiles, mammals, arthropods, amphibians, and fish	• Questions are related to the specific grade level of the class • Topics can include habitat, physiology, survival tactics, sources of food, and migration patterns
Math (mathematics)	Fractions, money, time, measurement, operations, geometry	• Teachers provide problems for each of the topic areas as homework tasks • These problems are presented to students individually
Native American (social studies)	• In the United States, the Indian tribe is a fundamental unit, and as of January 2017, 567 Native American tribes were legally recognized by the Bureau of Indian Affairs • Teams might focus on those tribes in their geographic proximity	Where do the tribes live in the U.S.? What foods do they grow? Where do they shelter? What games do they play? How do they preserve their culture?
Diseases of the Oregon Trail (social studies)	Typhoid fever, cholera, dysentery, diphtheria, measles	What were some of the hardships on the Oregon Trail? What was the most common cause of death on the Oregon Trail? What happened in 1843 on the Oregon Trail? Why was the Oregon Trail so important? What is camp fever?
Continents and countries (social studies)	• The seven continents (Africa, Antarctica, Asia, Australia and Oceania, Europe, North America, and South America) can constitute the major groups across classes • Countries in each continent can make up the individual teams	Once students have selected their country, they can be asked relevant questions from their grade's course of study, for example, capital, population, currency, languages spoken, type of government, famous athletes, climate, industries, etc.
Solar system (science)	Team names represent the eight planets, Mercury, Venus, Earth, Mars, Jupiter, Saturn, Uranus, and Neptune	How many moons does your planet have? How did your planet get its name? How long does it take to orbit the sun? How far is your planet from the sun? How hot or cold can it get on your planet?

sciences tasks were team tasks, while the math questions were given to the individual students. In this latter case, while it created more work for the teacher in terms of providing feedback, there was a stronger level of within-team accountability for the completion of the work.

A teacher in another school used a Native American organizing theme with a combination of both strategies. First the same set of questions was given to all teams, but then individual students were responsible for completing the different topics. Examples in this case included identifying shelter, cultures, games and sports, and food. As students fulfilled their responsibilities, their artifacts were added to their team poster board and points for completion were awarded.

Determine the Contribution of Classroom Tasks Toward the League Table

It is recognized that, in classrooms, accountability drives whatever task system is operating; this is equally true in physical education. Without accountability, there is in fact no instructional task, and students work only at the level they are motivated to work at. On the other hand, when there are rewards or consequences for certain levels of performance, student compliance is higher. If the teacher wants students to consider the integration of academic tasks valuable and important, the products of their work need to count toward the season championship and hence be part of the season league table. The teacher has complete flexibility in determining the point values of these tasks, as well as deciding whether group or individual contributions are required.

Integrate the Organizing Theme With the Culminating Event

Aspects of the organizing theme can be included within the culminating event in numerous ways. These are particularly well suited when there are a number of transitions between individual contests (as in a gymnastics event or a fitness season), as when teams are moving between different stations or when different students are switching from competitor to the role of judge. Some of these can include having students dress as the mascots of their team, or incorporating interviews during transitions when selected students are asked questions about their team.

In one of the biome seasons, the teacher used the app Kahoot! to provide an extra challenge to those students who were not competing or judging during a particular rotation. Kahoot! is a free game-based learning platform where multiple-choice questions are projected onto a large screen. During each event, the questions and up to four multiple choice answers were displayed on the main screen. Every answer corresponded to a distinctive color and shape. On the screen of the participants' devices, there were at most four rectangles with the color and the shape on each, and the students had to click or tap on the rectangle representing the correct answer. Each team was issued with an iPad and responded to various multiple choice questions taken from the team poster boards. After each question, the app provided the correct answer and the percent of correct answers, current team scores, and current team rankings.

AN OLYMPIC VALUES CURRICULUM

One of the tenets of the International Olympic Committee (IOC) is that sport is a school for life. With this in mind, the IOC has developed the Olympic Values Education Programme (OVEP), which aims to blend sport with education and cultural expression. The OVEP is based on the philosophy that learning takes place through a balanced development of body and mind, and encourages young people to experience life values such as excellence, respect, and friendship. These Olympic values are founded in the principles of the Olympic Charter, which states that the purpose of the Olympic movement is to educate young people through sport in a spirit of better understanding between each other and of friendship, thereby helping to build a better and more peaceful world.

The OVEP is based on five educational themes:

- experiencing the joy of effort,
- learning to play fair,

- practicing respect for oneself and others,
- the pursuit of excellence, and
- living a harmonious and balanced life of body, will, and mind.

An integrated curriculum around the big idea of Olympic values, then, would focus on the principles of participating, overcoming obstacles, and striving to be the best you can be. Table 21.2 shows an example of how a high school basketball season could be arranged to include these key Olympic values.

Key Elements of the OVEP Season

The standard format outlined in the next paragraphs could be adapted to local needs while still maintaining the underlying structural principles. Some schools might want to have more but slightly shorter seasons. Some schools might want to keep students on teams for an entire semester or school year. Some teachers might want to emphasize personal growth in the curriculum and downplay the aesthetics or global education. Some teachers will find it difficult to integrate art, music, and literature as fully as they desire. None of these restrictions or differences in outlook need detract from pursuing the main goals of the Olympic curriculum.

- *Using national teams as the affiliation format.* Teams represent nations (preferably spread across all the continents). Nations can be chosen by teams or assigned by teachers. Teams remain intact for that season, and then new nations are chosen and teams can be reorganized to provide even competition or for other reasons.

- *Forming Olympic committees.* Many teachers include a sport committee or sport board as an added student responsibility in Sport Education. This is a particularly beneficial feature in middle and secondary school because it provides a major role for students and creates a mechanism whereby decisions can be made and disputes arbitrated by students themselves, thus contributing to the curriculum goals of personal growth. Using the Olympism theme, the sport board would function as an Olympic Committee.

- *Integrating academic work to meet global, multicultural, and aesthetic education goals.* During the season, students learn about the country their team represents as well as those countries represented by classmates. This feature allows for substantial integration with social studies, art, music, and literature. National colors and anthems can add to the festive atmosphere. Music, art, and poetry from the various nations can be incorporated as appropriate. Much of this can be done as homework or integrated with the classroom teacher's work. Students can also learn about the national sports and major sport figures of each country, and they can create Olympic awards as art projects.

- *Formalizing the personal development goals of the curriculum.* Olympism is dedicated to creating a more peaceful world, working together, friendly competition, and striving to be the best that you can be. The personal and social development goals of Olympism are central to its overall purposes. Chapter 10 details the fair play approach to behavior and social development that is consistent with the goals of Sport Education. The fair play systems described in that chapter can easily be adapted to an Olympic fair play system. This system could also include player and referee oaths that are given formally by a representative at the start of each competition.

- *Creating a festive Olympic atmosphere.* The Olympic movement provides many symbols and rituals that can be easily incorporated in the Olympic curriculum to develop and sustain a festive atmosphere. Suggestions include using the Olympic rings and creed as large, permanent posters in the gym, using the athlete and referee oaths

Table 21.2 A Sport Education Season Encompassing Olympic Values

Lesson	Sport Education content	Olympic values content
1	• Introduction and outline of the unit • Announcement of teams • Divided into eight groups with six students in each • Election of captains	Pierre de Frédy, Baron de Coubertin, and the Olympic movement OVEP: • Respect for others • Balance • Fair play
2	• Review of game skills • Shooting, passing, dribbling • Whole class skills practice	Hosting an Olympic Games OVEP: • Balance • Pursuit of excellence • Fair play • Respect for others • Joy of effort
3	Introduction to three-on-three games in team practice	
4	Three-on-three cutting and passing	The Olympic symbol OVEP: • Respect • Excellence
5	Three-on-three mini games	
6	Shooting clinic	• Flying the flag: Understanding the significance of a flag in reflecting identity and values • Igniting the spirit: the Olympic flame • Understanding the value of the Olympic flame as a symbol that inspires hope and is connected to common values around the world OVEP: • Respect
7	• Rebounding clinic • Three-on-three mini games	
8	Three-on-three mini games	Logos and mascots OVEP: • Balance • Respect • Joy of effort
9	Three-on-three defensive tactics	
10	Skills test	
11	• Team practice • Duty team responsibilities	• Living by the rules of fair play • Recognizing the importance of fair play not only in sport but also in life
12	• Team practice • Duty team responsibilities	
13	Preseason competition	• The Olympic Games opening ceremony • Recognizing the power of Olympic symbolism • Learning how the Olympic Games opening ceremony can be used to make a statement about the culture, history, and spirit of the host nation OVEP: • Fair play • Respect • Balance
14	Preseason competition	

(continued)

Table 21.2 *(continued)*

Lesson	Sport Education content	Olympic values content
15	Tournament round	• Sport and art in the modern Olympic • Developing visual art skills that help communicate key messages of Olympism
16	Tournament round	
17	Tournament round	OVEP: • Pursuit of excellence • Balance • Respect for others • Fair play
18	Tournament round	
19	Tournament round	• The Olympic Games closing ceremony • Recognizing the importance of traditions and protocols in the Olympic Games • Recognizing how Olympism is celebrated and the values that are put forward though this ceremony
20	• Championship game • Awards and presentation • Closing ceremony	OVEP: • Pursuit of excellence • Balance • Respect for others • Fair play

before the beginning of each season's competition, and playing the Olympic hymn during the award ceremonies. Teachers can also use materials from the countries represented by national teams to build and sustain a festive atmosphere. Suggestions include using national flags and national colors, having students develop bulletin boards providing information about and pictures of their home countries, and using national anthems in medal ceremonies.

USING SPORT EDUCATION RESOURCES TO ENHANCE CLASSROOM LEARNING

The process of connecting classroom work with physical education need not be a one-way street. During a Sport Education season, a significant amount of material is generated by the students, such as score sheets, statistics sheets, and match reports, to name just a few. Likewise, there are game rules, playing areas, and equipment that are part of the sport or activity. All of these aspects of Sport Education can be used by classroom teachers in their subject areas. Some specific examples are included next.

Applications in Mathematics Lessons

Many of the artifacts from gameplay in Sport Education lessons provide resources well suited to helping students develop problem solving and mathematical reasoning skills. Table 21.3 shows how a number of Sport Education artifacts could be applied in math lessons. The University of Cambridge in the UK has a fascinating website called "Maths and Sport" (https://sport.maths.org/content/) that includes math activities, articles, and video challenges.

Table 21.3 Possible Translations of Sport Education Content to the Classroom

Sport Education artifact	Application	Samples
Match statistics	Percentages	• What percent of your team's total score came from free throws in today's basketball lesson? • What percent of the total possible score did the Lions team shoot in their archery practice today? • What percent of that score did each team member contribute?
	Fractions	• Express as a fraction the weight you lifted on the bench press today compared with the weight you lifted on the leg press. • John scored one third of his team's points, and Jennifer scored two fifths. What was their total contribution?
	Graphing	• Draw a line graph of your time for today's mile run, using each of the four laps as the horizontal axis labels. • Based on the graph for the Eagles' football scores for the past week, which day did they have their best defensive effort? • Produce a pie graph of the number of birdies, pars, bogeys, and other scores from today's round of minigolf.
	Operations	• If the pool is 25m long, how many lengths would I have to swim in order to swim 50m, 100m, 250m, and 500m? • Create equations of your team's curling score using multiplication and addition functions. • Calculate the equation that best fits the Devils' scoring trends from touchdowns and field goals.
Game rules	Geometry	• Identify all of the shapes you can find on the basketball court. • How many total rectangles are there on the badminton court?
	Measurement	• Calculate the area and perimeter of the handball court you are using for your Sport Education season. • Given the circumference of the shot put is 100mm (4 inches), calculate its radius and volume. • Your discus circle is 2.13m (7 feet) in diameter and the complete throwing pad is a 3.05m (10 feet) square; what is the area of the pad outside the throwing circle?

Writing Game and Match Reports and Journal Articles in Language Classes

One of the strong growth industries in sport has been the increase in sport journalism. Newspapers and websites no longer simply report scores and game highlights but also offer detailed explanations of sporting events. Because team practices and competitions in Sport Education are so authentic, language arts teachers have a ready supply of material that students may use. Consider the following examples:

■ *Game and match reports.* Using the format found in most major newspapers (e.g., headlines, bylines, stories), write a report on the game your team participated in today as either contestant or official. Prepare a press release headline of the major outcome of your Sport Education lesson today.

■ *Essays:* It has been suggested that team harmony is important to team success. Write a one-page essay describing the level of team harmony on your Sport Education team this season.

Because team practices and competitions in Sport Education are so authentic, language arts teachers have a ready supply of material that students may use.

■ *Letters:* Write a letter to a potential sponsor of your orienteering team. Include the correct address format, the appropriate formatting, and the acceptable ways of addressing the reader (depending upon whether she or he is known to you or not). Try to convince the potential sponsor of the value of providing resources to sponsor your team.

■ *Speaking and listening:* Next Tuesday, you are to conduct an oral interview with the referee from one of that day's floor hockey matches. Prepare your list of questions, and be prepared to include any specific incidents you might witness during the match that day.

Using Sport Education Data and Experiences in Science Classes

Science teachers may use data collected in Sport Education to enhance explanations and understanding of science content. In a number of sports, human physiology is significantly related to athletic success. Indeed, studying scientific concepts through their applications to sport may be the most effective way of presenting the content matter. Consider the following examples.

■ *Anatomy and physiology.* The link between human anatomy and physiology as studied in science classes and physical education is clear cut. It would not be difficult for students to record their heart rates during and after exercise over multiple classes and estimate their aerobic capacity as a science project. In a Sport Education fitness season, this connection would be even stronger. Science teachers could use a strength training season to teach both the anatomy of the body and the muscles that move the bony structure at joints. The focus would be on the lifts themselves and on identification of the muscles involved in each lift or in using particular machines. Teachers and students could explore how the body adapts to strength training in terms of muscle changes, flexibility, and the impact of strength training on metabolism.

■ *Health-related physical activity.* Students could plot their steps per day as recorded on pedometers or chart their repetitions and weight lifted in a series of strength exercises. One elementary physical education teacher in Columbus, Ohio, worked with classroom teachers to have students plot all their walking over the course of a school year. The goal for students was to choose another city called Columbus in another state and see if they could walk to that Columbus during the school year. A walking trail was created at the school, and classroom teachers had their students measure the distance from school to their homes so that when they walked to school, they could count the steps they accumulated.

■ *Levers and mechanical systems.* During a gymnastics season, teachers could ask teams to analyze the key mechanical systems involved in a balance, roll, or somersault. In weight training seasons, the effects of levers are particularly relevant since some lifts are performed standing while others are performed from a prone position. The differences in the mechanics of lifts would be investigated.

SUMMARY

The possibilities for teaching across different subject areas using Sport Education are endless, because the model is grounded in the idea of persisting small groups who work together to complete challenges. The key to this integration, however, is remaining true to the appropriate content of both subject areas, while at the same time, not trivializing either one. Done well, the collaboration can produce a whole that is greater than the sum of its parts. Done poorly, the content of both physical education and the classroom subjects can be distinctly compromised. The best chance for success exists where there is a significant commitment from all the stakeholders.

References

Ackerman, D. B. (1989). Intellectual and practical criteria for successful curriculum integration. In H.H. Jacobs (Ed.), *Interdisciplinary curriculum: Design and implementation* (pp. 25-38). Alexandra, VA: Association for Supervision and Curriculum Development.

Alexander, K. (1994). Developing Sport Education in Western Australia. *Aussie Sports Action, 5,* 8-9.

Alexander, K. & Luckman, J. (2001). Australian teachers' perceptions and uses of the Sport Education curriculum model. *European Physical Education Review, 7,* 243-267.

Alexander, K., & Penney, D. (2005). Teaching under the influence: Feeding games for understanding into the Sport Education development-refinement cycle. *Physical Education and Sport Pedagogy, 10,* 287-301.

Alexander, K., Taggart, A., & Medland, A. (1993). *Sport education: Try before you buy.* ACHPER *National Journal, 40*(4), 16-23.

Alexander, K., Taggart, A., & Thorpe, S. (1996). A spring in their steps? Possibilities for professional renewal through Sport Education in Australian schools. *Sport, Education and Society, 1,* 23-46.

Almond, L. (1986). Primary and secondary rules in games. In R. Thorpe et al. (Eds.), *Rethinking games teaching* (pp. 73-74). Loughborough, England: University of Technology, Dept. of Physical Education and Sports Science.

Alonzo-Zaldivar, R. (2016). *$10,345 per person: U.S. health care spending reaches new peak.* Retrieved from http://www.pbs.org/newshour/rundown/new-peak-us-health-care-spending-10345-per-person/

Araújo, R., Hastie, P. A., & Mesquita, I. M. (2016). The evolution of student-coach's pedagogical content knowledge in a combined use of Sport Education and the Step-Game-Approach model. *Physical Education and Sport Pedagogy, 22,* 518-535.

Araújo, R., Mesquita, I., & Hastie, P. A. (2014). Review of the status of learning in research on Sport Education: Future research and practice. *Journal of Sports Science & Medicine, 13,* 846-858.

Australian Curriculum, Assessment, and Reporting Authority (ACARA). (2015). *Health and Physical Education: Sequence of content F-10.* Retrieved from http://docs.acara.edu.au/resources/Health_and_Physical_Education_-_Sequence_of_content.pdf

Australian Curriculum, Assessment, and Reporting Authority (ACARA). (2017). *The Australian Curriculum: Health and Physical Education Year 10.* Retrieved from http://docs.acara.edu.au/resources/Health_and_Physical_Education_Sequence_of_achievement.pdf

Beets, M. W., Rooney, L., Tilley, F., Beighle, A., & Webster, C. (2010). Evaluation of policies to promote physical activity in afterschool programs: Are we meeting current benchmarks? *Preventive Medicine, 51,* 299-301.

Beets, M. W., Shah, R., Weaver, R. G., Huberty, J., Beighle, A., & Moore, J. B. (2016). Physical activity in after-school programs: Comparison with physical activity policies. *Journal of Physical Activity and Health, 12,* 237-246.

Bell, C. (1994). Elementary gymnastics. In D. Siedentop (Ed.), *Sport Education: Quality PE through positive sport experiences* (pp. 47-60). Champaign, IL: Human Kinetics.

Bell, C., & Darnell, J. (1994). Elementary soccer. In D. Siedentop (Ed.), *Sport education: Quality PE through positive sport experiences* (pp. 37-46). Champaign, IL: Human Kinetics.

Bennett, G., & Hastie, P. (1997). A Sport Education curriculum model for a collegiate physical activity course. *Journal of Physical Education, Recreation & Dance, 68*(1), 39-44.

Biggs, J. (1996). Enhancing teaching through constructive alignment. *Higher Education, 32,* 347-364.

Black, K. (2004). *Disability education program activity cards.* Disability Sport Unit, Australian Sports Commission.

Blocker, D., & Wahl-Alexander, Z. (2018). Using Sport Education in a university course. *Journal of Physical Education, Recreation & Dance, 89*(2), 56-61.

Borghouts, L. B., Slingerland, M., & Haerens, L. (2016). Assessment quality and practices in secondary PE in the Netherlands. *Physical Education and Sport Pedagogy, 22,* 473-489.

Branch, T. (2011). The shame of college sports. *The Atlantic Monthly Magazine.* Retrieved from http://www.theatlantic.com/magazine/archive/2011/10/the-shame-of-college-sports/8643/

Brock, S. J., Rovegno, I., & Oliver, K. L. (2009). The influence of student status on student interactions and experiences during a Sport Education unit. *Physical Education and Sport Pedagogy, 14,* 355-375.

Brown, S., & Hopper, T. (2006). Can all students in physical education get an "A"? Game performance assessment by peers as a critical component of student learning. *Physical and Health Education, Spring 2006,* 13-21.

Bryan, R. R., McCubbin, J. A., & van der Mars, H. (2013). The ambiguous role of the paraeducator in the general physical education environment. *Adapted Physical Activity Quarterly, 30,* 164-183.

Bunker, D. J., & Thorpe, R. D. (1983). A model for the teaching of games. *Bulletin of Physical Education, 18*(1), 5-8.

Bygren, M. (2016). Ability groupings effects on grades and the attainment of higher education: A natural experiment. *Sociology of Education, 89,* 118-136.

Caillois, R. (1961). *Man, play and games.* New York: The Free Press of Glencoe.

Calderón, A., Hastie, P. A., Liarte. J. P., & Martínez de Ojeda, D. (2013). El modelo de educación deportiva y la enseñanza de la danza: Una experiencia en bachillerato (The Sport Education model and dance education: An experience in high school). *Tándem, 41,* 93-98.

Carlson, T. B. (1995). "Now I think I can": The reaction of eight low-skilled students to Sport Education. *ACHPER Healthy Lifestyles Journal, 42*(4), 6-8.

Carlson, T. B., & Hastie, P. A. (1997). The student social system within sport education. *Journal of Teaching in Physical Education, 16,* 176-195.

Carlson, T. B., & Hastie, P. A. (2003). The infusion of participatory democracy in a season of Sport Education. *ACHPER Healthy Lifestyles Journal, 51*(1), 17-20.

Casey, A., & Dyson, B. (2012). Cooperative learning in physical education. In B. Dyson & A. Casey (Eds.), *Cooperative learning in physical education: A research-based approach* (pp. 166-175). London: Routledge.

Casey, A., & Hastie, P. A. (2011). Student and teacher responses to a unit of student-designed games. *Physical Education & Sport Pedagogy, 16,* 295-312.

Centers for Disease Control and Prevention (CDC). (2001). Increasing physical activity: A report on recommendations of the Task Force on Community Preventive Services. *Morbidity and Mortality Weekly Report, 50*(RR-18), 1-14.

Centers for Disease Control and Prevention (CDC). (2013). *Comprehensive school physical activity programs: A guide for schools.* Atlanta, GA: U.S. Department of Health and Human Services.

Centers for Disease Control and Prevention (CDC). (2017). *Increasing physical education and physical activity: A framework for schools.* Atlanta, GA: Author.

Charlesworth, R. (1994). Designer games. *Sport Coach, 17*(4), 30-33.

Cheon, S. H., Reeve, J., & Moon, I. S. (2012). Experimentally based, longitudinally designed, teacher-focused intervention to help physical education teachers be more autonomy supportive toward their students. *Journal of Sport and Exercise Psychology, 34,* 365-396.

Coakley, J. (2017). *Sports in society: Issues and controversies* (12th ed.). New York: McGraw-Hill Education.

Cohen, E. G., & Lotan, R. A. (2014). *Designing groupwork: Strategies for the heterogeneous classroom* (3rd ed.). New York: Teachers College Press.

Collier, D. H. (2011). Instructional strategies for adapted physical education. In J. P. Winnick (Ed.), *Adapted physical education and sport* (5th ed.) (pp. 119-150). Champaign, IL: Human Kinetics.

Cooper, J. O., Heron, T. E., & Heward, W. L. (2007). *Applied behavior analysis* (2nd ed.). Upper Saddle River, NJ: Pearson Merrill Prentice Hall.

Corbin, C. B., & Le Masurier, G. (2014). *Fitness for life* (6th ed.). Champaign, IL: Human Kinetics.

Corbin, C. B., Le Masurier, G., & Lambdin, D. (2018). *Fitness for life: Middle school* (2nd ed.). Champaign, IL: Human Kinetics.

Darkes, J., Collins, R., Cohen, J., & Gwartney, D. (2013). Performance-enhancing drug use (including anabolic steroids) among adolescents and college students: Etiology and prevention. In P. M. Miller (Ed.), *Interventions for addiction: Comprehensive addictive behaviors and disorders* (pp. 833-842). San Diego, CA: Academic Press.

Darnell, J. (1994). Sport education in the elementary curriculum. In D. Siedentop (Ed.), *Sport Education: Quality PE through positive sport experiences* (pp. 61-71). Champaign, IL: Human Kinetics.

Davis, R. W. (2011). *Teaching disability sport: A guide for physical educators* (2nd ed.). Champaign, IL: Human Kinetics.

Den Duyn, N. (1997). *Game sense-developing thinking players: A presenters guide and workbook.* Belconnen, ACT: Australian Sports Commission.

Dodge, T. L., & Jaccard, J. J. (2006). The effect of high school sports participation on the use of performance-enhancing substances in young adulthood. *Journal of Adolescent Health, 39,* 367-373.

Drape, J. (2018, September 12). The youth sports megacomplex comes to town, hoping teams will follow. *New York Times.* Retrieved from https://www.nytimes.com/2018/09/12/sports/youth-sports-costs.html

Dugas, D. (1994). Sport Education in the secondary curriculum. In D. Siedentop (Ed.), *Sport Education: Quality PE through positive sport experiences* (pp. 105-112). Champaign, IL: Human Kinetics.

Eichberg, H. (2006, January), Sport as festivity: Education through festival. Paper presented at the Akademia Wychowania Fizycznego (The Josef Pilsudski Academy of Physical Education), Warsaw, Poland.

Ellery, P. J., Rauschenbach, J., & Stewart, M. (2000). Impact of disability awareness activities on nondisabled student attitudes toward integrated physical education with students who use wheelchairs. *Research Quarterly for Exercise and Sport, Supplement, Abstracts of Completed Research, 71*(1), A-106.

Farias, C. (2017). Promoting equity and social responsibility within Sport Education. *Active + Healthy Journal, 24*(2/3), 35-43.

Farias, C., Hastie, P. A., & Mesquita, I. (2017). Towards a more equitable and inclusive learning environment in Sport Education: Results of an action research-based intervention. *Sport, Education and Society, 22,* 460-476.

Farias, C., Hastie, P. A., & Mesquita, I. (2018). Scaffolding student-coaches' instructional leadership toward student-centred peer interactions: A yearlong action-research intervention in sport education. *European Physical Education Review, 24,* 269-291.

Farrey, T. (2008). *Game on: The all-American race to make champions of our children.* New York, NY: ESPN Books.

Finkelstein, E.A., Khavjou, O.A., Thompson, H., Trogdon, J.G., Pan, L., Sherry, B., & Dietz, W. (2012). Obesity and severe obesity forecasts through 2030. *American Journal of Preventive Medicine, 42,* 563-570.

Fittipaldi-Wert, J., Brock, S. J., Hastie, P. A., Arnold, J. B., & Guarino, A. J. (2009). Effects of a Sport Education curriculum model on the experiences of students with visual impairments. *Palaestra, 24*(3), 6-10.

Foley, J. T., Tindall, D. W., Lieberman, L. J., & Kim, S. Y. (2007). How to develop disability awareness using the Sport Education model. *Journal of Physical Education, Recreation & Dance, 78*(9), 32-36.

Friend, M. (2008). *Special education: Contemporary perspectives for school professionals* (2nd ed.). Boston, MA: Allyn & Bacon.

Gelernter, J. (2016). Make the Olympics great again. *National Review.* Retrieved from https://www.nationalreview.com/2016/07/rooting-corruption-out-olympics/

Gilbert, C., Grossekathöfer, M., Kramer, J., Ludwig, U., Pfeil, G., Weinreich, J. & Wulzinger, M. (2009). The price of gold: The legacy of doping in the GDR. *Spiegel Online International.* Retrieved from http://www.spiegel.de/international/germany/the-price-of-gold-the-legacy-of-doping-in-the-gdr-a-644233.html

Ginsburg, K. R. (2007). The importance of play in promoting healthy child development and maintaining strong parent-child bonds. *Pediatrics, 119,* 182-191.

Grant, B. C. (1992). Integrating sport into the physical education curriculum in New Zealand secondary schools. *Quest, 44,* 304-316.

Grant, B. C., Sharp, P., & Siedentop, D. (1992). Sport education in physical education: A teacher's guide. Wellington: Hillary Commission for Sport, Fitness & Leisure.

Graves, M. A., & Townsend, S. (2000). Applying the Sport Education curriculum model to dance. *Journal of Physical Education, Recreation & Dance, 71*(8), 50-54.

Greenberg, J. D., & LoBianco, J. L. (2020). *Organization and administration of physical education: Theory and practice.* Champaign, IL: Human Kinetics.

Gréhaigne, J.-F., Godbout, P.G., Bouthier D. (1997). Performance assessment in team sports. *Journal of Teaching in Physical Education, 16*, 500-516.

Gréhaigne, J. F., Richard, J. F., & Griffin, L. (2005). *Teaching and learning team sports and games.* New York, NY: Routledge Falmer.

Harvey, S. (2007). Using a generic invasion game for assessment. *Journal of Physical Education, Recreation and Dance, 78*(4) 19-25/48.

Harvey, S., Cope, E., & Jones, R. (2016). Developing questioning in game-centered approaches. *Journal of Physical Education, Recreation & Dance, 87*(3), 28-35.

Harvey, S., Kirk, D., & O'Donovan, T. M. (2014). Sport Education as a pedagogical application for ethical development in physical education and youth sport. *Sport, Education, and Society, 19*, 41-62.

Hastie, P. A. (1996). Student role involvement during a unit of sport education. *Journal of Teaching in Physical Education, 16*, 88-103.

Hastie, P. A. (1998). Skill and tactical development during a Sport Education season. *Research Quarterly for Exercise and Sport, 69*, 368-379.

Hastie, P. A. (2000). An ecological analysis of a Sport Education season. *Journal of Teaching in Physical Education, 19*, 355-373.

Hastie, P. A. (2010). *Student-designed games: Strategies for promoting creativity, cooperation, and skill development.* Champaign, IL: Human Kinetics.

Hastie, P. A., Martínez, D., & Calderón, A. (2011). A review of research on Sport Education: 2004 to the present. *Physical Education and Sport Pedagogy, 16*, 103-132.

Hastie, P. A., & Sharpe, T. (1999). Effects of a Sport Education curriculum on the positive social behavior of at-risk rural adolescent boys. *Journal of Education for Students Placed at Risk, 4*, 417-430.

Hastie, P. A., & Sinelnikov, O. A. (2006). Russian students' participation in and perceptions of a season of Sport Education. *European Physical Education Review, 12*, 131-150.

Hastie, P. A., & Sinelnikov, O. A. (2007). The use of web-based portfolios in college physical education activity courses. *Physical Educator, 64*, 21-28.

Hastie, P. A., Sinelnikov, O. A., & Guarino, A. J. (2009). The development of skill and tactical competencies during a season of badminton. *European Journal of Sport Science, 9*, 133-140.

Hastie, P. A., & Trost, S. G. (2002). Student physical activity levels during a season of Sport Education. *Pediatric Exercise Science, 14*, 64-74.

Hastie, P., van der Mars, H., Layne, T., & Wadsworth, D. (2012). The effects of prompts and a group-oriented contingency on out-of-school physical activity in elementary school-aged students. *Journal of Teaching in Physical Education, 31,* 131-145.

Hastie, P. A., Ward, J. K., & Brock, S. J. (2016). Effect of graded competition on student opportunities for participation and success rates during a season of Sport Education. *Physical Education and Sport Pedagogy, 22*, 316-327.

Healy, S. (2013). Adapting equipment for teaching object control skills. *Palaestra, 27*(4), 37-42. Retrieved from https://www.chronicle.com/article/In-UNC-Case-No-Watchdog-for/241448

Huizinga, J. (1955). *Homo ludens: A study of the play element in culture.* Boston, MA: The Beacon Press.

Kanters, M. A., Bocarro, J. N., Edwards, M. B., Casper, J. M., & Floyd, M. F. (2013). School sport participation under two school sport policies: Comparisons by race/ethnicity, gender, and socioeconomic status. *Annals of Behavioral Medicine, 45*, 113-121.

Kelderman, E. (October 2017). In UNC case, no watchdog for major academic fraud. *The Chronicle of Higher Education.* Retrieved from https://www.chronicle.com/article/In-UNC-Case-No-Watchdog-for/241448\

Kinchin, G. D. (2001). A high skilled pupil's experiences with Sport Education. *ACHPER Healthy Lifestyles Journal, 48*(3/4), 5-9.

Kinchin, G. D. (2001). Using team portfolios during a Sport Education season. *Journal of Physical Education, Recreation & Dance, 72*(2), 41-44.

Kinchin, G. D. (2006) Sport education: A review of the research. In D. Kirk, D. Macdonald & M. O'Sullivan (Eds.), *The handbook of physical education* (pp. 596-609). London: Sage.

Kinchin, G. D., MacPhail, A., & Ni Chroinin, D. (2009). Pupils' and teachers' perceptions of a culminating festival within a Sport Education season in Irish primary schools. *Physical Education and Sport Pedagogy, 14,* 391-406.

King, M., & Rothlisberger, K. (2014). *Family financial investment in organized youth sport.* Research On Capitol Hill 2014. *Research on the Hill (Salt Lake City).* Paper 17. Retrieved from https://digitalcommons.usu.edu/poth_slc/17

Kirk, D. (2010). *Physical education futures.* London: Routledge.

Knowles, A., Wallhead, T. L., & Readdy, T. (2018). Exploring the synergy between Sport Education and in-school sport participation. *Journal of Teaching in Physical Education, 37,* 113-122.

Kohl III, H. W., & Cook, H. D. (2013). *Educating the student body: Taking physical activity and physical education to school.* Washington, DC: National Academy of Sciences.

Landis, R. B. (2013). *Studying engineering: A road map to a rewarding career* (4th ed.). Los Angeles, CA: Discovery Press.

LaPrade, R. F., Agel, J., Baker, J., Brenner, J. S., Cordasco, F. A., Côté, J., & Hewett, T. E. (2016). AOSSM early sport specialization consensus statement. *Orthopaedic Journal of Sports Medicine, 4*(4), 2325967116644241.

Laughlin, M. K., & Happel, K. (2016). Developing an appropriate goalball unit for secondary physical education. *Strategies, 29*(1), 16-23.

Launder, A. G. (2001). *Play practice: The games approach to teaching and coaching sports.* Champaign, IL: Human Kinetics.

Launder, A. G., & Piltz, W. (2013). *Play practice: Engaging and developing skilled players from beginner to elite.* Champaign, IL: Human Kinetics.

Layne, T., & Hastie, P. (2014). Active involvement and accuracy of calls of novice referees during a season of sport education. *Physical Educator, 71,* 459-472.

Ledingham, D., & Cox, R. L. (1989). Games-making evaluated. *Scottish Journal of Physical Education, 17*(3), 14-16.

Ley Orgánica 8/2013 de 9 de diciembre para la mejora de la calidad educativa (LOMCE) [Organic Law 8/2013 of 9 December to improve quality of education (LOMCE)] http://www.boe.es/boe/dias/2013/12/10/pdfs/BOE-A-2013-12886.pdf

Lieberman, D. (September 2017). An evolutionary perspective on how and why humans move. The Rainier and Julie Marten Lecture. Presented at the National Academy of Kinesiology Annual Conference. Chrystal City, DC.

Lieberman, L. J., & Houston-Wilson, C. (2018). *Strategies for inclusion: A handbook for physical educators* (3rd ed.). Champaign, IL: Human Kinetics.

Locke, L. F. (1975). The ecology of the gymnasium: What the tourists never see. *Proceedings of the Southern Association for Physical Education of College Women.* ERIC Document Reproduction Service No. ED 104823.

Loovis, E. M., & Loovis, C. L. (1997). A disability awareness unit in physical education and attitudes of elementary school students. *Perception and Motor Skills, 84,* 768-370.

Lorenz, K. A., van der Mars, H., Kulinna, P. H., Ainsworth, B. E., & Hovell, M. F. (2017). Environmental and behavioral influences of physical activity in junior high school students. *Journal of Physical Activity and Health, 14,* 785-792.

Lounsbery, M. A., Holt, K. A., Monnat, S. M., Funk, B., & McKenzie, T. L. (2014). JROTC as a substitute for PE: Really? *Research Quarterly for Exercise and Sport, 85,* 414-419.

Lund, J., & Veal, M. L. (2008). Measuring pupil learning: How do student teachers assess within instructional models? *Journal of Teaching in Physical Education, 27,* 487-511.

Lytle, R., Lieberman, L., & Aiello, R. (2007). Motivating paraeducators to be actively involved in physical education programs. *Journal of Physical Education, Recreation & Dance, 78*(4), 26-30, 50.

MacPhail, A. (2015). International perspectives on the implementation of standards. In J. Lund & D. Tannehill (Eds.), *Standard-based physical education curriculum development* (3rd ed.) (pp. 21-36). Burlington, MA: Jones & Bartlett.

MacPhail, A., Kirk, D., & Kinchin, G. (2004). Sport education: Promoting team affiliation through physical education. *Journal of Teaching in Physical Education, 23*, 106-122.

Mager, R. (1952). *Preparing instructional objectives*. Palo Alto, CA: Peron.

Masters, A. (2017). Corruption in sport: From the playing field to the field of policy. *Policy and Society, 34*, 111-123.

Mayo Clinic (2015). *Performance-enhancing drugs and teen athletes – Tween and Teen Newsletter*. Retrieved from: https://www.mayoclinic.org/healthy-lifestyle/tween-and-teen-health/in-depth/performance-enhancing-drugs/art-20046620

McBride, R. E., & Xiang, P. (2004). Thoughtful decision making in physical education: A modest proposal. *Quest, 56*, 337-354.

McKenzie, T. L., & van der Mars, H. (2015). Top 10 research questions related to assessing physical activity and its contexts using systematic observation. *Research Quarterly for Exercise and Sport, 86*, 13-29.

Midura, D. W., & Glover, D. R. (2005). *Essentials of team building: Principles and practices* (Vol. 1). Champaign, IL: Human Kinetics.

Ministry of Education (2007). *The New Zealand curriculum for English-medium teaching and learning in years 1-13*. Wellington: Ministry of Education. Retrieved from http://nzcurriculum.tki.org.nz/Curriculum-documents

Ministry of Education (1998). Programa educação fisica-plano de organizção do ensino aprendizagem [Organizational plan for teaching-and-learning: Physical education program]. Retrieved from http://www.dge.mec.pt/sites/default/files/ficheiros/eb_ef_programa_2c_ii.pdf and https://www.dge.mec.pt/sites/default/files/ficheiros/eb_ef_programa_3c.pdf

Mitchell, S. A., & Oslin, J. L. (2002). *Assessment in games teaching*. Reston, VA: National Association for Sport and Physical Education.

Mitchell, S., Oslin, J., & Griffin, L. (2013). *Teaching sport concepts and skills: A tactical games approach* (3rd ed.) Champaign, IL: Human Kinetics.

Modell, S. Collier, D., & Jackson, I. (2007). Paraeducator-teacher relationships: Creating positive environment. In L. J. Lieberman (Ed.), *Paraeducators in physical education: A training guide to roles and responsibilities* (pp. 25-34). Champaign, IL: Human Kinetics.

Mohr, D. J., Townsend, J. S., & Bulger, S. M. (2001). Pedagogical approach to Sport Education season planning. *Journal of Physical Education, Recreation & Dance, 72*(9), 37-46.

Mosston, M. (1992). Tug-o-war, no more: Meeting teaching-learning objectives using the spectrum of teaching styles. *Journal of Physical Education, Recreation & Dance, 63*(1), 27-31, 56.

National Association for Sport and Physical Education (NASPE). (1995). *Moving into the future: National standards for physical education*. Reston, VA: Author.

National Association for Sport and Physical Education (NASPE). (2010). *Guidelines for participation in youth sport programs: Specialization versus multiple-sport participation*. [Position statement]. Reston, VA: Author.

National Council for Curriculum and Assessment (NCCA). (2018). *Physical Education Framework*. Retrieved from https://curriculumonline.ie/getmedia/bc195f63-5ba0-4053-92f0-2796fefa23c5/SCPE_Framework_en.pdf

National Physical Activity Plan Alliance (NPAPA). (2016). *National Physical Activity Plan* (2nd ed.). Columbia, SC: Author. Retrieved from http://physicalactivityplan.org/docs/2016NPAP_Final-forwebsite.pdf

Niland, E., Barry, M., Dempsey, O., & Daly, J. (2010). *Best start: Inclusive schools project,* Dublin, IE: Irish Wheelchair Association – Sport. Retrieved from http://activeschoolflag.ie/wp-content/uploads/2015/08/Irish-Wheelchair-Association-Best-Start-Schools-Inclusion-Project.pdf

Nocera, J. (2016). *Indentured: The battle to end the exploitation of college athletes*. New York: Penguin Random House.

Novak, M. (1992). The natural religion. In S. J. Hoffman (Ed.), *Sport and religion* (pp. 35-42). Champaign, IL: Human Kinetics.

O'Donovan, T. M. (2003). A changing culture? Interrogating the dynamics of peer affiliations over the course of a sport education season. *European Physical Education Review, 9*, 237-251.

Ogden, C. L., Carroll, M. D., Lawman, H. G., Fryar, C. D., Kruszon-Moran, D., Kit, B. K., & Flegal, K. M. (2016). Trends in obesity prevalence among children and adolescents in the United States, 1988-1994 through 2013-2014. *Journal of the American Medical Association, 315*, 2292-2299.

Owen, D. (1996). Dilemmas and opportunities for the young active citizen, *Youth Studies Australia, 15*, 20-23.

Panagiotou, A. K., Evaggelinou, C., Doulkeridou, A., Mouratidou, K., & Koidou, E. (2008). Attitudes of 5th and 6th grade Greek students toward the inclusion of children with disabilities in physical education classes after a Paralympic education program. *European Journal of Adapted Physical Activity, 1*(2), 31-43.

Paralympics.org (2013). Policy on eligible impairments in the Paralympic movement. *The International Paralympic Committee Handbook*, Section 2; Chapter 3.13. https://www.paralympic.org/the-ipc/handbook

Pate, R. R., Davis, M. G., Robinson, T. N., Stone, E. J., McKenzie, T. L., & Young, J. C. (2006). Promoting physical activity in children and youth: A leadership role for schools. *Circulation, 114*, 1214-1224.

Pearce, S. (2016). Authentic learning: What, why and how? *E-Teaching: Management Strategies for the classroom*. Retrieved from http://www.acel.org.au/acel/ACEL_docs/Publications/e-Teaching/2016/e-Teaching_2016_10.pdf

Petersen, S., & Cruz, L. (2004). What did we learn today? The importance of instructional alignment. *Strategies, 17*(5), 33-36.

Pill, S. (2008). Involving students in the assessment of game performance in physical education. "Play to Educate" Sport in Education Conference digital proceedings, January 21, Flinders University.

Pill, S. (2013). *Play with purpose: Game sense to sport literacy*. Hindmarsh, SA: ACHPER Publications.

Pill, S. (2016). Game sense coaching: Developing thinking players. In M. Drummond and S. Pill Eds.), *Advances in Australian football: A sociological and applied science exploration of the game* (42-49). Hindmarsh, SA: ACHPER Publications.

Placek, J. (1992). Rethinking middle school physical education curriculum: An integrated, thematic approach. *Quest, 44*, 330-341.

Polikoff, M. S., & Porter, A. C. (2014). Instructional alignment as a measure of teaching quality. *Educational Evaluation and Policy Analysis, 36*, 399-416.

Pope, H. G., Khalsa, J. H., & Bhasin, S. (2017). Body image disorders and abuse of anabolic-androgenic steroids among men. *Journal of the American Medical Association, 317*, 23-24.

Pope, H. G., Wood, R. I., Rogol, A., Nyberg, F., Bowers, L., & Bhasin, S. (2013). Adverse health consequences of performance-enhancing drugs: An Endocrine Society scientific statement. *Endocrine Reviews, 35*, 341-375.

Pressé, C., Block, M. E., Horton, M., & Harvey, W. J. (2011). Adapting the Sport Education model for children with disabilities. *Journal of Physical Education, Recreation & Dance, 82*(3), 32-39.

Pritchard, T., Hansen, A., Scarboro, S., & Melnic, I. (2015). Effectiveness of the Sport Education fitness model on fitness levels, knowledge, and physical activity. *The Physical Educator, 72*, 577-600.

Pritchard, T., & McCollum, S. (2009). The Sport Education tactical model. *Journal of Physical Education, Recreation & Dance, 80*(9), 31-38.

Purcell-Cone, T., Werner, P., & Cone, S. (2009). *Interdisciplinary elementary physical education* (2nd ed.). Champaign, IL: Human Kinetics.

Qualifications and Curriculum Authority (QCA). (2007). Physical education: Programme of study for key stage 3 and attainment target. London: Crown. Retrieved from http://media.education.gov.uk/assets/files/pdf/p/pe%202007%20programme%20of%20study%20for%20key%20stage%203.pdf

Real Decreto 126/2014, de 28 de febrero, por el que se establece el currículo básico de la educación primaria [Royal Decree 126/2014, 28 February of the establishment of the basic curriculum of primary education]. Retrieved from https://www.boe.es/boe/dias/2014/03/01/pdfs/BOE-A-2014-2222.pdf

Real Decreto 1105/2014, de 26 de diciembre, por el que se establece el currículo básico de la educación secundaria obligatoria y del bachillerato [Royal Decree 1105/2014, 26 December of the establishment of the basic curriculum of Compulsory Secondary Education and Baccalaureate]. Retrieved from https://www.boe.es/boe/dias/2015/01/03/pdfs/BOE-A-2015-37.pdf

Reeve, J. (2009). Why teachers adopt a controlling motivating style toward students and how they can become more autonomy supportive. *Educational Psychologist, 44*, 159-175.

Richard, J.-F., & Griffin, L. (2003). Authentic assessment in games education: An introduction to the Team Sport Assessment Procedure and the Game Performance Assessment Instrument. In J. Butler, L. Griffin, B. Lombardo, & R. Nastasi (Eds.). *Teaching games for understanding in physical education and sport* (pp. 155-166). Reston, VA: National Association for Sport and Physical Education.

Richard, J. F., Godbout, P. & Gréhaigne, J. F. (2000). Students' precision and interobserver reliability of performance assessment in team sports. *Research Quarterly for Exercise and Sport, 71*, 85-91.

Richard, J.-F., Godbout P., Griffin L.L. (2002) Assessing game performance. An introduction to the Team Sport Assessment Procedure (TSAP). *Physical and Health Education Journal, 68*(1), 12-18.

Richardson, M., & Oslin, J. L. (2003). Creating an authentic dance class using Sport Education. *Journal of Physical Education, Recreation & Dance, 74*(7), 49-55.

Rink, J. E. (2006). *Teaching physical education for learning* (6th ed.). New York, NY: McGraw-Hill.

Romar, J.-E. (1995). *Case studies of Finnish physical education teachers: Espoused and enacted theories of action*. Abo, Finland: Abo Akademi University Press.

Roth, K., Zittel L., Pyfer, J., & Auxter, D. (2017). *Principles and methods of adapted physical education and recreation* (12th ed.). Burlington, MA: Jones & Bartlett Learning.

Scheibler, I. (1999). Art as festival in Heidegger and Gadamer. *International Journal of Philosophical Studies, 9*, 151-175.

Siedentop, D. (1980). *Physical education: An introductory analysis* (3rd ed.). Dubuque, IA: W. C. Brown.

Siedentop, D. (1994). *Sport Education: Quality PE through positive sport experiences*. Champaign, IL: Human Kinetics.

Siedentop, D. (1998). What is Sport Education and how does it work? *Journal of Physical Education, Recreation & Dance, 69*(4), 18-20.

Siedentop, D. (2002). Sport Education: A retrospective. *Journal of Teaching in Physical Education, 21*, 409-418.

Siedentop, D. (2004). *Introduction to physical education, fitness, and sport* (5th ed). Boston, MA: McGraw-Hill.

Siedentop, D. L. (2009). National plan for physical activity: Education sector. *Journal of Physical Activity and Health, 6*(s2), 168-S180.

Siedentop, D., Hastie, P. A., & van der Mars, H. (2011). *Complete guide to Sport Education* (2nd ed.). Champaign, IL: Human Kinetics.

Siedentop, D., & Tannehill, D. (2000). *Developing teaching skills in physical education* (4th ed.). Mountain View, CA: Mayfield.

Siedentop, D., & van der Mars, H. (2012). *Introduction to physical education, fitness, and sport* (8th ed.). St. Louis, MO: McGraw-Hill.

Sinelnikov, O., & Hastie, P. (2008). Teaching Sport Education to Russian students: An ecological analysis. *European Physical Education Review, 14*, 203-222.

Smarter Scotland-Scottish Government (2016). Curriculum for excellence: Health and well-being. Retrieved from https://education.gov.scot/scottish-education-system/policy-for-scottish-education/policy-drivers/cfe-%28building-from-the-statement-appendix-incl-btc1-5%29/Experiences%20and%20outcomes

Smith, A. F., & Hollihan, K. (2009). *ESPN the company: The story and lessons behind the most fanatical brand in sports*. Hoboken, NJ: John Wiley & Sons.

Society of Health and Physical Educators of America (SHAPE America). (2013a). *National standards for K-12 physical education*. Reston, VA: Author.

Society of Health and Physical Educators of America (SHAPE America). (2013b). *Grade-level outcomes for K-12 physical education*. Reston, VA: Author.

Society of Health and Physical Educators of America (SHAPE America). (2013). National standards and grade-level outcomes for K-12 physical education. Reston, VA: Author.

Society of Health and Physical Educators of America & the American Heart Association. (SHAPE America & AHA). (2016). *2016 Shape of the Nation: Status of Physical Education in the USA*. Reston, VA: Authors.

SPARC (Sport and Physical Activity Research Centre). (1995). *Report on the 1994 trial of Sport Education*. Canberra: Australian Sport Commission.

Sport New Zealand. (2017). *Roles of officials*. Retrieved from https://sportnz.org.nz/managing-sport/search-for-a-resource/guides/roles-of-officials

Stripling, J. (2018). Inside Auburn's secret effort to advance an athlete-friendly curriculum. *The Chronicle of Higher Education*. Retrieved from https://www.chronicle.com/article/Inside-Auburn-s-Secret/242569

Su, Y. L., & Reeve, J. (2011). A meta-analysis of the effectiveness of intervention programs designed to support autonomy. *Educational Psychology Review, 23*, 159-188.

Sweeney, J., Tannehill, D., & Teeters, L. (1992). Team up for fitness. *Strategies, Mar-Apr,* 20-23.

Tannehill, D., van der Mars, H., & MacPhail, A. (2015). *Building effective physical education programs*. Sudbury, MA: Jones & Bartlett.

Tindall, D. W. (2013). Creating disability awareness through sport: Exploring the participation, attitudes and perceptions of post-primary female students in Ireland. *Irish Educational Studies, 32*, 457-475.

Tindall, D. W., & Foley, J. T. (2011). Assessment modifications for students with disabilities in Sport Education. *Journal of Physical Education, Recreation & Dance, 82*(7), 30–37.

Tindall, D. W., Foley, J. T., & Lieberman, L. J. (2016). Incorporating Sport Education roles for students with visual impairments and blindness as part of a sport camp experience. *Palaestra, 30*(3), 31-36.

Tousignant, M., & Siedentop, D. (1983). A qualitative analysis of task structures in required secondary physical education classes. *Journal of Teaching in Physical Education,* 3, 47-57.

Trust for America's Health (2013). *F as in Fat: How obesity threatens America's future*. Washington, DC: Author.

Tudor-Locke, C., Lee, S. M., Morgan, C. F., Beighle, A., & Pangrazi, R. P. (2006). Children's pedometer-determined physical activity during the segmented school day. *Medicine and Science in Sports and Exercise, 38*, 1732-1738.

U. S. Department of Health and Human Services (USDHHS). (1996). *Physical activity and health: A report of the surgeon general*. Atlanta, GA: Centers for Disease Control and Prevention. Retrieved from https://health.gov/paguidelines/guidelines/

U.S. Department of Health and Human Services (USDHHS). (2001). Increasing physical activity: A report on recommendations of the Task Force on Community Preventive Services. *Morbidity and Mortality Weekly Report, 50*, 1-14.

U.S. Department of Health and Human Services (USDHHS). (2008). *Healthy people 2020 objectives*. Washington, DC: Author. Retrieved from https://www.healthypeople.gov/2020/topics-objectives

U. S. Department of Health and Human Services (USDHHS). (2010). *Healthy people 2020*. Washington, DC: Author.

U.S. Department of Health and Human Services (USDHHS). (2018). *Physical activity guidelines for Americans* (2nd ed.). Washington, DC: Author. Retrieved from https://health.gov/paguidelines/second-edition

van de Pol, J., Volman, M., & Beishuizen, J. (2010). Scaffolding in teacher-student interaction: A decade of research. *Educational Psychology Review, 22*, 271-296.

van der Mars, H. (2017). Viewpoint - Breaking news: High schools surpass elusive goal for PE minutes per week. *Journal of Physical Education, Recreation & Dance, 88*(4), 3-6.

van der Mars, H. (2018). Policy development in physical education… Our last best chance. *Quest, 70*, 169-190.

van der Mars, H., McNamee, J., & Timken, G. (2018). Physical education meets teacher evaluation: Supporting secondary school physical educators in formal assessment of student outcomes. *The Physical Educator, 75*, 581-615.

van der Mars, H., Timken, G., & McNamee, J. (2018). Systematic observation of formal assessment of students by teachers (SOFAST). *The Physical Educator, 75*, 341-371.

Vidoni, C., & Ward, P. (2009). Effects of fair play instruction on student social skills during a middle school Sport Education unit. *Physical Education and Sport Pedagogy, 14*, 285-310.

Vogan T. (2015). *ESPN: The making of a sports media empire*. Champaign, IL: University of Illinois Press.

Wahl-Alexander, Z., Curtner-Smith, M., & Sinelnikov, O. (2016). Influence of a purposefully negotiated season of Sport Education on one teacher and his pupils. *European Physical Education Review, 22*, 450-464.

Wallhead, T. (2017). Developing competent games players: Roles of the teacher and the student-coach. *Active + Healthy Journal, 24*(2/3), 21-24.

Wallhead, T. L., & Ntoumanis, N. (2004). Effects of a Sport Education intervention on students' motivational responses in physical education. *Journal of Teaching in Physical Education, 23*, 4-18.

Wallhead, T., & O'Sullivan, M. (2005). Sport education: Physical education for the new millennium? *Physical Education and Sport Pedagogy, 10*, 181-210.

Wallhead, T. L., & O'Sullivan, M. (2007). A didactic analysis of content development during the peer teaching tasks of a Sport Education season. *Physical Education and Sport Pedagogy, 12*, 225-243.

Ward, J. K., Hastie, P. A., Wadsworth, D., Foote, S., Brock, S., S.J., & Hollett, N. (2017). A Sport Education fitness season's impact on students' fitness levels, knowledge, and in-class physical activity. *Research Quarterly for Exercise and Sport, 88,* 346-351.

Weaver, R. G., Beets, M. W., Huberty, J., Freedman, D., Turner-Mcgrievy, G., & Ward, D. (2015). Physical activity opportunities in afterschool programs. *Health Promotion Practice, 16,* 371-382.

Wiggins, G. (1987). Creating a thought-provoking curriculum: Lessons from whodunits and others. *American Educator: The Professional Journal of the American Federation of Teachers, 11*(4), 10-17.

Wilson, S., & Lieberman, L. J. (2000). DisAbility awareness in physical education. *Strategies, 13*(6), 12, 29-33.

Winnick, J., & Porretta, D. (2016). *Adapted physical education and sport* (6th ed.). Champaign, IL: Human Kinetics.

World Anti-Doping Agency (WADA). (2018). The World Anti-Doping Code-International Standard. Retrieved from https://www.wada-ama.org/en/resources/science-medicine/prohibited-list-documents

World Health Organization (WHO). (2010). Global recommendations on physical activity for health. Retrieved from http://www.who.int/dietphysicalactivity/factsheet_recommendations/en/

Zimbalist, A. (2016). *Circus maximus: The economic gamble behind hosting the Olympics and the world cup.* Washington, DC: Brookings Institution Press.

Zirin, D. (2016). *Brazil's dance with the devil (Updated Olympics Edition): The world cup, the Olympics, and the fight for democracy.* Chicago: Haymarket Books.

Index

Note: The italicized *f* and *t* following page numbers refer to figures and tables, respectively.

About the Authors

Daryl Siedentop, PED, is a professor emeritus at The Ohio State University. He created the Sport Education model in the 1980s and published his first book on the subject, *Sport Education,* in 1994. He is also the author of several books on physical education, curriculum planning, and sport coaching. Dr. Siedentop earned the 1984 International Olympic Committee President's Award (Samaranch Award), which is the highest honor for work in sport pedagogy. He is a fellow in the National Academy of Kinesiology and has received numerous awards, including the Distinguished Alumni Award from Hope College in 1991; the Alliance Scholar Award from American Alliance for Physical Education, Recreation and Dance (AAHPERD) in 1994; the Curriculum and Instruction Academy Honor Award from the National Association for Sport and Physical Education (NASPE) in 1994; the School of HPER Distinguished Alumni Award from Indiana University in 1996; and the McCloy Award from the AAHPERD Research Consortium in 1998.

Courtesy of Daryl Siedentop.

Peter A. Hastie, PhD, is a professor at Auburn University and has conducted numerous seasons of Sport Education in schools. He also has published more than 40 papers on the topic. He completed the first series of empirical studies on the Sport Education model and has presented keynote speeches on the topic at the conferences in the United States and throughout the world. Dr. Hastie is a fellow in the National Academy of Kinesiology as well as the International Association for Physical Education in Higher Education (AIESEP).

© Peter Hastie

Hans van der Mars, PhD, is a professor of physical education at Arizona State University. He also taught at the University of Maine and Oregon State University. He has published extensively on teaching and teacher education in physical education, coauthoring 100 research and professional papers, books, and book chapters. He also has made over 220 invited, keynote, research, and professional development presentations at international-, national-, regional-, and state-level conferences. Dr. van der Mars is a fellow of the National Academy of Kinesiology and a research fellow of SHAPE America.

Courtesy of Hans Dijkhoff, KVLO.